FULL OF HOPE AND FEAR

FULL OF HOPE

AND

FEAR

THE GREAT WAR LETTERS
OF AN OXFORD FAMILY

EDITED BY

MARGARET BONFIGLIOLI

AND

JAMES MUNSON

OXFORD
UNIVERSITY PRESS

Great Clarendon Street, Oxford, OX2 6DP,
United Kingdom

Oxford University Press is a department of the University of Oxford.
It furthers the University's objective of excellence in research, scholarship,
and education by publishing worldwide. Oxford is a registered trade mark of
Oxford University Press in the UK and in certain other countries

First Edition published in 2014

Impression: 1

Published in the United States of America by Oxford University Press
198 Madison Avenue, New York, NY 10016, United States of America

British Library Cataloguing in Publication Data
Data available

Library of Congress Control Number: 2014934423

ISBN 978-0-19-870717-2

Printed in Great Britain by
Clays Ltd, St Ives plc

ACKNOWLEDGEMENTS

The editors have received generous help in their researches from many individuals and organizations, especially libraries and archive collections, and are grateful for the friendly welcome, patience, and interest of the following people and institutions, libraries, and archives:

In Cambridge, Michael Frankl, Chairman of the Beth Shalom Synagogue, Barry Landy of Fitzwilliam College, Val Nurse, of Beth Shalom Administrators, and Kate Senter of KVT BusinessCare.

In Chatham, the staff and volunteers at the Medway Archives and Local Studies Centre.

In Chennai, Sivaraj Munusamy of OKS Group, Dr S. Narayanan, Research Fellow, Institute of Advanced Study and Research, University of Madras, and Professor Vedagiri Shanmugasundaram of the University of Madras.

In Duxford, Martin Boswell at the Imperial War Museum.

In Gillingham, David Howlett, Membership Secretary of the Gillingham Baptist Church.

In London, Jane Dawson, Friends' House, Euston Road, Peter Elliott, Senior Keeper, Department of Research and Information Services, Royal Air Force Museum Hendon, David Jacobs, Chairman of the Jewish Historical Society of England, Hero Johnston at The Heatherley School of Fine Art, Hugh Petrie at Hendon Library, East Barnet, and Prof. Derek Taylor, OBE.

In Newcastle-upon-Tyne, the staff at the Tyne and Wear Archives.

In Oxford, Roger Ainsworth, Sally Jones, and Jessica Hughes at St Catherine's College, Elizabeth Boardman, archivist at Brasenose College,

Geoffrey Fouquet, Acting Archivist of St Peter's College, the Revd Peter Hewis, former Chaplain of Harris Manchester College, Timothy Metcalfe at the *Oxford Times* and the *Oxford Mail*, Audrey Mullender, Valerie Moises, Ray King, and Kate Beeby at Ruskin College, Rebecca Roseff at Magdalen College School, Elizabeth Sloan and Frances Stott, Librarians at the Oxford High School for Girls, David Smith at St Anne's College, Gay Sturt, archivist of the Dragon School, Michael Woods at the Bodleian Library, and the staffs at Oxford City Library and the Oxfordshire History Centre.

We are also most grateful to the following individuals for their advice, encouragement, and assistance: Lionel Bolton, Chris, Catriona, and Amanda Bonfiglioli, Martin Ceadel, Nicholas Chadwick, Fiona Clarke, David and Sue Cockram, Tony Essan, Gabrielle Fletcher, Tony Hancox, Ismene and Fenella Howse, Alexander Kerr, Vanessa Mildred, Richard Mullen, Susan Partridge, Ann Pasternak-Slater, Keith Randall, Charles Sale, Martin, Michael, and Nicolas Slater, Clover Southwell, Sarah Thomas, Eithne and Adrian Thornton, and Priscilla Tolkien.

We are, finally, deeply indebted to the Readers at Oxford University Press who recognized the importance of these letters and who made many valuable suggestions, and to our editor, Matthew Cotton, for his unfailing encouragement and assistance. We are grateful to those who have allowed us to use material of which they have the copyright. In a few cases the editors have been unable as yet to trace the current copyright holders even after considerable detective work. Despite all efforts, in some seven cases where the writers' full names are known (Maurice Adams, Violette Bossy, Joan and Maude George, the Revd G. H. Grinling, L. R. Sofield and M. P. Wilcocks) our researches have yet to discover descendants. The editors would greatly appreciate any information as to their whereabouts.

CONTENTS

LIST OF ILLUSTRATIONS

All images courtesy of The Slater Family

PREFACE

Margaret Bonfiglioli

This book has emerged from the considerable archive of family papers stored in my house in the village of Cassington, 5 miles north-west of Oxford—a kind of rich family compost. As the eldest son, my father, Owen Slater, had the responsibility of settling the final affairs of his parents, Gilbert and Violet, and of his two longest-lived aunts, Gertrude and Maud. Hence the tin trunks and deed boxes. Then there was a damp suitcase unexpectedly delivered by my Aunt Lydia Pasternak Slater when I was still living in Oxford. Occasionally a letter has surfaced and its content has taken me by surprise. A worried Gilbert writes to Owen in the days before he set off for training: 'Our hearts go with you, always a little bit anxious full of hope and fear, for your being well, and doing well, and living a good life,' while Violet used the same phrase in October 1918 when discussing talk of a peace settlement. Then there are the phrases that catch the eye: 'What shall I do with my socks?' 'Yesterday I took my Prisoner for a walk.' Can this be my father writing to his mother from the Front during the Great War? Not as I imagined him or his situation! So began the slow build-up of curiosity, discovery, and further questioning behind this book. In 2008 I began to work sporadically on a seemingly overwhelming task of sorting and transcribing and in 2012 I asked James Munson to help. His teaching experience and his work on Andrew Clark's famous three million word diary of the Great War meant he would be a good co-editor.[1]

A new impetus two summers ago made clearer the possibility of a book of letters from the 1914–19 period showing my father's growing up from the self-styled 'Homesick Babe' to the resourceful Royal Engineer at

FIGURE 1 Violet Oakeshott the art student: self-portrait oil sketch early 1890s.

its centre. First a major collection of letters emerged from the Louis Vuitton trunk on the landing (supposedly full of theatre programmes). Then last autumn my son Chris, who was shifting stuff about in the attic, unearthed a shoe box in which mouse droppings mingled with many more letters, most in their original envelopes. Then there was the small carved pine box, the sort used to store cotton reels. It proved to be Violet's private treasure of courtship notes from Gilbert in the 1890s—small, folded letters concerned with his struggles with work and money and with their complicated arrangements to be together. This gave me the strength to open the suitcase, to face my guilt and anxiety about its deteriorating contents, and to deal at last with the fluffy white mould eroding letters and increasingly brittle papers.

The trunk yielded letter after letter written during the war. This collection was a complete surprise. Owen, without ever mentioning it, had quietly kept letters which he had written during military service, as well as letters to him from his parents and brothers. In addition there were fifty other letters from Oxford, written by school friends and yet others

from a family named Brown who had cosseted him during his training at
Chatham. There were letters from Joyce Cockram and her younger brother
Hugh and from a girl named Joan George who called him 'Tufty'. References
were made to another Joan, Joan Anderson, whose father worked for the
Oxford Canal Navigation Company, but no letters from her have survived,
assuming any were written. Mrs Cockram, Mrs George, and Mrs Brown had
all written as well and there were letters from his friend Basil Donne-Smith
who used coloured paper, described his adventures with girls, and wrote in
a more intimate and literary way than other school friends.

These discoveries brought home the truth that few things take us nearer
to what actually happened in the past, and to what people actually thought,
than letters which were never intended for publication. In their privacy and
immediacy, their inconsistencies and false hopes, we come as near as we can
to understanding what people thought, feared, and hoped for at the time.

FIGURE 2 Violet Oakeshott
'the dowerless maid' c.1897.

FIGURE 3 Owen Slater aged 8
in 1907.

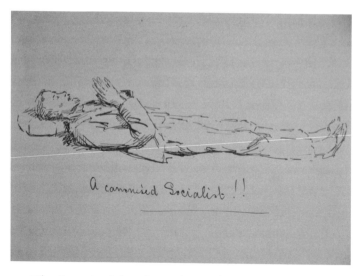

FIGURE 4 'The Canonized Socialist': ink pen drawing of Joseph Francis Oake-shott, a founding member of the Fabian Society, from Violet Oakshott's sketch book.

FIGURE 5 Dr Gilbert Slater: one time Socialist Mayor of Woolwich and later Principal of Ruskin College Oxford 1909 to 1915.

INTRODUCTION

James Munson

The First World War has survived as part of our national memory in a way no other war has ever done. The war's sheer scale, the horrendous number of casualties, and the collapse of three mighty European empires ensure this. Even though a century has passed, we are still surrounded by war memorials, films, news reels, and radio and television programmes about the fighting. We are also surrounded by myths and simplifications so tempting to journalists and television producers: the 'missing generation' and the unremitting horrors of trench warfare. We need constant reminding that the vast majority of soldiers and sailors were not killed nor were they injured and that war on so vast a scale can never be simplified. For Austrians it was very different from what it was to the British, not just in justification but in experience, just as to Russians it was seen differently than it was by Turks, Romanians, Serbs, or the French. Even within a specifically British perspective the war meant different things to different families, classes, areas, and age groups, let alone to different parts of the Empire, as Gilbert Slater's letters from India show.

The Slater family of Oxford were, like most families, both typical and unique. On the one hand, they were a middle-class family, comfortably off but far from rich, with three young sons. On the other hand they were far from typical. Owen's parents were from radical Nonconformist stock and were committed members of the Labour Party. Gilbert, very much the head of the family, was an academic, historian, and economist, who supported the war, while his wife, Violet, became a passionate opponent of all war as well as a supporter of conscientious objectors. As Violet's hatred of fighting developed into pacifism she illustrates how, why, and when people like her came to oppose the war and how this affected her political views when, after 1918, she got the vote. Likewise Gilbert's support shows how he accommodated his radical, anti-Establishment background to this new world.[2] The letters between Gilbert and Violet became a platform on which the war and the peace were debated with commitment. When combined with those from their friends and relations in England, Switzerland, and even Germany, the collection shows how varied and constantly shifting were views of the war and how dangerous it is to simplify people's feelings or to regard them as fixed.[3]

Gilbert's arrival in India in December 1915 started a correspondence that would continue throughout the war, a correspondence that not only supported Owen once he had been called up but kept alive a love marriage, by providing family support for one another in hard times. In the letters the tragedy of war and the daily chores are intermingled. The letters also helped Gilbert, by then an academic teaching in India, to find a way of being a father to young boys across space, cultural distance, and time, when letters could take up to six weeks to arrive, assuming the ships had avoided German submarines. For Violet, letters point to momentous educational decisions, her everyday difficulties with three lively boys, a recalcitrant stove, fuel shortages, and rationed goods in the shops. For both of them there was a constant exchange of views on war and international upheaval, suffering, and the question of how they and each of their children could work to enhance the renewed world which they hoped would emerge. Gilbert's and Violet's letters are private exchanges for they wrote as lovers, but they are, as we have noted earlier, also a forum for debate. Of necessity they also wrote about money while some are 'budget letters' to be enclosed with others or read aloud to visiting friends and relations. As a young officer, Owen's letters to his parents give us a very different perspective on the war from the usual one. In addition to the letters from Owen are those *to* Owen not just from his parents but from his younger brothers, aunts, uncles, friends, girlfriends, and cousins. Likewise these letters illustrate the importance of mail to men at the Front because they gave them the emotional link to a reality they did not want to leave behind.[4] They give us glimpses into what life on the Home Front was like for young people and children and provide some insight into the nature of letters to soldiers. They give us a first-hand, day-by-day account of the beginning and impact of the influenza pandemic of 1918–19 which killed more people than the war. Finally they give us some insight into the role of dreams and of the use of the word itself to describe the effect of the war on those caught up in it.

As in any exchange of letters within a family the pace and nature of letter-writing changed over the months. Most of the surviving letters are between Owen and his mother because Owen promised Violet he would write every day and so his letters, like hers, took the place of diaries, describing their daily lives. As the service was so much better between France and Britain than between France and India it was agreed that Violet would forward Owen's letters to Gilbert. Gilbert's letters describe his activities and life in India and give a unique first-hand Indian perspective on the war. They remind us that, as Professor Sir Hew Strachan has written, 'Britain fought this war as a global empire.'[5] What happened in Melbourne, Ottawa, Cape Town, Christ Church, or Calcutta was as much a part of the war effort as what happened in Manchester, Edinburgh, or Belfast. Violet's were an impassioned outcry against the war and increasingly against war in general, an outcry that led her in 1919 to move even further to the Left politically. Her protest was never a voice crying in the wilderness because she quickly joined national organizations opposed either to the war or to the growing demand for a punitive settlement based on German 'guilt'. Just as Gilbert's letters discuss events in India, Violet's give us insights into these networks of opposition politics. Her letters from 1918–19 also show us the political radicalism unleashed by the war and by the discussions about a post-war world.

As in any private correspondence, personalities emerge through the written word. Gilbert's letters give us the dispassionate analysis of a trained academic practising detachment. Having said that, it is ironic that Gilbert, for all his education and analytical abilities, accepted the propaganda that German 'militarism' had 'planned' the war for many years and that unless this 'militarism' were crushed, victory would be meaningless. It was Violet, if one discounts her impassioned religious rhetoric about sin and guilt, who actually ended up with a more balanced view of the war's causes. Her language may be uncomfortably simplistic to 21st-century readers but it points to the fact that the origins of the war lie in an extraordinarily wide range of interacting events, policies, and personalities. The question of war 'guilt' was an understandable reaction among the Allies to the atrocious behaviour by some Germans in Belgium and France, the execution of Edith Cavell, the sinking of the *Lusitania*, the 'crucifixion' of a Canadian soldier, and unrestricted submarine warfare.[6] 'War guilt' also gave Allied propaganda a valuable moral edge because it was also the language of law and religion. But the term has bedevilled our understanding of the war ever since.

But what about the letters from Owen's friends, Joyce Cockram, Basil Donne-Smith, Hugh Cockram, or Joan George, or those from Ida, Edna, and Marjorie Brown? In all these letters only twice do we come across reflections on the war, on warfare itself, or on the effects of war. Joyce Cockram asked Owen in February 1918, 'Don't you think this war has turned the rising generation into Cynics (I don't know whether this applies to you). You get that awful feeling, that nothing matters, & that one might just as well do—well, needlework, or something equally useless, as go on working.'[7] (Of course one could argue that this was more a reflection on the war's duration than on the war itself.) In that same month Basil Donne-Smith wrote to Owen from Oxford and said that he had taken part in a Junior Common Room debate at New College. The motion was that '"War is necessary for civilization".' Basil added, 'A moment's reflection revealed the fact that I thought it was but still I gabbled amiably for ten minutes & sat down in a chair & much confusion.'[8] But in most cases writers do not 'go on' about the war and when they do touch on it, it is only to describe what they were doing: volunteer nursing, agricultural work, or entertaining troops. Even when Hugh Cockram talks about being called up or Basil Dunne-Smith describes his military training, the war seems to be taken for granted, as part of the mental landscape. Opinions are not offered.

If we now turn from the letters to the family at their centre we find that the Slaters had put down roots in Plymouth and shared a common concern to record their history. Daniel Slater (1832–1902), Owen's grandfather, began a memoir in his old Sanskrit exercise book in the last January of his life. He was at pains to construct family trees to include all possible relations by marriage. As the schoolmaster son of a poor Nonconformist minister (himself a teacher and ardent preacher in what was then Wootton Bassett), whose life Daniel had already researched, the interventions of Providence were a key to his understanding of life. Sometime after 1917 Daniel's three longest-living daughters, Owen's formidable unmarried aunts, constructed their own individual chronologies with comments. Providence did not feature. Gertrude had started her memoirs more than once, first in 1910. Her last entry was in July 1953. Maud and Gertrude regularly wrote for the local newspaper and Maud was the only sister to have a book published. As with historians and sisters, Maud and Gertrude both wrote memoirs challenging and sometimes defending each other's accuracy. Their brother Gilbert's last letter, cheerfully written in sickness and pain, expresses just one regret—at not having yet written his own contribution to family history. The writing, sharing, and keeping of letters were family habits and almost inherited duties without which histories could not be constructed.

The one constant theme in all these letters, memoirs, and chronologies, and one that crops up again and again, is the Slaters' passionate pursuit of education for themselves and others. Their learning always became teaching as well as a way of earning a living. Though driven by economic necessity their studies also took them into new worlds of interests and pleasures. Great-grandfather Daniel, apprenticed to an uncle, knew he needed formal education to open his own school and attended the Congregationalists' Western College in Plymouth. There, after struggle and delay, he earned his external London BA but his long-desired higher degree was never achieved.

In 1858 Daniel married Ellen Augusta Trevor, who spoke French and German fluently and had been an assistant at her elder sister, Emily's, School for English Ladies in Bonn. Daniel and Ellen were married there and once back in Plymouth the new Mrs Slater proved a skilful manager, eventually catering for the boys at Daniel's new school, Cheveley Hall, 'on a liberal scale'. Like most such schools this was near the coast and boasted 'large and well-ventilated Schoolrooms...and very large and airy Dormitories—all enjoying a South aspect'. (All this was to reassure parents worried about illnesses such as tuberculosis.) Boarders over 16 paid 50 guineas a year with laundry, a seat at church or chapel, Greek and Latin, French, drilling, drawing, German, shorthand, land surveying, and book-keeping, with music as an extra subject. A black cloth suit, a straw hat with a band displaying the school colours (orange and black), towels, and a silver dessert fork and spoon were required.[9]

The couple had three sons, Gilbert, Howard, and Eric, and four daughters, Lilian, Gertrude, Maud, and Edith, none of whom ever married. Learning dominated the family and allowed the children to take considerable strides up the social ladder. Gilbert, Lilian, and Edith read for Cambridge degrees: Lilian and Edith in Classics and Maths at Newnham while Gilbert went up to St John's in 1882 to read for the Maths Tripos. Maud remembered stoning currants at the kitchen table for the weekly plum duff, her Greek grammar propped open in front of her at irregular verbs. Gertrude and she both learned the new technology of 'type-writing' and often typed Gilbert's manuscripts. Maud went on to set up a typing and shorthand school with her friend Hilda Baker in Plymouth and to publish *Isabella Price, Pioneer*, a biography of an aunt who died as a missionary in what is now Cameroon in 1860. Howard and Eric qualified as a doctor and chartered surveyor respectively.

All the children expected to work hard and to enjoy good summer holidays with plenty of bathing, picnics, long walks, and visits to each other's houses. Rivalry between them was combined with assumptions of loving concern and a willingness to rush to one another's aid in times of sickness or need. The example and influence of Ellen—'Mamma' in the family—were the keys to traits that continued strongly in Gilbert and later in Owen. Her benign acceptance of people and her extraordinary capacity to keep calm would be gifts of great value in a teacher, a parent, or a young officer. She weathered a series of events which had distressed her greatly and which perhaps had also endangered her reputation as a respected matriarch but weather them she did. Clever, bossy Lilian became a Roman Catholic nun while Maud involved herself in the suffragette movement and Gilbert became a socialist. Daniel's and then Gilbert's overwork undermined their health while Eric's financial problems were exacerbated by two 'unfortunate marriages'.

Gilbert Slater (1864–1938), whose life always consisted of some combination of researching, writing, and lecturing, returned to Plymouth after Cambridge in 1885 to teach (not altogether successfully) in his father's school. He joined the Fabian Society the next year and got leading fellow Fabians such as Sidney Webb to travel down to give lectures.[10] He helped to organize unskilled workers into unions after the London dock strike of 1889 and threw himself into local politics. He stood as a Labour candidate for the Plymouth School Board in an election which, like most Board elections, included a debate over the provision of religious instruction in the schools.[11] To radicals such as Gilbert the schools were seen as the beginning of a national system of state education. To show their independence from the past, their radical supporters demanded the abolition of all religious instruction, as well as the provision of free meals. Young Mr Slater got very few votes.

Gilbert left Plymouth in the early 1890s for London. At first he lived and worked in Toynbee Hall, the earliest and most famous of the 'university settlements'—teaching and welfare centres set up by Oxbridge graduates in deprived areas, at first in London. Toynbee Hall was in Whitechapel, one of the poorest parts of the capital. Despite financial difficulties Gilbert began to get a good reputation as a lecturer on history as well as social and economic problems, first at Liberal and Labour venues and later on other platforms. In 1897 he married Violet Oakeshott, daughter of Joseph Oakeshott of East Barnet and Eliza

Maria Dodd of Stoke Newington, for many centuries a Quaker centre and home to a number of Dissenting schools in which opportunities for girls' education abounded. Indeed, one such school was run by a Sarah Dodd. Violet's childhood in London was followed by seven years in Sunderland where her father had been promoted Postmaster in 1883. Here she continued her art education, and sketches show painting excursions to Scotland and Switzerland. The Newcastle Art Society exhibited *Off Duty*, her impressive portrait of a miner (still in the family). Joseph's retirement from the Post Office, where he had earned a reputation as 'a man of tact, courtesy and efficiency',[12] took him back south. This gave Violet the opportunity of studying at the Heatherley School of Fine Art, the first school to admit women on an equal basis to men. A 'special feature is the French sketch class, consisting of studies from the life, with frequent changes of the pose of the model'. The story goes that this was a matter of anxious concern to her eldest brother, Joseph Francis, with whom she was living in Thornton Heath and that he 'kept her on a tight rein'. His house, listed in *Kelly's Directory* as a 'kindergarten', explains Violet's many sketches of small children made before she had any of her own.

Violet and Gilbert's marriage was undoubtedly a love match between two people determined to have a partnership of equals. His ever sardonic sister Gertrude claimed he had thrown over a better match and, unlike other 'needy Socialist young men'—she cites George Bernard Shaw and Sidney Webb—he had married 'a dowerless maiden' who was almost a socialist and whom Gilbert called 'my dearest comrade'. They set up house in Woolwich and the next year Violet gained a distinction in LSE courses in 'Economics and Political Science' taken through Woolwich Polytechnic. These studies would lay the groundwork for her committed interest in politics in the debates over the post-war world. In 1899 they began a family: Owen was born that year, Eliot in 1904, and Patrick in 1908. The couple involved themselves in protest movements, committee work, and the local Labour Party. Gilbert was elected to the Woolwich borough council in 1903 and two years later became mayor. He was also involved in converting the local Labour Party paper, *The Pioneer*, into a successful weekly.[13]

Gilbert committed himself to the movement to extend adult education to those who could never afford to go to university. He became a lecturer in the expanding University Extension movement pioneered by London University. These lectures, which were open to all for a small fee, had begun in London in 1872 and in 1876 the London Society for the Extension of University Teaching was set up by the Universities of Oxford, Cambridge, and London to supervise the courses offered. Lecturers had to be accredited by the Society and stipends were set: £5 a lecture was not unusual. Sometimes courses attracted large audiences and in one academic year (1901–2) some 15,000 people came to the fifty-nine centres providing lectures. Indeed the years leading up to 1914 have been described as a 'golden age' of extension lectures in the social sciences.[14] In addition to his lecturing and political work Gilbert started research for a doctorate and in 1905 got the higher degree, for which his father had so longed, when he was awarded the D.Sc. for work done at the new London School of Economics.[15] (His thesis became his first book, *The English Peasantry and the Enclosure of Common Fields*.) For her part Violet emerges through her sketch books: 'All so enchanting and so impossible!' are her pencilled notes on shadows and reflections in a sketchy river scene. For her, sketch books took the place of the chronologies kept by her sisters-in-law: babies, toddlers, young boys, flowers, seascapes, and even a pen drawing of her recumbent brother as 'The Canonized Socialist' with his hands joined in prayer like an effigy of a mediaeval knight. But beneath the art lay a commitment to improving the lives of the poor as strong as her husband's, if not stronger.[16]

Gilbert's careers as political activist and lecturer were prospering but there was no security and the work was demanding. Then in 1909 he was appointed lecturer and later Principal of Ruskin College, set up ten years earlier in Oxford to educate working men. This must have seemed the fulfilment of all his dreams of social reform and education for all, not to mention life in a city with good schools for his three boys. However, the salary of £200 a year was not very generous even if it was 'to be considered' after the first year, and Gilbert's tenure was not to be an easy one. In a fragment of a letter written in 1916 he admitted that 'I don't like myself much, and it is always easy for me to see why other people find me unattractive.' Fortunately he was left free to lecture outside the college. They let their house in Woolwich and Gertrude rushed up to help them move to Oxford. Gilbert threw himself into promoting the college and travelled round the country to raise money. On the academic front he taught and supported the college's developing connections with the University of Oxford: to him, working men deserved nothing less. He continued his writing career and in 1913 Constable published his *Making of Modern England*, one of his most popular books. (A US edition would appear in 1915 and the book is still in print.) In that same year life got even better when accommodation for the Principal's family finally became available in Ruskin's impressive new premises. Gilbert's mother praised the building as 'very suitable and nice—simple and plain, but well planned and convenient and every modern appliance for health and comfort', especially the facilities for hot baths.[17] (This reflected a family passion for water—boating, swimming, or even splashing about in baths—that would feature in their letters.)

Owen, the first born, was not given one of the names traditional in either parent's family. Instead he was named after Robert Owen, the famous social reformer.[18] His second name, Richard, came only at his grandfather Daniel's special request, to commemorate his brother, yet another Slater schoolmaster. So we have O.R.S., sometimes known as 'orse. Like his brothers he began his education at the Oxford Preparatory School (the 'Dragon School') before entering Magdalen College School as a day boy. Getting to know Owen as a growing boy has had a special fascination for his children, seeing how early significant traits, habits, and interests began, some lasting all his life, some modified by other pressures. His keen interest in photography and his love of music were surprises. His love of dancing and the spirit of delight, often in small things, lasted all his life as did his gift for finding unconsidered trifles. His practical understanding of how things worked and of how to mend them were lasting characteristics honed by his experiences in France.

On 29 July 1914 Owen's family, now comfortably established at Ruskin, left Oxford for their annual summer holiday in the West Country and for their now customary reunion with their Plymouth relations. Owen, after seeing to his guinea pigs and helping with arrangements for departure, had to start writing and illustrating his holiday diary, an annual school task. Picnics, bathing in the sea, walks, playing on the beaches with cousins, hunting for mushrooms, visiting museums and the Coast Guard Station with its powerful telescope, taking a steamer to look at the Eddystone Lighthouse, and even enjoying two visits to the cinematograph—all are recorded in detail. Violet had time to do some particularly vibrant pastels of Bigbury Bay while Owen sat beside her working on watercolours to illustrate his diary. The declaration of war against Germany on 4 August did not alter their plans and it wasn't until September that the family was back in Oxford although Gilbert was already 'very doubtful as to the future of Ruskin'.[19]

For the Slaters, as for most people, the war, now in its sixth week, was something to be read about and, at least in Gilbert's case, to be supported. On 22 September his name appeared under a brief letter in *The Times* in which 'writers who have interested themselves more especially in the history and progress of democratic ideas' said they desired 'to associate themselves' with the declaration written by the country's leading writers. This had been published four days earlier and labelled by the paper 'Britain's Destiny and Duty. Declaration by Authors. A Righteous War.' With Gilbert's name were those of G. D. H. Cole, G. G. Coulton, R. C. K. Ensor, A. G. Gardiner, J. L. and Barbara Hammond, H. W. Massingham, R. H. Tawney, and Professor George Unwin.[20] With the passage of time this detachment from the war would change for Violet, the boys, and Gilbert. The extent to which the war affected every person's life, the question of a 'total war', is one that has confronted historians in recent decades.[21] The experience of the Slater family, as seen in their letters, sheds welcome light on this vexed and immensely complicated question to which there are as many answers as there were families and localities. With each month, the war gradually had a greater impact on the Slater family but it did so in a variety of ways and tempos—rationing, Violet's growing involvement in radical politics, the deaths of friends, the fear of Zeppelins when in London, and, most important of all, the endless discussions between Violet and Gilbert as how best to keep their son out of the trenches, if not out of the war itself. These discussions, and the actions Violet and Gilbert considered, show that the war was never so 'total' that they became victims of forces beyond their control. Even after their son entered the army they did not relinquish their right to intervene and in 1919 Violet took it upon herself to get Owen demobilized and back into university. The family's 'autonomy' remained intact.

As these developments unfolded what had been a spectacle gradually became something in which all the family were involved. Yet at other levels, in personal relationships, social life, schoolwork, or pleasure-seeking, the war seems to have had far less, if any, effect. Most family routines—sports, holidays, and visits—were maintained and the boys' schooling carried on largely as before. For the Slaters the war became part of their lives in October 1914 when 200 Belgian refugees arrived in Oxford. While these were only a fraction of the estimated 200,000 reaching Britain their presence was still a major event in the city. Ruskin, which had already decided to delay opening the new building to students until 1915, now became a temporary home for thirty working men, one of whom arrived with seven children. The 10-year-old Eliot found the Belgians 'fine fun'.[22] Eventually the college would become a hostel for nurses working in the city's new military hospitals. Violet's mother was anxious about the family's future and a little sceptical concerning new ideas about compulsory baths for miners and better wages for farm labourers which Gilbert had discussed in the *Ruskin Collegian*, the college magazine.[23] Equally sceptical was Gilbert's own mother, who wrote to her daughter Lilian at her Cambridge convent. She doubted all the talk about the war's being 'over by Christmas' and described her financial worries about hard times to come. Should she put her savings in War Bonds or in a Post Office account? Either would yield 4 per cent but which was safer? Which was more patriotic?[24]

By April 1915 the security and prospects which Ruskin had offered were things of the past and Gilbert told his mother that the college had recently decided not to open in the autumn of 1915. Worse news followed: 'As I also have a difficulty with some of the staff, who have been behaving badly—Furniss,[25] I find, has been intriguing to get rid of me for some two years—I resigned. I shall now get some pay for the past six months, & my salary till September, and I hope that I shall during the coming winter get lecturing enough to make ends meet.' The family's hope to carry on living in Ruskin for 'another year' came to naught and they now had to find a new home with the help of a loan from Gilbert's mother.[26] There was some good news when in May Constable published his short book *Peace and War in Europe*, in which he expanded on the views expressed in the letter published in 1914. In this, according to his obituary in *The Times*, 'he showed himself to be, in the best sense, an Imperialist, and the spokesman of a large and then growing body of democratic opinion'.[27]

But the family could not live on royalties or on lecturing in the midst of a war and Gilbert therefore accepted a five-year appointment as the first Professor of Indian Economics in the University of Madras at £1,000 a year. To help him prepare for his new position he had friendly talks with fifteen Indian students still in residence in the University. Once in Madras he would flourish and be regarded ninety-three years after his retirement as 'one of the greatest economists and the founder of the Department of Economics'.[28] In 2009 a portrait of him was placed in the library of the University of Madras, where it was unveiled by the Finance Minister of Tamil Nadu State. But all this lay far in the future and in November 1915 he set out for India and wrote his last feature for the *Ruskin Collegian* on the boat train. As he travelled, the family was moving from temporary lodgings to 4 Park Crescent (later No. 20 Park Town), at the time a cold and uncomfortable house in the Park Town development in North Oxford. Gilbert's first stop was Marseilles where in November he received letters from home, including one from Owen: 'I hope & trust we will all get on well while you are away. I hope you have been having a good journey…I do hope you are keeping a diary. Bacon says that when on a sea voyage & there is nothing to see but sea & sky men very often keep diaries but when travelling on land & see lots of sights they very often don't keep one at all…There was a first match away & I didn't play in it…Poor Eliot's not feeling well…He's been trying to write a poem but it isn't at all a success. I've finished my lessons but it's getting quite late so I'll have to go to bed.'[29] In late December Gilbert arrived in Madras while back in England the war became part of Owen's own life when he joined the Officers' Training Corps at school. The OTCs, membership of which was voluntary, were not new, having been started in certain public schools and universities in 1908, but they were new to Owen and his family. It was a step that could lead to the trenches.

The letters in this collection begin in earnest in January 1916, but what do Owen's tell us about Owen and about the war? His letters as a soldier are mainly concerned with everyday life, practical problems and situations: the frequency of the post, the number of letters received and books read, homesickness, clothes, family matters, sleep or the lack thereof, other soldiers, the French, and plans for his life after peace. Owen's parents had openly debated how to keep their eldest son out of the fighting, so much so that his father, who supported the war, even raised the option of his son's becoming a conscientious objector in order to join the Friends' Ambulance Unit as a driver, but 'about that you must ask your own conscience'. Owen went so far as to agree that 'anything [is] better than France or Flanders',[30] but he did not become a CO. It is fairly certain that at this stage of the war, neither fully understood the harsh treatment sometimes handed out to COs. When in training he wrote to his mother that 'everyone here is enthusiastic about the war' but he did not mention his own views.[31] At first glance this reluctance to comment may seem strange for a young man who had been brought up in a politically radical environment but Owen was wisely reserving judgement.

When Gilbert wrote to Owen about the fear of injury or death— 'I wonder how you all take it?'—he answered his own question: 'Rather fatalistically I fancy.'[32] This 'fatalism' probably describes the attitude of thousands of young men, as does Owen's comment when setting out for the Front: 'All one can do is to do one's best & trust to Providence.' But within this 'fatalism'—or acceptance that one was being carried forward by forces beyond one's control—the fruit of his mother's teaching, driven home in almost every letter, was ripening. It manifested itself in a dislike of 'militarism',[33] by which in July 1918 he meant the rituals of officer life in the mess at a camp where he admitted that he did not like the other men. (In addition these rituals may well have had something to do with his discomfort when having to cope with a formal and upper-class way of life which was alien to him.) Once he was at the Front a new element was added. In October that same year he had his 'first experience of shell fire & I admit it fairly unnerved me'. Later on in the same letter he told his mother that 'one cannot realize in the slightest what war is like until you have seen a little of it. I am sure I have seen quite enough & what little it was has made me feel quite different. I am afraid I can't explain in the slightest what I mean. Probably I shall have recovered completely in a couple of days.' At the end of this letter he returned to his experiences: 'I hope & pray that the war will be over this year. It is such a ghastly waste of everything & I am perfectly sure that if the militarists in England experienced just a little bit of it they would seize any reasonable opportunity for making peace.' His use of 'militarism' and 'militarist' had now expanded to include those who supported the war's continuance and was a common enough reaction among soldiers. Having said that, his feelings in this letter are interspersed with talk about his accommodation, his horse, the quality of French coffee, and the post. In his next letter to his mother, written the following day, he had recovered his spirits and did not return to the subject at all. But the experience, however limited, had left its mark and within a fortnight, while his unit was still at the Front, he openly questioned the Allies' war aims. His thoughts were crystallized in another letter to Violet:[34]

The end of the war seems very close now, most people here put it at about a fortnight to a month. I hope they are right. Though I am certain that we are absolutely defeating our ends in asking for unconditional surrender. That will just about firmly establish militarism in all the fighting countries. International socialism is the obvious remedy but everyone I have met out here so far is so unutterably pig headed. Speaking with the men you get on all right up to a certain point. Then they will suddenly make a remark that dashes one to the ground as far as internationalism applied to war is concerned.

Owen's idea of 'Militarism' had matured from a dislike of extended dinners, loyal toasts, rowdy drinking, starched linen, and regimental silver to a horror of the fighting and 'waste' and then to a view that many came to share after the war: by totally destroying the German Empire through unconditional surrender one would not in fact destroy militarism. His solutions, 'international socialism' and 'internationalism', are vague and simplistic, not that unusual in a 19-year-old who might have been, in part at least, anxious to please his mother. While he did not, like his mother, adopt religious language, oppose the war per se, or denounce warfare in general, he did approximate her view that crushing Germany would not crush militarism—the use of force to achieve national aims—but only entrench it in all the warring nations. Oddly, when he could do something practical, by voting for an anti-Lloyd George coalition candidate in the general election in December, he did nothing even though he was entitled to vote. (All he had to do was to ask for a postcard ballot.) Of course this apathy was very marked among many men still in uniform but in Owen's case it walked hand in hand with quite radical views.

Through these letters we are given a unique entrance into a country and a family at war, a country and a family that were both full of hope and fear—the hope of victory and the fear of its cost. In their range of interests, backgrounds, ages, prejudices, hopes, and fears, in what was said and in what was not, in what was accepted and in what was doubted, in what was assumed, in what was unquestioned, in Owen's slowly ripening radicalism, in Gilbert's acceptance of propaganda as truth, and in Violet's outcry against the killing, these letters add immeasurably to our understanding of what the war that was meant to end war was like to those who actually lived through it.

NOTES ON THE TEXT AND ON CURRENCY

In preparing this collection, the editors examined 503 letters, memoranda, and postcards written between the summer of 1914 and the autumn of 1919 and of these they used 404 in whole or in part. They have kept the text of letters and cards as close to the original as possible. They have retained original abbreviations, capitalization, punctuation, and spelling. Those who complain about the low standard of spelling in 2014 will find consolation in the plenitude of incorrect spelling we see here: even Joyce Cockram, a well-educated medical student, spells medicine as 'medecine'. In those very few cases where keeping the original writing or punctuation would have caused confusion we have made silent corrections. Corrections by the writers themselves have been shown where these are of interest. We have provided corrections and brief explanations within square brackets immediately after a name, word, or phrase when these were necessary but in most cases we have confined background information to end notes. A query within square brackets indicates that the text or date immediately preceding it is not clear or certain while all ellipses are the editors'. We have also used asterisks to identify those letters that only survive in fragments, that are missing pages, or that are damaged. Given that letters were passed round to family and friends, sometimes thousands of miles away, it is not surprising that some were damaged or went missing. Where dates are not given we have inserted them within square brackets and when we are not certain about a date we have inserted a query after the suggested day, month, or year of writing. As subscriptions to letters tended to be the same we have omitted them in most cases although they do show how customs were changing:

the older generation still signed with their Christian name and surname, even when writing to a wife, husband, or child. Some younger people, such as Owen, Basil, or Joan, would simply sign their Christian names, while others, such as Joyce Cockram, signed their full names. Frequently Violet used her initials, V.O.S., for Violet Oakeshott Slater. As with all correspondences that extended over a long period, the flow of letters altered with the passing of time. The letters start in November 1915 when Gilbert leaves for India, and at first the majority are between him and his family. After January 1918, when Owen is called up, the pattern changes and most letters are between him and his mother.

At the start of the First World War the pound (or sovereign) was divided into twenty shillings (s.) and each shilling (5p) was divided into twelve pence (d.) which meant there were 240 pennies in the pound. Each penny (1d.) was in turn divided into two half-pennies (ha'pennies) and then into four farthings (½d. and ¼d. respectively). In addition there were five other coins: a half-sovereign, worth ten shillings (10s.) or 50p, a half-crown (2s. 6d.), worth 12½p, a two-shilling piece (2s.), worth 10p, a sixpence (6d.), worth 2½p, and a three-penny (3d. or thru'penny bit), worth 1¼p. The sovereign and half-sovereign were gold while the half-crown, two-shilling piece, shilling, sixpence, and threepence were all silver. Pennies, ha'pennies, and farthings were bronze. (As today, crowns or 5s. (25p) pieces were only issued for special occasions.) The lowest denomination note was for £5 although in 1914 Parliament authorized the issue of £1 and 10s. notes. The half-crown was often referred to as 'half a dollar' while the two-shilling piece was usually referred to as a 'florin' or a 'two bob piece'. The shilling was often called a 'bob' and sixpence was referred to as a 'tanner'. A guinea (21s. or £1.05p) was a coin last minted in 1814 but the name survived as a colloquial term. Five guineas were written as 5 gns. Guineas were usually used by professional men or smart shopkeepers who sought in so doing to enhance their standing.

Thus one pound, four shillings, and sixpence was written £1 4s. 6d. although sums were often expressed solely as shillings so that this same amount could have been written as 24*s*. 6*d*. or 24/6. When in December 1918 Violet Slater was outraged at the cost of turkeys—two shillings and eightpence a pound—she wrote 2/8.

In terms of a pound's 'purchasing power' the 1914 pound may be said today to be very roughly equivalent to £75.00, which means that a 1914 shilling would today be worth some £3.75. [<www.measuringworth. com> for 1914/2010].

CORRESPONDENTS AND PEOPLE FREQUENTLY MENTIONED IN THE LETTERS

Maurice and Ada Adams were friends of the Slaters who lived in Coulsdon, historically a Surrey village north of the North Downs but now part of Croydon. Maurice sometimes gave Violet financial advice.

Joan Anderson, whose father Octavius was the Secretary of the Oxford Canal Navigation Company, was a friend of Joyce Cockram and, to a lesser degree, of Owen. The Andersons lived in a company residence, The Stone House, in New Road, Oxford, near the canal. Joyce had a room in the house during term time. Joan also had a sister and a brother, Eric.

Mlle. Violette Bossy was from Serrières, near Neuchâtel in Switzerland. At some stage before 1914 she had stayed with the Slaters in Oxford.

The **Brown Family** lived at 29 Stuart Road, Gillingham, Kent, and were involved in a 'Rest Room' set up in 1914 in the Sunday School of Gillingham (Baptist) Tabernacle, which they attended. It was a home from home for soldiers from Chatham, 3 miles away. George Edward Brown owned a factory producing confectionery and pickles. He had four daughters (Marjorie, Ida, Edna, and Dorothy) of whom we have letters from the first three (who regarded themselves as Owen's 'sisters'), and one son, Norman, who did not write. The girls' mother also wrote to Owen, Gilbert, and Violet Slater.

The **Cockram Family** lived in Lloyd's Bank House in Wallingford, a market town on the Thames some 12 miles from Oxford, where Mr Reginald Cockram was the manager of the Bank. **Hugh Cockram** was a year behind Owen at Magdalen College School and after Owen left he became

Senior Prefect. He followed Owen into the University of Oxford, in his case to Queen's College. When war began (Ella) **Joyce Cockram** was at the Oxford High School for Girls. After leaving school she became an undergraduate at Oxford through the Society of Oxford Home-Students (later St Anne's College) where she began her studies in medicine. Having been born in April 1899 she was one month older than Owen. Joyce and Hugh's mother, Ella Cockram, wrote both to Owen and to his mother.

Basil Donne-Smith was senior to Owen at Magdalen College School and was Senior Prefect in 1916. At this time his surname was simply Donne.

The **George Family** were Oxford friends who lived at 25 Polstead Road. The daughter, Joan, was perhaps a girlfriend of Owen. Her father, the Revd T. P. George, worked with the Church of England's Men Society until his death in 1918. Her mother, Maude, occasionally wrote to Owen as well.

Amne Grafflin was a wealthy American and a close friend of the Slater family. Her much younger husband Walter Vrooman had been one of the founders of Ruskin College in 1899, two years after their marriage. They were divorced in the USA in 1903 and Amne Vrooman reverted to her maiden name of Grafflin. Her former husband stayed in America where he gradually lost his mind and died in 1909, aged 40. Amne Grafflin gave £1,000 to Ruskin's new building, laid one of the four foundation stones in 1912, and continued to give financial support. With the death in 1915 of Miss Giles, the woman responsible for the correspondence side of the College's work, Amne Grafflin took on her work without pay. During the war she also lived in Park Town.

The **Revd C. H. Grinling** was a man of independent means and one of the first residents of Toynbee Hall. After a spell as a curate in Nottingham he moved to Woolwich in 1889 where he became a Labour activist and where in time he became an agnostic. He was editor of the Woolwich *Pioneer*, the local Labour Party newspaper, and had taken the young Gilbert under his wing while Gilbert did valuable work on the paper. The Slaters remained friends of Grinling and his wife who lived in Woolwich and continued to take an interest in the journal.

Israel and Annie Hersch were Cambridge friends. Israel Hersch had read physics at Cambridge and by 1915 was a maths teacher at the Perse School in Cambridge while Annie was a keen suffragette. Israel established Hillel House as a house for Jewish boarders at the school in 1904 and was the House Master until his retirement in 1929. Mr Hersch was sometimes referred to as Ira. They had two sons, Robert and Laurence (Laurie), who was Owen's age and became a flight lieutenant in the Royal Air Force. Annie wrote as 'Aunt Annie'.

L. is an unidentified German woman who seems to have been a friend of Violet Slater before her marriage. It appears in 1919 that she was a recently retired teacher from the *Gymnasium* in Waren, Germany. L. was also a friend of Maurice and Ada Adams.

Harold, Joseph, and Philip Oakeshott were Violet Slater's brothers.

Mary (also referred to as **Mollie** in the letters) was Violet Slater's second sister.

The **Slater Family** consisted of Gilbert and Violet and their three sons, Owen, Eliot, and Patrick. When the letters begin in November 1915 Owen, aged 16, was at Magdalen College School, Oxford, while Eliot, aged 11, and Patrick, aged 7, were day boys at the Oxford Preparatory School, Oxford (later known as the Dragon School). Violet and Gilbert were both 41 years old when Gilbert left for India.

Ellen Slater was Gilbert's mother while Lilian, Gertrude, Maud, and Edith were Gilbert's sisters, none of whom had married. He had two brothers, Eric and Howard, a physician in the Royal Army Medical Corps.

Agnes Peacock was Violet's sister who lived in Leyburn in Yorkshire and was married to James Peacock, a family doctor.

Betty Slater was Owen's cousin, the daughter of Gilbert's brother Howard, a doctor in the Royal Army Medical Corps.

Mavis H. Starkie was an Oxford friend of Violet Slater. By the summer of 1918 she had moved to Oswestry.

THE LETTERS

In November 1915 Gilbert Slater left for Madras where he arrived on 20 December. Once there he began a new career as well as a new passion for improving the lives of the Indian people. Back in England Violet created a new home for herself and the boys, helped financially by Gilbert's mother and Violet's brother Joseph. Back home the war news was grim. On 15 October Bulgaria had entered the war as an ally of Germany and Austria-Hungary thereby allowing Germany to continue reinforcing her ally Turkey. On 28 December the Allies began evacuating the surviving troops from the disastrous Gallipoli landings, which

FIGURE 6 (*From left to right*) Owen, Eliot, and Patrick Slater: the children left behind in Oxford in 1915.

had taken place in April. *By the end of 1915 Britain had endured a year of Zeppelin raids and the effects of unrestricted submarine attacks on all shipping. This included the sinking of passenger liners including RMS Lusitania on 7 May with the loss of 1,198 lives. At the Front, Germany had started using poison gas in the Second Battle of Ypres.*

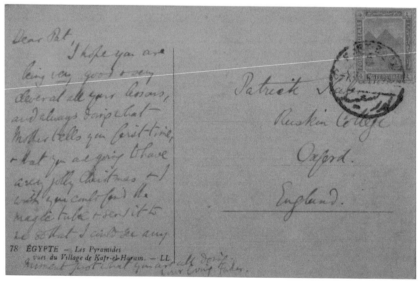

FIGURE 7 Postcard from Port Said: first news to his sons from Gilbert Slater in transit to his Professorship in Madras.

Gilbert to Violet, 31 December 1915

One or two things I can't remember whether I told you—first, that I did find your little note in my pyjama pocket on board the steamer, and it warmed my heart... Second the apparatus the boys gave me I use continually. It is invaluable in a country where you are warned against all ordinary unboiled water to have the means of boiling up a little drop in a minute or two. I shall take it with me wherever I go in India. You must now be settled in our house... I do hope you will get to like it... I have just done two Governor of Madras functions—a concert last night and a garden party this afternoon. I distinguished myself on each occasion by being the only person to go on a bicycle. Every body else went either in a carriage or motor... The deeds of the house—doubtless you have already ascertained, are deposited at the Bank, and remain there until we notify Cockell [the bank manager] that we don't want an overdraft any more.

Gilbert to Violet, 1 January 1916

Your letter starts Dec. 8 and is rather a melancholy one... but with better news at the end that Bella [Barnes][1] has promised to come & help in the move. I do hope things begin to get better after that. *And don't stint money on getting domestic help*... & try to get the good of the money I earn. I enclose my draft of the syllabus for the Economics. If I can get this through the Board of Studies it will begin to operate immediately in the transformation of the examination... The exams previously have been on English text-books—quite abstract & incomprehensible to the Indian. I have arranged to start lecturing at the Presidency College[2] on Jan. 17 & have also requisitioned for an office & a typist. In this way I shall have a regular meeting place for students and a sort of economic laboratory... Chadwick, Director of Agriculture... put me on to a young man who is engaged in re-settlement in Madurai, which involves thorough enquiry into the economic facts relating to a village; & we have fixed up provisionally for me to accompany him when the term is over. I am also making similar arrangements with the weaving expert of the Indian Govt. He goes round the villages with improved looms & demonstrates. The great curse of the whole country appears to be the money lender...Another man I have had a talk with is a young botanist...I am hoping through him to get a better grip of the sanitary problem of Madras...I met Lord Pentland, the Governor[3]...a day or two ago, & had a word with him, and he said he would arrange for a talk...It is interesting to note that in Southern India English is the medium of communication between natives speaking different vernaculars....

I don't think you must feel that I am shirking responsibilities by coming out here. So far as I could see there was nothing I could do in England to help bring the war to an end, and here if I do my work well I shall certainly be helping to prevent future wars...and for carrying my family through the period of war difficulty & poverty & depression of trade afterwards—could I be very sure of success at Home? I feel I should have *deserved* to lose your love if I had not come (absurd. V.O.S. [marginal note]) and the feeling that I had failed to do what I was quite clear was my duty would have poisoned our relations. I should have been a morally broken man. (bosh! Rot! V.O.S. [marginal note]) But don't think I do not feel the separation, and not seeing & being with you and the boys & the long time it takes for letters to come & go—and most of all, the last addition to the barriers between us through the loss of the 'Persia'[4] and all that it implies. But I am hopeful that the end of the war is not so far off now. I think the German people must be beginning to be tired of it in spite of all their victories and the German Government beginning to doubt whether after all their long planned resolve to plunge the world into such horrors was not, from their own point of view, a mistake. Until the aggressor repents there can be no peace; but I fancy repentance is beginning. So, sweetheart, let us pray for a much happier New Year than the old one.

Patrick to his father, 1 January [1916]

We had a lovely time on Christmas I got up a 3.30 to see what was in my stoking I had a book called 'The Trail of the Sandhill Stag',[5] a pair of gloves & a toothbrush, a drawing book & some sweets [word indecipherable] & an orange & 2*d*…A little while ago Mrs Grafflin came to tea & we played cards, so she invited us to come to tea & play cards & we had a lovely game & a glorious tea of tarts & bread & Irish butter & cakes all of which I had 8.

Gilbert to Eliot and Patrick, 7 January 1916

Yesterday another mail came in, and this time it brought a letter from Mother, and one from Owen, but none from either Eliot or Pat, though Mother did say that Eliot would have written if he had not had so many lessons. I am very sorry, and I think Mother should have written an excuse for one of the lessons. And there were no [school] *Reports* in the letter, and I want to see the bad *Reports* as well as the good ones. I don't expect reports to be as good as if I were at home to help with the lessons. And I don't so much mind about whether you are high up or low down, as long as you work steadily and try to do your best every day without getting worried or flurried. Sometimes luck is good, and sometimes it is bad.

I have been getting hold of people and making them tell me things, and getting hold of big books which contain a few interesting facts amid pages and pages which are no good to me. One morning I got a man who lives in this hotel to play me a game of tennis before breakfast, and we played three sets…I got very hot, and had to stop every few minutes to wipe off the perspiration, but I felt afterwards as though it had done me a lot of good.

Did you ever read the story in the *Jungle Book* called Rikki-Tikki-Tavi?[6] All about a mongoose which fought with cobras and killed them? A man came to the hotel yesterday and wanted to sell me a mongoose, it looks rather like a hairy snake with little short legs itself, but I would not buy it. I should if I were going to have a house of my own. I think I shall soon buy a motor bike, and when I bring it home I shall have a side car, and then we shall have some jolly excursions—Mother will sit in the car, and Pat [can] curl himself up between her knees, and Eliot shall sit behind and away we will go.

Goodbye, dear boys, and remember that I do love to have letters from you.

Gilbert to Violet, 13 January 1916

The mail which should have come since I last wrote went down in the 'Persia'...When next I get a letter it will tell me, I hope, all about your Christmas, which I do hope went well. What a pity I can't send you some of our bright sunshine! The Syndicate of the University met on Tuesday and agreed to what I asked—i.e. an office, a shorthand clerk, & necessary furniture and equipment. This will enable me to work by dictation & mimeographing...I have been having my 'moonshee' [Munshi or language tutor] regularly this week. He is rather a funny old man, but he has a very good idea of teaching. One great difficulty about Tamil is that the book Tamil taught in the grammars is very different from what is popularly spoken...I do for him one exercise a day out of the handbook & then he gives me dictation—dictates common phrases, which I try to write down by sound. It is very difficult, as I suppose English dictation is to children & foreigners...As the Tamil speaker ordinarily speaks fast & chews his words—they never open their mouths properly in ordinary talk, and they slur over the last syllables of all long words—the whole job of learning Tamil is very difficult. I am almost inclined to think that English will gradually supersede the vernaculars over South India; but it may turn out that Hindustani will prevail...Last week my bank here sent

£20 to our account in Oxford... It seems probable that I shall have to buy a motorcycle, and if so, I shall be a bit short of money & shall have to cut down my remittances somewhat... I had a more vivid dream of you last night than usual, sweetheart. I dreamt we met at Marseilles, but when I put my arm round you to kiss you, I perceived you had on rather stiff stays, and then that your manner also was rather stiff... God bless you, sweetheart, & send happier times, & peace. Ever your loving husband, Gilbert.

Owen, having been appointed a prefect, became a boarder at Magdalen College School.

Owen to his father, [January 1916]

Well I'm quite settled here now. Old Brigger[7] had me down before term began & jawed me & asked me to be a 'prefix'. Wretched fellow he couldn't help making the joke. He'd made it the day before to Mother, so I knew quite well what was coming. I just managed to get my play box finished before I came down. I felt rather strange on the first night, 20 beds in one dorm, very different from a room to yourself. Another thing is getting up. We have prayers at 7 am & we are called at 6.45. Which makes it pretty quick work as it usually takes about 5 mins. to get out of bed. So far I've had a cold bath every morning. I found that that was the only way of waking me up at all. We have just had a most awful essay to do & it has taken me ages though I found it very interesting. 'A dialogue between Socrates & another on Total Abstinence'. I have just been doing a Greek prose perfectly & we are just beginning to go full speed ahead on Plato's *Crito*... I expect I shall get into Greek fairly well soon... They have put me in the second four & we have been told by a very pessimistic coach that we are not so very bad after all.

Gilbert to Owen, 14 January 1916

You are well into the term by the time you get this and I wonder how you are liking it, & how you are getting on with Brigger…And I suppose you are nearly at the top of the school, and a Prefect and altogether a person of importance…There is a lot of very interesting agricultural work going on in India. I don't know whether Mother showed you my little memo. on cow dung, about the practice the people generally follow of burning the dung as fuel. That is one of their agricultural sins. Another is that they grow precious little fodder for their beasts, & let them starve & half starve in the hot season; they take no trouble about breeding, with the consequence that an Indian cow yields only a quarter of the quantity of milk, that an average English cow gives. The whole agricultural work is rather in its infancy, but a lot of different plant & animal diseases have been studied and remedies found…Other things that are going on are improved breeds of cotton plants, of sugar cane & indigo, and propaganda among the peasants to induce them to give up all sorts of wasteful & stupid methods of cultivation; and to form cooperative societies to help one another to get free from the grip of the moneylender. I am wondering whether we could arrange for you to get some months in India sometime—say during a Cambridge long vacation—and go round and visit the various agricultural stations…It seems to me very fascinating work…What a nuisance you have to mug away at Greek! But never mind, it is like my having to mug away at Tamil which is ever so much harder…Goodbye for this time, old chap …

———⁂———

On 27 January 1916 Royal Assent was given to the Military Service Act 1916, which would come into force on 2 March. For the first time in British history the Crown had resorted to conscription. All single men under the age of 41 were now liable to be called up when they turned 18 although later the upper age was raised to 51. Married men, ministers of religion, those working in reserved occupations, and widowers with children were excluded. In May the exclusion of married men was ended. The Act allowed men to seek exemption from military service for various reasons including a conscientious objection to war. By 1918 these 'conscies' numbered some 16,000. The Slaters' work for the Labour Party and Violet's

*increasing involvement with the Society of Friends meant that COs played a larger role in
her life than was the norm.*

Gilbert to Violet, 6 and 9 February 1916

Next week I shall be in a village, and cut off to some extent from communication. I might miss next Saturday's mail unless I post before going. I think I told you before that a man who is a sort of student-lecturer at the Christian College has arranged to work with me in making village surveys, beginning with his native village, and then going on to others. I am hoping that a good many students of the Colleges will do the same; and I am starting with him in order to be in a better position to direct the whole thing...With regard to money—I have sent £10 each month to my mother, and also £18 8s. in payment of Owen's school bill...I should like to know how you are getting on for money—make a rule to pay everything by cheque, & to pay promptly, then the bank will keep all your accounts for you & you can find out any time how you stand...Goodbye, my dearly beloved wife...Always your loving husband, my dearest, Gilbert.

Gilbert to Owen, 9 February 1916 from Hotel Connemara, Madras

Mother says...that you were just off for a week at the Smiths, & then going on to Ealing. All that time I was so glad to know there were no Zeppelins over London though since, I see there was a fleet of them over the Midlands. Very glad to see that one, apparently, never got back to Germany...I suppose by now you will know your Matric. Result[8]...And by the time you get this you will have got through the greater part of the most wearisome term of the year.

As you have had such a working time, one way and another, through the Christmas holidays, I should very much like you to get a good holiday at Easter. I think it would be very good if Mother would take Auntie Gertrude's house at Yelverton…spring at Yelverton is often very delightful…Would you like this? If so talk it over with Mother on Sundays & persuade her to arrange it…I am off now in a few minutes for the village of Eruvellipet, to begin my village surveys. I will write to you to tell you all about that—it may be interesting.

Gilbert to Owen, 9 February 1916 from the Madras Club

Mother has sent me on a letter from Annie Hersch about their plans for Laurie. She thinks there will probably be industrial conscription soon & says that they will try to anticipate it by getting Laurie into engineering works where he can be learning something, as otherwise he may be compelled to work at something which will not help him in his career, & she says the same principle applies to you. It occurs to me that as the University (Oxford) Professor of Chemistry is working at chemical research for the Government he might take you on, on Manley's [the science master's] recommendation, and that this would be the best way out of the difficulty for you if it is possible. It would be the most useful thing you could do for the country, and could also be educational for you & very helpful in your career, and also useful in case you missed an Agricultural Scholarship & had to go in for something else.

Gilbert to Eliot, [9 February 1916]

I wonder whether you would have liked to be at my inaugural address yesterday? It was given in a very splendid hall, with Lord Pentland taking the chair, and telling the people that I am a very learned man, and had hundreds of students there. Indian students in Oxford look like English people, except that they are dark, but in India they wear white cotton petticoats, something like ladies' hobble skirts[9] and have bare feet, and some have their hair quite long and hanging down their backs, while others twist it into a knot at the back of their heads, so that they look more like young women than young men. Most of them study very hard and go to lots of lectures, but they also play cricket, & hockey, and soccer & lawn tennis…The tennis courts are a sort of sand with something to bind it and make it hard. If Mother were out here she ought to do lots & lots of painting. The sun shines brightly every day, & the sea is as blue as it can be, and the rivers, and the trees are very pretty. There are always people catching fish in the river with nets—or trying to…I wonder how you get on with your lessons this term; and if you like living so close to the school. Now that Owen is at school, you are the man of the family, and I hope you are taking very good care of Mother.

Violette Bossy to Violet, 10 February [1916]

It is true enough that we live now as in different worlds. Your and Owen's letters tell me things I could never dream of. Ruskin college *désaffecté*, Dr Slater in India, it is all like an impossible fancy. I cannot imagine what brought such a change. I only hope that it is for something better. However, you must miss Dr Slater dreadfully, he is so much the father & the chief in the house. Can he well bear the new climate? And he arrived just in the hottest days, I think…I believe that I know à peu près were [where] your new house stands…Do you continue to go to Ruskin for the ill?…Each day, prisoners of both parties are comming to Switzerland to re-establish their health. They are so wellcome…You don't know how I long sometimes for a day in Oxford. It remains so much for me the very place of young things.

Owen to his father, [February 1916]

I do hope this will get posted in time. For the last two or three days I have been terribly rushed. The 2nd IV have been going out every day & will continue to do so until the race. I am rowing 3…We are doing Plato's *Crito* & the *Apology*…Gym is going on quite well & I have been told by Haliday the instructor that I'm the best boy he's had for 15 years, that with a little coaching I might get into a public school team. I'm rather bucked at that…there is not much else to do but to work & keep alive & boat…thanks awfully for your letter, it was very interesting indeed. I've got a suggestion for you about cow dung. Don't you think their superstitions may have something to do with their disliking to use it for manure. The old theory of magical influences by contact?

I like the organ very much indeed though I have not done so very much yet. Not learnt enough to take the school service with any success yet. I had a sudden fit of working the other day. I did a Latin prose in about an hour, at any rate not more & got 12 for it, which is my top mark & an essay in less than ¾ & got β+ for it. I'm afraid I must leave off now as I've got to row in a few minutes. Your loving son Owen.

PS. N.B. I don't advise you to buy a motor bike, but if you do, whatever you do buy a good one. There's nothing worse than a rotten one.

Gilbert to Violet, 18 February 1916

Now about that stove—if the Kitchener[10] won't work get one that will—though I wonder if…the thing would work all right if you understood it…the third thing to remember [is] that the intensity of your feelings makes you a rather overpowering mother, and creates a sort of timidity in the children which may lead into deceitfulness. You must try to allow for this & be cautious in uttering words of reproof…Now don't think that

I am scolding you unjustly, especially with regard to the boys, & accusing you of making them untruthful. The intensity of your desire that they shall be brave and honourable is bound to tell in the end; but you do…make it awfully hard for people who love you to tell you things that are unwelcome to you. My dear girl, do try all you know to cultivate calmness of soul. The circumstances are awfully trying, I admit.

Gilbert to Eliot and Patrick, 18 February 1916

I have just had *three* letters from each of you…I am very glad you both have good reports and are getting to be clever boys…And I want you also to be very brave and truthful and honourable…Last week I went away into the country to see what the villages are like…when we got to the station called Villapuram, and there we found hundreds of people on the platforms and outside the station with their beds on the ground asleep…there was a bedroom in the station, so we went to bed…We got up at half past six next morning,…and there two bullock carts were waiting for us…Nearly all the land is rice fields. These are quite small and perfectly flat…When we got to the village we drove up to the house of the richest man…It was a new house, not quite finished, though he has been 14 years building it!…He is well educated, and speaks English quite well…Tom stayed there and cooked meals, while Sundaram Reddi and I explored the fields and talked to the people…The people asked me into their houses to have meals, and then they made me sit down to a table all by myself and burnt sticks to make a sort of incense, & gave me weird spiced cakes fried in ghee…Now goodbye, my dear Boys. I do hope you will be as good and kind to your dear Mother as you possibly can, and make her very happy. Always your loving Father.

Gilbert to Violet, [18 February 1916?]*

I got your first letter, and the boys' three letters before breakfast. It is *so* nice to get them, it seems to bring you all so near. Dearest I like what you say about my complexion. I don't like myself much, and it is always easy for me to see why other people find me unattractive, not quite so easy to see why one person loves me. My darling, I too ache to see and hold and kiss you again, & I love to think of your little curls on the back of your neck, and your peaked nose, and slim height & swift movements.

⎯⎯∞⎯⎯

On 21 February the Germans launched their massive attack on the French fortress of Verdun. The fighting continued until December with a horrifying number of casualties on both sides. The Germans never achieved their goal, which was the capture of the city and fortress of Verdun.

Gilbert to Violet, 22 and 24 March 1916

Whether it is to be depended on or not one cannot say, but there seems to be a sort of impression forming that the war will not be many months longer. Tirpitz's[11] resignation seems a good sign; if any thing effective had been done towards securing a German naval victory they would hardly have sacked him, and if nothing yet has been done, it is probably too late now. If all goes well we may even have peace by October. There seem to be increasing signs that the Germans are finding victory like the Dead Sea apples.[12] But of course by the time this reaches you important things may have happened—e.g. the new German loan may be a great success—that will indicate that the people are still backing up the military.[13] Or the German offensive may succeed at Verdun or...Czernowitz [the capital of the Austro-Hungarian province of Bukovina].

So far as I can judge Indian opinion, it is, among all the educated classes heart and soul for the British Empire. The Brahmins would like to supersede British officials, non-Brahmins generally prefer the British official; but, so far as I can see, nobody really thinks of British rule as alien.

16

Mrs Besant[14] talks of it as if it were, & no doubt her talk is mischievous as well as malicious, and it flatters Indian vanity to be told that Hindu civilisation is so much older, wiser, more beautiful & saner than that of the West. And the people have a wonderful power of deluding themselves with words. But, nevertheless, they think of various officials as individuals & weigh them up. And their general impression of the ordinary Collector—who is magistrate & administer of a district corresponding to an English county & who rules it with the help of one or two deputy collectors and native officials—is that he is a good sort, unbribable and just in intention, but (sometimes) peppery in temper, and (frequently) rather easily imposed upon by an ingeniously constructed story...I am hoping for good personal news in your next letter...Don't drift, sweetheart, in matters of health...Try to relax your mind & snatch at pleasures as they pass. It is too exhausting to be always at high tension. I can only try to help you and take care of you by advice, and I am afraid advice may seem like unwelcome sermonising. Don't take it so, take it as the nearest thing I can do to folding you in my arms and trying to comfort you to sleep.

Gilbert to Violet, 29 March 1916 from Palni

I have just received the English mail sent on from Madras, with the good news that Owen got through Matric. first division. Like you and Owen I feel awfully bucked. You also tell about Dr Carlyle[15] for baptism, and godfathers and godmothers. I hope Grinles [the Rev. C. H. Grinling] will be able to come. I am sure he would know how to say the right things, and it would be very fine for Owen to get the infection of his spirit. But when you wrote me before about Owen joining a class to prepare for confirmation I did not at all realise it meant baptism first.[16] I think one effect of living in India is to give one an increased dislike of all religious ceremonies, there is no end of it here and it is all divorced from morality—in a number of cases positively immoral.

17

While this terrible war is raging one can hardly make plans. Your letter is about the beginning of the great Verdun battle—when I write this the battle has been going on for over a month & Verdun has not fallen. But be sure I shall get home when possible…I have just read of the 'Sussex'[17] being torpedoed & 100 lives lost. That looks very bad. I'm afraid that the idea that is strongest in my mind in reading war news is 'Will the war be over by March next, my earliest chance of getting home!'

Gilbert to Violet, 12 April 1916 from Madura

Your letter written just after Owen's baptism & confirmation has been waiting here for me some days…Next week's mail is, I believe, the one that was on board the *Sussex*, so whether I get it or not is doubtful. I hope you are not overdoing it with visitors; but very glad that you enjoyed having Annie Hersch so much. For all our sakes, don't you go getting into prison!…I am very sorry Brownrigg thinks Owen has no chance at the Greek for the Higher Certificate[18]…It would be such a blessing to get that Greek disposed of & out of the way. I think however hopeless the chance Owen had better have a try. Get him cribs for the set books…and let him go right through with the crib several times not long before the Exam.

With regard for the future the choice is very difficult. I think on the whole I should prefer him to try to join the Friends' Ambulance service[19]…But I would not press him in the slightest—nor would I press it against your wishes. I think the best alternative is for him simply to stay on at school for another year…When you get this you had better talk matters over with Owen & try to come to a conclusion. Geddes started for home by the mail before this. You might consult him…Arthur Geddes is with one of the Quaker organisations…With lots of love. It is I fear a long time of sadness & dreariness we have before us—but I have not given up hope of peace within the twelvemonth, and of meeting then. I am always looking forward to that meeting. I picture the ship coming in to the quay at Marseilles & your waiting there—& then—Try to be happy, sweetheart.

—∞∞∞—

Gilbert to Owen, 22 April 1916

I have felt quite cut off from you, as last mail but one you did not write, being doubtless too full up with Baptism & Confirmation, and last mail went down in the *Sussex*... You have now gone through the Christian form of a worldwide ceremony, among primitive people called 'making man', among the Greeks, Eleusinian mysteries—but always fundamentally the same thing, that the boy should realise that he is a boy no longer, but a man, with a man's powers and responsibilities: that he has entered into the tribe, and taken on tribal responsibilities, or the Church and religious responsibilities. I should like to know how you think & feel about it. If you would let me know, be sure that I would sympathise. It is my job now to be the very best friend I can to you, to give you advice and help, but to recognise that now your life is your own, and that your own will and judgement must have the ultimate decision in what you choose to do. This must particularly be so in relation to the war, and what you do with regard to that. You know I should best like you at the end of this summer term to either join the Friends' ambulance corps or to do something else definitely helpful. I think in after years you will always be glad to feel that you have put your brain and muscles to the service of the country in the midst of its great and terrible danger, and of the still more terrible danger to civilisation and humanity in case we should be beaten in the war. *But* you must do this of your own free will & choice or not at all. Either do it because you feel it is the right thing to do, and because you want to do it; or don't do it at all.

If you say *no*, then I will arrange for you to stay another year at school and you can go on with your school life & studies just as if there were no war and I don't suppose anybody will ever reproach you. When you are 18 you will then come within the military net for home training, but we may

19

well hope that the war will be over before you are actually called upon to serve. You must choose which course. If you choose to leave school, in order to help the country, there may be a great variety of things open to you besides the Friends' Ambulance corps. But look into your own heart, and determine what is your answer to the choice for the coming year— school or national service, and let me know. Your very loving father, Gilbert Slater.

<hr>

On 24 April, Easter Bank Holiday Monday, the 'Easter Rising' broke out in Dublin but was over by 30 April, leaving behind a divided Ireland.

Gilbert to Eliot and Patrick, 5 May 1916 from Gray's Hotel, Coonoor

Here I am, up in the Blue Mountains, nearly 6,000 feet above sea level…this little railway twists its way up the slopes, which are…in most places forest, a good deal of it bamboo, which looks like grass from a distance, and lots of different sorts of trees…In these forests people say there are a good many leopards. A lady was bicycling on the road quite close here, and she had a dog running behind and a leopard jumped out and snapped up the dog, and the lady scooted as hard as she could go. A few days ago a leopard was seen just below this hotel, & some men fired at it, and missed it, and at Kotagiri…another holiday place 16 miles away, there is a tiger hiding in the woods. Perhaps I shall see one of these beasts, but if I do, I don't think I shall be clever or lucky enough to snapshot it.

<hr>

Gilbert to Owen, 11 May 1916

I have just got yours about your [cycle] ride to Hunstanton…I see from the school bill that you are in the football group & the rowing group—

and I have to say 15s for the two photos! I am *very* glad to see Brigger has given you a better report than ever before…I have been doing some riding like yours—62 miles in 2 hours or more…It is a big ride to do 62 miles against a strong southwester, I hope you took no harm. I am so glad you have liked being a boarder…Tomorrow I am going to cycle to Kotagiri and should get some nice views…A short time ago I am told that a young man & young woman went for a stroll in a wood at Kotagiri—11 miles from here—and were attacked by a bear. They ran for their lives, and fell into a deep ditch, where the bear lost them, & while he was nosing round looking for them, some natives passed by, so they shouted & the natives drove away the bear & picked them out of the ditch. Then we hear a good deal of talk of tigers, leopards & wild elephants. I have seen no trace of any of these beasties.

I don't think I need write further this week about your future. Let me know what you settle on, after talking it over with Mother. But take my advice, & seize any opportunities you get of learning to ride a horse & manage a motor car.

Gilbert to Owen, 19 May 1916

Tomorrow will be your birthday! The manly age of 17 reached! By the time you get this you will be quite accustomed to the feeling of being 17, & drawing nearer to the Certif. and to the great decision you have to make about how you will use the next year of your life. Here I am on holiday; but not entirely…preparation for the coming year's work has to take a good deal of time, and more goes to Tamil. I have some hopes of getting a useful grip of that language, though hearing English all round makes it much more difficult. All my story for the week is in the letters I have sent to Mother & Eliot & Pat—so you must see these and take this merely as a birthday greeting.

Gilbert to Owen, 25 May 1916

Now when you get this you will be close to the Certif. I have previously re-commended you towards the close of the time to get a translation and go over the set books very carefully and two or three times, with the translation. If you have not done so yet, it is high time you did. Perhaps it is not a satisfactory way (though of that I am not sure) of studying Greek, but you don't want to study Greek only to squeeze through the Exam. Don't give up hope of passing till the Exam is actually over. It would be a great save of bother for you to pull through. I don't think I have anything to add to what I have written before about the most important question of what you could do after the end of term. The only new idea that has occurred to me is that it might be worthwhile to consult Uncle Howard about your getting into the R.A.M.C.[20] in case you do not get into the Friends Ambulance Corps. I wonder whether it would be good for you to try to catch the Skipper[21] and have a talk with him. It might be worth trying, though he must have many anxieties on his mind. I will write when I am sending my cheque for his bill.

⸎

Between 31 May and 1 June the Battle of Jutland was fought. It was at the time, and arguably remains, the greatest naval engagement in history. It also remains one of the most hotly debated aspects of the war. The Royal Navy's Grand Fleet was joined by ships of the Royal Australian and Royal Canadian navies. They were attacked by the German High Seas Fleet in an attempt to destroy part of the Grand Fleet and weaken the Allied blockade of Germany. While both sides claimed victory, the British suffered more casualties and ships lost while the Germans failed in their purposes. Three days later, on 4 June, Russian forces began the massive Brusilov Offensive against the forces of Austria-Hungary.

Gilbert to Owen, 8 June 1916

I got yours of May 11 last Sat … I also got the *Draconian & The Lily*,[22] and see that you won your race with Worcester [College], and also that the Editor congratulates you on Matric … We only heard last night of the naval battle of May 31st, and the first news we got seemed very bad indeed—as

22

we heard of *very* heavy British losses, and only some guesses at much smaller German losses. Subsequent information makes it look better; but no doubt it is all ancient history for you.

⊷⊶

Gilbert to Violet, 15 June 1916

I have this week received two mails…You did *not* send—at least I have not yet received, your directions about washing woollens. I put on this morning a shirt my boy washed, it was rather awful, and, I fear, a good deal shrunk. About pyjamas—Some people, Collins for example, get into their pyjamas immediately after dinner, and receive visitors in them. I don't. So the question of decency does not arrive, except in travelling by train and then I do sleep in pyjamas.

Now with regard to Owen. I am feeling more hopeful now that the war will end before he is 18, or before the period of grace is up. And I don't in the least believe that there will be any conscripting of boys of 18 immediately after the war is over. The country can't afford it…It therefore really comes to this, I think. (1) If the war is going to last on beyond his time next year [after 20 May when Owen become eligible to be called up]. In that case I think there will be a very material advantage for Owen to have before hand got into the Friends' Ambulance service. The Friends are such a powerful body that I don't think their service will be blocked or interfered with. (2) If the war ends before advantages are much more equally balanced, true Scientific agriculture will be very badly needed; and to go straight ahead with the programme we planned would in many respects be best; on the other hand the educational value of the ambulance training would be very considerable, and the taste of real & useful work I think would be excellent for the development of his character.

The last week's news, of the great Russian advance in Galicia, seems to bring better hope than anything we have heard for a long time of an end to the war within twelve months—but, of course, next week's news may

23

reverse that.[23] You might have another try to talk it over with Dr Gillett.[24] I fancy it may need some influence to get Owen into the Ambulance, and Dr Gillett's personal recommendation should count.

⸺oᴥo⸺

Gilbert to Violet, 22 June 1916

I was talking with a Miss Miller the other day…she told me that her younger brother has been allowed to continue at school in order to pass certain examinations, and get his military training in the school cadet corps instead of in the army, and she thought the same course would probably be open to Owen. This seems to me a possible new light on the problem…All the recent news of the war seems to confirm the hope (though by the time you get this there may be as much news of a contrary tendency) that the war will be over before lads of Owen's age are used. It would probably be a great pity for him to be called up for military training, and herded with a miscellaneous lot of youths of all sorts of characters in barracks, waste time, and get no good, even if never sent out in active service. It is quite a different matter going on at school and drilling with Oxford V.T.C.[25]

I cannot argue it out, but my feeling on the matter has gradually changed…my preference was for Owen to join the Friends' Ambulance Corps—now my preference is for him to stay on at school, try for the science scholarship we originally planned for him if he is permitted to do so, do as much agricultural work in the holidays as possible. Perhaps the change of feeling comes from the fact that I am more and more looking forward to peace and thinking over the problems of the condition of things when peace is established. I shall join the Council for Combating Venereal Diseases (or whatever name it calls itself)[26] out here, and shall hope to do something for it when I get home next spring. I think you might spare a guinea a year to it, and try to enlist members among your friends…War, the greatest of all evils, is also the greatest of opportunities, and the special opportunity granted by this war is, I think, to appeal to those people who have shown a certain willingness to die for their country. When the war is over, to give birth to an untainted generation. Possibly it may be practicable to found a Madras branch. India is, apparently, very much worse than England.

Life here passes easily and even frivolously. We have 'chota' [*Chota haziri*, the Hindi term for 'little breakfast'] at 7, usually go up to the [Madras] Club[27] at 8 or half past, for tennis, see the papers of the day before (Madras), take a turn on the lake, come back to breakfast at 11.30 probably stay indoors till tea—3.30—then tramps or more tennis or boating till dark. Dinner at 8, and after dinner there is pretty regularly one four playing bridge. There is no piano here, which is rather a pity…I am afraid this is not an interesting letter. After all, play is so much less interesting than work, and the only work I have done here is preparation of my course to begin next month. This is half England, rather than India—tea just now, for example, bread & butter, seed cake, toast, jam, marmalade, on the table hydrangeas, petunias, antirrhinums…Always your lover, Gilbert Slater.

Gilbert to Violet, 28 June 1916*

It seems to me that Owen really wants to stay on at school, and that you think that is best; I am now inclined to think so too. I am hoping that the end of the war will be in sight before he is 18; and there will be a great advantage if he can go straight to preparing his chosen career.

Before I forget it, I have arranged to move into the Madras Club…one nuisance will be that I shall have to dress for dinner every day. But it is central, and a good deal cheaper than an hotel, and conveniently situated, very free from mosquitos, and has various little advantages, e.g. I can get a game of tennis early in the morning & then a plunge in the swimming bath, before breakfast

The series of engagements called collectively the 'Battle of the Somme' began on 1 July 1916. While advances were made, this joint Anglo-French attempt to break through the German lines ultimately failed by the time the offensive ended in November. On the first day there were over 60,000 British casualties and by November the total had grown to over one million among all the armies involved. Only in February 1917 did German forces leave the Somme to pull back to the recently finished and heavily fortified Hindenburg Line. This was to allow their depleted forces a better defensive position.

Gilbert to Owen, 21 July 1916

I don't know where you will be in August, so I am sending this to Auntie Agnes, in case you are at Leyburn [Yorks.]...Last week end I was at Coimbatore Agricultural College[28]...They have a variety of agricultural work in the college & have to do 3 hours actual work per day, the rest of the time being given to study. Some interesting things are being done, not exactly by the College, but beside it. One man is busy with sugar cane. For an unknown period sugar cane has been grown by planting bits of cane, usually the top three joints below the leaves. The sugar cane man has succeeded in getting the cane to produce fertile seeds, & has been selecting from the seedlings, which vary enormously, for vigour of growth, hardiness, yield of cane per acre, & sugar content of cane. Another man is doing similar work on rice. But the chief object is to train men to serve in the Agricultural department, in which they will have to advise peasants on methods of cultivating, manuring, implements etc. I met here, besides the College staff & other people I had met before, the man who has just come out to take up cattle-breeding— which is perhaps of all branches of agriculture what the Indian does worst...I am now settled in at this house, which I share with Arthur Davies. Have a chota—tea, toast & bananas—at 7 am—breakfast at 9, a sort of combination meal, lunch & tea, at 2.30, and dinner at 8...A tennis ground is being got ready, & should be fit for play in about a week's time...Since the time of the naval battle, up to now, the war news has been such as to make me much more hopeful of an ending before many months have gone. But I fear submarining may get even more acute.[29]

<hr />

In the summer of 1916 Violet's growing opposition to the war, noted in Gilbert's letter of 12 April 1916, led her to join the International Committee of Women for Permanent Peace, later the Women's International League for Peace and Freedom.[30] This had been formed at a women's peace conference in The Hague in April 1915 and campaigned for a negotiated end to the fighting and for votes for women.

Gilbert to Violet, 21 July 1916

I don't know much about the Women's International, but I am glad you have joined it. I shall like to know who are the other members of the Oxford branch. It is flattering that you should be made chairman. (I don't think your gifts run much to Chairmanship.) Mind, *the* great thing a Chairman has to do is to secure fair play and full opportunity for the expression of all points of view particularly (a) those of the minority, & (b) *those with whom he least agrees.* But while it is flattering, it also rather suggests that the branch is small, or its members not very influential. One thing you should see is done at every meeting—discuss possible new members, and detail somebody to look up each likely person. It just gives the members something to do in between, and keeps live their interest. You should see 'New Members' down on the agenda for each meeting… I… have begun my lectures to Madras students, & given a lecture at the Kellett Institute, Triplicane, a Wesleyan Missionary effort[31]… I have got into the limelight again immediately, I find. I was pressed to speak at Coimbatore, to explain what Economics is. I said, incidentally, that the vocal Indian opinion was quite right in demanding further expenditure in education, sanitation, agricultural progress, & industrial progress, but wrong in simultaneously demanding reduction of taxation. That it is worth while to pay an extra anna, if you get back an extra rupee, & that there are lots of ways in which a Govt. expenditure reckoned in annas will bring back a benefit to be reckoned in rupees (16 annas = 1 rupee, 1 anna = 1^d). The *Madras Times* gave this their first leader, & *New India* a leaderette.[32]

[J. A.] Hobson's letter is characterised by his admirable spirit; but one thing he leaves out of account, the necessity of getting such terms as to give reasonable security against another war following quickly on the heels of this one. These terms, I think, must include (1) compensation to Belgium & Serbia, (2) the unification of Poland & Serbia, (3) the liberation of Slavs & Romanians in the two Central Empires. Further France will rightly demand the restoration of Alsace-Lorraine, and I think should have it; we, I think should get the Heligoland back,[33] in view of the use Germany made of it, and our colonies will not permit German colonies in their neighbourhood. Also we must not in the treaty of peace sign away our fiscal freedom. Now as soon as we can get these terms we should make peace, but I fear that will not be until the war has turned more against Germany. After that I think every great power in Europe will have a salutary conviction that war is a horrible & undesirable thing, and the prospects before the world will be brighter.

When our tennis ground is ready we shall be at home to Indian students every Sat. afternoon, & regale them with tennis, fizzy drinks & conversation. This, I hope, will be continued after Mrs Davies returns—i.e. I hope it will still be our joint home. It makes things much easier than it was with Ruskin students...8.20—must scoot! Lots of love, Gilbert

---

Gilbert to Owen, 29 July 1916

I have just had Mother's letter of June 30th telling me about the arrangements for you at Moor Farm. It seems rather mean of them not to give you full board & lodging in return for your labour; but you must bear in mind that even if they do make some measly profit out of you, you are working really to feed the country and to gain knowledge and ability. I hope you will have a good time, and develop your muscles, and learn enough to make it worth while. I am earnestly hoping for Turkey to be knocked out soon, & then the pressure put upon Austria to become overwhelming and then Germany will surely not be able to hold out long. Flies, stinks, & most of all the deafening noises are said to make life in the trenches unendurable. It is only right & fair that all should take their part in the miseries & sufferings, but I cannot help being selfish enough to hope & wish that you may be spared.

University politics are quite exciting, owing to the fact that Mrs Besant is always getting hold of the Indian members of the Senate and stirring them up to make themselves as troublesome as possible, & then writing inflammatory articles in her paper New India. She is always trying to make trouble somewhere or other. Thus some time ago the Indians petitioned that in certain trains there should be separate carriages for the Eurasians, because the Indians didn't like travelling with them. The R.M. Co. agreed & labelled two carriages, out of about 12 or 15, for 'Anglo Indians'. Now she has stirred up the Indians to say that it is illegal tyranny that they should not be allowed in those carriages, & to enter finally, & the day before yesterday a mob of students collected at the station and, being much more numerous (they never attack unless they are about 10 to 1) attacked the Eurasian passengers, & injured some so much that they had to be taken to hospital. Then Mrs Besant comes out with articles applauding their valiant, courageous spirit—the martial spirit of old India etc. It will not be surprising if she finds herself under lock & key pretty soon.

The farm work to which Gilbert referred was at Moor Farm (now Harmby Moor Farm) 2 miles outside Leyburn in Yorkshire where Owen's Aunt Agnes Peacock lived. The work allowed him to follow the advice given by his father, and by schools round the country, to do his bit to help the war effort. The visit also created a desire to become a farmer and allowed him to become confident in handling farm horses.

Gilbert to Violet, 4 August 1916

I have got Brigger's letter … [and] understand that by putting his name down for a particular college Owen would not necessarily pledge himself to go to it if he gets a scholarship elsewhere. I think it is rather important that he should go to Cambridge rather than to Oxford. The degree course is 3 years instead of 4—that makes some difference. And the teaching is very much better in Agriculture & allied subjects at Cambridge … I wonder where you are going for the holidays. I have heard something from Agnes about your going to the sea-side with Annie Hersch. I think that would be a very good idea.

The 2nd anniversary of the beginning of war! Again, after a month or two's interval we read of Zeppelins over England. They do not wait for the nights to shorten much. We are told this time that there are no casualties. I wonder how it will be thorough the winter? I think all the romance & false [?] glamour has gone out of war now—I do really think that there is a good chance that this is the war to end war—if only we can get Germany well beaten.

Owen to his mother, 6 August 1916 from Moor Farm

Today's Sunday & I'm down at Aunties. I came late last night … I've been having a very happy time, very busy & very hard work & I simply haven't had a minute to spare till today … I've ridden quite a lot & driven horses a good deal but not done any milking yet. The work is very much the same & not very interesting & at times I get quite tired & rather bored but that soon passes. Mr Tweddell, pronounced exactly as it's spelt, is an absolute nigger for work … all the work so far has been with the hay but when that's finished we are going to cut bracken on the moor & bring it in which will be great fun. They've got no corn land at all here all grass & cattle. They've got the dearest pair of young foals you can imagine & lots of little pigs, young turkeys & baby chicks & calves & lambs so its all very interesting…I don't make a sou out of that 10/- really as it will all go as pocket money.

Owen to his father, 9 August 1916 from Moor Farm

I'm afraid this will only be a very short letter as at present I'm working on a farm. We work from morn till night almost without a rest, only stopping for meals. The other day we had a day of fourteen hours. The work is mighty hard & in consequence I sleep from the end of one day's work to the beginning of the next. It's doing me a world of good I'm sure, in fact I don't believe I've worked so hard & for such a long time before in my life…We have a glorious view across the valley to Pen & beyond & it is ripping to see the mist in the valley in the early morning hiding all but the top of Pen…The family consists of Father, Mother & four children two boys, 20, 14 & two girls, 16 & 14. Also a grandmother. They are all very nice and kind but at times it is almost impossible to understand them…I'm very sorry but I shall have to leave off now as I shall be working all day at getting the hay in & there is only one chance of getting a letter posted, by the post girl. So much love from your loving son, Owen.

Gilbert to Eliot and Pat, 12 August 1916*

I sent off this mail a shawl for mother, and with it a few sea-shells for Eliot which I picked up on 'Eliot's beach'. Davies and I motored here last Sunday. You go south from Madras till you come to the river Adyar, & cross it by a bridge. And then you go through a great sandy waste which has been reclaimed. People began by planting casuarinas trees in the sand; they are like fir trees, and grow very quickly, and make good fire-wood, & they drop their needles which make a sort of manure & bind the sand together, and then after the casuarinas are cut down, all sorts of crops can be grown, & plantains (i.e. bananas) and palm trees. The Theo-sophical Society has a great estate here of some hundreds of acres. At the end of this you come out on the sandy beach…It used to be the fashion for English people in Madras to motor or drive out and bathe. But when-ever the Indians see English people do anything they hurry to imitate them, & so the Indians came out too, & then English ladies did not care to undress on the beach with a crowd of natives looking on, & so the beach is nice and nearly deserted.

Gilbert to Owen, 12 August 1916

Last week I had no letter from you…But I had one from Brigger, from which it appears that he did not at all think that the Greek in the Higher Certif. was too much for you if you dug in at it, and he thought you were disposed to think you could do it without a special effort, and has been trying to stir [?] you up to make that special effort by exaggerating the difficulty! I wrote and told him that he quite misunderstood you, & that he should have let you know that it was quite possible, & the more he made you feel that you had a chance, the more you would have tried. So now I suppose you have failed in Greek, and very likely purely on ac-count of this misunderstanding. If you had believed me & not Brigger you would probably have got through. But when he said 'It would be a miracle if you passed' he only meant it would be a miracle if you passed without putting in more time at the Greek. Well, it can't be helped now. But you will know better another time how to take what he says. And let this be a lesson to you in future to have more faith in your own powers… I have been hampered all my life by that undue under-estimate of my powers, & have only got cured of late years, & still have it in my instincts, if not in my calculations, & I have no doubt you have it too. It is a far greater handicap than thinking too well of yourself.

Well, I hope you are having a good time, & putting on muscle & feeling fit, & with a grand appetite & yet not forgetting to chew up your food well.

Owen to his father, 15 August 1916 from Moor Farm

Today is the first wet day we have had since I've been here & in consequence we can do very little hay work. We have still got 80 pikes [stacks] or more to lead in...It is perfectly glorious to do work manually instead of trying to do work mentally. And besides I'm getting considerable biceps, a thing I've never had or needed before...I'm feeling perfectly gloriously fit all over though I haven't had a bathe for over a fortnight now.... Its great fun feeding the horses, driving them & riding them particularly.

Gilbert to Violet, 16 August 1916*

I have signed the covering statement to the 'Basis for a Just Peace' and have sent it with a covering letter to Dr Carpenter.[34] I think it is now about the right time for the public discussion of peace terms; and the fundamental idea of aiming at a just settlement in such a way as to remove the provoking causes of future wars, is on the one hand obviously right & on the other, necessary to enforce.

I doubt now whether we can arrange any thing better for Owen to do than to go right on at school, just as though there were no war. If you can do anything for wounded, well & good; otherwise I don't think there is any good in your going to see him brought in.

When you get this your summer holidays will be over—and I know so little as to what they are. I shall be watching Zeppelin reports most anxiously. Poor Annie Hersch appears to have been having a fearful grind—and poor Martin [Owen's cousin], by the time I write this, I suppose, is back again at the Front. Pushing back the German line is truly a terrible business. But what fiends to have planned and planned & planned all these horrors for years, & then schemed to bring about the crisis, & have done it so shamelessly.

⸎

Gilbert to Owen, 19 August 1916

I am sending this to the School, as I suppose you will be back when it arrives. I wonder what sort of holidays you had and I hope you put on muscle & filled out a bit, & had *some* jolly days, in spite of hard labour. At last the war seems to be going better, though with horrible casualties. Somewhere or other the enemy must begin to crumble up soon, one would think, if the pressure is continued as now. So I am quite hopeful of peace in twelve months. I am hopeful, too, of being able to get home next March (leaving March, arriving April).

⸎

Owen to his mother, 20 August 1916 from Moor Farm

We've been having bad weather too but no remission of work, the only difference is that it has been much more varied. I did a good two hours of proper riding yesterday. It was great fun, we went over the moor after sheep. We brought them home, separated the lambs from the mothers & marked the sheep & counted them about fifteen times & finally got it the same three times so we took it at that, 116 with about 50 lambs or more. Lately I have been looking after the calves, feeding them & parafining them where they have got ringworm. Its usually an awful job catching them & they simply wont keep still when they are caught...I'm afraid I

34

shant get any bathing before I get back to Oxford. The moors are simply glorious here now…They are awfully nice people here & they seem to want me to stay on.

———⚭———

On 27 August 1916 Romania declared war on the Central Powers. The next day Italy, anxious to seize territory from Austria-Hungary, followed suit.

Gilbert to Owen, 8 September 1916

I have been very glad to get your letters from the Moor Farm, & to see that you have enjoyed it so much…I see from your report that Brigger thinks you go to North Oxford too often. He does not add 'to see Joan George' but I suppose that is what he means. I hope to make that young lady's acquaintance next spring. But you should be careful to use the special liberties you enjoy as prefect with moderation. If you haven't done so already let me know your weight, so that I shall know what you have put on since the race. I hope this term you will get your colours for socker. I am still very nearly the worst tennis player in Madras…I am earnestly hoping that the war will end in about six months from now—Rumania's intervention should make that possible. What is your own idea of what to do after Christmas? How would it do for you to see the Skipper and ask him what he thinks? I think that after it is all over you will be glad to think that you have done something to help. Hay-making is *something*, but a few weeks' haymaking is not very much. I very much hope that you will not be called upon to go into barracks or into the trenches, in fact that would appear to be very unlikely, I am glad to think; but there are a lot of other things possible. I have seen something about some sort of volunteer corps organised by the Govt.[35] Do you know anything about it? If you can find out anything, let me know.

———⚭———

Owen to his father, 21 September 1916

I have been quite busy all the time, mostly with the garden…[which] is beginning to look really a little ship shape…by the way Mother says she's sorry she didn't send the boys accounts but they put down a charge of one guinea entrance fee for Pat & she protested. I have been having extra organ lessons during the last week & yesterday Mrs Briggs gave me a piano lesson & another one today. I shall be in the football eleven & I hope to get a nice lot of matches though I don't expect there will be very many. I had my last early morning bathe on Saturday, its horribly cold now & I don't expect I shall bathe again this year.

Gilbert to Patrick, [September 1916]

I have had your letter this week in which you ask me why I did not get into the palm tree and pick a coker-nut. Do you know, I think if I had tried to get it I should have broken my neck, and then what would have been the good of the coker-nut?

To-day something happened that might interest you. A man came to the hotel with a cheetah kitten. The Cheetah is a sort of spotted leopard that sometimes the people of India tame and use to catch deer…He wanted to sell it to somebody to keep for a pet. If you had been here, I think you would have wanted to buy it. It was about twice as big as a big cat; but of course it will grow a great deal bigger, and then what could one do with it? It would get to be quite dangerous…I was glad to get so nice a letter from you, with all those kisses. I can see from your writing that you are fast getting to be a big boy. Perhaps next time you write it will be all about school

X   X   X   X   X   X

Tell mother to give you lots of kisses from your loving Dad.

Gilbert to Owen, 22 September 1916

I wonder how much you forget me while I am away. In six months from now I shall be on my way home—& in six months from your getting this I shall, all being well, be with you. We must soon, after this, make up our minds as to what you are to do after Christmas. Do you know what the Hersches are going to do about Laurie? Of course he is somewhat younger than you, but they may be making up their minds. Are you drilling with the V.T.C. now?

I have had a chat with my host Charlton, who was in England this summer; & he expresses the opinion (1) that the war will very likely be over by May, (2) that nobody can be sent to the Front, under the conscription law, under the age of 19. When I get back to Madras I will look the matter up in the files of the *Times*, if they have it in the Club, so that we know where we stand.

Gilbert to Owen, 6 October 1916

I have heard from Mother & Brownrigg that you failed in Greek, in Physics & in Chemistry. I should have liked it better if I had heard it from you...I have also heard that last term you persistently cut the cricket to go up the river with Joan George or other folk. And you tell me you would dearly like to be a farmer...Now you must realise that there are 3 ways of getting into any sort of agricultural work—one is to be a labourer on a starvation wage & that would kill you. The second is to be a farmer, and that is impossible without capital, and capital I cannot supply you with; and the third is the way we planned—by means of a science scholarship and the Agricultural course at Cambridge. That is all there is in England. Of course there is the alternative of emigration, which you may be driven to.

But apart from emigration, so far as I can see, your chance of getting into the sort of work and life that you would like depends on your grinding successfully at your school work. You must pass Little Go [the first examination for the Oxford B.A.]...this term, and then really dig in at the science, & whatever other subject you take up as an extra. I should like the extra subject to be French...But this term it is the Greek...You must regard that as the *first* thing you have got to do to avoid having to be a clerk in an office, or a schoolmaster, or something else equally distasteful. Show your grit, and stick at it...And do please try to open your heart to me, & tell me things about what you think & do sometimes when you know I shall not like to hear them, as well as when I shall. I want you to be able to get some good out of *my* experience of life & to avoid the mistakes I have made, without making all those that I have avoided...So plug away, old chap, till I come home.

Gilbert to Owen, 27 October 1916

I have just heard that you failed in the Certif. In *Maths* as well as in Greek & Science. Now what is the explanation of that? I do wish you had written to me all about it. I have just had a letter from Brownrigg, saying that Donne [Basil Donne-Smith] is Senior Prefect. I think you wrote about him before, & that you thought him a very undesirable Senior Prefect. Please let me know. I have sent back Brownrigg's letter to Mother, and I want you to see what he says. I have no doubt he is quite right about your being *very* sensitive to other people's opinion. But you must bear in mind that to *get* their good opinion you must stiffen your resolves & steel your nerves to act *regardless* of their opinion. You can only win respect by showing that you respect yourself, & that you think a great deal more about your own opinion of what is right than what other boys say or think. This is really a tremendous matter & will make an enormous difference to you throughout your career.

Further, do try to work steadily & well.

Brigger thinks it would be well for you to join the Volunteers. If you have to go into the Army, it will be a lot better for you if you can get in as an officer instead of as a private, and, I think, if you join the Volunteers, & do your level best, you may use that as a step towards getting into the O.T.C. My own hope is (1) that in that way you will escape certain difficulties & dangers, & have a better chance of being whole & sound in body when peace comes & (2) that the military training of an officer is likely to be more educational to you than that of a private, & (3) that it will be good for you to have to *give* commands sometimes & not merely obey them.[36]

I am awfully anxious about you, & longing to see you again, and *do* write and tell me not only things that you know I should like to hear about your doings, but also things that you know I shall not like to hear, anything there is to tell about your difficulties with masters & other boys, & how it was you did so badly in the exam.—and also you own feelings about your career, & what you want to do if the war ~~is still on~~ lasts. I want you to be master of your own fate, and to get the benefit of all that I know about the world.

Gilbert to Owen, 4 November 1916

I have had a brief note from Brigger about the O.T.C. which I have sent back to Mother, & asked her to talk over with you. I think there must be a tremendous advantage in getting into the O.T.C. if you can, rather than being in the ranks. But perhaps it would be better again to get into the R.A.M.C. I presume you cannot get instead into the Friends Ambulance service without becoming a Conscientious Objector. About that you must ask your own conscience. Don't let the whole matter slide. I cannot decide for you, though if anything remains to be decided when I get home, I can help. I am glad that that will be before you are 18.

Work away well & steadily, my dear boy. Don't let outside distractions put you off. Make up as far as is possible for your failure in the Certif.—

though I am afraid that failure will, one way and another, cost you a good deal.

—∞—

On the night of 6–7 November 1916 Gilbert had a dream. He woke at 3.30 a.m., wrote a memorandum about his dream, and entitled it 'The Voice in the Night'. It is not clear whether or not he sent the Memorandum to Violet.

I was sitting on the edge of an abandoned quarry overgrown with wood, enjoying the dappled sunshine and shade, and propped against a tree; and then I saw all the trees round me being burnt and destroyed, and soon my tree too would be a shrivelled stump. I asked 'How is this?' and ~~the answer came~~ a voice answered 'Man~~kind has~~ is mad, and bent on destroying all that is useful and beautiful in the world in which he lives.' And I remembered the war, and perceived that it was the destruction of war that was spoiling my wood.

So I said 'I must see about this. I must speak to Germany.' And immediately I went to Switzerland, and standing on the edge of Switzerland and looking over Germany I said 'Never mind your rulers, but tell me, you common people of Germany, in what terms you are willing to make peace.' And the German people answered 'You must pay us two hundred and forty-eight millions.' I replied 'You want a war indemnity of two hundred and forty-eight millions? You will not get it. But I will speak to the English people, and find out in what terms they will make peace, and come back to you. And perhaps after I have taken many journeys to & fro, you and they will have abated your demands and peace will be possible. Meanwhile the war must go on.'

But as I was going away, the voice whispered to me & said 'Why not amalgamate?' And I cried out aloud 'Why not amalgamate?' and all Britain and Germany heard me. And straightway Queen Victoria and Kaiser Wilhelm answered, 'Why not? We shall be delighted. We only serve our states, we do not care what becomes of our jobs.' And all English & Germans all joined in the cry 'Why not amalgamate?' And I said 'What an accursed idiot am I not to have thought of that before. What horrors might I not have prevented!'

Then I realised that I was in bed and had been dreaming. Nevertheless the whispering voice of my dream continued to speak to my listening mind, now proving more critical. The dialogue went:-

'Why *not* amalgamate?' —

'Because we cannot desert our allies' —

'Let them join too. Why should not all the belligerent states amalgamate?' —

'Because it is impossible.' —

'But would it be impossible if people asked themselves the question "Why not amalgamate?" It is what business men would do. If two great trusts were fighting and things came to this pitch, they would amalgamate. Why not States and Alliances? Why should not *you* ask that question, and keep on asking it?—Then by degrees other people will ask it too.' —

'Because people would think me mad.' —

'Why mind? Plenty of people have been thought mad who were not. They will not put you in a lunatic asylum, nor really injure you.' —

'But *how* to amalgamate?'

Gilbert to Owen, 18 November 1916*

I have just seen the report of a question in the House of Commons suggesting that the troops who are hanging about in India should be transferred to France, and their place be taken by boys of 18–19. It is the sort of proposal out of which something might come—& this might mean your coming out. There also is the idea conveyed that boys under 19 should not be sent to the Front—which is only common sense because they have not yet attained their full strength and endurance—that rather encourages me.

On 21 November Gilbert's brother Howard, a doctor serving in the Royal Army Medical Corps, was aboard the hospital ship Britannic when it was torpedoed by the Germans in the Aegean Sea. While some 50 of the crew were killed, 1,106 survived. Howard was mentioned in dispatches because he was the last man to get into the last of the thirty-five lifeboats. (By tonnage the Britannic—a White Star liner—had been the largest British ship afloat.) It was said that it was his actions, which included organizing the lifeboats, that allowed so many men to be saved. He eventually reached England via Athens, Malta, Marseilles and a three-day trip across France. On 28 November German air raids on London used aeroplanes for the first time.

Gilbert to Violet, 6 December 1916

I am afraid that my letters are arriving very irregularly; the renewal of submarining in the Mediterranean causes much delay.[37] This should reach you by New Years Day. Sweetheart, I wish you for 1917 and always a very much happier year than the one that is passing.

I found all my Madura friends well & thriving, and stopped there two nights long enough to sleep off the fatigues of two nights spent in railway trains. There were various competing attractions [to Gilbert's lectures] including a 'Home Rule' lecture by a Mr Wadia, Mrs Besant's right hand man;[38] & consequently my audience suffered, but was larger than I expected in the circumstances.

On 7 December 1916 Lloyd George ousted Asquith to become Prime Minister in a re-organized coalition government dependent mainly on Conservative support. On 18 December the US President, Woodrow Wilson, asked all belligerent nations to state their war aims to see if there were grounds for negotiations. On 22 January 1917 he told Congress that the Central Powers had declared themselves willing to attend a peace conference without preconditions while the Allied Nations insisted on certain points such as reparations. For his part Wilson insisted on an independent Poland and a peace without victory. Without some common ground there was no point in having talks. In Britain, a Labour Party Conference voted overwhelmingly in favour of carrying on the war and of participating in a coalition government.

Gilbert to Owen, 17 February 1917

Yesterday I went to the fort to get my passport signed...I have now to go to the French consul to get it viséd for going through France, & my preparations, bar packing, are done.

All 'British subjects in India of European parentage' have to register & are liable for military service. It is supposed that they will get 90 hours drill & training per month, but it is not known exactly what they will have to do. Anyway, it is one of the compensations of old age that I am free, & free to go home to be with you for a bit. I am longing for a long day up the Thames...So far as I can make out all from 16 to 60 are liable to compulsory service at home now and I wonder whether you have been allowed to go on with your school & university course. I suppose nothing very serious will happen before I get home...I wonder whether you have altered your opinion about the war lasting on for years & years. Don't you think now that it is very doubtful

(1) whether Germany can hold out till Xmas
(2) " Bulgaria " " " " "
(3) " Austria " " " " "
(4) " France " " " " "
(5) " we " " " " "

And is there not good hope that the Germans will soon begin to think that the terms they can get now are as good as they are likely to get later? Why pay a larger price for a worse article?

The following letter refers to the work of women in the manufacture of munitions. Gilbert's sister Gertrude, as an older woman, worked on the clerical side which was tiring but not dangerous. Younger women, often those who had left domestic work for higher wages or because they had been 'let go', had to endure hard and often appalling conditions on the factory floor due to the chemicals involved and the introduction of shift work. There were also several major explosions at Faversham, in 1916, Silvertown, in 1917, and Chilwell, in 1918, killing among them some 315 workers. It is estimated that by the end of the war 950,000 women were working in munitions. Most were paid far less than the male workers they had replaced.

Gilbert to Gertrude Slater, 19 February 1917

We have just had two mails arriving simultaneously, one having been 25 days on the journey & the other 33…It is very nice to hear that Howard was personally thanked by the W.O. [War Office]. The whole thing is quite characteristic of him, always as a small boy he had that combination of pluck and the dramatic sense which this exemplifies.

We are just now in a time of good news—super-submarines apparently defeated, important victory at Kut, another small advance on the Ancre, and great success of the War loan all reported simultaneously.[39] It looks as if Asquith *was* kicked out in time after all—I was much afraid that he has been allowed to cling to office so long that the injury might be irredeemable. He is a good example of Shelley's

> Rulers who neither see nor feel nor know
> But *leech-like* to their helpless country cling[40]

people call him a 'limpet'—leech is the true word for him. Since he got the sack the prospects of a safe and easy run home for me have brightened very considerably; and I am losing my apprehensions on the subject, the more so as I hear Violet is getting an insurance out. I have some hope that things may be over or nearly over when I go back to India, & perhaps in the autumn Violet will be able to come out. You do not say anything about your munitions work, I hope you are continuing to stick it all right & not getting too fagged.

Very little has happened since I got back from my tour in the west…perhaps the most interesting thing was the visit of Mr Curtis of the Round Table.[41] That certainly helped to crystallise one's political opinions. I am now pretty well convinced of the necessity of giving India representative institutions—a sort of statutory Parliament, the constitution & functions of which may be regulated from time to time by Acts of the Imperial Parliament [Westminster]. It would of course take a long time to set out the arguments for & against. One good effect of the war is that it has demonstrated that India was already much more loyal than had been supposed, and secondly, it has greatly increased Indian loyalty. It has satisfied all intelligent Indians that they cannot stand alone in a world of such highly developed militarism, and also that the British Raj is far better than any other alien rule. The Germans, no doubt, had been pegging away underground, using both missionaries and prostitutes as political agents, but they had not accomplished as much as they supposed, and the war came too soon for them from the Indian point of view. It is wonderful to see how all their exact and careful calculations about the rottenness of the British Empire, the feebleness of our maximum display of military strength, and the degeneracy & effeteness of the British character, have been falsified by the result. One little thing that cheered me—perhaps it was a false cheer—was that I wrote to the *Times* to urge that food exports from home to India should be prohibited, & have heard recently that this is to be done.[42] I have not however, heard that any prohibition has actually been imposed. But it did make one feel that the power of acting, & not merely waiting & seeing had been recovered.

All British in India from 16–50 are now liable to military service, and all Indians invited to volunteer.

⊸⊶

Gilbert to Violet, 19 February 1917

I am glad you feel that you *could* put off my coming home if necessary, but I do not think there is any necessity. So far as we can guess from news up to date the super submarines have been met by super-counter-measures, with remarkable success. It seems to have had a splendid effect to kick out Wait-&-See Asquith,[43] & to get real men, who consider it necessary to do their best at the head of things. It reacts right through the services &

general public...On Sunday I got Sir John & Lady Wallis[44] to dinner. Sir John Wallis was Vice Chancellor of the University when I came out, but he has ceased to take any share in University work or administration; Lady Wallis is an extraordinarily elegant lady, about 50, I imagine, trying to retain the appearance of 25. She used to go by the nickname of 'The Hardy Annual!' because she had a baby regularly once a year for a good many years running...When I am back home for good, and agitating the British public on Indian subjects, I shall contend for the principle that those who go to Dravidian districts, in general in educational service, shall know something about Dravidian culture and literature[45]...We went to a meeting of a little discussion society called 'The Twelve'! to discuss a paper by Kandeth on the limits of State action. There were 3 English & 5 Indians present. The theory that Indians are unfit for self government, & therefore must not have it, seems to me to be quite natural & inevitable in people who do not realise how unfit for self government our own people are. These folk were a bit abstract and unpractical in their way of talking, but that appeared to be the result of lack of practice, not lack of capacity. In education, sanitation etc the Indian government appears to have turned the prow of the ship of State in the right direction now, what is wanted is to get a bit of a move on. I find the belief with which I came out confirmed, that the biggest thing we can do for permanent peace is to turn the British Empire into a league of nations, self governing in their internal affairs.

The Govt. besides compulsorily enlisting all Europeans, has invited Indians to volunteer, & Mrs Besant has turned into a recruiting agent.[46] The Indian *spokesmen* are very pleased but whether any volunteers likely to be of use will be obtained is doubtful...Just think, a fortnight from today, or tomorrow, I shall be starting on my journey home! I sometimes wonder whether something may not happen to prevent my return to India according to arrangements. It seems not impossible that I may be called upon to do something or other till the end of the war.

Gilbert to Owen, 20 [?] February 1917

So far the super-submarines of the Germans do not seem to have [been] so very effective; and by all the news we get here the navy seems to be getting a grip on them very nicely. Anyway the Mediterranean appears to be actually safer than when I went out; and the crossing of the Channel not much less safe.[47] ... People here are *now* surprised when I tell them I am going. They say 'How will you get exemption?' I say, 'Oh that's all right, I am over 50.' They say 'Have you got a medical certificate to prove that?' So I suppose my appearance is fairly youthful. Everybody under 50 has to serve, & is liable, if under 40, to be sent to Mesopotamia, if between 40 & 50 only to serve in India. They are going to give the lot 90 hours drill in the first month, & then 4 hrs per week, with a period in camp.

We hear of greatly enhanced income tax coming—25% off our salaries. I wonder whether the University will stump up a little more to make up for it! If not, I shall have to manage to make something out of my travelling allowance. But it will be hard to make up for a loss of £250 per ann. It will make a good deal of difference in what I shall be able to do for you, & later on, for Eliot & Pat. Let us hope that the report is exaggerated.[48]

I start from here in a fortnight—so, in a fortnight more or less, from the time of your getting this, I shall be with you, though only for a brief time... I hope you are getting decent hockey & good rowing, & plugging away as hard as you can at French, Maths & Sci. seeing you are now quit, thanks be, of Latin & Greek.

On 24 February Britain sent a copy of the Zimmermann Note to Washington. In this document Germany proposed an anti-American alliance with Mexico through which Mexico would regain territory lost to the USA. Mexico did not take up the offer. On 12 March revolution broke out in Petrograd and on 15 March Tsar Nicholas II abdicated. A Republic was formed which carried on the war. A renewal of Germany's unrestricted submarine warfare in the Atlantic, combined with the Zimmermann Note, caused the United States to declare war against Germany on 6 April. On the first day of registration for national service almost 10,000,000 American men came forward within the first twelve hours. On 9 April the

Second Battle of the Aisne began and the Canadians scored a success at Vimy Ridge. Later that month Gilbert arrived in Oxford for his first home leave and letters between Oxford and Madras ceased for the time being. That spring Violet became even more involved in anti-war work by distributing handbills issued by the Society of Friends' Peace Committee. These advocated universal disarmament and the creation of a League of Nations.

Violet to Owen, [May 1917]

I gave away Pacifist leaflets and a lady came and asked me for my name and address and said did I know that I was liable to be put in prison. I refused my name and address and told her I realised I ran the risk of imprisonment. I asked her by what right she demanded my name. She was fairly young and pretty and a tiger! It is the wicked one-sided press that creates this spirit. Another Friend [Quaker] was taken to the police station by a soldier who apologised for doing so but said they were given orders when home on leave to take to the police any one giving away pacifist literature.

———

On 20 May Owen celebrated his eighteenth birthday. He was now liable to be called up under the Military Conscription Act (1916).

Gilbert to Owen, 21 May 1917 from Coulsdon, Surrey

Tomorrow is your birthday and you will be 18!…We must celebrate your birthday on the first free day you have. It is rather a miserable sort of thing to have birthdays in war time, especially the 18th, so the best wish I can send is peace and an early discharge from His Majesty's service.

———

On 3 June 1917 a conference of the Independent Labour Party voted two to one for a negotiated settlement to end the war. Five days later General Pershing, Commander in Chief of the American Expeditionary Force, arrived in London. On 26 June the first American troops landed in France, leaving bewildered Frenchmen to wonder 'what in the name of the good God chewing gum may be'.[49] In July Gilbert set out for India.

Owen to his father, [12 July 1917]

Thank you very much for the picture post card you sent me from Marseilles. How interesting it must be to go travelling like you are all through the Mediterranean…I've very nearly finished my bike…I played in another match the other day, right half in place of another boy who has hurt his knee. It was a very good game, away against Leighton Park, the quaker school near Reading.[50] Its a pity they were quakers because they had two or three big fellows who otherwise would have been in the army or in some O.T.C.[51] There was a large swimming bath…After the game I had a bathe, it was horribly cold & took your breath away like anything but bucked you up beautifully. Only one other boy dared to have a bathe. By the bye we lost the match…Exams are beginning tomorrow. I hope I shall do respectably well.

Violet to Gilbert, [July 1917?]*

How should I get it [peace]? I would have a Peace Conference, keep an open door & try to get at the truth from all possible sides. I would attempt to bring about an understanding, whose business would be to get all the light possible thrown upon everything possible & bring about a speedy & satisfactory settlement of differences…I would have had the Stockholm Conference [of socialist parties which did in fact meet in September 1917 after much delay]. Why do we not do these things? Why do we always suppress everything but evil? Because when we have war we want war & we know we must hate—'you can't fight unless your blood boils' was one of our placards. Everything that is cruel & terrible must be shouted. And so we get an entirely unbalanced, distorted view of things…War brings this absolutely false view of things that arouses all the mean, cruel instincts & shrivels up the soul. And one of the most dangerous theories that war breeds is: You may do evil that good may come. Most people think that war is evil. Well supposing that the soldiers come home & for the common good (in their estimation) think that they must kill the Capitalists & those who want to keep privileges to themselves—the large landowners. Will they remember what they have preached and taught?

It seems to be quite hopeless if we are going to put the whole tragedy down to Germany, at least we must see that we all believed…in armed forces. It doesn't seem to me to make the whole cause a just thing [or] right…It seems to be useless to argue about the difference in guilt. We were all believers in armed forces.

Owen was able to take advantage of reforms which created the Officer Cadet Battalions. These had been set up in 1916 to replenish as quickly as possible the ranks of junior officers as this group had suffered the highest number of casualties. In the new OCB those who, like Owen, had been in their school or university Officers' Training Corps, along with those who had had sufficient time in the ranks, were commissioned as second lieutenants after an eighteen-week course. The Cadet Battalions were attached to various units such as the Royal Artillery or the Royal Engineers for which Owen tried but failed at first to get a place.

Gilbert to Owen, 28 August 1917

Yours is a nice meaty little letter—quite a lot of news in it. I am sorry you could not get into the Engineers, but the chief thing really is, I suppose not to be in the infantry, & so I am glad to hear you have been accepted for a cadetship in the R.A. [Royal Artillery]. I hope you enjoyed your farming—I expect you quite enjoyed earning a net 6s. a week and doubling your income. I wonder how much of the allotment got dug before you went off to Wallingford?

Things continue to go very successfully with me. The students who took part in the making of my book of 'South Indian Villages' all came up to scratch, over the correction of proofs, and some added a good deal of interesting matter. I really think it will be about the best book yet published on its subject, or anywhere near it. I have had a letter from some one writing from Sir Rabindranath Tagore's[52] house asking for a copy of my 'Village Questionnaire' as they propose carrying out investigations on my lines. I have had the Govt. of India Statistical Officer and another Simla[53] official asking for...copies of my Bombay lecture...If only I were informed as a certainty that the war will be over by 1st April I should feel very happy—no—I don't think I should because of the miseries while it does last. But it would be good to know that.

On Thursday 6th I go on tour...People who don't go on tour envy those who do—people on tour envy those that can stay quietly in Madras.

I have great hopes of getting to Calcutta for Christmas. When there I shall probably make a rush for Darjeeling in the Himalayas.

Eliot to his father, 17 September [1917]

My Darling Daddie...Yesterday we went to Boars Hill[54] the blackberries are just beginning to get ripe and we got quite a lot. Patrick and I stripped naked and had a Red Indian War dance. It did seem horrid to get into the thick heavy hot clothes again. Mother and I walked to the top of the hill while Owen cut rushes with which he is going to make a mat...I have just got a lovely box of shells from you picked up on Elliot's shore. They are sweet little things and it was awfully kind of you to send them to me. Yesterday afternoon we went to tea at the Grafflins Owen included.

Gilbert to Violet, 22 September 1917*

You ask what I think of [H. G.] Wells' article.[55] I think it is vigorous and timely—somewhat exaggerated of course. It is Wells' habit of mind to see the various aspects of a question very vividly...I think it is possible that very clear statements of the intentions of the Allies with regard to the 3 points Wells deals with:- Tropical Africa, the Turkish Empire, and trade after the war—might help the peace movement in Germany…At the same time it must be pointed out that Germany has, as ever founded on pre-war experience, to fear being shut off from tropical trade or influence in Turkey. German trade with India for example, has had all the help & encouragement that British trade has had, & has grown much faster. Curiously there has been no British monopoly preventing Germans from buying what they liked. But on the other hand in India and Australia there were German monopolies preventing any British purchase of certain metals except from the German monopolists…They have chosen to turn commerce into spying and to send out political agents fomenting sedition in the disguise of missionaries and prostitutes, & as a consequence, whatever terms Government may come to with regard to conditions of peace, suspicion and dislike will dog the footsteps of every German who comes to India…I don't think there is any fear with regard to Germany's commercial prosperity after the war. She will have a job to fix things up with the state creditors, but as this is all, or practically all internal debt, there is no insuperable difficulty in that, nor any which her rulers are incompetent to deal with. Her organizing power and internal resources which have given her such a tremendous rate of growth & wealth during the 40 years before the war, & which have been so wonderfully demonstrated during the war will remain unimpaired, if only she will abandon her idea of conquering the world & economise on army & navy, she has every reason to anticipate an even more rapid growth in wealth in the future than in the past.

It is so nice to hear of you having a good time, and that Owen 'is such a cheerful and active spirit'. You ask me what I read—I fear practically nothing except the daily telegrams and stuff throwing light on Indian questions…I do brood over you in the midst of England in her toil & trouble, & long for reunion. Your loving husband, Gilbert

Gilbert to Eliot and Patrick, 22 September 1917 from Travellers Bungalow, Kumbakonam

My dear Eliot,

Only a few days ago I got your letter written a fortnight before with the school reports. It was not quite such a good report as I should like. This year you are not only in VI a1, but in the top division of that class...and so you are, or ought to be, one of the top boys of the school, and you must remember that, and remember that you set an example...I want you to learn boxing this term, as it will help you to stand up for yourself and what you think right when you go to a public school. [Kumbakonam] is considered a very sacred city and has a lot of temples to all sorts of gods...It also has a sacred river, the Cauvery [Kaveri], which people worship like the Ganges at Benares. One of their ways of worshipping it is to put all sorts of filth in the river and drink the water. They are funny people. There was a debate at the College on Tuesday, on Indian Home Rule, and by a big majority the students voted that India is quite fit now to govern herself without any help from Englishmen. You see how it is. English people say that Indians require somebody to teach them not to drink filthy water, among other things. Indians say the water is not filthy, it is sacred, and immediately filth gets into it, it is cleaner, and to drink the water makes everybody who drinks it very clever, and they don't want a lot of ignorant English people who don't know Sanscrit, and who have not read the Vedas, interfering with their wonderful and ancient civilisation and all the wisdom that has been handed down from the Rishis, the great magicians who lived thousands of years ago. So the English people can only convince a very few, but they say to one another, 'If we *do* clear out, what a high old mess there will be.'

My dear Pat,

I have just had a nice little letter from you...This place...is in its way very pretty, it has lots of coconut palms waving their graceful fronds in the sunshine, and there are trees planted along the sides of the roads, a good many being mangos...But it s a most wonderful place for mosquitos, and my young men say that the mosquitos are as big as flies…I have been going to the College to play tennis…The lecturers play a good deal, and they look very funny. They wear a sort of short nightshirt, and underneath that a white petticoat that hangs down from their waists to the ground, but they manage to tuck it up so as to make a sort of divided skirt. They have bare feet, and to play they take off their turbans, and you can see their heads are all shaven except a little nob at the back of the head near the top. They do look funny, but they play rather well.

Gilbert to Violet, 29 September 1917

I do not think my attitude, in principle, has at all changed since the Boer war.[56] I should then have considered all Boers who refused to help defend their country as either very undesirable characters from the point of view of courage, these being the rule, with exceptions to be accounted for in various ways. But if military service had been enforced in England I should have been a Conscientious Objector then. Every man ought to be a C.O. when his country engages in [an] aggressive, unjust & unnecessary war. No man ought when his country is defending liberty & right & civilisation. So now every German ought to be a C.O. & no Briton. It is all very well for you to say 'We are all miserable sinners', and if you point that at me, I admit I have made no display of courage entitling me to throw a stone at the C.O.s. I am a bit of a coward myself and have a lot of sympathy with them, though that does not prevent me from seeing that the *result* of their conduct is to make them aiders and abettors of military aggression & tyranny…I can't help thinking you really mean '*They* are all miserable sinners' namely the allied as well as the German & Austrian governments. Now each government has its own sins, but the vital fact is that the allied governments tried to avoid this war, and are trying to bring it to such an end as to preclude as far as possible future wars, while the German (& Austrian to a less degree) forced it on, and are trying to produce such a conclusion that they can shortly resume it and complete the victory…We are reaping the penalty of our sins as a nation for betraying the Danes in 1864 to Bismarck & the French in 1871.[57]

Now every man, whatever his character and motives, who fights against Germany is a true Pacifist so far as the *results* of his actions go…we must have patience. The necessary preliminary is that the German people smash their present government, & they may do that when it is defeated. I fear it is very improbable that they will do so first. You write 'You and others who dream that war will end war—' I don't dream any thing of the sort. I say war breeds war, as a rule…Victory of the aggressor breeds more war, victory of the peaceful nation wantonly attacked breeds peace. Victory of the allies in this war will not ensure peace, but victory for Germany will undoubtedly breed more & even worse wars…You never seem to remember that we were never given a choice as to whether this war should take place or not, it was Germany that chose, our only choice is as to what the course of it and the end shall be.

Eliot…is now at something of a crisis…I very much doubt if you are right in thinking he reads fiction too much…The more you can ignore and laugh at lapses of conduct at home the easier it will be for him to be steady and diligent at school. And, what is more important, his affection for you will grow, and your *permanent* influence over his life and character increase. Don't think, because I am away, you must play the stern father. Let the school do that. You be the loving indulgent mother, who what they call 'spoils' her boys…Lots of love, my dearest sweetheart. I think of you & the boys continually, & long to be with you to help you through this winter.

———

While still boarding at Magdalen College School Owen was matriculated in Michaelmas Term into the University of Oxford through the Delegacy of Non-Collegiate Students.

Owen to his father, 3 October 1917

I have been…working fairly solidly & regularly at the allotment. It is most horribly tough but I'm gradually getting through it…I am going to dig a pit or rather a trench where the central path is to be & fill it with the rubble & cinders & put gravel that I have discovered, on the top of that. It will be absolutely a causeway by the time it is finished. As regards my Divers[58] that is progressing slowly but it is a most awful bore. Last Monday I rode over to Harpenden for a few days. I had a ripping ride…I rode over to Luton via Dunstable on the Tuesday to get a bath at the Luton baths but we found it was a ladies day only. It was most abominably annoying. On Wednesday we didn't do much except to go over into St Albans. It is a ripping old town with a most beautiful cathedral. I spent all Thursday in the hospital with Aunty Maude helping & doing odd jobs—mainly accounts & filling in various army forms—it was rather interesting but I should imagine one would get awfully tired of it after a time. Our wretched old lawn mower simply won't cut. I took it to pieces & tried to make it better but without very much improvement…Last night I went to the theatre with Jack Thorburn. We saw the 'Man Who Stayed at Home'[59] an impossible absurd detective story of German spies really it was quite amusing & I enjoyed myself very much. J.T. is just off to a cadet battalion in Cambridge. I wish I knew where I was going. There's an R.F.A. [Royal Field Artillery] cadet battalion at Berchampstead [Berkhamsted]. I might possibly go there—I'm afraid I shall have to go before the end of term but I may get leave for exams & perhaps I might not have to go before December after the exams are over. One last bit of news. Mrs Briggs is giving me singing lessons.

Violet to Gilbert, [mid-October 1917]

I am sorry to only write a few miserable words. Yesterday I had a truly dreadful headache which lasted longer than usual but today I am much better…I heard from Katie Barnes that their Leonard has been very dangerously wounded they are terribly anxious. But are not allowed to go to him. Poor things it is ghastly and cruel, and then you read of the 'Peace Offensive' articles in the *New Statesman* by men who seem to have no heart or imagination.[60] I cannot understand it...You yourself said in a letter to Owen last time that [the Germans] had been driven back across the Aisne 'We hope with great loss.' Think what it means in agony and pain to the poor soldiers and agony and pain to the poor Mothers or Wives. It is useless to pretend it could not be prevented! We have never tried any other way...No other way but cruel war is left untried. I suppose that there will be a time when a more advanced human being will be evolved and we have learnt not to behave in this spirit individually towards each other. If we kept knives & pistols & clubs perhaps we should still use them.

Yesterday Pat & I went blackberrying and then I went alone to Yarnton[61]...the only ripe ones were up high so I valiantly mounted the hedges regardless of scratching as if I were 12 & I got nice ones. Then I went to the Food Control counter & at last got 5 lbs. of sugar...It was quite a victory we have to contend with this sort of sport & victory consists in contending with obstacles.

[P.S.] Owen writes every day dear boy.

<hr />

On 24–5 October 1917 the Bolsheviks overthrew the Provisional Government in Petrograd. On 26 October the Second Congress of the Soviet of Workers' Soldiers' and Peasants' deputies adopted the Decree on Peace which demanded immediate Russian withdrawal from the war. While the Bolsheviks' power did not extend throughout Russia, the future for the Allied Powers was now thrown into doubt.

Gilbert to Violet, 10 November 1917 from Kobe Lodge, Royapettah, Madras

I am now let up after ten days in bed, and have been allowed a little variety of food. Apparently what has happened to me was that I caught an attack of dengue, a sort of ten days' fever, & that made active a little dormant dysentery trouble…I stayed in bed till it was time for me to appear at the Senate House to lecture, gave my lecture, then came back, went to bed and telephoned for the doctor. He said straight way 'its the usual—we'll soon put that right'…On Tuesday last…he suggested shifting me from the club here—this is a nursing home…The doctor's chief reason apparently was the administering of enemas…The gout appears to have gone during these last few days, and I hope & fear…. when one comes to think of it, have nothing to complain of—though it does feel as though fate had dealt me a scurvy trick to let me be ill and away from my dear wife. What's the good of illness except to make a man duly thankful for having a wife? Perhaps it is some good for going over old times again in memory; but that makes one beastly homesick…On Monday I hope to be able to get to the bank for business, and then I shall send off what money I can spare…Goodbye, my dearest beloved, Gilbert Slater

<hr>

Gilbert to Violet, 13 November 1917 from Kobe Lodge, Royapettah, Madras

To-day the doctor told me I could leave this place, and go back to the Club. I thought it a little abrupt to go without any notice, so told him I would go to-morrow. It so happens that to-morrow my room is wanted for another patient; so the people here are quite satisfied. I have no notion how much I shall have to pay, but both nursing and medical attendance are necessarily very costly to Europeans in India. However, I hope I am now out of the wood.

On Monday I got to the Bank, & cashed my cheques and telegraphed home £150 to you, with my love. This contains my Christmas money, as I shall have to keep something in hand out of next month's salary…it will be about the middle of January that I shall send rent, probably by telegraph, and as large a sum as I can manage. This really seems to me about the only expression of my love which can carry much actuality and conviction with it.

You will like to know about Kobe Lodge, which has sheltered me for just a week. It is a very ordinary sort of Madras bungalow, with a central windowless room, lit mainly through the front room which is a sort of lounge, separated from the garden by pillars only; a third big room behind, used as a dining room (you understand Madras houses are free from passages, and the walls have such big & wide door-ways, without doors, that they approximate to pillars). Out of these 3 rooms various little bedrooms open, & there are others upstairs...By the way they only charged me Rs 8½ per day, and as hotel charges are at least Rs 7 per day, this leaves only Rs 1½ or 2s. per day for the nursing; which seems to me extremely moderate...This was begun on Tuesday, & is being continued to-day, Wednesday. I have now returned to the Club and feel reasonably fit...my gout *did* disappear, in any recognisable form, during my lying in bed, but now I am up, it appears to be slightly active again...the root trouble that caused the gout must have been some germ in the bowels, which, when encouraged by dengue, gave the dysentery...Yesterday Messrs Blackie's man (Blackie act as Indian agents for Constables) came to see me about pushing the new edition of 'Making of Modern England' in India. Something may come of this—nothing very important, but it will be helpful to getting fairly well paid writing work when I come home. It is quite likely that after my period is up here, the writing of books will be my main occupation. This will have the merit that the income accruing will outlive me.

There is a possibility of my getting some vacation lecturing in Ceylon in case I cannot go home next spring...Of course I shall not let anything interfere with the possibility of getting home in case peace is made. Before you get this presumably the Russian situation, apparently now more dubious than ever, may have cleared up, and anything may result therefrom, including peace before Christmas. In that case I fear it will be a 'German peace,' and a continually arming peace—but it might not. And I have always held that even armed peace is better than war. Lots of love...ever your loving husband.

Gilbert to Owen, 14 November 1917

It is quite a long time since I had a letter from you, and I am wondering what is happening to you about your military service; whether it is to be R.E. [Royal Engineers], or R.A. [Royal Artillery], or infantry. I do hope not the last. I almost think I would rather you were in the flying corps than the trenches.[62] When this gets to you I suppose you will be in a Cadet School with a host of other young men, something like going back to boarding school…but with harder work, and more liberty as to what you may *drink & smoke*. I don't think you are very likely to take to getting too fond of whisky, but it is a terrible thing when this does happen to a man. Only a few days ago a man came into my room and confessed to me that he was bound to go blind before long if he continued to drink and smoke, but he could not stop. He will lose his work, and…then he will be completely ruined…It is no good being an ostentatious teetotaller or non-smoker, it only puts other peoples' backs up and does harm. But it is very necessary to be quite resolved on always being moderate in both drinking and smoking. I heard it remarked of a man the other day 'He never refuses a drink, but he always calls for a small soda or lime squash.'—a very good plan—at any rate in India, where there is practically no limit to what you can drink.

I do hope you will be in good company, & I think you probably will, on the whole, though no doubt there will be a mixture. And I do hope you will try to write at least once a week—send a common letter to Mother & to me, which she can send on to me, & put on a special slip anything that is for either of us separately. Try to tell us the little unimportant details that enable me to get an idea of your life. Off you go from your home into your own individual life, the more independent the better; but our hearts go with you, always a little bit anxious, full of hope and fear, for your being well, and doing well, and living a good life. So try to be as communicative to us as you will want your sons to be when they are your age.

Gilbert to Owen, 16 November 1917

It was a joy to me when the last home mail came, to see your handwriting on one of the envelopes, but Alas! When they were all opened there was not a word from you. When I am separated so far from you in distance and in time, and the days are speeding us to your leaving home, and going to cadet school, and then passing into the Army, and the chance of my seeing you before you enter in to all sorts of new experiences, and perhaps into deadly dangers gradually disappears, I do feel this separation very keenly, and I do want very much to know what you think and feel about things.

I scarcely feel there is much hope of an early peace, but I still cling to the hope that your training may not be hurried through very quickly. And that before you actually go to the Front, peace will come. Yet month by month as the war is prolonged the probabilities against my hopes increase. With the cloud over the future I can quite realise that you find it hard to plug away at Divers & French & Chemistry—yet this would have been a splendid chance for you. To have worked very hard & done your utmost, would not only have had its academic reward, what is far better, it would have given you *power over your self*, which you must steadily endeavour to acquire.

Goodbye my dearest boy. All my heart goes with you.

Owen to his father, 21 November 1917

I have great news to tell you this week. Some time ago I sent up to the War Office through the Adjutant an application to get into the R.E. Some time afterwards I had to interview some big bug in the R.E. who had come down from Birmingham practically only to see me. He asked me various questions about my knowledge & self & on the whole seemed fairly pleased, 4 days afterwards I heard that I had been accepted...To-day I received a notice telling me to report on Sunday in four days time at Newark. Of course this is positively beastly because it would mean breaking up my term & perhaps missing my Exam. I went & saw Claypole at once also Dr Pope⁶³ & both have written to the W.O. Claypole says that in any case I should probably be allowed to come back for my exam & possibly might get leave to join at Newark a month later...All this is horribly exciting & makes one feel tired all over...As regards the O.U.O.T.C. [Oxford University Officers' Training Corps] I think the sentimentality of military training must have affected me because on the whole there is a satisfaction in doing a drill movement well. I believe it appeals to one's sense of geometry. I have just been made a lance corporal which doesn't mean very much except that one is a senior member of the corps & is supposed to know a little more than the common fry. Besides it puts one more on the level with the officers & it is possible to get more familiar with them than otherwise...We have been doing compass work lately & on Monday night we did compass marching in Wytham Park⁶⁴ by night. It was quite fun but my party had to walk for about 500 yds over a ploughed field—steam plough— much worse than ordinary. Thank goodness it hadn't been raining or it would have been awful.

Owen to his mother, [24 November 1917] from Shalem Lodge, Newark-on-Trent

I got here quite well considering all things at about 5.45 & have just had a good tea. Mrs Quibell met me at the station & brought me home,—here rather...There always seem to be interesting people travelling with one. In my carriage there were two R.F.C. [Royal Flying Corps] officers— brothers or brothers in law, one with his wife & two kids 1 boy & girl. Both wore sailor hats, both kids were hefty, about 7 & 5, especially the boy. He was called H.M.S. *Colossus* which was rather a joke, the girl H.M.S.

Minotaur. Also in the same compartment was a musical land worker. I really had a very good journey & the Quibells are awfully nice.

[P.S. from Violet:] Mrs. Quibell…has a daughter in Oxford that I must find out. They met O. at Newark & kept him until Sunday afternoon.

Owen to his father, 5 December 1917

I've just been through a harrowing experience—my chemistry exam…I don't think I've done so badly…You know I had a month's leave—till December 30th…As a matter of fact…I'm not dreading it in the slightest—only a little bit excited. From what I've heard the work will be very interesting—building bridges & then blowing them up & every kind of work dealing with signalling & explosives…When I raise some cash from actual earnings I shall buy one of those Vest Pocket Kodaks—they are awfully good little things…I am so sorry your gout has lasted such a beastly long time…If I ever get the chance of going out to India as an Engineer would you like me to take it? I think its a case of anything better than France or Flanders.

Violet to Gilbert, 7 December 1917

Owen & I are hurrying to catch the post…& we are anxious to let you know at once that he has passed his exam. We are very 'bucked' you may be sure. He is always very modest about his attainments & did not think he had done very brilliantly in the exam & then today after the viva he came home quite hot & pink feeling like a 'maggot' & said he got wind up because they started asking him questions he could not answer, he only knew vaguely. Its awfully nice to know so soon & a real comfort that he has passed…I hope he will not have the year's military training that will exempt him from other exams. I wish he had been able to take Divers for the sake of the work. It would be interesting to know something of the Greek testament…Did you do anything with the Syriac Christians with regard to Bishop Herford's commission?[65] You never said. He is anxious to know about it.

On 8 January 1918 Woodrow Wilson set out the United States' war policy in his 'Fourteen Points' speech before Congress. His ambitious, some said unrealistic, proposals for a new world order included: the abolition of secret treaties, freedom of the seas, free trade, worldwide reduction of armaments, adjustment of colonial claims with consideration for the 'interests of the populations concerned', the evacuation of all Russian territory by other nations' troops, the restoration of Belgium as an independent nation, the restoration to France of all territory seized by Germany after 1870, the readjustment of Italy's borders along 'lines of nationality', the autonomous development of the provinces in the Hapsburg Empire, the restoration of Serbia, Montenegro, and Romania with a guaranteed adjustment of their disputes and access to the sea for Serbia, the autonomous development of the non-Turkish parts of the Ottoman Empire with security for Turkey, an independent Poland incorporating 'territories inhabited by indisputably Polish populations', and a general association of nations to protect all countries' independence and integrity. Back in England, on 13 January 1918 the war truly became part of the Slaters' family life when Owen, already enlisted as a private (30844) in the Oxfordshire and Buckinghamshire Light Infantry, left Oxford for the Royal Engineers Officer Cadet Battalion at Kelham Hall[66] in Nottinghamshire.

Owen to his father, 9 January 1918

This week I am off to my Cadet Battalion at last. Really they have treated me very well. I…have not had to go before January 13th. Isn't it annoying I shall have to go to Newark on Saturday in order to report on Sunday at 4 pm. Its most abominable having to go the day before. I am rather funking it all now my time has come but I don't really expect it will be at all bad when I get there. The work is sure to be interesting whatever happens. I have been having quite a gay time the last 10 days or so. There has been more or less continuous skating & also I have been to three dances & a party…Do you remember Bishop Herford who lives at the Woodstock Road end of Lathbury Road & has a little private chapel? Well I fell into his clutches & he asked me to take a Sunday school for him or rather help him with one. I had to accept as he was in such a hole but it was not altogether pleasant. The school was down in St Ebbes[67] & an awful hole with terribly dirty kids who made abominable rows. It was perfectly horrid because really I had no authority over them. Not like school where you could give lines or a licking at a moments notice. The worst you could do was to say 'Hush!!' or in very exceptional cases kick the kid out of the room. I'm afraid I did the latter most of all...I very much disappointed the dear old bishop. Ever since the first class he has been lending me books—very kind of him I'm sure. However I got bored—terribly bored with the class & only managed to withdraw with the greatest difficulty...The next letter you get will probably be from Newark. With love from your loving son, Owen.

P.S. I wish you would tell me my character from my writing. I'm afraid it would not be at all complimentary.

Owen to his mother, 14 January 1918

I would have written to you before but I have been so busy...We started on Monday, today, by being woken at 6.0 am, parading at 7.15, breakfast 8, parade 9.0, dinner 1.0, parade 2.0, tea 5.0 then dinner at 7.45...I share a room with 5 other cadets all old soldiers & quite nice people. The class I am in—just starting—consists of approx. 80 cadets nearly all old soldiers...O.T.C.s like me. We all dine in one room at small tables, 7 each & the food is quite plentiful & good. Language too is surprising—much better than at school...the people seem to be quite a decent lot...We get riding in a day or two. Hurray...I shall find a bycicle very useful if you will send me mine...the river Trent runs round two sides of the grounds & is very swift—no bathing allowed. Please give my love to everybody. I must leave off now. I hope to catch the last post. Much love, your loving son, Owen

Violet to Owen, 14 and 15 January 1918*

We are so delighted to have your letter & to hear how kindly you were received by Mrs Quibell. I hope we shall hear more tomorrow…Winnie did not turn up at all so we have had everything to do…Yesterday…I went with Mrs Grafflin to the Friends Meeting. It was a particularly nice one & three people spoke…it is too bad of Winnie not to turn up. I told you didn't I that she wants to leave in a months time & go on the land.

We want to know so much about you & your surroundings. I hope you will try to tell us the leading things. I must send you a list of questions if you do not. I thought of you specially at 4 oclock & wondered what sort of a ceremony you went through. Tell me if you want your vests etc…*Do you want your sugar ticket* [ration coupon]. Of course I shant use it. I hope you will get enough to eat.

God bless you my dear boy. Keep a straight path & try to help all the lame dogs you can.

[PS] Tuesday. No letter has come so I will send this one. Don't forget that we want to hear. Of course at the beginning there is so very much we want to hear…1 Anything about the Quibells. 2 When you left them. 3 Your [induction?] at 4 pm in Kelham Hall. 4 What you did afterwards. 5 What sort of rooms you have to live & sleep in. 6 Any chance of privacy? 7 What times off? [8] What time you get up. [9] Go to bed. [10] Duties.

⸺◦⸻

Joyce Cockram to Owen, 22 January 1918 from Oxford

Thanks most awfully for your letter. The only stipulation I make about writing is, that you've jolly well got to write too…I am afraid I can't find the negative of me punting, & I can't remember anything about it…As printing is so expensive in Newark, I should suggest that you let me undertake anything for you here. (It sounds official, doesn't it?) I used your camera, to take a photo of Eric Anderson…but as films are expensive, I'm being very sparing...Thank you so much for lending me it...Hugh took Joan [Anderson] & me to the George,[68] the other day, for tea. He really managed it most awfully knuttily,[69] & was a first-class host. He is getting very blasé, even more so than usual.

I had to drill the VI on Monday. We started quite gaily, but when I had to stop, I broke down completely, into a fit of hopeless hysterics, by having to say 'Attention Halt, one, two.' When I'd recovered slightly, I made the class open files. They did it rottenly, so I had them back again. I couldn't remember the right command & said 'As you were'. Peals of laughter from every one, of course!...What sort of a place is—(bother all interfering people, Mr Anderson wants the shutters shut, some one else rings a bell!)—Newark? When you write, tell me what you're doing. It is no good stuffing me with tales of equipment & button cleaning. It simply doesn't act.

<hr />

Gilbert to Owen, 25 January 1918

By the last mail I got two letters of yours, Nov. 21 & Dec. 5, one telling me about your getting into the R.E. & the other about your leave till Dec. 30...I am jolly glad you will get into the R.E. A lot of the work will be interesting and instructive. You ask how I should like you to come out as an engineer to India. I don't suppose that you will have any choice where you go during the war; but after it is over you might if you choose probably get into the P.W.D. (Public Works Dept.) which is the engineering branch of the Government of India. But I don't think I should recommend India for a young man unless he has given up hope of a satisfactory career in England or the Colonies...fruit farming in Tasmania is a job that looks fascinating to me. I do hope to hear before long that you have passed your Chemistry Exam...Somehow I think we are just now on the brink of negotiations, whether we go forward or slip back into a fresh outburst of war is, of course, a question in which it is no good offering predictions., Still, I think, the pressure towards peace in Central Europe is getting more & more powerful, so I have a good deal of hope that the war will be over by the time they are thinking of sending you abroad. In that case you may get some clearing up & re-constructive work to do in France & Belgium, which would be very interesting and instructive. Unless you get sent to India, it will be some 15 months at the shortest, I suppose, before we can meet. I am *so* glad to get your photos, & to see you all looking so well.

⸙

Violet to Gilbert, 31 January 1918 from her sister's house in Leyburn

Here I am at Leyburn after a long journey of 12 hours...Nowadays everyone carries his own luggage so the place is chocked with luggage as well as people...You know Annie [the maid] has left. She went at Christmas. Went to 'Munitions' but did not like it and is now doing temporary work as cook in...Ealing...I may stay here until Saturday week, then go on to Newark [to] see Owen...I do want to see the dear boy and his surroundings...Then I shall go to London & stay one night either with Mary [her sister] or Bella so that I can do a little shopping at Jaegar[70] and see Joseph. One doesn't want much to stop in London because of raids...Shopping is increasingly difficult. I sincerely hope the Oxford Co-operative Soc. will show a little more energy for I simply can't stand more than ½ an hour in a queue. Edna [domestic servant] and I went last Saturday...& got to the Maypole [grocery and dairy products] at 10 to 8 o'clock; already there were about a 100 people! Edna who walked got much further back; we got 1lb of margarine each; & that with suet will last about a week & later the street was almost full, Liptons [provisioners] on our side and Maypole on the other. Women carrying babies, & a long line outside on the road of prams with small children it was really pathetic so I expect in the end some would get nothing. They were 8 abreast.

68

Meat we can get twice a week just what the butcher can allow. I can get tinned food but no one is allowed much.

On Sunday we went to hear a Mr Tatton who is with Relief work in connection with the Friends' Relief Com.[71] He came over to get money to pay for Siberian wheat because famine has already begun...He told of the truely awful suffering of the Siberian women and children and old men of their patience and stoical bearing of pain and privation, the men starving themselves for the women & children and the women for the children so that often only one child would survive of a family of 20 odd...People all hurried off to tea and only one or two asked personal questions, so we heard nothing about the Revolution tho' he offered to tell what he knew and had come through Petrograd...Mind you tell me how you are. I have ordered some butter beans and shall send them if they come...Much love dear heart...ever your loving wife Violet.

Joan George to Owen, 2 and 12 February 1918

Dearest Tufty, Thank you very much for your letter. I nearly wrote to you last night only I thought I would leave it another day or two.

Owen dear,
I am so sorry I found this beginning of a letter to you today—goodness knows if I have written to you since—I hope so, if not I am awfully sorry and humbly apologise etc Mrs Delap has gone out to supper and to the theatre...tonight...at present I am sitting with the door wide open—expecting every moment to hear Peter being violently sick upstairs, because he complained of a pain at tea. Heaven grant it does not happen. He is usually sick at nine o'clock when he is and it is just that now so...At ten o'clock I shall retire to upstairs and get in my 'jamas and put on my skirt and sports coat and perhaps my out-doors coat and come down again to get her water boiling etc so that she may have Bovril if she wants and then go to bed.

Oh Tufty there are Organ Recitals every Sunday until March 2ⁿᵈ. I do wish you were here and that we might go together—but c'est impossible!!…Now I am going to tell you something which you may be quite pleased over or you may be quite annoyed about and that is we may be leaving '25' [Polstead Road, Oxford] or rather mother is, and we are going to live at no. 8 Grove St…Grove St turning is just next to Hall's that Gentleman's tailor who always has vivid coloured handkies and socks in the window. Mother has the house for three years—it has six rooms and the cellar all perfectly dry…I think mother will be very comfy there although it is so tiny and has no garden or Bathroom…Oh there's Peter coughing!! It's alright it was only a cough!!!

You dear priceless transparent old thing I knew all the time that you were feeling rather fed [up] at having to walk back with Miss De Brisy that night after the dance. I was rather a little beast to you I believe—too— Tufty I don't mean to be ever, only I think I am a weeny bit shy and afraid of your somehow sometimes—besides being an awful little snob—I am actually getting to mind what people say—I'm one!!…Now dear old thing I must go. Goodnight! Ever your loving Joan

P.S. There is a book of Horace's *Odes* here—I am vastly interested in the translation of one certain one—about a certain girl—do you know it— her name is—Pyrrha.⁷²

Violet to Gilbert, 5 February 1918* from Leyburn, Yorks

My little holiday is speeding away. I have now three days & then I go on to Newark. I got your letter dated Dec. 10ᵗʰ *only* one, so it took nearly 2 months…the Labour papers & the D.N. [*Daily News*]…demanding an International conference…there is a great deal of Labour unrest…the problem [about food] is…becoming more acute…at present Agnes does [not appear] to have any difficulty in getting butter, fats, eggs…I do not know whether things will get [better] after we are rationed but it will be much more satisfactory. I did not say that we could not get brown bread. Every now and then the Coop: get out of brown bread & then I go round [to buy] Dr Allinson's bread[73] but the Coop bread is still very good…I only get about 2 loaves a week…Annie's lover came home from the Front & was in Oxford [for] 4 days before he went to Portsmouth. Edna gave Annie much less time than I should have & said that [the two of them] seemed quite satisfied!

Gilbert to Owen, 9 February 1918

I have been so glad to get your two letters of Dec. 7th & 18th and to hear of your success in passing the chemistry; and also that you got the extension of time & to know where you are…I am looking forward to your letters which I hope will make me realise how you are living.

Well, my dear boy, I am thinking of you continually, and hoping for your happiness and welfare. I have some hope that your course may be longer than the 4 months. I fear now there is small chance of peace before there has been bitter fighting on the west front, and little chance of peace before you are on active service. I wonder what your feelings are. I don't think I ever funked death for its own sake, though I do on other accounts, the missing a finish of my work, and the possible pain, and, very much more than these, the results to my wife & bairns. I don't know whether at your age I should have felt that I was losing much in the enjoyment of life, not as much as I hope you do. I fear you will have to go into peril of wounds, disease and death, yet perhaps the greater chance is that you will escape all three actually; and, I hope, when you have come through, you will feel that you are not sorry to have played your part.

Violet to Gilbert, 11 February 1918 from Kentish Town, London

Here I am on my way to Mary's and doomed to wait more than an hour for the next train…I told you (probably twice) that I went to Leyburn and stayed with Agnes and Jim for 12 days and then went to Newark to see Owen…Maude was there for a week having taken a week off from the hospital (you know that she is Commandant and feels herself to be a quite indispensible person)…I reached Newark at 1.20 and Mrs Quibell met me…The Quibells have a very comfortable modern house with a nice big garden. They are Wesleyans, he undertakes local preaching; they are middle aged with one son in the war, one has been killed, the eldest. Mr Quibell, his father and brother have a factory for artificial manures and other things. He is evidently very desirous to treat his work force well and feels rather bitter at the trade union attitude of hostility. I suppose the same sort of feeling we had at Ruskin. They are really religious people and so delightfully warm hearted and hospitable. They keep quite open house to Owen and are most kind to him. Unfortunately Owen was feeling poorly; he had been inoculated the day before and was done again on the Sunday. He came over on Saturday…[and] stayed to tea and supper and came the next day in the morning. I went with Mr and Mrs Quibell to the Wesleyan chapel. It seemed so old fashioned—hymns and all; I felt dropped back 30 years.

⸺∞⸺

Basil Donne-Smith to Owen, 12 February 1918 from New College, Oxford

I am doing half-time…We are going compass marching & it is all very exciting: soon it will be very dark & hard breathing men will fly through the night down Botley road[74] of many bridges & more memories. In the stillness of echoing Wytham [Woods] will they creep out in muttering groups & go their ways & there will be no sound. Yet all the while steadily, stealthily unseen will the magic needle point & point them on & there will be ceaseless moving in the gloom. I shall be dead with terror & the weird notion of that pilgrimage in the dark. And meantime perhaps the silken Peggy plays with a new lover in the glamour & music of some luxurious, dazzling café & the Belgian sleeps peacefully in a maiden bed …

The next two pages are written later (on Thursday) … Thursday arrived with the dreary prospect of a days map reading yet I tell you *in earnest* that with an encouraging letter from Peggy I would have read maps on windswept Shotover[75] for years & years without a murmur. It was too bad for map reading however (today is Thursday) & we were dismissed—the others to joyous freedom, I to morbid ponderings & Hamlet-dreams. To night I waited & at 5.0–6.0 she came accompanied by two men … At Cowley road[76] one man was dropped & your humble servant was well up behind the other two. Near the Cowley road P.P.[77] the other man departed & like a Greek athlete I stepped into the arena with a prayer for help. Venus was with me; *she* (P) stopped at my call, eyes told the rest. As dear, as kind, as ever, she laughed at the idea that I had been morally rejected & for a long time we walked in the seventh heaven of delight and the Cowley road: and I am to see her at 8.15 to-night—There is a debate on the Labour question in the J.C.R [Junior Common Room]. Ah its a good life lads its a good life … I must stop. With love Basil

---

Patrick to Owen, 20 February [1918]

I am so sorry you have got jaundis it sounds and seems so horried.

I have been first twice in Latin and the master gave me a penny each time as well as mother.

The term is going so quickly it was half term yesterday. Lots of love from Pat

---

Violet to Owen, 20 February 1918

I *am* so sorry that you have jaundice. I wonder what gave it to you. I hope you are already feeling better & will soon get your leave. I suppose if you do not get it for Friday week you will only have to postpone it a week.

Of course about medicine you will not take Eastons[78] until after you have finished with the doctor. As for the little pills they might be good *if you need them* but I think that you had better not take them without asking the doctor while he is giving you med.…I suppose you have had to stay in doors & could not visit the Quibells. I am sorry that you will not be able to act the French maid. It is such fun…I hope you haven't forgotten to write to him [Gilbert]…At the end of this letter I will put a few addresses & you must write them down in your note book, or invest in an address book & enter them.

I hope to send off the pants & soap box. Mind you take care of your music—keep it in the case & mark it with your name…Mind you get your things from the Quibells & bring them in your sack. Perhaps you could take it to the station the day before. Don't you think it wd. be nice to take Mrs Quibell a really nice pot of flowers. Get some plain cards & yr. name in case you find them out.

Joyce Cockram to Owen, 25 February 1917 [1918] from Oxford

Thanks awfully for your letter. I'd wondered if you were ill—in fact, I thought you were probably a victim to that Arch-Enemy of the Youth of this world—Measles. Is Jaundice painful? I've no ideas on the subject at all. I can simply imagine you revelling in sheets. There is something peculiarly attractive about a good slippy linen sheet, isn't there?

Can you manage sick leave when you come out of hospital?…Joan [Anderson] and I went home on Friday and returned this morning, as Joan had to go on duty this afternoon…Don't get a wrong impression of

Joan. A Grown-Up Age has got to come to most people—it's practically as inevitable as The Ice Age & Prehistoric Times. Joan does it exceptionally well and hasn't tried it on me, thank goodness! At present, when I'm listening to her, I get a fit.

Don't you think this war has turned the rising generation into Cynics (I don't know whether this applies to you). You get that awful feeling, that nothing matters, & that one might just as well do—well, needlework, or something equally useless, as go on working.

And somehow it seems frightfully mean that people like me should go on for our degrees, when people like you can't.

I like your quotation about civilization very much. Have you read 'Familiar Studies in Men & Books' (R. L. Stevenson)? If not, try & get hold of it. The one on Walt Whitman is extraordinarily good. I never finished *Pendennis* [by Thackeray] I'm sorry to say. I've just finished 'Redgauntlet' (Scott) and enjoyed it thoroughly. There are some most exciting smuggling scenes in it. I am at present reading 'Everyman and his Music',[79] which is extraordinarily good, and most amusing in parts. Do you want books to read, or have you plenty?

Joan and I went 'On the bust' the other day. We took Hugh & Fletcher to tea at the George; came back here for music and then we took the boys to see 'David Garrick' (Martin Harvey's company).[80] Joan and I are still Martin Harvey mad, which is sad. He is simply splendid; and has the proper receding forehead and the other outstanding features of a tragedian.

I enclose a 1½ minute time exposure I took…of that man who came to stay here…I believe I have paid about ⅙ or some vast sum like that for you at Druce's.[81] I simply daren't have an account. But for goodness sake, don't worry about what I pay for you. Don't I use you Camera gratis.

Josephine Morrison has cut her hair short!

The Olive Skinned Belgian M. de Boeck is very flourishing. Prepare for a shock. She is engaged to be married to an American. Poor old Donne! I haven't seen him this term—at least I did see him, but he stolidly refuses to see me. Please write soon. Letters are wonderfully exciting, whoever they may be from.

[P.S.] 26–2–18. I got packed off to bed at this point…Mrs Slater seems to expect you home this weekend. You simply must manage leave of some sort soon.

Mrs Maude George to Owen, [February 1918]

It is *my* fault that Joan's letter has not reached you—I wanted to send you a line—was knocked up. Joan was worse & now it is days old. I am so sorry. Why have jaundice? It is better than the blues I grant but not pretty at all. I do hope you are better dear boy.

Joan has been & is still ill (don't tell her) congestion of the brain & a chill on top with a great deal of pain poor child—if you have time to do so write to her—it cheers her up so much & she needs cheering pretty badly.

FIGURE 8 Owen Slater (*right*) with jaundice outside a military hospital with a nurse called Joan and an unidentified officer.

I am sitting on the floor in the drawing room & do wish you were coming in to tea! I do miss your dear old cheeky face (don't strafe me!)

So glad you are comfortable in hospital…Good-bye dear boy; we never forget you.

Basil Donne-Smith to Owen, 27 February 1918

I am in a dreadful state, on the horns of a dilemma, on the verge of the pit of destruction—to carry your metaphor further. Fortune has lifted me with her sugar tongs out of the sugar bowl of sweet happiness, preparatory to plunging me in a tea cup full of swirling misfortune. It is thus—a) Under the influence of Prestaggers[82] I am reforming & have become a server (one who assists the priest at Communion); b) the girl in the picture shop is frightfully beautiful…[and] has been a long acquaintance (in a merely slightly interested way)…Furthermore she will exercise a good influence & keep me from the clutches of the less reputable of her sex. You ask about Prestaggers in your last interesting letter…he is no dodderer. I should say he was about 25–30…He stroked the House togger[83] & rowed 7 in the eight, but, oh so fortunately, he is not one of the 'healthy Englishman' type…he is a thorough good man 'of the High Church persuasion'…On Saturday mornings at 7.30 I serve for him at the Convent Church. Last Sat., was my first go off. The ritual is complicated & I don't know how many howlers I made…If I may criticise, your letter wasn't it a trifle unfortunate that one passage read as follows:- 'I've met another Joyce who's a nurse here. I'm in a ward of three beds!!' Do you want as many as that? What an *utter* ass I am; didn't catch on at first; see now; sorry…We had a debate the other night; there is a regular debating society here now & I opposed the motion that 'War is necessary for civilization.' A moment's reflection revealed the fact that I thought it was but still I gabbled amiably for ten minutes & sat down in a chair & much confusion…Later. We go down on the 16th, that is if I am called up by then.

Otherwise I may do a vac course, but this is very improbable...I have always associated church with dry sermons, teaching in dreary Sunday Schools, best uncomfortable clothes & piety & so on. Then the force of the thing struck me. Christ came to earth with divine power subjected to mortal temptation...endured the conceit of nonentities & hardest of all smiled as they killed him. Granted this, what a wave of admiration must come over one...that's what I am trying to realise. Awfully sorry to bore you with all this—what a rotten letter! Write soon, Yrs ever, B.

Gilbert to Violet, 27 February and 7 March 1918

There has appeared a statement that the worst is passed with regard to shortage of shipping; I hope it may be true, but I rather doubt it. Things are looking awfully black just now, with the Bolshevik treachery consummated, and the prospect of Germany controlling the resources of Russia. It is hard to see how peace can come unless the common people in Germany kick, & that just now they seem less likely to do than ever. There is just a possibility that the threat of a Great German offensive is bluff, and intended to be a lever to extort the most humiliating terms from the Allies; and it is also possible that the partial taste of the blessings of peace will make the Germans keener on getting complete peace. They are only fighting now for what will be very bad for them if they get it—domination over people who hate them. But I fear it is most unlikely that they will see that.

This time last year I was preparing for home-coming—this time next year I hope I shall again be. This year I have only a visit to the hills to look forward to, with plenty of work to do there. The director of Education of Ceylon has just come through Madras, &...told me that they are anxious to have me...It would be nice to go to Ceylon and also to get a little extra money to wipe off debts. I am very short of cash just now...I hope to be able to send about £120 in the beginning of April.

On Wednesday evening I went to Mysore City to fulfil my lecturing engagement for the Mysore University...The change bucked me up, and I am feeling better than any time since my visit to Kumbakonam...Mackintosh, the young London Scot who was at Gray's Hotel with me at Coonoor in May 1916 is on the staff of the Maharajah's College. He came round in the afternoon & fixed up a game of tennis for me...I had a big audience my first night...The three lectures were all on Indian village problems, I will enclose a syllabus. On the Friday I went to the Maharani's college for girls & women and the Maharajah's College in the morning. The former is remarkable for its range. It has kindergarten, up to B.A. classes, and also as a sideshow music (the native instrument, the vina [veena]) and drawing, & bamboo basket making. It is divided into two sections, the Canarese and Anglo-Vernacular. In the former all instruction is given through Canarese, but English is taught as we teach French. In the Anglo-Vernacular section English is the chief subject in the lower classes, & the medium of instruction in the higher ones. There are 400 altogether. Mackintosh got me to take the B.A. class for him. There were four girls in it, three Indians, hopeless duffers, one Eurasian & Christian, an intelligent, nice-looking girl.

Mackintosh victimised me the same way at the Maharajah's College, and there it was a big class to whom I talked about methods of studying Indian Economics. The acting Principal...is a Maratha Brahmin...a native of Mysore, and a student of the Christian College, Madras, & of St John's College, Cambridge. So as fellow Johnians we had a good deal to talk about...He wanted me to undertake to write an elementary textbook of English Industrial History for Indian Students; I wanted to book him to come to Madras and help in my Diploma work. The more you give the students a variety of *supplementary* teachers the better.

[7.3.1918] We have got our mails, your letters of Jan. 17 & 22, & the first that have come from Owen since he went to Newark. He has not written direct to me; but I am very glad to find that he is in good company, I hoped he would be. I have also received...the *Ruskin Collegian*...I agree with your remarks about the *Ruskin Collegian*. But do try to think as charitably of old Furniss as you can. He is academic and commonplace to a degree, but he is industrious & well meaning & I believe was swept into a treacherous line of action quite alien to his own disposition by Mrs. Truly our Ruskin students have a poor record compared with the Dragons, though some of them have shown themselves men—either as volunteers or Conscientious Objectors…We fear that at least one mail, & probably two consecutive ones, may have been lost…If the mails actually were lost, I shall try to recover as much as possible of what I write and repeat.

[P.S.] Very glad to get the butter bean notes. I have had then copied & sent to the chief agricultural people all over India.

———✸———

On 3 March the new Russian Soviet Federated Socialist Republic signed a peace treaty with the Central Powers at Brest-Litovsk, having begun negotiations on 22 December 1917. To gain peace the Russians ceded almost a quarter of the old Empire's territory to Germany, Austria-Hungary, and the Ottoman Empire. Russia also promised to compensate Germany for the repudiation of German-held tsarist bonds. In November Germany renounced the treaty as part of the Armistice negotiations. The Allies assumed this treaty would release a large number of troops for the Western Front.

Violet to Gilbert, [3 March 1918]

In the afternoon Owen & I cycled into Cheam [Nottinghamshire] & a little beyond. We went round Kelham Hall but Civilians are not allowed inside…There is a nice little church within the grounds and we went in there & talked. Owen says his course is lengthened to 13 weeks & then he will have a long week end in the middle. He has done the riding course…& is now doing trenching, bridging etc. He says that…the right & only thing to do [is] to lie, you are always losing your equipment & must take anything you want that you come across & stick to it. It doesn't seem an altogether good model for Civil life! There are 3 sorts of R.E.s & he's R.E. 'Field!' I fear it is the most dangerous but it is no use worrying until the time comes…I have not seen the papers but I hear that Russia has made peace & I cannot believe it somehow…I very much enjoyed my little visit to [word indecipherable]…I had a very comfortable, pretty little bedroom & a hot bath almost as nice as the Ruskin one!

―――∞――――

Gilbert to Owen, 7 March 1918

I was so glad in getting your two first letters from Newark to find that you are in good company, and that things are so nice as far as you describe them. I should like a little more detail, so that I could picture you in my mind in your new habitat. I hope you will like the riding. If a certain part of your skin retains the toughness it acquired in boating it will be good—it will all be wanted!

For news about me you must trust to having letters forwarded—owing to the close fit between the arrival of the mail & its departure, & a sudden access of University business, I am very cramped for time for writing. I do hope you will have a fine time at Newark & make some real good friends; & that there will be no hurry about sending you to the Front. Every day's delay is something to the good for your parents, whatever you may think for yourself…Write direct to me if you can find the time—otherwise send messages in your letters to Mother.

―――∞――――

Violet to Owen, 7 March 1918

It was very naughty of you to keep us so long without a letter—one a week—& I did not know if you were still in hospital. We are *very* delighted & excited at the prospect of having you so soon. I hope the leave will come off…Be sure you bring a great coat or trench coat. Don't go & catch cold. I suppose you will have to bring your old sack for your things. It's rather a nuisance…Winnie's [Owen's cousin's] young man has been home from the Front & she had been here very little so that I have been kept at work pretty hard & in consequence am rather tired out. He goes back tonight poor fellow—perhaps we shall have more help & more leisure seeing as you know there is always plenty to do with the difficulties of shopping. If you come at once you will just get your holiday through before the actual rationing comes in force. I don't understand it & I suppose shall not until we have the experience.[84]

[P.S.] Two things dear boy. Mind you bite up your food well (Forgive me for mentioning it!!!) Also wash well especially your feet. Never have stale perspiration on you, & try to wear clean underclothes. If they do not allow you to have things washed send them home sometimes, it will be worth the carriage.

I will send pants when they come back from wash & I have mended them. Early next week with a bit of P's [Patrick's] birthday cake. I purposely do not attach names to this document, as if you lose it, it may be a word in season to someone else. VOS

I was just going to!!!

[P.P.S.] Jolly glad you are coming home. Hope you will help us mend the bikes. The Et ceteras are playing this afternoon, but alas I am not in the match. Must go now, Eliot

---

Joyce Cockram to Owen, 9 March 1918 from Oxford

Thanks awfully for your last splendidly long letter…To be perfectly honest, I was very glad to hear Mrs Slater turn Revolutionary, as you put it. So few people of our Mother's & Father's generation have any sympathy with the Lower Classes. My Mother and your Mother are the broadest minded people—in that way—that I know. It's so rotten to say that a woman or man is common, just because his people are garage people or factory owners—and then dub them as thoroughly bad—the

'Impossible to know' style of thing. Don't you think so?...I don't think you quite hung on to what I meant about taking exams now. I really mean to imply that the quicker people like you can get back to work the better for the world in general, because anyhow during the rise of our generation men are bound to be of greater use than women; so it seems rotten that people like me can't be doing something definitely for the war, so that it's over quicker. Things like—well, passing London Inter. Science [the University of London Intermediate Examination in Science] etc don't seem to count. See?

Josephine looks quite nice. I'm beginning to think it suits her. It is absurd to do such a thing, all the same, and it seems to be the fashion. I think I shall cut mine off too!...What surprised me so about 'Men & Books' was that it was interesting although I knew nothing about the man in question. I'm now reading *Travels with a Donkey*, which is good in part, but gets dull because you don't know any of the places. We had to read 'Dr Jekyll and Mr Hyde' last week at school. Have you ever read it? Personally I was disgusted. The plot is thrilling and exciting enough, but the idea of the whole thing is—unhealthy to say the least of it. I like your idea of people's mental development depending on what they read. Since then I've noticed that it's jolly true. So, 'congratulations!'[85] I believe you said something about wishing you were here, to enjoy the good things every-body mentions in their letters. But you see we only mention the good times we have. If you like I'll write a letter full of all the rotten things which happen. You'd be jolly glad to be out of Oxford then!

Oxford has done awfully well this week. We only asked for £150,000 and this morning we had £300,000; so we've got two destroyers, instead of one. It's rather brainy, isn't it? Everywhere the excitement has been intense. There is a tent in St Giles and another on down at the Plain,[86] where you buy War Bonds. There is also a model pill box in St Giles...I saw Patrick in the town the other day. I was biking back from O.H.S. [Oxford High School for Girls, 21 Banbury Road] and suddenly I heard a shriek. I jumped out of my boots, but took no notice (as a matter of fact I had shoes on). A 2nd yell followed and I did look up then and saw Patrick standing in the road waving his hand as if mad. I nearly had a fit, of course. He is the limit…The school play—*Julius Caesar*—is taking place after Easter. It ought to be quite good; but I am utterly sick of *Julius Caesar* and think it's a rotten play for girls. Don't you…Please write soon. The postman has neglected me lately!

Gilbert to Owen, 14 March 1918

We have two homeward mails going at short interval—one last Thursday, and one today; but in between we have had no mail arriving from home—so I have another opportunity of writing to you, without having any letter to reply to. Here is a little tip which I think is very valuable for maintaining health, which I recommend you to keep in mind. When you buy a toothbrush, pick out the one with the hardest bristles; & *rub very energetically* when you use it. An extraordinarily prevalent disease, which brings on general weakness & bad health, is little ulcers in the gums, and I believe a sure way to prevent it developing is to rub your gums so hard that unless they are quite sound you create a sufficient flow of blood to get rid of infection. Blood is an antiseptic, & the only one that can be applied quite effectively from inside.

The war prospects look worse and worse, but one never knows when there may be a change. When you get this it will, I expect, be about the end of April, & you will be in your fourth month in the Cadets. I do hope to hear soon what the prospects are. I cling to the hope that Engineers officers get a good long professional training before they go to the front. I am awfully glad you can speak so well of your companions. But for the dangers ahead you must be having, on the whole, a very enjoyable time, & I hope a time that you will be able to look back upon in after years with great pleasure. God bless you, my dear boy. Write.

On 21 March Germany began die Kaiserschlacht, *the Emperor's Battle, the first of a series of massive offensives along the Western Front, with the Battle of Picardy in the British sector. In February Gilbert had suspected that talk of these battles was a 'bluff' but in the event they were the Central Powers' final attempt to defeat the Allies before American troops and resources arrived en masse.*

Gilbert to Owen, 24 March 1918

I am hoping you will still be in the Cadet Battalion in Newark...but you may be moved on, and so I am sending this home so that it shall reach you wherever you are. The war news has been very bad, and while on the one hand the prospect of beating the Germans gets more remote, on the other, the hope of there ever being any real or tolerable peace in the world if the Germans are not beaten has got to be very faint indeed. When the prospect is so dark there seems nothing for it except to go on from day to day trying to do one's duty, whatever it may be. All my duties have really reference to the needs of the world when peace is re-established, & it is rather sad to be doing so little to help in the great crisis.

Next Sunday I leave for Kodaikanal [a popular hill station resort]. I leave here in the evening, arrive at Kodaikanal Road station about 10.30...I suppose I shall have a quiet and uneventful three months boating & playing tennis, and doing examination papers, and writing my next book for the Madras University Economic series, while you are doing I wonder what? I have had so far the barest glimpse at your life in Newark only that the company & food are good, & that you are going to have riding [lessons]. Now I suppose you are learning all sorts of things, & becoming a young man of vast abilities. It is so good that hitherto things have gone so well with you; I have that to be thankful for, while anxieties increase. Just now the war seems to be reaching a final climax. People at home must have much to bear.

I do want you to feel how constantly my thoughts are with you, and my hopes and fears for your well-being. Always your loving father, Gilbert Slater.

Basil Donne-Smith to Owen, 1 April [1918] from 57, Cranes Park, Surbiton

Qu'en pensez vous? Guess I'm on a winner this time! You must have been rather surprised: a bit of a change after Peg. By the way I hope you know what I'm talking about. Well I was awfully glad to see you, I hope when I'm in an O.C.B. [Officer Cadet Battalion] I get as much leave as you do…what I want is an opinion from you. I received 3 letters this morning…one from Pat that's her name: I think we ought to think of a better name though, just for you & me. 'The girl in the Picture Shop', is far too long, but I can't think of anything better at present.

Violet to Gilbert, 3 April 1918*

This time last year you were with us. We thought of you a great deal on Easter Monday—we walked in the same direction that we all walked in last year…Joan George came round…after supper for an hour (she shared in the lemonade)…I think I told you that they had news…that…[Joan's father, the Revd T. P.] George had died suddenly. It is very sad, they had…cheerful letters since the news & they cannot hear details for some little while. Joan is doing some agriculture & going daily. She gets 15/- a week…Owen went off in wet feeling depressed—he certainly doesn't care for the Army. He, Hugh Cockram & I cycled in the teeth of a wind to Wallingford on Sunday to see his people. Joyce cycled back with us—she was coming back to work…Goodbye my own darling. God bless you. Your loving wife, V.O.S.

On 5 April Owen's friend Basil Donne-Smith entered the Cadet Battalion attached to The Kings Royal Rifle Corps. Four days later on 9 April Germany launched the second spring offensive, the Battle of the Lys, this time in the British sector of Armentières.

Violet to Gilbert, April 1918

This time last year you were here & brought me this pen that I am using as a wedding present. I wonder if you will remember the day...21 years ago...It seems a very long time ago. I never expected to be parted thousands of miles apart & the horror of a terrible war going on...I did not think it would be possible for such sad times to continue. All the wrong people are being killed & millions groan...I thought Labour would have done it but it lacks faith.[87] I long for a new spirit to get past all the fatal complications & to simply let the people get at each other & learn the truth...It is terrible to think of the ground that cost so much human life being again & again a sacrificial altar...I wish America had never come in then perhaps we should have tried other means & not closed up every avenue but force...Yesterday I went out early by the 8.40 train to Banbury to the Friends Quarterly meeting held there. I met & had a long talk with a master of Leighton Park Reading it seems a modern school...I asked for a prospectus...I think if he [Eliot] fails in the Winchester, L.P. Sch. is on high ground & has splendid grounds, libraries etc. [George] Cadbury & others do a good deal for it. Many of the Leightonians are fighting & some are C.O...I feel very much drawn to something more like this for the boys. I am not sure that the Public schools are worth while. What we want in the future is public spirit that will want to help in the building of a very different world, we do not want the old traditions. Eton suits ought to go & all that they stand for. We want to really live as if we believe in the Fatherhood of God & the Brotherhood of man.

Owen to his mother, 14 April 1918*

I would have written to you before but I expected a letter & a parcel from you any day...do please send me the things, the most important is the marmite...I have had an awful craving for grub the whole of the week. I hope I shall recover before long…I can't tell you how tired I have been…last week we have just started drill & riding again; it is ghastly. On Saturday we had to wear full equipment with water bottle, ride & drill for two hours & do physical jerks for another two hours. Everyone was pretty fed up by the time we had finished. If matters go on like this I would give anything to be in hospital, still more to be out of the abominable show altogether. The effect of military training & discipline is to make you forget everything that is not essential to your work. I discovered an old essay of mine the other day. I'm sure I couldn't write one like it now. I'll send it to you & see what you think of it.

Now as regards things of a more cheerful nature. On Friday evening I went into Newark & had dinner with…Frank P.…We didn't do anything but we had quite a jolly little evening. F.P. is going up to New College next term & is going to join the O.T.C. so naturally we discussed that & Oxford. At about 10.0 pm the gas went out & there was an air raid warning. I left at about 10.15. Newark was pitch black & I got hauled up by a Bobby for not having my lights *out*. Everyone was riding with no lights at all. It was rather beastly in the town…When I had got back to Kelham I definitely heard three shells explode in quick succession. I found afterwards that they exploded near a racecourse & aerodrome at Lincoln.

Yesterday I rode over to Brant [Broughton, Lincs.] & over to the Morleys. Miss Morley was of course at the Hospital & asked me to go with her. Her pater is an old country squire & a magistrate etc. Her mater is very nice too…They are all very jolly & I went round the village sights. A ripping old church & a Quaker meeting house…They provided me with a scrumptious tea, home made bread & butter & egg sandwiches. Afterwards also with an equally good dinner finishing up with a huge piece of cream cheese. I got back to Kelham at 10 o'clock & saw the last half of a…concert…At about midnight we heard more explosions either gunfire or bombs…I am very anxious to hear how you have been getting on. How is the kitten?…My course is going to end on the first of June when I shall get three weeks or 10 days leave.

Agnes Peacock to Owen, 19 April 1918

I am sending you a pair of thin socks, they look hairy but Uncle Jim says they are soft & light & very good so I hope they will be a treat when you wear your 'joy rags'. The toffee can be worn at any time & will alas! disappear all too quickly. I hope your grub hunger is dying down. Mollie & her confrères boil potatoes nightly to fill up gaps. From what she says I think they are rather meanly supplied with bread & fats. She is enjoying Cambridge immensely but was very anxious to do some war work instead & is I believe to do six weeks flax picking in the long vac. Yours is the harder part to do drills etc. against the grain but however much we hate war I cannot see what else can be done now. Years ago we ought to have worked against its possibility—now it seems to me unbelievably impossible to leave the Germans to triumph, what would life to anyone be worth. It is sad beyond words to be an armchair critic, one can only do as the old hymn says 'Trust in God & do the right'.

I don't want to read you a sermon but it is infinitely sad if we are not inspired to just go on to the best of our ability in the nearest duty at hand. I am so glad you have riding & engineering feats to break the monotony... It is just about post time & I hear an apologetic cough from the kitchen which means our young letter carrier is waiting to post this. Much love & lots of loving thoughts & prayers from your loving Auntie Agnes

Owen to his mother, 20 April 1918*

Thank you so much for sending me the parcel particularly the marmite & the gingerbread... Grub is short at present though we are getting a messing officer & things ought soon to become much better. I wish you had sent a larger pot of marmite. I am afraid that what you have sent will not last very long... Please don't trouble to send any more clothes or pants until I ask because I have loads of things & probably my zephyr [light shirts or trousers] & rowing bags [trousers]...Also I had plenty of rocks [rock cakes] & some scrumptious toffee from Aunty Agnes...we have a riding exam, tomorrow...I am going to the Quibells...again. Poor Arthur Quibell was wounded...three days ago & is in London...I went in last night. They had not heard how serious it is at any rate he will be out of it for a long time; poor fellow I hope he won't lose his leg...At present I am waiting in a queue for a hair cut...the cadet Bulmers is a very nice lad. We are quite comrades; as a rule we do our schemes[88] together. Please give my love to the kitten, cat rather & her kittens. I wish I could see them...You have not told me what you are doing about a servant. When does Edna come back. I do hope you are not over working yourself & getting too tired. It rather sounded like it from your last letter.

———⊱⊰———

The need for a Royal Engineer to be able to ride seemed odd to some of Owen's relations but good horsemanship was essential if officers were to get about quickly behind the lines and over difficult terrain. In addition, good horsemanship was still the mark of an officer and a gentleman. The end of cavalry charges meant that the work of horses was largely confined to transport, especially moving artillery. The importance of horses in the war has been more appreciated in recent years. This is not surprising when one remembers that by 1918 Britain had over 1,000,000 horses and mules in service. Losses were horrendous: almost half a million British horses were killed between 1914 and 1918.

Owen to Patrick, [20 April 1918]*

Many happy returns of the day. I have written to Mother & asked her to give you [1s] don't spend it on sweets at once. I will try to send you a cake or a pork pie or something like that.

We have got an examination in riding so today I am very busy looking up...in fact I am tchacooning[89] like anything. Yesterday we went for a ride, just twenty of us. After we had gone about three miles we had to take off our horses' saddles & ride, trot & gallop. One or two fell off but no-one was hurt as we were riding on the grass. It was huge fun but rather uncomfortable as all the hair came off on your clothes, & so you had to groom yourself as well as your horse.

There was a concert last night and two men pretended to be dustmen. They brought out a carpet & started to beat it. One got underneath to hold it up & got smothered & they started wrestling & fooling about & made a terrible dust. Just then the lights went out & we had to have God Save the King in the dark & there was a frightful muddle getting away.

<hr>

Owen to his mother, 23 April 1918

Thank you very much for the parcel—it was a great surprise & very good. The ginger only survived two days but I've kept some fruitarian cake. Rations are probably better now. I haven't been spending so much cash on grub…We have had a busy week, one riding exam came off in the middle. For a practical, I got on fairly well but [I had] a horse I couldn't quite manage which rather spoilt the effect. On Friday we went up on Beacon Hill & were drilled in putting on gas masks. It is absolutely devilish & makes you look as ugly as sin. We had to go through the gas chambers with our masks on, you couldn't smell anything at all. But the masks were abominably tight & uncomfortable & made you slobber like a teething baby.

Arthur Quibell has been wounded jolly badly in his thigh & in fact it has to go. Two days ago the report was 'just his own'. But he is better now…Next week is going to be worse—exams in Drill, Physical training, Musketry…[The officers have] brought out an abominable order about flannels. Cadets are encouraged to wear flannels, but they will only be permitted in the grounds of Kelham Hall. Under no circumstances will cadets leave Kelham while wearing flannels! It means that I can't go to the Quibells wearing flannels. No. 1 Company has just gone down & I was invited to the breaking up concert. I think if I had not had jaundice

I would...Everyone here is enthusiastic about the war...When you do send me a parcel will you send me the best cricket bat you can find. By the way will you send on this letter to father? So sorry Pat chopped his finger.

Joyce Cockram to Owen, 26 April 1918 from Wallingford

Many thanks for your letter...I am sorry you're so utterly fed up—so am I, for various reasons. We've been spring cleaning all this week, while Mother has been away...It is extraordinary, how much brass there is in this house. I am sick of the smell of Brasso and as to washing china & pictures, I loathe the job...I've started a button campaign since Mother has been away. Two buttons come off Hugh's trousers periodically, about once in two days, and the days when it isn't trousers, it's shirts! Dad manages to make a hole...in the toe of his sock, when I'm the only one who has the opportunity to darn it, and he forgets to tell me until I've just got thoroughly interested in something...The more I'm at home without Mother the more honestly and sincerely I admire her 'excellent virtues'. All this is just to impress upon you that we have our minor worries & troubles, & life isn't all roses.

Don't get too skittish about late passes. It would be awfully awkward if you were caught one day. Is it worth the risk?

I expect Hugh told you all the news on Sunday, when he wrote. You may be interested to know that he and I have got on together splendidly, these holidays. Honestly, we've made great strides, & it is mostly due to you, too. He has said something at times about the R.A.F. and still seems rather set on the idea, says he's got a lot of the right kind of endurance for the job. I think the only thing to be done is to deal very gently with him, because he certainly won't stand being driven, at any rate by me. Dad thinks that the chances of his having to join the Army are very remote, he said last night that that he thought the war might be over this year even now, because he considers this last feat of arms on Germany's part to be a gigantic bluff. Of course, I don't know what he knows about it, and he's rather given to optimism, but he's often right. I wonder whether he'll have to join the army himself? He'd find it jolly hard in the ranks, his family have always spoilt him so! Wouldn't it be killing if he were to become your servant.

Up to this week, my work has been going well. Unfortunately I haven't done a stroke this week. I *hope* I get through that exam. New ideas are cropping up about my future which are rather complicated; the main thing is, that, to my huge delight I shall probably begin to 'bring grist to the mill' (Dad's expression) after next term. This has been agreed upon between us for two very different reasons; Dad's is that he's afraid he can't afford to keep me any longer, and mine because I've been longing to *do* something for the last year, ever since I took in the fact that medecine was out of the question for the present. Dad wants me to take up work in London under Government.

I saw your Mother before I came home. Unfortunately I was too late from school (We had the play that night, if you remember.) to get to that lecture. I thoroughly enjoyed a long talk with her on Education etc…Hugh & I both go back to Oxford on Wednesday. He says he'll be writing to you in about a week & would like a letter from you!

Don't get too fatalistic, will you?

―⠀⠀―

Gilbert to Gertrude Slater, 27 April 1918*

I have just received yours of March 13, & have also yours of Jan. 29th received last mail to answer…You ask after Mrs Geddes. She died just over a year ago, of some fever caught in India. They had not gone home for the summer. The oldest son, Alasdair, who was a Major in the Flying Corps— the youngest major in the British Army it was said—was killed while walking through a village by a cannon shot just about the same time. Mrs Geddes died without being told.

All this time not only my own appointment, but the Chair itself has been provisional and temporary, maintained out of a non-recurring grant from the Government of India (not the Madras Gov^t). I hear now that the Syndicate has resolved to approach the Gov^t. of India with a view to making the Chair a permanent matter. This is practically a declaration that my appointment has proved a success.

I am up here [at Kodaikanal] for three months, April, May & June…It is hardly a holiday, as while I am relieved of a good deal of my ordinary work, I have a lot of exam. papers to mark. They specially appealed to me to take this on this year & in view of enormous prices one wants all the money one can get.

The Diploma regulations have now been sanctioned by Government, so the beginning of a University Dept. for teaching Economics has been made. All next Session the working of that will be my first job, though the lecturing to University B.A. students will continue.

***

On 27 April the German army launched the third offensive in its Kaiserschlacht with the Third Battle of the Aisne in the French sector along the Chemin des Dames. Within three days German casualties reached 31,000 killed, 20,000 missing, and 190,000 wounded. By the same date Allied casualties (killed and wounded) reached 160,000 while 90,000 men had been captured. By 1 May the Germans were in possession of some 1,000 square miles of territory previously in Allied hands.

Violet to Gilbert, [c.28 April 1918]*

I am not very keen on St Edwards [School, Oxford] though the Sturts find it to their taste. It is very Churchy & very Military[90] Besides if I do come to India, it would mean Eliot becoming a boarder…Of course I wish very much indeed that I could consult, & that you could do something in the matter. It is a miserable thing to be so far separated.

I shall telegraph anything important, for instance 'Eliot' & the name of the school. And when dear Owen's training is over—in 5 weeks!!

I shall tell you where he is sent. So do not worry about things of that sort.

Our garden is looking so nice just now—beautiful I might say. Picture to yourself the lilacs just coming out, the white & blue hyacinths covering the beds, the apple trees in full bloom & the little cherry tree a nosegay of white blossom. We have not finished up the wood you chopped—we have had plenty of coal, though we have been very careful indeed about coal. I cannot bring my mind to look into the future. I do not suppose I shall get to India but of course if you come back, anyway I shall get in coal soon only we have had such abominable coal, slate & rocks: it is very difficult to make good fires with it…It is late & I must to bed. Goodnight my dearest Dear. How I wish you were here.

P.S. I have not mentioned the war. Most terrible fighting is going on—all the ground that cost such millions of lives—such millions of gold & money lost. Can it be possible that people shall still think that the only reasonable way is force. Surely there must be even from the military point of view, a better way: it just seems incredible that people should allow it. You say what can we do? Well this certainly is a failure. Why not call a truce, state war aims [word missing]. Secure treaties & see what we really all want.

<hr />

Violet to Gilbert, 30 April 1918

Your last written on the 14th March arrived in a little over a month. I am enclosing 2 or 3 letters. One from Owen…You will see that I am joining the Friends,[91] their comment simply means that one's 'name' has to be submitted to a half yearly meeting or something before it is put upon the books. I do not suppose that they will refuse me though I have definitely stated that I do not pledge my self to believe in any creed and I claim freedom of religious thought. I think it will be a great help to me. I hope so and it will make it much easier to explain my position. I hope I may be some use to the Society, but in many ways I am an unfit person. Last Sunday Prof. and Lady Gilbert Murray[92] came to the meeting. The place is usually quite full. I have been thinking a great deal about Eliot's education…and I am determined to see the Friends school at Leighton Park…I propose to let Eliot go in for the Winchester schol. as you wish. I hope if he gets in it will be really a good thing for him…but I have never been anxious for him to go there—I don't like the ordinary Public Schools, apparently they are frequently a hot bed of vice [homosexuality] and that it is too awful to let a child run the risk of coming in to such an atmosphere. No doubt there are good points, but it seems to me that the old fashioned Public Schools are played out…Do not imagine that I am joining the Friends so that I could send the boys. I did not think of it until I saw what is being done to militarise education. I think probably the boys at such a school would be much better, less snobs…One thing may interest you. They have an O.T.C. in connection [with the school]. The boys are not all Friends' children. I am not anxious to have Eliot do nothing but Classics all his education.

⸺❦⸺

Joyce Cockram to Owen, 5 May 1918 from Oxford

Thanks so much for your two letters. It was rather brainy of you to remember my birthday…I hope you didn't get into an awful row about your pass. It struck me afterwards that you'd think it awful cheek on my part to give you any advice. It is rather a good sign that Hugh said nothing to you about the R.E.'s. He's rather a hopeless freak to deal with, because he absolutely refuses to be driven into anything…I'm sorry that he has to leave school at the end of this term. It's awful hard luck on him, really. Work is something terrific for both of us, at present…If I don't get through this exam I don't know what I'll do, the disappointment to every one will be terrific. I very much hope that after this term, I shall start on my own & hope to get work in London until the end of the war then possibly I may take up medicine again, hope to at any rate... We have got to read a novel of Dickens before Thursday, I have chosen 'Martin Chuzzlewit', which is too long, I find; and I haven't begun it yet. It wouldn't be a bad idea to start now.

Cheer up! Yours sincerely, Joyce Cockram

Owen to his mother, 7 May 1918*

I am so glad you have seen Leighton Park School. I have been over there twice to play them at soccer... I wonder I never thought of it as a school for Eliot before. It is a ripping place altogether, fine swimming bath, & all the boys so far as I remember were quite nice. I don't think I should like Eliot to go to the M.C.S. I wouldn't mind so much if Cockram would be there to keep an eye on him. I'm afraid that without that he would get slack as the standard is not at all high.

Poor Arthur Quibell had to have his leg off two or three days ago & was very bad indeed. The doctor was with him the whole night & he nearly died twice, since then he has just been holding his own. I heard this on Saturday & haven't been in to Newark since... After I leave Kelham, if I get through everything, I get about 10 days leave & then go to Chatham[93] as an Officer for a fortnight's course in heavy bridging. After that I go for a month at least, possibly longer, to one of about six places: Chatham, Newark, somewhere in Wales—Ganway [Conway] I think, or else in Yorkshire... We have been having any amount of exams last week. I have done well in most of them, but I have failed in riding.

Eliot to his father, 8 May [1918]

In the last two games of cricket I caught two people out and very nearly caught out a third...I think I will be top this week. We had a Latin Unseen and I got 65...The two little kitties are great fun, they can manage to tumble out of their box now which is about 4" high. They are very inquisitive and playful. On Sunday [we had] a service and I read the first lesson...It was in the Hall. Hum[94] took the service and it was very nice. He seemed to think that Labour was going to have its turn now and said that there must be sympathy.

[P.S. from Violet] Eliot read very clearly & with some feeling. He read it to me several times before & once to Hum. Hum was most liberal in his view—we had such nice hymns...Of course we ended off with 'God Save the King'. I wonder if we shall utter that barbaric 'anthem'. I hear the soldiers won't sing it. It's worse than absurd the second verse [is] abominable. I wonder who wrote it.[95]

Gilbert to Violet, 8 May 1918 from Kodaikanal

It is more than a week since I last wrote...Henceforth we are not to be told beforehand of the departure of the mails. I hope that will add to their safety, in which case one must bear with the inconvenience. Similarly, I suppose, we shall not know of the arrival of mails till we get them, which is the position you have been in...The Bakers had a little 'Sale of Work' for blinded soldiers this afternoon, and I promised to go and help with the miscellaneous side shows—e.g. Aunt Sally[96]—which they proposed to have in the garden. But the rain prevented all out door items in the programme, so I was relieved of the duty.

All our activities seem to be of the character of fiddling while Rome is burning, but what can we do? Just now a few convalescent soldiers are being sent up, & Kodai is asked to organise hospitality for them. It is not much to do, but people are all jumping at the chance to do something.

The great calamities of the war, the progress of German domination in Russia, and the German advance in France, have greatly eased the political situation, the most anti-British of Indian political leaders are quite clear that they don't want British rule replaced by German, and are throwing themselves into the recruiting campaign. It seems a very wise course on their part—corresponding to Mrs Pankhurst's[97] policy in the outbreak of the war; and I anticipate the result will be a similar but not so complete a victory. Anything like complete Indian self-government must take a long time to come, if it is not to bring disaster; but I think the time is ripe for a beginning, and for the pronouncement of a definite policy of developing self-government as fast as possible.[98]

———

In May Eliot went to Winchester to sit his scholarship examination while Violet enlarged her anti-war work by joining the Fellowship of Reconciliation, a Christian pacifist movement.

Violet to Gilbert, 10 May and 13 June 1918

Both Owen & Eliot have gone & we are such a quiet little family with just little Pat. Owen went to Chatham on Sunday & on Saturday he and I went up to town [London]...Edna wanted me to stay for the weekend, but as Eliot was to go off to Winchester on Monday I said I should return by the 7.30 train. So I did &...on Sunday morning Eliot came home to say that they were to start for Winchester on Sunday afternoon. So we had a mighty rush...Mary had arranged to go & see Barrie's 'Dear Brutus'[99]... We reached the theatre just in time & were fortunate enough to get into the Pit...Owen's new boots made his feet rather tender. Poor little chap he was a little oppressed with the new dignity of being an officer. Its stupid. I believe he ought not to have sat in the Pit & ought to have travelled 1st class. One almost feels as if it is wicked to forget the war even for an hour. I always feel that [John] Rus-

FIGURE 9 (*Clockwise from top left*) Hugh and Joyce Cockram, two of Owen's principal correspondents who became family friends with the Slater brothers and Violet; Basil Donne Smith, a Magdalen College School friend; Ida (with rabbit) and Edna, two of the Brown sisters from the family who befriended Owen in Gillingham.

kin's [?] suggestion that all should wear black & all places of amusement be closed would very much help to make war intolerable which it
ought to be. Instead there seems more extravagance & self indulgence.
Owen did not hear of his commission until Friday, or indeed that he
was to go to Chatham.

Thursday, June 13th My dearest Sweetheart. Your parcel came yesterday
& I immediately wore the coat which is very delicate & pretty & beautifully
worked . . . That naughty boy Eliot has not written as I can't tell you a bit
how he has got on . . . I do wonder if he will get a scholarship. I would much
rather that he went to Leighton Park School, but I fear it cannot be. I see
that at Oundle the boys are making munitions. Isn't it abominable! If they
want to do useful work why not let them do agriculture.[100] I feel more &
more that if we want a different world we must give our boys & girls a different education. Asquith came & held forth here the other day. Lord
Selborne said that he had always lived a pure & honourable life!! What
does he know about Asquith [words indecipherable] & perhaps one or
more women![101] . . . the use of this perpetual humbug in every department
of life.

We had our [F.o.R. or Fellowship of Reconciliation] meeting at Keble
College. Dr Lock & Dr Carpenter & Selbie[102] all spoke well & there were
about 40 odd people, some women & a fair number of clergymen & ministers . . . Dr. L & C. both emphasised the fact that we are not allowed to
know what is happening in Germany. They quoted various movements
that news of which had come through Holland. We are not allowed to
know what happens in England . . . I feel that it was worth while . . . Directly
I know about Eliot I shall cable . . . He & Pat are very disobedient—they do
not seem to realise that there is any claim on my part for obedience . . . I do
wish you were here when I go to the allotment; I specially want you there
when I have to carry 3 cans of water to water lettuces cabbages &
marrows!

Owen to his mother, 15 May 1918

I had the last exam of my course this morning. I think I did fairly respectably at any rate I'm sure I got through…In No. 1 company 5 public school boys are having another course here so I wouldn't be a bit surprised if I had to also, I don't think I should mind very much, in fact I know I should have quite a good time but it would be abominable going over all the old work again. However I can't tell what will happen to me for at least a fortnight. I think I shall get all my kit in Oxford, it's the best plan on the whole. By the way do look out for a pair of boots for me…Just think of it I shall be home on Saturday June 1st. Hurray. Unfortunately I shall get only about 7 days leave if I go down to Chatham. If I come back here [Kelham] I shall get about a fortnight I hope.

I told you last week that I had moved into a tent which I share with another cadet…I cannot stick the man…One thing that annoys is that by an elaborate system of tipping he gets his bed made and his half of the tent brushed & his buttons & boots cleaned. He has a very persuasive manner also which increases the unpleasantness…Tennis is in full swing. I have had quite a lot of play. I didn't get any today as I wandered into Newark on my bike. I hope to be able to get time for a game every evening now that our exams are finished…We go on trek for three days before we leave. It is great fun we go about 15 miles a day & do schemes. We take it in turns to be somebody for a day. For instance I might be company Commander for a day, cook the next & a driver on the third. It is generally pretty hard work…About the bob I'm sorry but you will have to wait a bit as I've only one or two bob to last me 10 days as I've got to fork out 10/- for the farewell dinner next pay day. I hope Eliot is working well & not getting stale or his wind up.

Patrick to his father, 18 May 1918

We went to 'boar's hill' this morning, Eliot and I.

We found a lovely place and had dinner at about 12.30. Then we went to look for sticks and we found two lovely ones it took us about an hour to cut them as we only had two picknick knifes wich were aufly blunt.

After that we picked bluebells and I found a lovely...little place in the shade under a Sicamore with a lot of bluebells round it and beautifully if mossy, it was nice and cool there to, and it was aufly hot every where else. I lay down there and had a rest and then we went and both had rests and then we came home. With lots of love from Pat

Harold Oakeshott to Owen, 19 May 1918

I am afraid this won't reach you in time for your birthday...I suppose this is an extra momentous occasion for you, as I imagine it sees you a fully fledged combatant. I should like to know just how you stand and what you think your prospects are: let's hope that the next birthday will see an English Peace...On arriving home [from holiday in 1899] we heard the news of your safe arrival...to think this is all of nineteen years ago and that little squalling piece of Humanity has now reached Man's estate and is taking its place in its country's work...It has been a beautiful day today...Dorothy [Harold's wife] stayed at home to prepare for tomorrow's picnic. I hope the day will be as fine. We had hoped to gather bluebells but others had been before us and there were precious few for our bag; what with the difficulties of travelling nowadays I'm afraid our poor kids won't get an early experience of vistas of bluebells and clumps of wild primroses as naturally the woods round Croydon are very overrun...Croydon is a great place for aeroplanes and the air has been thick with them all day;[103] one gets rather tired of the continuous drone—it seems to destroy the privacy of the country—we had some retreat from the motor car but there is none from the aeroplane. Well goodbye old chap...Your loving uncle, Harold Oakeshott

Owen to his mother, 20 May 1918

Thank you very much for your letter & the gingerbread. I have nearly finished the latter…We start on trek on Monday…Did I tell you I had to pay 10/- dinner sub? Well I am horribly short of cash. Can you send me £1 to come home with?…As for the trek we have three days & have to march an average of 13 miles a day. Thank goodness I shall be bicycling one day & another I am Batman to one of the officers. It is going to be great fun if the weather last, which I doubt…Sorry I haven't a moment to spare. Inspections are showered on us by dozens.

Violet to Owen, 20 and 23 May 1918

Many happy returns of to-day…I expect you had several letters & I hope you got a cake. Auntie Agnes said that she was sending some gingerbread…It is nice to know that things arrive safely & are appreciated…Your time is drawing very near & you will be sorry to say goodbye to the Quibells & other kind friends you have made. I hope you have been in to the Q's, even if Mrs Q. is the only one at home. They must have been through a terribly anxious time poor things & it is very sad to think that poor Arthur will be a cripple all his life & deprived of the power of rapid motion. I hope he will otherwise quite recover. I want you to say goodbye to the maids there & give them each 2/6—just say Goodbye & shake hands & say 'Will you buy yourselves a little present from me.' As for Mr and Mrs try to express your gratitude for their friendship; say it had made a great difference to you which I am sure it has. When you come home we will try to think of a nice book that they will like & you shall send it to them. I should like them to have something to remember you by.

Yesterday Joyce came in to tea. She looked so cool & nice in a pretty muslin frock. She invited us—Edna and I—to come to tea then & in the end we fixed up that she should come here & give the boys their tea today & we go there so we did. We found some people called Anderson, Mr & Miss. Joan was at home & we had some music, she played & sang & Mr Anderson also played. He played with sympathy & is artistic. Joan played well but with less artistic feeling…I was glad to meet her. She is quite a pretty girl but I like nice little enthusiastic Joyce best…. Mind you get your birthday letters answered.

[PS. from Pat] Please write as soon as possible. Pat.

[PS. from Violet] Letter from Father he says that he received in one mail five…letters & no from you & you understand that there were 5 from each of us. *Do* try to write regularly. V.O.S.

Joyce Cockram to Owen, 21 May [1918] from Oxford

I meant to write to you yesterday for your birthday—and I simply hadn't a second in which to do a thing. Anyhow, now, the best of luck & many happy returns.

Your present state seems to be rather like mine—somewhat unenviable. You say you are nervy—so am I. You are working hard—so am I, so I'm sorry for you because it is so appallingly warm. I should think the worst of sleeping in camp is that you get awakened by the birds early in the morning…I had a horrid shock last week, because there was some muddle about Registration…[for the London Intermediate examinations] before May 1st, and of course I hadn't done anything in the registering line, because it wasn't referred to in the Regulations. Miss Haig Brown [Headmistress of the Oxford High School for Girls] and myself thought I wouldn't be able to take it at all—for 2 whole days. However, I think it's going to be alright now. Six weeks today 4 of my papers will be over!

By the way, it isn't settled that I will take up Government Work unfortunately. I wish something was settled for a change. However anything might happen during the next six months, so I just rub along, & manage to enjoy life, more or less…How long leave do you get? And do you begin on June 1st?…I am going to see your Mother tomorrow & will take her those snapshots to see. I am enclosing one of the drawing room for your benefit (I don't quite see how it benefits you, but still—)…Words fail me—so I stop. Good luck in all your exams; you are a lucky pig to be finishing at the end of next week. It jolly well isn't fair. What happens to you after your leave?

Violet to Gilbert, 22 May 1918

I have been spending a good deal of time in seeing people…about the proposed 'International Christian conference'. It is a very little piece of work but one feels it might lead to an awakening. We hope to get the Bishop of Oxford.[104] Dr Lock is holding an invitation meeting in his drawing room on June 12th or 14th…I wonder whether—when—there will come a great wave of desire for a possible settlement of the war. Now we are in the position that after years of fighting we are no further forward than we were after the first week…and all those millions of men dead or injured and homes desolated and yet on the whole we think there is nothing to be done but to go on fighting and pray God that victory may be ours!! I went to see Dr [A. J.] Carlyle. He has been lecturing at the Front on Reconstruction after the war. He said the men were inclined to ask what we are doing at times…I can't get anyone to dig our allotment meanwhile the weeds are becoming a nuisance…Owen will be home in the first week in June…We have been having a spell of hot dry weather but when it breaks we ought to be quick and get things in. I have bought scarlet runners, and French beans, and cabbage lettuces.

Eliot to his father, 22 May 1918

I am very sorry I am writing in pencil but somehow or other all the pens seem to have disappeared.

Just as I am writing the two little kittens are jumping down off the couch on to the floor (about 1½ feet, they themselves are about 3" long); They are coming on by leaps and bounds. They are very plump and active except in the middle of the day when they sleep for most of the time under the iron steps leading from the dining room onto the verandah. It is most oppressively hot except in the evening and early morning.

There was a match this afternoon between the Dragons and Herne Bay College this afternoon. Hearne Bay College is a school that has come to Oxford out of [the] Raid Area as you may have already guessed from its name.[105] We won scoring 88 runs four people only out...I was not in the match itself but I was scoring which is something.

[P.S. from Violet] We have to be very careful of paper. When I went out to buy envelopes I was told I could only have *one* packet [?] as they were rationed.

Joan George to Owen, 23 May 1918 from Watlington, where she was doing agricultural work

Thank you so much for your letter—did you think I was never going to write to you? I am awfully sorry I have been such a time about it but it's not my fault really dear! I am now supposed to be having my dinner & never have I wanted a meal less since I started this job...I suppose I must eat it though or I shall 'faint by the potato rut!!' Yes we are at it again—started potato planting again today—after a whole solid fortnight of it two weeks ago! When one does 8 hrs on end for *three* days one gets rather sick of it. I think this must be my 11th week here...When are you coming back old man? Surely its pretty soon now?

I am just going to see if my tea has come yet—no it hasn't. Did I tell you the Boss always sent us a jug of tea out at 12.30? I wish you had been here on May Day[106]—I did not get up altho' I wanted to—its no fun going alone…The tea has just come.

Later. I am so sorry I haven't any more time as I must go out for Mother—so will post this & write again soon.

[P.S.] Dear, I am *awfully* sorry, I have only just realised what the date is—please forgive me Tufty & I really do wish you *very* many happy returns of the day—altho' I am three days late over it. Mother sends her love & best wishes too. Dear Tufty I *am* a pig—a *very* repentant pig too—& I can only ask you to forgive me, yours Joan

<hr />

Joan George to Owen, 26 May 1918

Thank you very very much for your letter—you are a dear to write when I was such a brute in not realising the date [of Owen's birthday] & not writing.

S'ure & I have had a grand time!! I worked *hard* all yesterday & at 4 o'clock Geoffrey Newman suddenly turned up—he has two days leave—goes back tomorrow. Mother gave me an opal & diamond ring of hers—& a little *beauty*! Miss Hill sent me three pounds—a cheque (!!!!!!)…Hubert & Ken Bartlett & Phyllis a little book 'The Princess' by Lord Tennyson—do you know it? *Wasn't* they nice?

I am trying to wangle a weeks leave from the Boss…Do write again soon—I don't like Gargoyle for you—Gorilla is better!!! Much love, Joan

<hr />

On 27 May Germany opened the third stage of the Kaiserschlacht *with the Third Battle of the Aisne. This latest offensive continued until 6 June.*

Patrick to his father, 29 May [1918]*

Owen is comeing back on Saturday [1 June] and I hope we shall have a good time. He is comeing for seven days. The Kittens can lap and eat porridge and bread soaked in milk. With lots of Love from Pat

[P.S. from Violet:] I want to get rid of them!! I have to feed all three & it is difficult to get meat also they are not clean & kept indoors & so I let them all sleep on the verandah. Don't forget I shall telegraph when Owen goes & also about Eliot

---

Eliot to his father, 29 May [1918]

We had such an extraordinary Latin Prose to do the other day. It was a letter from a boy at Winchester to his brother. It tells how he went out of bounds to get some grub for another chap. How he met the 'bear' and was ordered to come to him at 4.30; How that ass Philip hit him in the wind and made him feel very sick; how when he did go to the Bear he was half an hour late; how in the midst of his castigations (and because of them) he felt so sick that he made a dive for the door and how the Bear becoming hugely enraged was at the point of expelling him when he vomited forth and spoilt his best Turkish carpet. It then goes on to make remarks about keeping fit for sports and asking what was happening at home. I could do it all fairly well except just at the end when he talked about not eating too much in case of spoiling his wind for the mile.

I have got rather an interesting Essay to write. 'In an (imaginary) county called Euwhone (or something similar)[107] a decree was issued abolishing all machines worked by Electricity or Steam'. I have got to make out the case (a) for this decree (b) against it.

Owen is coming home on Saturday. I am looking forward to it frightfully.

[P.S. from Violet:] I have not heard about the Leighton Park School yet. I do not quite know when the Winchester scholarship exam. comes off. I suppose about the 10th or 16th of June.

—⚮—

Basil Donne-Smith to Owen, 29 May 1918

Thanks awfully for your letter…Well I have a great deal to tell you…On Saturday I was on a 'loose end'; my idleness led me down towards Magdalen College via the High Street. A damsel past & eyes met—I think somewhere, on some dim red mountain in the land of damned, Satan laughed, once, harshly. At that second—but I turned and it was only the broken sudden start of a barrel organ when the man stops to pick up a copper thrown him from a window. The damsel passed on—I followed—Magdalen Tower leaned wearily over us in the heat, there was a drawling noise of people chattering & eyes met again—smiles brought words in their train; 'was she free?' 'yes'; 'did she care for the river' she preferred a walk. The return walk to Carfax[108] provided me with an opportunity of studying my companion, & combined with the conversation carried on I gathered the following facts. Ida Constance Ireland lived at Watkins Farm Northmoor[109] near Eynsham. Her father owned several farms near by. She had been to Somerville College & was 18 years of age (the last two items appear to be rather incompatible with one another). Her face is full & young with masses of dark brown hair. Very well: long & rapid strides were made by the river-bank in the Parks that afternoon:-

'We lipped it 'neath the green leaves in the shade.'

She finished a) by making me late for rowing b) by bagging my handkerchief. The following Wednesday produced a similar but more affectionate meeting & then came a letter which showed the I.C.I. was 'head over heels'. The next Saturday…I went over to Northmoor and we spent a luxurious afternoon miles from everybody, very close. Then came another letter full of 'novelette' 'passion'.

Meanwhile what about the Shrew? Heavens! False deceiver! In a kind of don't care, 'want-to-show-off' fit I exhibited Connie's handkerchief which I had bagged—the thunder cloud grew black on Cynthia's brow—here was a challenge! I realised too late as the showers of ill hidden sarcasms came whizzing at me. I turned if off by getting praised for owning up & saying I never thought my conduct meant anything to her. Eventually after some work I got her to admit it did & promised to choke Connie off...I wrote a long penitent plausible letter to Connie & saw her this afternoon Weds. As the Shrew predicted it was *dreadful*. She (Connie) has had 3 proposals in her life, 2 actually since she has known me. There were two outbursts of weeping & [a] sort of hysterical stifling of sighs, a confession that she 'loved me better than anyone she had ever known' (*what* a cad I felt) & so on. Of course she is a sentimental girl but still, I felt I had rather put my foot in it.

Now I introduced Jack Metherell, a Charterhouse[110] boy who was a cadet at New College, to the Shrew & he came up several times. Well I don't mind telling you in the social line he absolutely cut me out. The Shrew when (after preparation of course) taxed with it assured me that I was top dog still. You see on Sunday last I had a good straight talk with her about the Connie affair & the Metherell fascination. Well such is my opposition I can't really say I care much for either girl...I wish I could meet a girl similar to those in Rosetti's pictures tall with a beautiful cool purity, & a knowledge of fair things & poetry & music...where are they? E. A. Poe[111] was always writing about them but I think they must have died out or taken to munitions or something...We are going on exeat [leave] on June 7th but I hope you will be in Oxford before that. Be sure to look me up won't you or write a note or letter making an appointment.

C. J. Evans, Headmaster of Leighton Park School, to Violet, 31 May 1918

I am sorry to have to report that the decision of the Scholarship committee is that it would not be fair to other candidates to set a special examination for a boy between the advertised times of examination: this means that we shall have no scholarship examination until February 1919, and your need I take it is for September of this year. I much regret to have to write this as I sympathise so strongly with your feeling of the danger of the pull towards militarism that good schools, indeed one may say the best Public Schools of the country, give to boys who go to them.

P.S. There is just the chance that the full Board of governors, meeting early in July, might possibly take a responsibility that the Scholarship committee does not take. I suppose that this will be too late for you; it certainly is too weak a string for you to rely on, and to give up the chance of entry to another school.

Eliot to his father, 2 June [1918]

Owen came home last night for a weeks leave before he goes to Chatham and does some heavy bridging. It is awfully nice to have him back. At present he is helping Pug to mend the spring board. He is going to do all sorts of things for us, mending the mowing machine and pump and bike.

I have been rather poorly these last five days and…I have not been bathing lately, and that is rather boring as after games I am always frightfully hot. We have just arranged for one of the kittens. We are going to give the one with the white spot on its breast away to a friend of Mrs Toinbee, our next door neighbour.[112] The one we are giving away is the more greedy, and strong and warlike. The other is pure black and more gentle…Perhaps we will give it away afterward to someone whom we know and like better like Joyce Cockram.

―◆◆◆―

Patrick to his father, 2 June [1918]

My Dearest Darling Daddy, Owen has come back and we had a bathe in the evening and I just got permission because Owen and Mother and Miss Algar were there and Mother wanted badly to see me dive. We have found a home for one of the kittens already. I took a top board on Friday and I did a hopeless flatter which was awfly boaring. We have just got my berthday letter which is lovely. I hope you are injoying your holiday. We are looking foreward to haveing a boat for a day now Owen is here, and going up the river and haveing a jolly good time.

[P.S. from Violet:] I do not know which day as there is always school.

―◆◆◆―

Owen to his father, 5 June 1918

My course at Kelham is now over & I am home on leave before getting my commission & going to Chatham for a 10 days heavy bridging course. The leave in army terms is called L.P.G. leave pending gazette…My last week at Kelham was just one tremendous rush…each course finishes up with 3 days trek. We marched out to Sherwood Forest, & through for a certain distance & then back again. The different duties & positions were held by different people each day, only I was unfortunate in having a marching job each day…It was very hard work as most of the way we marched with full pack & rifle. We put up at a pub at E[dwinstowe] the officers & acting officers having proper officer's quarters & the remainder

FIGURE 10 Second Lieutenant Owen Slater ready for service in France.

sleeping in a huge long attic. For bedding we had a waterproof sheet & four blankets, so we weren't so badly off. The second day was rather easier...we billeted at another pub at T[uxford] & gave an impromptu concert at the assembly room in aid of the military hospital at Newark. It was a great success...I was lucky. I scouted round & found a straw loft where I slept beautifully...The last day from Tuxford to Newark was by far the worst...we were pretty done in by the time we got back. Each day

I had to march the whole way but thanks to soap in my socks my feet did not suffer in the least.

The next evening…we had our farewell dinner & concert. Both were a great success…Of course you can realise what it was like: small tables with smokes & drinks provided in consequence I was up till 1.30 putting & trying to put people to bed. Two hefty Australians who were absolutely tight got annoyed at something & pulled down half a dozen tents; the occupants for the most part sleeping soundly till the next morning. However though it was rather disgusting I didn't think we were nearly as bad as the two classes before us.

Altogether my course…was most enjoyable though rather spoilt by overbearing atmosphere of supervision & discipline. You may be dropped on or given the sack for almost anything…apart from that everything is ripping, particularly tennis etc. I very much wanted to get up some rowing but nobody was keen…I have got to buy all my officer kit, & a beastly job it is too: horribly expensive. At least now I shall be earning my own living & I hope saving to a certain extent though what my wages are I don't know.

By 6 June the Germans' spring offensives had cost them some 130,000 men in killed, wounded, and captured while Allied casualties numbered about 137,000. Three days later the Germans launched their fourth push in the Battle of the Matz, once again in the French sector.

Owen to his mother, 9 June 1918 from Chatham

I arrived here this afternoon…I can hardly realise that I am an officer at Chatham. It seems an absolute impossibility—a bad dream in fact. Thank goodness I am in civvy billets, rooms attached to a pub in fact—very comfortable two to a bedroom & sitting room for four with a quite respectable piano. Will you therefore please send the following pieces of music to Lieut. Slater, 19, Wood Street, Old Brompton, Chatham

1. Chopin Preludes also if you like & it doesn't make the parcel too heavy
2. Grieg Lyric Suite 12 [Op. 12] including Rustle of Spring [by Christian Sinding]
3. Chaminade Serenade [aux Etoiles]

Gilbert to Owen, 10 June 1918

I think of you continuously as I read the newspapers, in which the news from month to month continues bad; and I wonder where you are now and what you are doing. I do wish I could have come home this summer—one wonders what will happen before next. I have been doing a little work, and playing tennis, & chess & having walks etc., and there is no news to tell, & what there is I have put in the other letters which I hope Mother will send on to you. I just add this to send you my love. Always your loving father, Gilbert Slater

---

On 13 June Owen received his temporary commission as second lieutenant in the Royal Engineers dated as of 1 June.

Eliot to his father, 13 June [1918]

I have just had my Winchester Exam…On Monday, as we had nothing whatsoever to do…we went all round the town…Then in the afternoon we went to a very old Church, it is a most beautiful place and the only thing that spoils it is that just by the altar, all that end of the church, every thing has been painted the most brilliant colours. The man who was responsible for it was Butterfield,[113] the same man who was responsible for Keble. It is very much the same as Keble except that it is painted, the most brilliant colours. Otherwise it is the loveliest old Church imaginable…It is called St Cross…I got into the viva voce and I also was one of the six boys who had a math viva…There were 73 boys in for the scholarships and only 30 got into the viva…Skipper came down on the last day and we all came back together. I shall simply be off my head with joy if by any chance I do get a scholarship…I shall know on Saturday afternoon.

[P.S. 16 June] I turned out fourteenth. There are thirteen scholarships given. But it is quite probable that there will be another vacancy and I will get a scholarship. It has happened several times before and of course it is more likely to happen in War Time. For in ordinary times boys leave at 18 and a half or 19 but now they are called up at 18. So if the war continues I will be more likely to get a scholarship than if it does not.

[P.P.S. from Violet, 17 June] The Skipper has gone down to Winchester to find out all he can. He wants Eliot to go in for Westminster. I do not know anything about Westminster. But I have written to Mr Evans at Leighton Park & asked if Eliot will be eligible to enter for their scholarships in February & if so I shall let Eliot wait at school (if the Skipper will allow him to) & chance either L.P. or Winchester.

———— ✦ ————

Hugh Cockram to Owen, 14 June 1918

Only a p.c. because I shall have to answer you rather soon—the letter which you said you'd send on Tuesday with the 10/-. I have been to Alcotts [music shop in the High Street, Oxford] and taken the thing round to Joyce, she is very bucked with it. Alcott's would not let me have it without paying for it. It was 8/6 so if you have not already sent your cash, so much will be sufficient. Otherwise will add the extra 1/6 to the bike money. The latter goes splendidly…I put it to the supreme test on Sunday, by cycling home [to Wallingford] for the day…You ask for a respectable list of wants. There is nothing, my dear chap, that I don't want—Camera, bicycle, books of any description, set of soft collars, ties, cash, tie pin, a photo of thee, a picture, well—you see anything from a rhinoceros to a 1*d* whistle or a bayonet to a tie pin! My similes are rather unique are not they? I am supplying Joyce with exactly the same list, so please put your heads together before communicating with me... Yours, G.H.H.C.

―――∞∞∞―――

Joyce Cockram to Owen, 16 June 1918 from Wallingford

I should imagine you must be thinking me a 1st Class specimen of 'Girls with Extraordinary Habits and Customs' by now. I ought to have written at once to thank you for the perfectly delightful edition of 'Iolanthe'. Joan [Anderson] and mother and went all through it last night. Thanks awfully.

One of the reasons that I haven't written is that I wanted to enclose the prints... I also enclose one which I took. I'm afraid I must have moved the camera... I haven't finished the film & one simply daren't waste a single negative nowadays... Joan and I biked over by way of Stadhampton, Berrick Salome, and Benson on Friday evening. It had been wet more or less all day and the country was just beginning to look topping again. The dog roses were lovely; you know that kind of mixed scent in the air after rain, don't you... Today... Hugh turned up about 3 and stayed till 10 to 4. He managed to eat *some* tea, a pork pie & some bacon, half a gooseberry tart & custard, but I will not go into details!... I shall... be in London from June 29th to July 9th, having exams on July 1st, 2nd, & 3rd & on the 8th... I saw your mother on Wednesday. She had just got a topping present from Mr Slater, of a sort of blue coatee embroidered with chrysanthemums... Everybody here is flourishing... Sunday school, bank, 'The daily round, the common task'[114] etc: I think 'Life' here must be the limit! I wish to goodness I knew what was to happen to me after this term. And won't it be ripping when the exam is over? Good luck! Have you developed extraordinary muscles in your arms yet? Yours sincerely, E.J. Cockram

[P.S.] I don't know why I signed myself with such a signature! Sorry!

―――⊗∞⊗―――

Eliot to Owen, 16 June [1918]

The results of the Winchester Exam turned out yesterday…and I turned out 14ᵗʰ. There are 13 scholarships given so I have just failed…While we were at Winchester every evening we climbed to the top of a very steep hill [St Catherine's Hill] which is really an old British Fort against the Romans. When we got to the top we ran a most excellent single lane maze which is about a thousand yards long and when we get to the centre we eat our oranges and rest a bit and then we run down the hill as fast as we possibly can go and we get to the bottom in about a minute and a half. The hill is about five hundred feet high I should think. It was extremely bracing on the top. Mind you write and tell us what you are doing at old Brompton.

―――⊗∞⊗―――

Violet to Owen, [16 June 1918] in same envelope as above

The Skipper & Hum think that there is a chance of Eliot getting a schol. They may hear now or even as late as Easter 1919…It is rather like E. to be just behind. My feelings are very mixed, poor little chap he of course is frightfully disappointed…The boys will probably stay on at Lynams until Easter…I hope I shall be able to arrange for Eliot…to stay until Christmas & then perhaps he can go in for the Leighton Park Schol: in Feb…I want you to write a nice letter to Mr & Mrs Quibell. Eleanor thinks that they would like that book Aunt Mary was talking about—'The Urban Labourer' by Mr & Mrs Hammond.[115] I will order it for you if you like me to & send it from you. Just ask after Arthur & tell them about yourself…I wonder if you would like to send the Quibells yr. Father's 'Making of Modern England'. I think Mr. Q. Would like it.

[P.S.] I am glad the Browns are nice.

[P.P.S.] Hugh & I have done a fair amount at the allotment, he came twice. Eleanor Q[uibell] came in to supper last Sunday after E[liot] went. Goodbye dear boy. How much are you earning? Tell us what you do. Much love from us all.

Owen to his mother, 23 June 1918

What an awful bother about Eliot. It would be an awful pity for him to have to go to school in London—it is such an unhealthy atmosphere both morally and physically. However! It is a great pity that L.P.S. is out of the question—it is such a good healthy all round school…On Friday my bridging course ended…and am now attached to F. Co'y. No. 1 Reserve Battalion R.E. I start my duties as an officer on Monday. I don't exactly know what they are & in fact I am tchacooning. It is mainly I believe supervising the training of recruits. I shall probably have a fairly slack time with occasional bursts of heavy work. I expect to have to go under canvas in a week or two…On the whole I expect to have quite a jolly time here…The more I see of the billet the better I like it. The piano is really an awfully nice one. The Browns too have turned out to be a delightful family though the boy—about 8–9—is a little fiend. I went out to Wigmore[116] with them yesterday in Mr Brown's car…I am going up there this afternoon perhaps…I enjoyed my bridging course very much, I only wish it had lasted a bit longer. There is an Army & Navy Cooperative stores here—quite useful. I hope to send you a few matches soon but when I don't know[117]…I am awfully pleased to have my music here. I can play every day & at times have actually managed to get in a little real practice…As regards work we do 8 hours a day, two hours of which consist of lectures: the rest is practical and most interesting—making & launching iron girders & things like that—all bridging &

useful anywhere. We have been going into the strength of materials a lot just lately.

There is a military swimming bath here—I have had one or two bathes already. It is quite small but beautifully clean & well kept. The only fault being that it has only one miserable diving board, nothing in comparison with the Cher[well River in Oxford]. I find I miss my bicycle—everlastingly walking or taking a train. I will see about having mine sent directly I hear definitely about leave. My course actually finishes on Friday & after that I have ten weeks at least training & probably more. They have started giving us some work & on Sunday I started work in the morning about 10.30 & went on. When I began to feel hungry I went down to see about dinner & found it was 2.30 so I had to go without but I made a jolly good tea I can tell you. My time tonight is limited—I always try to go to bed early though I don't always succeed I admit.

Owen to his mother, [late June 1918]*

As regards my leave I am very much afraid I shan't get any...I wonder if you have said anything to Woodwards.[118] On the whole now I think I had better have everything sent...as I can't tell how long I shall be here or what I shall be doing.

You ask me about my screw [salary]. Well it is difficult to say. Theoretically I get 10/6 a day but out of that I have to provide for my messing which will probably come to something like 20/- to 25/- a week. Beyond that I have no real necessary expenditure though tram fares etc run off with loose cash. I suppose then I ought to save something like £2 or £1.10/- a week. However living in civvy billets I shall have to pay something beyond the allowance.

Just next door is a small shop with a large placard in the window: 'Savery Pies'. I have often wondered what [is] 'savered' about them. Talking about grub, we are quite well fed. Breakfast: fish & bacon, porridge & bread & jam, so you see we do quite well. As regards that book for the Quibells I really don't mind in the slightest which book to give. Will you decide then & order…& I will pay you by cheque. As regards the letter I will write one at once & send it to you that you may suggest improvements. If you think none are necessary will you put the letter in the book & post it off to them.

I am enclosing the photos that I took, I'm afraid they are not particularly good—very amateurish indeed…On Saturday I went with the Browns to their plot at Wigmore…It was a glorious day & I had a ripping time. I think the most enjoyable thing about going up there is that one comes into family life & gets away from military bachlerdom. I am awfully pleased to have my music here [text ends]

Debates over how countries could learn from the war, as opposed to debates over war aims and peace terms, increased with each year of fighting. Among many people, especially radical intellectuals, the idea arose that mankind could actually avoid further conflicts through the establishment of an international organization with the power to prevent wars by intervening in diplomatic rows. This idea had been given an impetus in another speech by the US President Woodrow Wilson on 27 May 1918 when he started a public campaign for a 'league of nations'. The term was by no means unique to Wilson and was used by many including Gilbert, along with his friend Professor Gilbert Murray. In Gilbert's case he had used it to describe his vision of a reorganized British Empire in his letter to Violet of 19 February 1917. The term had also been used in the Quaker handbills Violet had distributed in the spring of 1917.

Hugh Cockram to Owen, [24 June 1918]

Rejoice with me; I am not leaving school at the end of this term after all—is it not ripping? And owing to pressure mostly from me last Wednesday and then from Brigger who helped it on and put the cap on it all by a letter from the Senior Tutor of St Johns to him saying that

I was too young. Is it not spifflicating—you see Dad could not refuse that but he's horribly bored, so I am to do my bit to lighten him up. Responsions next week and after that Certif.[119] Yours in haste, Do write soon, H.C.

Violet to Gilbert, 26 June [1918] from London

I have just seen young Eliot into the 'Challenge' as the Westminster Scholarship is called. For some time I sat outside the Abbey & then I found it so cold I went & had a cup of coffee & came on to Somerset House... O how I just wish I could send him to Leighton Park where it is so much lighter & brighter & beautiful & sensible as far as one can see. Fancy Eton with a top hat or cap or Khaki for a choice. 'Shades of the prison house'[120] begin to close about the growing boy with a vengeance!

I've seen a lot of very respectable middle aged Labour men up for the [Party] Conference.[121] I heard this evening that Kerensky[122] had come. I shall be glad to hear what happened only the papers only put in the parts they do not disapprove of. The co-op Women's Guild Congress was held in Bradford. According to the reports they only passed a resolution advocating a national milk supply. They really spoke upon a People's Peace—the resolution was not carried but had a good vote and did carry a resolution asking for a League of Nations and urging abolition of secret diplomacy and demanding control by Parliament & the people of foreign policy—only 20 dissenters.[123] It is getting cold & I must stop.

We got the Sergeant to show us over the school... It is interesting & picturesque, but one almost wants to get away from civilisation that has gone so far from nature in every way.

[P.S.] I will enclose a letter from Owen. Fancy only 10 days training in heavy bridging! He has fallen on his feet though & seems fairly happy. Dear boy.

Owen to Violet, [2 July 1918] from Royal Engineers Mess, Chatham

I am orderly officer for the company this week. It doesn't seem to entail much extra work. I have to inspect the rooms & the meals & everything else once or twice. On the whole it is rather fun. Last week I had to pay the men. I wandered over to the bank & cashed a cheque for £180 & afterwards took a cab back & paid the men. For a wonder it came out exactly right but before everything was actually counted up I felt rather nervous I can tell you. That was on Friday. On Saturday I went over to Wigmore with the Browns as usual & had a very jolly party. It was Edna B's birthday—age 15 ... Do you remember how much money I gave you. £12 wasn't it? I was wondering because I have not yet run out of my change. I am trying to send off a box of matches but I don't know whether they will get through. Also can you get Golden Syrup? I bought a tin the other day. If you can't I may as well send it.

My dearest mother, I am going bald! What shall I do? It is a terrible catastrophe isn't it? I am writing to Hugh to get him to send my bike. I hope it will come all right.

Mrs B. Told me the other day that I was looking fatter & better than when I first came so I suppose it must be the effect of good food & exercise. I have been doing quite a lot of walking lately. By the way they are Baptists. I went to chapel with them on Sunday evening. Quite a nice little service & sermon, a good organist but not very much of an organ.

Lamberts[124] shoes arrived all right, they are beautiful & fit very well but since I have been wearing them they seem to be a little too long. However that can't be helped though I wish I had known that they weren't made for me when I first had them.

Now for commissions. Please will you

1. Send my tunic.
2. Order two more ~~khaki~~ shirts from Woodwards... At present this is all I want.

—⧂—

Joyce Cockram to Owen, 2 and 3 July 1918* from London

Your letter was awaiting me... this evening, & I *was* glad to see it... Today's [exam] papers had been absolutely the limit & I was about fed up, I can tell you. I needed something to cheer me up badly... I am sorry I made such a fool of myself about your address. If you will put horoglyphics (?) at the top of your letter, what *do* you expect. It took Eve & me ½ hour to make that amount of sense out of it!

I raised flu from Eric's fiancée, a London girl, who was staying at Stone House. I wasn't able to go to school till last Friday, so you can imagine the state of my brains. I'm totally fit now, except for a cough which worries the other candidates & me & makes me hot & cross.

Wednesday [3 July]. Another day over!... I suppose Chatham is too far away for you to manage a Wednesday or Thursday afternoon isn't it? Because I shall probably be in town [London] from Monday 14th till Friday 19th.

The papers haven't been bad on the whole except yesterday's. On Monday the exam was at University College, Gower Street. I arrived about 9.50 feeling very lost and looking very silly. I've never seen such quantities of men & boys in and out of khaki in one University building before and there wasn't a female in sight when I arrived. About 2 mins. later (it seemed at least 5 mins.) I was seized by an appalling maid who said 'You go there'—politely? & I followed my nose down lengthy passages & around awful corners & down odd flights of stairs till I arrived at the Ladies Cloakroom. There were about 5 hats there & that was all. In an endeavour to find out what happened next, I lost my way & was addressed by [a] nice friendly girl (evidently an internal student) who escorted me along what seemed miles of passages & up thousands of stairs to the library. There I spoke to the man in charge [text ends]

Violet to Gilbert, 3 July 1918

It is dreadfully after 11 so I fear this is only a beginning. Eliot has got a 4th scholarship at Westminster...I have not cabled because I do not quite know what it means. The Skipper says that the expense at Winchester is about £21 per annum & at Westminster £35. The Bursar has written to me as if the scholarship was worth £35. I have written to him to ask exactly what the cost of board, & education, beyond the scholarship amounts to.

Gertrude Slater to Gilbert, 3 July [1918]

We were sorry to hear of Eliot's missing a scholarship by so little. If he had been fit, he would perhaps have got one: Violet said, just before the exam, he was looking very limp. I felt sorry when I read his last school report, that he was devoting himself so much to Greek. When he was younger we used to notice how good his mathematics reports were—such a much more useful subject. When you are choosing a new school for him there is one important point now that you may not think of—& that is to choose a school with a cadet corps & make him enter it & keep in it till he leaves. Then he passes straight into the O.T.C.

Eliot to his father, 3 July 1918 inside his mother's letter of 3 July

I am going in for a Westminster Scholarship and I have just had the first paper…So far I have had the Latin Prose Composition, Latin Grammar, General English and Latin Translation. The English was chiefly composed of questions about History, English Literature and a few definitions of words like 'moraine, estuary, watershed' etc…By the way we had a very good time while we were in London…Of course we saw a good deal of Westminster Abbey although we did not see the King's throne [Coronation Chair] and other people's tombs. We went up the Monument (over 300 steps which is more than it seems, 50 is a lot) and had a glorious view of almost all London. We saw St Paul's and the Houses of Parliament. By the way King's Scholars at Westminster have to wear Etons[125] with stiff collars and top-hats and they have a very grand invitation to the King's Coronation, marriage or funeral. Also they are allowed to attend Parliamentary debates.

[Letter continues in Violet's hand:] Pat slacks most of the time; he lives to play and is always enjoying life I believe in and out of school except when he gets into trouble which he does fairly often…Pat is frightfully careless, when he played in a match he enjoyed cricket but he would rather play in the hedges than play cricket and I fancy escapes…It is no easy task to bring up boys without a Father.

Violet to Gilbert, 4 July 1918*

Poor old Towser, Edna's dog, got knocked down & dragged along by a military motor lorry…it is horrid to have an animal suffer. Oh how much more a human being. It is always coming over one in great waves of indignant emotion that it is possible to let the war go on without any attempt to generate another way of settlement. One would imagine that some effort could be made to stop it even if the fighting had to go on all the time. That is the step I want taken. The Churches ought to use all their influence.

Then the other step is freedom of opinion & speech so that the minority should be allowed not only expression but the right to do all it likes to convert the majority…I heard last week of two young men—one killed when he had been at the Front 3 days another 6. What is the good of it all? It is an illusion like the belief in witchcraft. Unfortunately all sorts of people are becoming rich & getting jobs so that Peace will have its drawbacks…We have been on the river for meals & today most of the day I took my work & we just paddled about between dinner & tea…All the time one feels that people can be peacefully enjoying themselves when their nearest & dearest are being blown to pieces & murdered or are helping to murder other innocent men. You feel like this I know. It would be more satisfactory if one could devote one's whole time to some 'stop the war' work. It seems obliged to go on. I wonder how much longer it will take.

***

Hugh Cockram to Owen, 5 July 1918 (morning prep)

Many thanks for your 2 letters & the enclosure. I will send off your bike today according to your instructions, & I will not despatch this letter till I have so that you will know it is on the way. I will put the rest of the cash in 6d stamps. At present there is 5/- in, & there will be another 5/- about from this 10/-, so another 5/- would make up the sum, see, 15/6. As Deuchar is closing on the 12th, & bike money has stopped, & you are rolling in cash, so you may as well send at least 6/-, or 2/6 or 3/- or 6/-…[or] 15/6 or 6/- + £5 or 6/- + n [note for] £5. Where [there] is any positive whole no…. Your bike is now all 'packed up'. I am taking it to the station in a few moments. Smalls[126] have passed & I believe I have 'dudded' in the grammar papers; Brewis, who is examining, said that I was doubtful, & hence I presume I am a wash out. Blast! Damn!!! We don't hear the results till Monday, when Certif. starts.

Later: I have despatched your bike—all well & good.

***

Owen to his mother, 7 July 1918 from Aldershot[127]

You will see from my address that I have left Chatham. I have been sent down here for a three weeks course of riding, driving & mounted duties very suddenly. I only knew on Saturday morning & I left Chatham in the afternoon...as I knew Joyce Cockram was up for her exam I looked her up & found Joan [Anderson] was there too so we went into St James Park for a short time & then had lunch together at Lyons Corner house. Quite jolly really like a breath of Oxford & home.

My duties start tomorrow fairly early...I heard from M.T.O. [Violet's sister Mary] that Eliot had a 4th schol. at Westminster. I wonder whether he will go. It means wearing a topper & Etons doesn't it? I am longing to hear from home. In fact I'm abominably home sick & want leave at once as Peace still seems almost as distant as ever. I haven't found my legs here yet & am rather miserable.

Patrick to Owen, 7 July [1918]

We went on the river yesterday and we had some strawberries which were lovely we had Goosberries (ripe ones) and we envited Mrs Paul-Jones to come with us and we (Eliot and I) had a bathe before tea but after tea every-body had a bathe and a naval officer called 'Sargeant' showed them how to dive, he did swallow dives and Flying dives and Kangaroo dives and lots of fancy dives.

School is breaking up in 11 days not counting the Sundays.

Owen to his father, 8 July 1918*

I have suddenly been transported from Chatham to Aldershot. Both places are pretty bad as regards militarism but Aldershot is the worst...I have not

FIGURE 11 The Officer's Ride, Aldershot, detail from official photograph with Owen in the centre. His riding certificate states that 'Lieut R. O. Slater of the Royal Engineers, underwent a short course of riding as prescribed in King's Regulations, and can ride sufficiently well to perform the duties of a mounted Officer.'

told you why I have come to Aldershot. It is for a three week course of riding duties, very similar to my riding course at Kelham…on the whole I shall have a very jolly time. One rather unfortunate thing is that I don't know anyone at Aldershot & I dislike most of the officers here…I am billeted in what is called the C.O.'s [Commanding Officer's] House…I am sleeping in my valise[128] with the assistance of four blankets. It is not particularly comfortable but I don't mind the roughness a bit. In fact it is rather jolly. But what I do loathe about the whole thing is the Mess. The food is all right but the dinner & meals are horribly swanky, port & sherry after dinner etc: you know the style of thing & it is abominably expensive. At…Chatham I paid 2/- & no extras at all but here it is 2/- a day with any amount of additional expenses as mess subscriptions to entrances to different clubs nobody wants to belong to etc

Owen to his mother, 10 July 1918

I had two letters from you today…I have written to the Quibells…Poor Arthur is having a bad time of it. I do hope he will pull through all right. You ask me what attitude my men take. I have never come into contact like that with any of my men; the idea of the army is to separate men from the officers as much as possible. The only time I see them is when I am on parade or when I pay them & that is more or less a parade, i.e. only in an official capacity…I am so glad you have ordered the shirts. They are gloriously comfortable though they are huge round the chest & jolly long in the arms…Mr Quibell like Mr Brown is a manufacturer but I imagine has been rather hit by the war. His line is confectionary & pickles. They are not the same class of people as the Quibells, not nearly so aristocratic, in fact what some people would call not so well bred. But they are awfully jolly…I really don't know anything about my bike. I am waiting to hear from Hugh. I asked him to send it off last week but it hadn't arrived by the time I left.

Gilbert Slater's first and arguably his most important book on India was published this summer by Oxford University Press. His collection of essays by his students, Some South Indian Villages, *was richly illustrated with original photographs and was the first volume in the University of Madras's Economic Studies series. He had sent his students into their own villages in order not to upset local people. The students arrived with prepared questionnaires about villagers' lives and the information gathered gave government officials the raw facts they needed to improve farming. The book also did much to arouse public opinion about the dire state of village life.*

Gilbert to Owen, 10 and 13 July 1918

I am hoping in a day or two to get a letter from you, but I do not suppose it can contain much news beyond how you finish up at Kelham; and after that, as the next mail steamer was sunk, I shall get no more news till close on the end of August at best. We get various items of news indicating that things are bad in Germany & holding out hopes of peace, but mostly rather distrust such news, & now I suppose, the harvests are coming in...& their difficulties will be lessened a great deal for a considerable time. The latest talk is of a fresh Austrian onslaught on Italy—if it fails as completely as the last there may be some hope of a separate Austrian peace, and then the end may not be far distant. But other people are expecting instead a fresh German offensive in the West, or an attempted invasion; & I think most people expect that invasion will be the last card Germany will play, & playing it will indicate that things are desperate.

We have just received the Montagu–Chelmsford report on the proposed future government of India. Mrs Besant foams at the mouth over it, but the more respectable Indian leaders seem to approve of it. Practically it will probably mean handing over the control of education, agriculture, sanitation & road making to Indians, &, of course, increased taxation. I don't think education will suffer, agriculture may or may not, sanitation probably will, at least for a time.

Saturday 13 July. I have been waiting for the mail to come in—now it has come, but never a letter for me! I suppose mine have all gone to Kodaikanal. It is a great nuisance as it will take nearly a week for them to get there & come back again, and as that is in the midst of the Kallan (thief by caste) [Kallar] country, there is some chance of their being lost. 2 years ago I lost 3 letters from home between Madras & Kodaikanal.

You are coming nearer and nearer to the time when you take up work & responsibility—and a share in the task of restoring peace to the world. Any hopes that could have been entertained of getting peace otherwise than by some measure of victory over Germany are shown by the experience of Russia to have been mistaken. It is a terrible thing to go into the trenches, but that is the only way to stop the hell making that Germany has devoted herself to. God bless you, my dear boy, Your loving father, Gilbert Slater

Hugh Cockram to Owen, 11 July 1918

I hope the bicycle has arrived safely. I sent the bike off last Friday...I have passed Smalls...What about Cash for War Loan? Where's your £5? Could you advance me 2/- for myself? I am awfully hard up. Yours, G.H.H. Cockram

---

Ida Brown to Owen, 13 July 1918

Dear Home Sick Babe, We sent the cycle off yesterday. Hope it will arrive safely. We have not been able to see about the camera as we have had company staying with us, but will try to go over on Monday if possible.

29 [Stuart Road] is very quiet now that you are away. We girls will be glad when you come back as our health is suffering severely because we miss our usual walk to the 'Death's Head' at 11 p.m.

We are just off to Wigmore. Wish you were coming. All the family join in love.

P.S. Have you written to Mrs Bilson yet? I.B.
P.P.S. Thank you for breaking in with the chocolates. I.B.

Maud Slater to Violet, 14 July 1918

What a beautiful basket you sent me!...it looks so handsome. We are also pleased to hear of Eliot's success. It is really much to his credit. Grandma thinks as you do that the Friends' school would probably be the better. I expect he would be happier there & probably get a better education. It is difficult now-a-days to arrange for holidays; it is not only the high fares, but the restriction of trains is so great that all seem to be crowded. In

London the difficulty of getting to the coast is so great that we hear of people waiting 4 hours in a queue after getting their tickets.

I am giving up some of my outside work after this term; rather a bad time to give up as expenses will be so much heavier but I seem to have touched my absolute limit of work, & it is no use killing oneself over making a living. What makes me feel regretful is that the work, which I took over from a man, will lapse again into the hands of another man. I myself am teaching the new system of shorthand—Dutton's[129] & am learning shorthand all over again. It is a great improvement on Pitman's. Have you a Woman's Citizen's Association[130] in Oxford? We have formed one & I hear from Ada [Maud's sister-in-law] that she is on the committee at Newport [Isle of Wight]!

———

On 15 July the Germans launched the last of their offensives but after some initial successes they were halted by British, French, and American forces. On 18 July a French-led counter-offensive began and two days later the Germans started to retreat. This marked the beginning of the end of the war on the Western Front.

Violet to Gilbert, 15 July 1918

You will be sorry that I was in such a difficult position about Eliot. I generally find if I am awake in the night a solution comes. The solution was that since you are not here to consult I must make the choice so I determined to forgo Westminster & to accept Leighton Park…Westminster & Winchester are fascinating because of their historic interest & very probably they have good masters but we have got to have a different future…I hope you will not be disgusted. I suppose that even now if Winchester offers you could take him from Leighton Park…I told Mr Lynam and he is disgusted & feels sure you won't approve & said that I must take full responsibility…C.C.L.[131] said I was throwing away chance of a career for E.—scholarship to Trinity Cambridge & perhaps a Professorship.

———

The debate over conscientious objectors, men whom Violet had always defended, had inten-
sified during the war because of some men's harsh treatment by tribunals and in prison.
Tribunals always had the power to grant exemptions to COs ('Absolutists') who would not
enter the services as part of the Royal Army Medical Corps or Non-Combatant Corps or who
refused to do any work of 'national importance'. By April 1918, some 4,500 men had gained
such an exemption. In that same month the government brought in a new scheme that fur-
ther allowed COs who had worked for twelve months and had good records to undertake work
of their own choice so long as it was still of national importance and was approved by a gov-
ernment committee. On 30 April Lord Peel told the House of Lords that some 2,971 men had
taken this option. How the new scheme worked is described by one of Violet's friends.

Mavis H. Starkie to Violet, 16 July 1918* from Oswestry

Thank you very much for your kind letter & birthday wishes. I am still
here with Bert. and I know you will be very glad to know that he has been
applied for by a farmer in sympathy with the C.O.'s—his [the farmer's]
own son was court martialed yesterday at Shrewsbury for refusing military orders and [Bert] started work with him last Monday. The farm is
about 5 miles from Oswestry & they lend him a bike; he cycled home
4 times last week and had Sunday off altogether. For the last 8 weeks I
have been working at the farm & get home each evening about 7. I don't
go on Sundays so we get the week end together. Work in a shop seemed
impossible to get and was very badly paid. I am now helping in the house.
They are very kind & I get plenty of butter & milk to use at home.

Berts brother that was with him in France has been brought to England
sick, & is now at home on sick leave, we expect he will be sent to Oswestry
on Thursday. The brother that went to Wakefield Prison has been discharged on the new Home Office Scheme.

Your news of the boys is very interesting. I hope Eliot will be happy at
school…I cannot think of Owen ordering men to kill their fellows. How
one longs for it to end.

Basil Donne-Smith to Owen, 16 July 1918
from Keble College, Oxford

An Oxford communiqué received this morning states:- 'Between 10.0 p m and 10.15 p m of the night of Saturday July 13th Mary Mildred Josephine Powell was kissed three times without coercion of any kind.' (Since then I have used no other). She decided that although it was her belief that kissing should only be a prelude to matrimony & she objected to being the subject of a wager (I bet her I should succeed before I finished)—yet when I propounded a theory of a different nature she would be sufficiently self sacrificing to grant my request!

We went to Magdalen [College] Chapel some time ago and they placed us up in the top row where you have a big book on a cushion and nobody minds if you go to sleep …

Pat was glad when I turned up at 'Grey Gable' in the afternoon, & I took her a new book of Stephen Leacock's[132] & we read it together.

My next ambition is to get her home for a week-end! Things will look rather business like then won't they—but I can keep my head & she, well, she's all right.

I encountered dear old Peggy last Friday in New College Lane,[133] she is going to London for 10 days. I wonder if its anywhere near you. She swore to write me an exact and detailed account of her experiences.

―――

Patrick to his father, 23 July [1918]

My Dearest Darling Daddy,

Many happy returns of the day! I am aufly afraid this will be frightfully late.

I have started collecting butterflies and I have caught … 9 all together. I have got 3 prizes, 'Songs of the Blue Dragon', 'Masterman Ready' and 'the life and Death of Jason', the first was for my Dairy [Diary], the second was for French, and the third was for my Holiday task Drawing.[134] With lots of

[P.S. from Violet:] The naughty little chap shot off. I shall encourage the collection & buy a book about butterflies. Eliot does not like the idea of killing at all…Mrs Harper didn't come all last week & only once this. She wants [to] give up. She has taken in more washing & finds it & our work too much. I should have thought our work when she comes & goes at stated times & has 6^d an hour would have actually paid her better. What shall I do when Eliot goes to school & there is only Pat & me [?] Its a problem…Fruit is almost unobtainable &…clean cherries [cost] 2/2 a lb. We had one lb of strawberries & one of ripe gooseberries & yesterday I got 1½ rasberries. We are going to look out for crab apples!!!…There are plenty of potatoes.

Eliot to Owen, 23 July 1918

We enjoyed your visit awfully. It did seem funny after you had gone only to have three people in the House. On Monday afternoon Miss Quibell came to take us on the river. But as it continually looked as if it was just going to rain, in the end we stayed at home and played all sorts of games. We played Animal Grab, and then Happy Families with the same pack. In happy Families it was awfully amusing because each time you won a card you had to say 'thank you' and when you did not your adversary could claim back the card or cards he had just lost and get the turn of asking into the bargain…Ever your loving brother, Eliot.

Violet to Gilbert, 23 July 1918

I have ached to have you. Mr Evans would not let me decide straight off & indeed I thought I ought just to write to Mr Gough of Westminster & ask to be allowed to resign the scholarship. In the end I did…I heard this morning that he had no objection, that the scholarship would be given to the next candidate. It has been a terribly painful time. I do wish I did not feel everything so much; one can't have as much capacity for pleasure without the same for pain. I ended up with a dreadful sick headache.

Owen came home on Saturday [20 July], dear boy. He cycled from Aldershot on Saturday and cycled back on Sunday. It was delightful and did us all good, especially me…I do want to have every moment of Owen's time if he has a holiday. I do dread intensely the time when he has to go. It's too awful.

We spent the morning on the river. It was so beautifully quiet we enjoyed it so much. As we came off we met the Skipper; he stopped and talked to Owen, and then as I mounted my cycle came back, so I went on. Of course he wanted Owen to influence me about Westminster. Owen told him L.P. [Leighton Park] was a very good school. Owen thinks I have done wisely. I want you if you can to write carefully to the Skipper. I expect he washes his hands of me. A damned Pacifist who doesn't appreciate Public Schools. (From all accounts they are hot beds of vice.) It seems quite questionable what advantages they offer except the snobbish hallmark. I wonder if we are going to get something better—after the war. It does seem sad that we should throw our children into surroundings that only bring such temptations. (I fancy the introduction of women teachers which must come will be helpful—men shirk their responsibilities more than women.) We all regret evil we have done and perhaps it makes us humble to feel that we are so in need of forgiveness ourselves, but we want, so far as we can, to let our children have better chances…We need a new sense of honour in the new world that is to be built up & a much greater power of understanding.

I really felt broken in pieces with longing to confer with you…Also I really feel quite certain about it, though one cannot have all the good of both a big school, and a small one, a Public or a Private, a new or an old. Have you read the 'Loom of Youth'?[135] I should like to see it. Of course one is so attracted to the lovely old historical surroundings of Winchester & Westminster. Mrs Sturt told me that in the end one way or another Winchester costs a good deal. I presume if you like L.P. you will not want E. to leave at Christmas or Easter if he gets an offer of Winchester?

Violet to Gilbert, 23 July [1918] [This is a postscript to a letter from Patrick and Eliot Slater which has not survived.]

This is a tiny birthday greeting from the boys...As soon as I hear from Owen I shall try to arrange, I really think I shall go North [to her sister in Leyburn]. I do feel homesick for someone. It is such a depressing time. The growth of the determined hate propaganda is so awful. Such wicked posters, & all the news one feels is distorted. One feels almost baffled when one knows that nothing but the spirit of loss and forgiveness can put this poor world on to the right lines. The continued poison [text indecipherable] just to do harm. One can only hope that those who are responsible for it all will overstep the mark...I think that what sickens one most is the attitude that America has taken up. It seems as if they are quite prepared to go on indefinitely and determined to have no recourse to International conversation...God bless you my dearly beloved.

Gilbert to Owen, 25 July 1918

My dear Second Lieutenant,
It does seem strange to think that you are now a commissioned officer in His Majesty's army! But I think you are lucky to be in the Engineers...I hope you get on as well at Chatham as at Kelham & I am glad that on the whole you liked Kelham so well. I should think the heavy bridging must be quite interesting. I am wondering whether it is during an advance or retreat that Engineers get the dangerous work to do—I am afraid it is

both times. There is a Col. Churchill here in the [Madras] club. We were talking one day at dinner as to when the war was likely to be over, and he was saying nothing. So I turned to him and asked his opinion, & I was rather surprised when he answered very confidently 'This year.' He explained that he meant that he felt pretty sure than the final negotiations would begin before Christmas. I do hope it may be so... I think it is quite likely that it may be months yet before you go to the Front; & perhaps there your work will be cleaning up things. In the old days young men sighed for adventure & danger, even if hardship came with it—now I suppose you all see more danger ahead than you want. I wonder how you all take it? Rather fatalistically I fancy. Do you feel all the time as though you were living in a dream, and might wake up at any moment?

Your remark... about asking Joyce Cockram to have your plates developed made me turn up your photos of your time with the Cockrams last year. I noticed for the first time one inscribed 'O.R. Slater—smoking—naughty boy!' I hope you don't think that I think that it is naughty of you to smoke—but I do think that when you go to the Front it will be necessary to keep a watch on yourself lest you slide into the habit of excessive smoking. It is said that enormous numbers of men have injured their hearts that way—because one result of the war has been to make people smoke more than ever. It is wise, I think, to reserve tobacco for occasions when you are in discomfort, or being simply fed up with some tedious condition or occupation.

———⊙⊙⊙———

Gertrude Slater to Eliot, 29 July [1918] from Bull Point on the north coast of Devon

I was so very glad to hear that you had got a Westminster Scholarship. We are all very proud of you... Betty came home from Cheltenham last Friday, & Alec [Eliot's cousin] began his holidays... He has just passed the College of Preceptors[136] [examination]. Next term is his last at school &

then he hopes to get into Sandhurst. He goes off next Friday to the school camp to work for the farmers...Alec will be the Senor N.C.O., quite an important person...He may be at the camp 2 months.

I have just been moved to a high desk & stool from my former table, & given new work. It means learning such a lot of new stuff...My teacher is a youth a little younger than Owen, & it makes me feel so much inclined to laugh when he says to me so gravely 'But I told you that before!' I am afraid I am a slow pupil...I have to pick it up as I go along, & it is all so important too, if I give G.C.B. shells to a ship that should have B.C.F. shells the gun will be blown to bits! My teacher joins up in 2 months, so I must work hard & try to get most of it learnt by then.

Violet to Gilbert, 30 July 1918

I do so long for you in these sad times...I do feel sometimes that I should enjoy a little waiting upon. But when the boys are at their best we are very happy together. It was so delightful to have Owen & he is a dear boy. I feel that he will not get contaminated. It is nice that he and I can talk about anything quite naturally. I think he has a naturally chaste and simple way of looking at sex questions. It is interesting to see how his sympathies are so much more democratic now. The first thing almost that he said when he came in was have you got the *Herald?*[137]

He wanted to see about the Munition strike[138] from the Labour point of view. He said he was fed up with the only paper he sees...We went to the Friends meeting on Sunday morning & on the river in the afternoon. We went right up to the part near the shallows where there is a backwater on the right. We landed on the left where we used to bathe before they could all swim & we had our tea on the meadow. It was very hot but somehow beautiful. On Monday we went to the river in the morning. The boys bathed first…I have just heard that Owen got to Chatham & that he is in barracks & has a room to himself which is rather nice.

Tell me exactly what you think & feel if you feel. I love the truth best of all. It is very difficult to act without consultation but I have kept the vision which to me is all important. I don't think I have been unwise even from a worldly point of view.

[P.S.] Have you read 'The Loom of Youth'?

Patrick to his father, 31 July [1918]

Yesterday Owen went away and when he was packing up he found a 'Red Admiral' which he gave to me, he gave me 2/6 as well and told me to buy a book on Butterflies and Moths with it. When Owen went away we went down to the station with him and when we came back I got a book for 3/6, Eliot had 3/- too that Owen gave him and he bought a grey hat.

Maud Slater to Violet, 1 August 1918*

I must enclose a note to you in Eliot's. We shall be so interested to know which School Gill [Gilbert] chooses for him. One of Phene's [Howard Slater's wife] friends here sends her boy to the Reading School, & Lilian had heard all about it as a thoroughly good progressive one. I expect he would be better looked after there mentally & physically, but on leaving Westminster he would have advantages a new school could not give. I am glad he feels drawn to more modern studies now, it does seem a pity to waste boys' time now over such old fashioned studies as he has been spending it on.

I hope Owen will get leave soon, & come home, & then you will be able to get away afterwards…Poor boy, he seems to be having quite a good time, but we can't understand what an R.E. has to do with riding about.

Gilbert to Owen, 4 August 1918

As long as I don't get a telegram I shall think of you as being still in England, having some sort of training. I only hope Mother in wiring will not try to tell me too much, so that the Censor stops the wire…Also the last 3 days have brought better news from the Front. At the moment of writing the latest news of importance is the recapture of Soissons by the French, & we are hoping the enemy will be driven back across the Aisne with substantial loss.[139] Whether success develops or the next thing will be a set back, you will know when you get this. But the chance that it may be possible to go home under peace conditions next March is considered, in Madras Club, quite a good one…I wonder if you will get sent to India? I have had a letter from a second Ruskin man who has arrived at Bangalore…If they, why not you? You would not be allowed to come to Madras, but I could go up to Bangalore to see you.

On 8 August Canadian troops led a surprise assault on the Germans near Amiens and drove a 7-mile wedge into their line. This day became known in Germany as 'der schwarze Tag'—the Black Day—of the German Army, in Ludendorff's words. The Canadians' success began the 'Hundred Days Offensive' by Allied troops as they seized the initiative.

Owen to his mother, 11 August 1918

Thank you very much for sending on the parcel & for getting me the ginger. I have asked Joan [George] to lend me her camera—I don't know whether she will but at any rate if she does she is going to bring it round to you to send it on to me...Did I tell you that I got my Burberry?...The 'Nation'[140] you send me is really quite good & is at present in the mess, I have read it nearly all. Tomorrow I start a course of survey which lasts about a week & then I shall be on short courses for about a fortnight after. It will be great fun I think. Please tell me as soon as Mrs Bilson's baby arrives stating particulars as to sex, size & if possible names & complexion. I think I told you that Edna Brown has got measles—isn't it beastly!

On Friday my men marched up the hill—a couple of miles or so & then spent the day cutting brushwood; it was great fun & a glorious day. I have a new book on Oxford & its Colleges by someone or other & illustrated by Edmund New.[141] It is very good, both writing & illustrations. I don't expect to get leave until sometime after you return from Leyburn & then it will probably only be for a long weekend...There's really no news, I wish I was in Oxford, that's all. Much love to the boys & to yourself.

P.S. In your next parcel please will you send me the best white flannel shirt you can find. Also I should very much like my Burberry suit but perhaps you won't want to send it.

———⊗———

Owen to his mother, 19 August 1918

I have had breakfast & as before do nothing & wait for orders. I slept last night not on a good feather bed but on my valise. On the whole it was quite comfortable but the ground always bruises one's hips more or less though I had six layers of blanket under me...There is really nothing to tell you as I am doing nothing except eat sleep write letters & read...A man has just come up to me & said, 'Hellow Slater, still writing?' 'Yes. Why? Do you want to come?' 'Oh no but I saw you writing before breakfast yesterday morning & you've been writing ever since.' It's not quite true but nearly. I think I shall stop now & write to Father. My letters are not supposed to contain news but just to let you know I am well & moderately happy…Mind you get Hugh to help you with the allotment. I am afraid my mind runs round in circles when I think of home.

[P.S.] I am saving my own paper for an emergency. I shall probably nearly always manage to get paper wherever I am. O.R.S.

Owen to his father, 20 August 1918*

Mother has just sent me a batch of your letters…In one of them you go into money matters concerning the education of us boys. Well you know at present I am keeping myself and saving a certain amount…I earn 10/6 a day with lodging fee & out of that I have to pay everything else, messing comes to about 2/6 a day. Taking in to consideration all travelling expenses etc I reckon to earn or rather save about 5/- a day or say £2 a week. At present after just 3 months service I have got a bank balance of just over £40. So you see if the war goes on much longer I shall be getting a fair sized banking account…I told you about my courses of riding at Aldershot…Since my return to Chatham I have been through a course of survey. It was very interesting what there was of it, but it was so frightfully elementary. Talking about the Inter.[142] I believe I can take military sciences as one subject so that would be a distinct saving though of course it would be much better to take something else if I could.

I can't tell at all how long I shall be in England…a month longer at least but beyond that I can't tell in the slightest. It all depends on those kittle cattle 'Supply' & 'Demand'. I am back in civilian billets again & very comfortable. Though for a short time I was in the barracks which was not very pleasant. A bare room with no bed voila tout!

Violet to Owen, 25 and 27 August 1918 from her sister's house in Leyburn

I was very glad indeed to have your letter. Its a *fortnight* ! since you wrote. Yes we did get your parcel with the golden syrup & were very grateful for it. I hope that civilians are going to be allowed jam, up to the present we have not been able to get any.

27th. It is Father's birthday & we are going to cable 'Love' to him. 'Slater University Madras. Love. Slaters. Leyburn.' It will cost 5/10…I want you when you write to tell Father that you are saving money which will help towards the remainder of your University Course. I do not want him to think that he must stay out another 5 years in India. He mustn't. I shall not be surprised if not only you will have some money but that you will have special chances of getting into either College or some government dept. For instance Board of Agriculture of Forrestry…We shall go home on Thursday…I hope to have Edna. I hope too to have Bertha. She will be better than no one through the winter months & if she isn't she will have to go. She is v. anxious to get back to 'service' [from munitions work] so perhaps she has learnt some lessons.

Joan George to Owen, 3 September 1918

My very dear Tufty, Thank you very muchly for your letter which I got this morning. Firstly Mother sends her love & says she was most awfully pleased to hear of you again—she's very fond of you dear—[and] very amused at the cow chasing incident & some of your accounts of your work.

Isn't this writing *lovely* Mr Spider Legs? (that's what *your* letters always remind me of—the writing thereof I mean!)…You sound rather mixed Baby Tufty!! 'I do wish Oxford was a bit nearer Chatham as it was when I was at Aldershot.' Sounds as though Chatham & Oxford wriggled nearer to each other when you were at Aldershot & then when you went back to C. They regained their normal places!!!! Did she tease you then?!

146

How like you to get into trouble in that way Owen. I mean about the Farmer & his cows. How *absolutely* like you!! No I haven't read 'Profit & Loss' by J.O.[143] Is it worth getting?

I have had very little batheing this year at all worse luck…I *am* wild. Have started riding lessons. Have had my fourth today, no—fifth is it?…He seems very pleased with me & I am permitted to go away & trot & canter alone now. Oh you can guess how I love it so I needn't try & tell you—It's perfect…Geoffrey I *hope* is coming today week for 24 hrs or so. I don't know how long but it is still uncertain if he can get off. I am looking forward to Tuesday very much as there is a good bit to talk over with him—& scold him for!!!! You wait till you come home again—you'll go through the same—almost M'sieur Tufty!!!

Well it is nearly nine o'clock & so I must go I am afraid…Good night dear…much love, yours affectionately H. Joan Pyrrha George!!!

[P.S.] What an 'orrible name Owen!!!

Joyce Cockram to Owen, 8 September 1918 from Wallingford

Many thanks for your letter of—ages ago. Hugh and I (…Of course I know it is my turn to write.) have been wondering what has happened to you. Hugh says he hasn't heard since August 1st!

As a matter of fact, I'm having more cooking lessons than I intended…A fortnight ago Mrs Read reported sick & took five days holiday. Then I had to fillet the fish even! Then last Monday Mr. Read turned up from France & Mrs Read has gone to Oxford with him for a fortnight. We've got someone coming in tomorrow, but all this week we've been running the house. Hugh is perfectly splendid about helping with the washing up…on Wednesday I went with them [her mother and Hugh] & caught the 9.30 train to Uffington (station) (next but one to Swindon). From Uffington we walked up to Whitehorse Hill & endeavoured to find the famous Weyland's Smith's Cave but did a hopeless slow one and missed it. We then walked back to the Wantage R^d station through Wantage & altogether had a most successful day…Things don't get settled here; but I *think* I am going back as a Home Student for two years & work for the B.Sc.[144] Anyhow I can't teach—Isn't money the most appalling nuisance that was ever invented? I am going to vote for the most democratic democrat who exists when I get the chance.

What a life! One washes up all day. Please write to one of us sometime.

[P.S.] Monday. I wrote a letter to you last night which I enclose. Many thanks for the film. It was awfully decent of you to think of sending it me. By the way, was the cryptic epistle a sort of hint to me that I am an awful slacker?

I mustn't stop to write more. My dear little Papa wants the light put out here in the bank.

Please write to one of us soon. I begin work at the hospital at Mongewell[145]—tomorrow, hours 9–4. When do you expect leave?

In September Owen got his last leave before his departure to France which he spent in Oxford.

Violet to Owen, 16 September 1918. 4.30 a.m.

My darling Boy, I am awake & I have just heard you pull up your blind so for the minute you are awake too, but I hope that you will soon sleep. There are so many things that I should like to say just now when you are going—what I feel—'going down into hell!' My mind goes back to the time before you were born when I could feel your life developing within me, & I wanted to breathe only pure air, & think only pure thoughts, & see only beautiful things. There was not beautiful scenery in Woolwich, but always the sky & the crocuses & primroses—fruit blossom in our garden, & I wanted all this to become part of you. Then you came a—to me— beautiful & perfect little Babe…It is a supreme joy to be a Mother! And I believe too to be a Father…as you know our prayer has always been that you may be able to 'choose the good & refuse the evil'.[146] We named you Owen after a man who spent his life in trying to improve the miserable condition of the mill children, Robert Owen…and now as you are growing into manhood it is a great joy to me to see you beginning to think & to refuse to run the risk of the temptation of drinking & smoking. The very last thing we should have chosen would have been for you to enter the army. But…my son just try to live bravely & simply being if you can a father to your men…It is, I am sure, only what we *give* that we *have* & character is the one investment that pays & the things that matter are not those which we often think. There is a beautiful poem of Walt Whitman's on 'Prudence' where he talks of the 'Prudence that suits Immortality' & says something like this—that the young man who lost his life in trying to save a comrade has done very well for himself.[147]

Though we are separated from each other we are with you in spirit always. You will feel very strange & lonely especially at first, but you will find much that is new & interesting & I hope you will in spite of everything, be happy in the belief we are all in God's keeping & that even out of all this horribleness & wickedness good will come. God bless you & keep you my darling. Keep this letter, perhaps it will be a comfort to you sometimes when you feel homesick. God grant that you may come back safe & sound & help build up a better world.

[P.S.] And dear boy I know you grieve that I must bear the pain of this parting, knowing that I cannot even rejoice like some in your taking part in the destruction of evil by means of war…war is an entirely wrong & unchristian method of fighting evil. But I have a great joy, an unspeakable, quenchless joy in having had the vision & possessing the belief that God's plan is the Brotherhood of Man, since He is the Father of all & there is in everyone, however depraved, the Divine spark. And I believe that you & many many others will get this vision of the better way, having been in hell.

Betty Slater to Owen, 17 September 1918 from Oxford

What a pity I got here just one day after you left! I would so have liked to see you in uniform. Do you like it in the R.E's?...Auntie Edith...is coaching Alex for Sandhurst[148]—the poor old boy really has to work now & I don't think he likes it at all!...Last week he was vaccinated—simply terrified, & thought he would faint *at least* & so he was quite disappointed when he found it was nothing but a gentle scratch. It hasn't begun to 'take' properly yet, but he can't play football of course, & his language on the subject is quite lurid! He wears a neat little red ribbon round his arm sometimes when he wants to swank. This letter seems to go meandering on like a silly little stream—but you see I have nothing at all interesting to say. Auntie suggested we should all write to you, & at least this piece of paper will bulge out the envelope & make it look fat & exciting.

—————

Owen embarked for France on 18 September.

Violet to Owen, 18 September [1918]

My thoughts have been with you ever since you left. I hope you had a nice crossing. If you crossed at 4 o'clock you must have run through to Rouen when it was dark & so have seen nothing. If I remember rightly just coming into Rouen it is dirty & smoky & horrid. I hope you will find something beautiful & that you will be comfortably housed and fed. I hope you will take as much advantage of what French you have to use it. It is so different from what we planned when you were to learn French by going to stay in Switzerland with the Bossys.

Well now I must tell you of my adventures. Uncle Harold & I walked over Hungerford Bridge, the sky & the river looked beautiful, & I did wish that you & I had been going together to Charing X & there we said

FIGURE 12 Calais: 'Officers Only' cattle truck with French orange sellers. Owen's first photograph taken in France on his VPK (vest pocket [Kodak] camera).

goodbye & I went on to the C.S.S.A.[149]...I did various shoppings...London seemed chock full of people. I have never been in such terrible crowds as we were in going on the Metropolitan Railway from Oxford St. to Paddington. It was simply a living stream. It seemed almost dangerous—a sort of nightmare especially on the moving staircases. All buses were full so we had to go underground...Do write as frequently as you can dearest boy. It will make such a lot of difference. I feel so sad. Your going has made the war feel more real & terrible than ever. I shall try to write very often so that you may feel part of us still, though in such different surroundings ... Little Pat of his own accord prayed for you tonight. He said 'Keep Owen safe & bring him home safely & finish this horrible war as quickly as you can.' There has been some discussion of the Austrian Peace proposal, nothing very encouraging[150] ... Goodnight my darling boy. God bless & keep you from all evil.

Eliot to Owen, 18 September [1918]

It is now just a day and a half since you and Mother went off in the train. You must have been in France now for a day or more. I wonder what kind of place you will find it, and where exactly you are and what kind of grub you're getting and how you feel and tons of other things. We have suddenly discovered (much to our joy) that letters to the Front only cost a penny. Troops also for their letters home do not have to pay anything ... This morning I went & had a bathe at Lynams. Pat came too. The two Hoares were there also and the whole time we carried on a most lively conversation.

Owen to his mother, 11 [18] September 1918

At length I have reached my company but don't know exactly what position I am to hold or how I am to carry on. My valise is stranded somewhere. I only hope I shall get it again ... Last night I was fairly comfortable I had a waterproof roof above me & a dry tiled floor beneath, I managed to requisition a blanket which I wound round myself on top of my trench coat. I slept fairly well though the floor was awfully hard although I have slept under very much worse conditions ... Thank goodness I have had

Owen's orders posting him to France, 11 September 1918. Owen embarked for France on 18 September

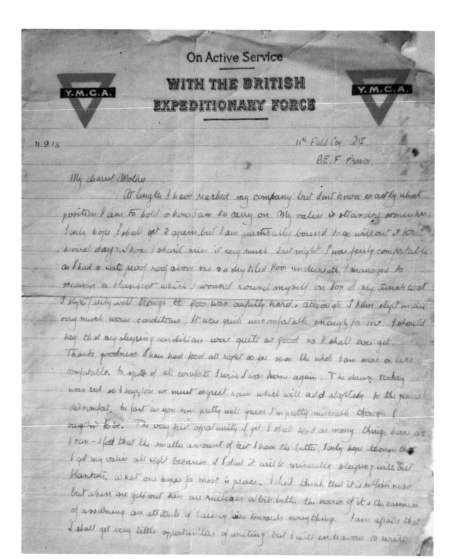

Owen to his mother, 11 [18] September 1918 (p. 152 in this volume)

fairly soon & it only be a field post cards. I am longing for a letter though I'm afraid I shall have to wait days before hearing. In that letter to you that you sent on to me he says nothing about my bike, not even that he has ridden it at all or whether it is safe all right. Please ask him from me to take care of it. & the more letters I get the happier & perhaps the less miserable I shall feel. I still feel as if I am in a dream & that nothing at all out here is real. I will write to Cox for my Pass book & see if I can send you any more money. Please tell me if you ever got that cheque as I haven't heard yet. I hope you have. When I am in the line I shan't have any chance of spending money & when I am in rest the place will probably be so smashed that there will be nothing to spend it on. Send my love & best wishes etc to Father. I wrote to him just before I left the base depot. All the officers in the company seem a decent a lot as I could expect to get in with – particularly the C.O. who is a sport. I suppose I shall be given a job soon which will keep me jolly busy. The censoring is a horrid nuisance as I can't tell you where I am, or what I'm doing. I'm afraid in this case not even by telegraphy. I have been told that I am to be put in charge of a section – hope I get on all right. I shall if I've got a good sergeant so I trust I'm lucky though I wish I knew a bit more about my job & how to carry on. All one can do is to do ones best & trust to Providence. I am sorry but my letters generally get cut off suddenly. When I'm in the middle of a sentence I suddenly find I've got to rush & get a move on. I shall have to start work in a few minutes so I will leave off. Though we can hear the guns firing continually, I haven't been under shell fire yet. I suppose that is an experience to come. Please give my love to everybody you think fit. My thoughts & mind are perpetually at home – in England. Very much love to you all from

your loving son

Owen.

8.10.18   Rouen.

My dearest Father

I have just had a couple of letters that you sent on to me from home, one which had just come & one which I had had when I was on leave. It was quite a treat to get them both. From the last one it seems rather as if you are overworking yourself. I do hope you won't try to do too much & make yourself ill. You appear to be working just as much as you possibly can.

In some other letter you talk about my photographs of the summer Vac & about smoking. So far I have really never had any inclination to smoke & what I have seen of others has rather disgusted me. It seems so hopeless to spend every available minute of the day smoking as a great many do here wherever there is a gathering of any number of men the atmosphere gets horrid in a very short time. Altogether I have not been stirred in the slightest by any of the officers I have met so far. Everybody seems to take advantage of every opportunity to indulge in drinking & smoking & dissipation of every variety. One hears young stars like myself saying "Hooray! Tomorrow's guest night & I can get tight" & they carry out their intentions.

On a guest night at Chatham one might imagine one was attending some ancient barbaric ceremony — a feast to such & such a god. To start with there are three long tables like this ⌐ & they are entirely bare except that down each side runs a narrow table cloth on which are wine glasses & the various impediments of eating. Down the middle of each table are placed various 'plots' & silver ornaments most sumptuous & grand. In my diagram, the spot over the centre of the top table represents the President

Owen to his father, 8 October 1918 (p. 178 in this volume)

While we come in & take our places the various waiters & waitresses all line up behind the top table & directly the president has said grace they turn to their right & file away to their different duties. About half a dozen WAACs. stand solemnly round the hall with their backs against various pillars. - absolutely motionless during the whole of the meal - only moving their eyes. Dinner progresses in the usual way course after course & always on guest night they are very to finish with. At the beginning of dinner one has two glasses, a tumbler & a wine glass, the wine glass is never under any circumstances used if you order a drink they bring you a separate glass suitable for the drink. When the eating is over these glasses are collected & the whole table cleared. Then at a given signal all the cloths are whipped off the table by a man standing at the end. Port wine glasses & finger bowls are solemnly placed on the table and — no more business of drinking the king's health is gone through. "The King" [illegible] [illegible] The King" thereupon the band plays & "God save the king's then everyone says "The King" & drinks. Then the smokers light up & this is where the WAAC statues come in. Each arms herself with a long silver snake with a methylated spirit flaming tongue & lights everyones cigarettes or cigars. Finally after the port has been round twice & one has sat smoking & talking & drinking for about half an hour the president rises & there is a general rush for the door.

Howard. That is all about Chatham. I would like to tell you a little about my life here though there is not much to tell. After I crossed the Channel I spent a couple of days in a rest camp & then came on here. where I have been waiting ever since to be posted to a company. For the first week were under instruction in fieldworks & had practical examples & schemes to work out. We used to get off about 4 PM & then have about three hours writing to do before the scheme was completed. The whole

7.11.18.

My dearest Mother

We have moved up towards the line but are still about the same distance away from it owing to an advance on the part of the infantry. We had an abominably long tramp, mostly cross country owing to traffic on the main roads. We have not done any work yet but will probably start tomorrow a uninteresting job of clearing roads. I have got hold of a pair of brown high boots, I don't know much I shall have to pay for them, not much I know. Actually after arriving in our billet this evening a mail came up & I had your letter of the 29th. which told me mainly about influenza I do hope Eliot & Pat will have completely recovered by the time this arrives. You ask about the stockings they arrived with the others & are glorious though I haven't worn them yet. I will try to give you a description of a shell some time when I am not so tired or so busy. The weather still continues glorious, I only hope it will keep fine.

Please take care of yourself.

Very much love to you all

Your loving son

Owen.

Owen to his mother, 7 November 1918 (p. 212 of this volume)

Marjorie Brown to Owen, 3 January 1919 (p. 247 in this volume)

7 Park Crescent
Oxford
8.1.19.

My dearest Father.

At last my leave has come through. I am home for 18 days, 19 days total leave. I say at last but that gives you an entirely wrong impression. In normal war time circumstances or if I was out my company I would have to stay in France for 3 months before getting leave but meanwhile came out some time ago - have to be every 3 months to bring at the Base I put in for leave forth.

I was very much afraid it would be cancelled because the times it was put back for a day. However I am now home again & it is very jolly, everyone is well, I told Eliot, Pat I have gone. I had a pretty

I have seen you. The girl forget to say jolly interesting, while the boy who is a quiet chum of mine is more or less quiet & reserved. But present he is working for a rebel, is matter.

I hope to see the boys in a day or two & will write at once when I have seen him & tell you what he says.

I am afraid I am more or less satisfied with my position in the army, besides 11/- a day is not to be sneezed at. All the same as soon as I get back I shall get out as quickly as I can & branch for civilian life & importunely.

Much love from

Your loving son
Owen.

Owen to his father, 8 January 1919 (p. 250 in this volume)

16.2.19.

My dearest Mother

Sunday is a fine day. My day off again so stayed in bed respectably late but got up for breakfast & went to a Communion service after church Parade. I spent the rest of the morning in rigging up an electric light in my cubicle which is a great success & a tremendous improvement. In that way I spent a very jolly morning, really enjoying myself. After tea I went for a short walk with the Major but it turned dark very quickly & miles away you could see heavy rain over the sea so we turned back. The country just round here is not pretty; the hill we are on is a plateau & very flat & the stray houses you see are hideously ugly like this & look very like one of those paper carved bricks kids play with. Very close to us there is a huge camp of German prisoners.

The picture below represents the tents enclosed by high barbed wire entanglements & then a path

Owen to his mother, 16 February 1919 (p. 271 in this volume)

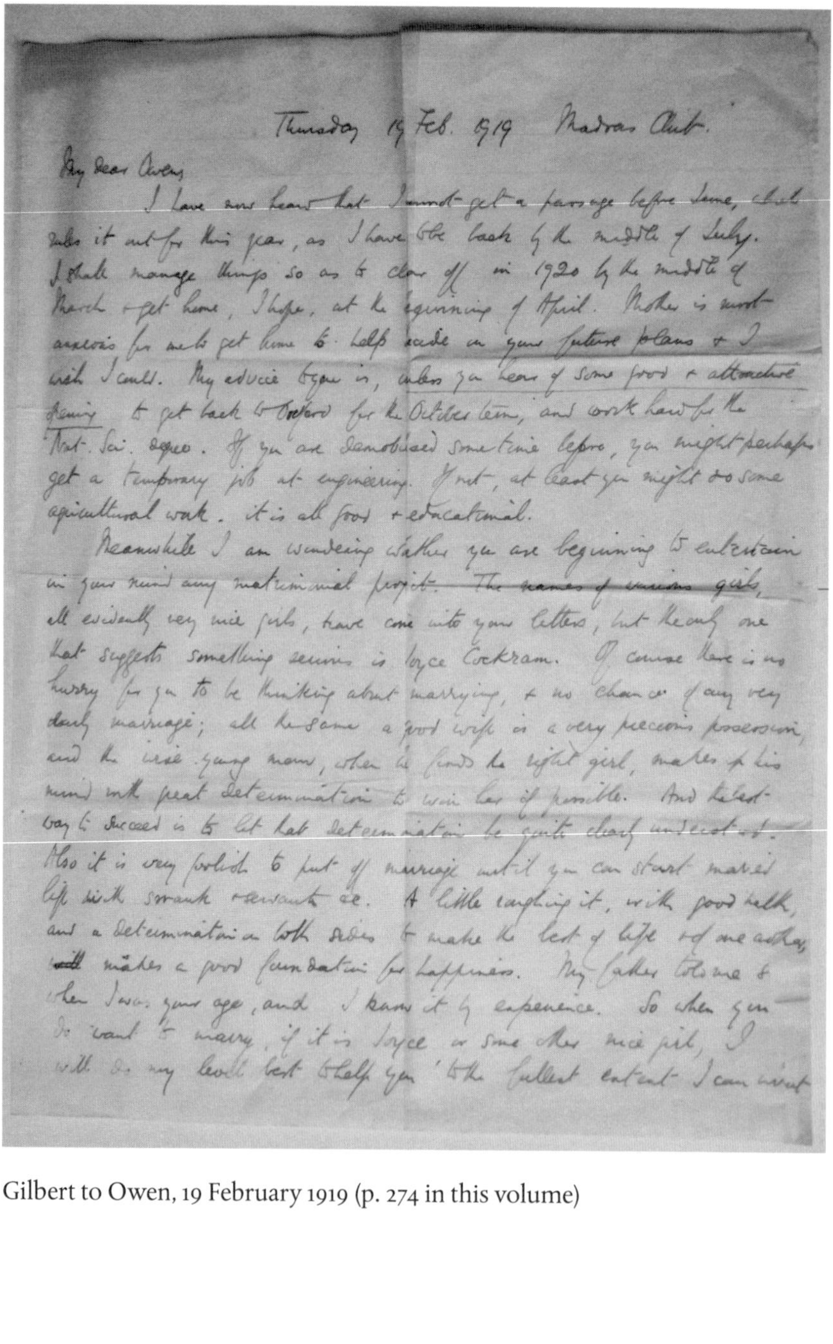

food all right so far. So on the whole I am more or less comfortable…as you can pretty well guess I am pretty miserable though I oughtn't to be. The first opportunity I get I shall send as many things home as I can—I feel that the smaller amount of kit I have the better…What one hopes for is peace. I don't think that it is selfishness but when one gets out here one realizes a bit better the horror of it & the easiness of assuming an attitude of laissez faire towards everything.

I am afraid that I shall get very few opportunities of writing but I will endeavour to write daily even if it only be a field post card.[151] I am longing for letters…In Eliot's letter…he says nothing about my bike not even whether he has ridden it at all or whether it is still all right. Please ask him from me to take care of it. The more letters I get the happier I shall feel & perhaps the less miserable. I still feel that I am in a dream & that nothing at all out here is real.

I shall write to Cox[152] with my pass book & see if I can send you any more money. Please tell me if you ever got that cheque as I haven't heard yet…When I am in the line I shan't have any chance of spending money & when I am at rest the place will probably be so mashed there will be nothing to spend it on.

All the officers in the company seem as decent a lot as I could get in with—particularly the C.O. [Commanding Officer] who is a sport. I suppose I shall be given a job soon which will keep me jolly busy. The censoring is a horrid nuisance as I can't tell you where I am or what I am doing…I have been told that I am to be put in charge of a section—hope I get on all right. I shall if I get a good sergeant…All one can do is to do one's best & trust to Providence.

I am sorry but my letters generally get cut off suddenly. When I am in the middle of a sentence I suddenly find I've got to rush & get a move on…Though one can hear the guns firing continually I haven't been under shell fire yet. I suppose that is an experience to come…My thoughts & mind are perpetually at home in England.

Ida Brown to Owen, 18 September 1918

Very many thanks for the book. It was awfully kind of you to send it. We shall always prize it, also the little note you enclosed. We are going to learn all the songs so that we can sing them to you when you come back. I hope this idea will not keep you from coming. If you meet any young officers out there you might ask them if they trained at Chatham or 29 Stuart Rd.

We were very sorry you did not come back again. We had all been looking forward to Tuesday night. Ever since you went we have been drinking tea just to see if the tea leaves foretold your return, but we could not find you in the bottom of the cup. Now we are all suffering from indigestion and bad nerves. You can't imagine how we miss you...Its hard to realise you have really gone...Its horrid to think we shan't know where you are or what you are doing. That censor is my pet aversion but I suppose I must not grumble at him if he is helping to win the war.

Lieut. Jeffries came to supper on Sunday, and this afternoon we have a Tommy coming to tea and two coming in the evening. In this way we are trying to fill up the aching void you have left.

Tomorrow I am going to Town [London] with Grandma. You know I made a bargain with her that I would escort her if she would take me to the Theatre...This will be my first experience of getting about London alone. I have always had the Pater to look after me, now I have to look after myself and someone else too. When you read my character did you say that I could calmly and unperturbed cross a road that was surging with traffic and that I should not lose my head under trying circumstances? I have no fear of losing my handkerchief on the journey which of course is a great comfort. Had you not read my character I should have been in a state of fear and trembling all the time dreading the loss of such a friend, but now I can rest assured that all will be well.

The Tommy arrived before I could finish this. Now it is past midnight. I have pushed them all off to bed...Its a pouring wet night and its just beginning to thunder. I wonder if you are under canvas or in a nice cushie billet...Horace [Marjorie's fiancé] wished to be remembered to you...We all send heaps of love and wish you the best of luck and a safe return, Your affectionate Sister Ida.

P.S. Don't forget that photo you promised us.
P.P.S. I find that my kilted skirt wants another hook and eye. If I send it out will you do it for me?...Its 12.30. We are going by an early train and I shan't want to get up tomorrow morning. So good night and *Cheer up.* Ida

---

Violet to Owen, 20 September 1918

It is delightful to have your letter and to know you are safely across...It must be very interesting to see 'foreign parts'. I hope you will try your French as much as you can. You will be able to read French newspapers. I wonder whether you will find out their politics from reading like you do from an English paper...Now I am on the train on my way to Wallingford, after having seen Eliot to his school. We cycled all the way and were fortunate in having good weather...I hope you will not have to go through terrible experiences. Though I know there are so many poor fellows that must. That's the worst of it...I'll send you the *Herald* and the 'Nation'. When you have read them leave them in the Y.M.C.A. or somewhere where someone else can see them...Joyce is doing work in a hospital hard by...Mind you try and see the interesting old buildings in Rouen. I believe there are some interesting and ancient Law Courts etc. I must cable to Father I have not done so yet. I know it will be a shock to hear that you are actually in France.

Joyce Cockram to Owen, 21 September 1918 from Wallingford

Your Mother asked me to write to you, so I suppose I must!...Your Mother turned up yesterday during lunch came back from Reading in the

evening…After supper (Menu—Rabbit Pie—French Beans and Potatoes. Stewed Cherries & Red Currants and Custard. Cheese Biscuits (it
ought to have been Biscuits but it was Bread) & butter. Coffee—I mean
Tea unfortunately; Drinks—Water). Miss Hedges came in and we had
music, of a deep & serious turn of mind…Mongewell still goes strong:
this morning we got into an awful row—the chief housemaid said we
didn't make the beds properly—only just because she couldn't find anything else to curse us for…However I said to Annie (the housemaid) that
we'd try our level best to improve—& she was so surprised that she
retired discomfited…Please write soon.

Violet to Owen, 22 and 24 September 1918

I…have sent several letters to Rouen, among others your Bank Pass book.
Mind you tell me when you receive it dear boy. I have now had three letters
from you…I had a letter from Eliot & it sounded fairly happy. Of course the
new boys have got to go through various ordeals. Eliot is in the Lower School
& in the lower 5th…Did I tell you that Bertha can't come & that Mrs Harper
leaves on Friday…I had a nice letter from Mrs Brown—she said that they
miss you very much & that you never came too often or stopped too long.

[24 September] I hope by this time you have got my letters. I have
written every day except Sunday…I'll try to write tomorrow & if possible
a few words every day. My thoughts are so much with you. Much love
dear boy, yr loving Mother

Hugh Cockram to Owen, 22 and 24 [?] September 1918

My dear Slater, I was so bucked to get your letter of the 19th posted on the
20th…and that up to now you are doing fairly well over there, and that in

spite of the paucity of berths, you managed to make shift with a table. I am wondering how your French stands. I hope it serves you well. Now in order to show you I don't forget instructions, I am doing many sums in geom: this weekend the one that stumps me is of this nature...two circles, of radius x are found to overlap if radii are drawn perpendicular to each other etc. You see the idea don't you?

[24 September?] Sorry I got no further yesterday, but I am terribly busy...I find the Senior Prefect's job is not all beer and skittles. Especially as I am combining with the onerous duties of Librarian, and President and Secretary of the Senior Common Room all rolled into one...Masson is Captain of footer and Clapperton Sec. I suppose you know this but I am blest if [I] know what to say. I thought I had heaps to tell you. Oh, by the way I have gone up to your place to see your mater, and she let me have the bike; I took it to Armsteads's[153] to have it done up and they said that the back wheel needs respoking; I am having that done at 9/6 which is pretty cheap. But I want to impress you [that] I owe you nought further...The inmates of this study are quite willing to help you in any way so long as you help us as much as you can.

Aunt Lilly to Violet, 24 September [1918]

I heard the other day through Aunt Annie, that which gave me really much sorrow on your account—that you eldest boy—Owen—was called up to the Front...Oh you poor Violet—it must be so dreadful for each mother, & is I know so dreadful for *you*, poor, poor Violet. I do feel so very concerned & grieved for you who have not Gilbert by your side to give comfort by personally sharing your grief.

Dear girl, one can say nothing to comfort but it is just true that (by his own choice?) Surely by his own choice he is joining in as noble a cause— an effort & aim, almost if not quite, as noble an effort as was ever engaged with...giving *himself,* in the struggle against Devilry—Righteousness against Evil, in the aim—Surely God in Righteousness against the Works of the Devil!—in *that light* this is a Holy War against [word indecipherable] wrong in High Places & everyone who goes with the purpose to bring Freedom & Peace to the enslaved & injured, is doing his Best in a Holy Cause & therein lies I think an immense comfort to every Mother— But oh! All this [word indecipherable] can't undo by a hair's breadth the agony of fear in the loss of him, & when gone to the midst of danger away from sight & sound—one can't say anything [word indecipherable] poor girl—except just, God Bless & Keep him & bring him safely back to you, having *helped* in this righteous effort...I have not had to experience this— but I *know* that [what] it would be to me—as for others...May he come back safely & happily again to all who love him—It is dark, Goodbye & Love from Aunt Lilly.

Owen to his mother, 27 September 1918

I managed to get to bed pretty early last night in spite of the scheme. We have got another this afternoon which may take any length of time...so I am sending this hurried letter in the dinner hour. For a change the Y.M.C.A. hut is perfectly quiet...I am sending you a cheque for £20 if you will kindly stick it in the Co-op as you suggested. I suppose you better pay some of my bills for me...Guest night was not so rampageous as I expected...Not more than half a dozen were ill afterwards...The weather has been glorious...Just beautiful for the Cher. [Cherwell River] etc. I'm afraid I miss Oxford very much, but my greatest physical hardship is to have to go without a bike.

On 29 September Ludendorff heard of the planned surrender of Bulgaria, Germany's ally, and advised Berlin to seek an armistice.

Violet to Owen, 28 [29] September 1918

It *is* good & sweet of you to write to me every day & it is a great comfort to get your letters however small & short they are. I am with you in spirit so often dear boy. And yet I have forgotten to get the R.E. note book. I will really try to do so tomorrow—you know how the time gets filled up. Mrs Harper has left & Edna is going so we shall be a very small family indeed. Eliot writes rather unsatisfactory letters. I don't mean as if he is not happy but not telling anything... Pat & I went to the Quakers this morning— there were quite a large number at the meeting in spite of rain... Certainly having so little domestic help makes everything more difficult. I find it so difficult to think of you in France. I wonder if you are within hearing of the guns. Are you with the lot of men with whom you went out or have you got scattered yet. I hope you will see something of Rouen & try to speak French. You will be pleased to hear that not only did we get some blackberries but have got an order to buy 5 lbs. of sugar to preserve them... I must stop now. It is getting late & the fire is nearly out. I have lost the post so will add a few words in the morning.

Monday. I went round Oxford to try to get your R.E. Notebook but couldn't get it so I ordered it... I hope you have plenty of warm things. *How about gloves.* I saw a rather jolly pair of gauntlet fur lined riding gloves at the C.S.S.A. for 25/- That is a lot to pay if you are going to lose them but if you will keep them I will get a pair & send for a Christmas present from Father & me. You might as well have them at once so tell me when you write... What are schemes I wonder? Perhaps I may not know. It is interesting to see something of the country round—it sounds rather beautiful. How one wishes you were visiting it in other circumstances. I went to see Mrs Grafflin yesterday & had tea with her at the hotel. There was a good looking & well mannered Canadian with a pretty girl. They had had champagne for lunch (Mrs. G. told me) & had just had liqueurs. Girls who encourage fellows to drink & spend money on them are a snare, & never nice. I am so glad you do not drink & I hope you will not. It will I feel sure save you running into many temptations. I do feel that you were fortunate to know the Quibells & Browns. I had a nice warm hearted letter from Joyce. Perhaps she told you that she is going to come to Oxford as a Home Student[154] for 2 or 3 years to study for medicine…I enclose a letter from Father…I fear he is working too hard…Goodnight dear boy. I think you are surrounded by prayerful thoughts. Every your loving Mother

—⬥—

Joyce Cockram to Owen, 29 September 1918 from Wallingford

I don't know exactly how to treat you, so you must be particularly lenient! It seems mean to write and tell you the splendid stroke of luck—or perhaps it isn't luck—I've had; but I think I must. Mother and Dad paid a flying visit to Oxford…and saw the Science Tutoress & the Principal [at the Society of Oxford Home-Students]…and what do you think? I am going to be a Lady Doctor. Isn't it too ripping for words…But I'm terrified in a way…It struck me on Friday that I shall have to dissect a frog and other cold blooded animals & I can't pretend I shall like that! So long as they keep clear of spiders I shan't mind half so much…I think it would be an awfully good idea, if you did have a thing like that degree to keep you occupied. There is nothing like work to keep one's mind off disagreeable things.

It's amazing, what rot one can write when one tries, isn't it? The hospital is still going strong but I can't say I adore housework; and the 'inmates' get on my nerves. I suppose I should stick it if I had to, but I'm glad in some ways that it isn't necessary…We are treated just like kids of two and were ordered off to church last Sunday and today. I like going to church, but I do object to being *sent* there…At present I am revelling in *Woodstock!*—I mean in the book.[155] Have you read it? Do you get many books? If not, is it permissible to send books? If so, would you like some…That artistic, poetic and romantic touch of yours—in other words, your remark that 'The hour of moonrise draws nigh when the faeries will dance over the heather and bathe in the fire buckets' filled my soul with gladness for it showed that the state of your soul after writing was better than before.

⸙

Owen to his mother, 29 September 1918*

We had no scheme to do yesterday so when we broke off at 4 pm we had definitely finished for the day. I had to issue tobacco to the troops between 5 & 6 pm and after dinner when I attempted to write I just managed to finish a letter to Aunty Molly & got so fed up with rotten music & billiards that I went to bed.

I have just filled up my pen with French ink. I don't know how it will act. But I dislike it intensely it is a purple black instead of a blue black, & not particularly nice to write with. This morning I started work at 8 a.m. as assistant censor officer.[156] Broke off at 9 till 10 to issue tobacco & then went on till midday. You forget what you have read generally when you come to the end of the letter, but three things struck me. Nearly every man said 'I hope you all are in the best of health as this leaves me in the pink' sometimes about three times in the same letter; also 'Cigs are cheap' & 'The beer here is rotten' & not a few of them make remarks at the censor. It is a pretty boring job on the whole. Issuing tobacco is as bad,—the men file past you, saluting twice & you stamp their cards. I was doing it with another officer & after we had finished we were presented with a dozen boxes of matches as a gift. I only wish I could send them on to you. I'm sure they would be useful.

Last night I went to an orchestral concert at the Y.M.C.A...I was the only officer there. I took my sketch book in the other evening & tried to sketch faces. I found it difficult to get much likeness. But anything is good practice & I could only get half a minute to a minute to each, they moved such an abominable lot...People speak very much against the railway strikes[157] here—officers & men—at least you never hear a good word for them. The only papers one sees are the *Daily Mail* continental edition & such things as the *Bystander, Sketch, Punch*[158] etc.

Patrick to his father, 30 September 1918

I have just had your letter from you asking whether I got any prizes and telling about the club mongoose and Mr Punnett, I do not know whether I told you or not but at any rate I got 3 prizes 1st being called 'Masterman Ready' by Captain Marryat, with [which] was for being first in the French exam, and 'The life and Death of Jason' by William Moris for painting a winter scene, and 'Song of the Blue Dragon', by some old boy for My Summer Diary.

I am sending you my report but the two things I am 2nd in are the same forms realy although I have gone up 2 forms in every thing, no more, and no less.

Mother has got a headache and is lying in bed all today.

We had a dayboy and a border match today and the dayboys won 12 points to 4, as they always do. With lots of Love from Pat.

Violet to Gilbert, [30 September 1918]

I m so sorry not to write, I have had a dreadful headache, one of my worst, but I am a good deal better now though I am writing this lying in bed. We had letters from you since I last wrote which was delightful. Only I am very concerned that…you must work such very long hours so that you have to forego your tennis. And that on top of that you want to put in extra work so as to earn more. Please do not think that you must do this. Eliot's school will only cost about £80…Poor dear Owen is no cost. So *do not kill the goose that lays the golden egg.* I do want you home well & strong. I have now a £100 balance…My darling your health is the balance we must try to keep…I do hope war will cease & you & Owen will be home next spring.

Owen to his mother, 1 October 1918

I have now completely recovered from my indisposition of yesterday as I expected. We are now on a course of riding & it is perfectly glorious. This morning we went out into the country which was beautiful in the autumn weather…We went part of the time through a pine forest keeping at first to the roads & then following curly paths & tracks. The roads themselves are of Roman straightness…You know how glorious a pine forest is with the sun on the trunks, dark green overhead, the green bracken underneath. The bracken has not turned colour at all yet, though the spindle berries are coming along rippingly…I enjoyed the morning immensely—riding, I think, stands equal to rowing as a sport. When we got back to the stables we had to groom our own horses & they were filthy, hadn't been groomed really properly for months so you could not do very much with them.

In the afternoon we did physical training which was huge fun, no set or fixed exercises but all combined in various energetic games. We had one game of rugger which was horribly energetic played with entire disregard for nearly every rule. Never the less it was most enjoyable & left you pretty exhausted.

We have now taken up the continental system of time, having a day of 24 hours instead of a day of 12 & a night of 12. It sounds horribly strange when first you hear it. 'Gentlemen you will parade again at 13.50.' Tonight is guest night & I believe after dinner we are going to have a concert there will probably be 'high jinks' though I hope without disastrous results. I had a ripping hot bath this evening—much better than one ever gets at home. However I hope you will get that bathroom made respectable sometime though at present everything is so horribly dear. Don't forget to tell me when you get my £20 cheque. I don't quite know when I will be able to send another—in about a month's time probably.

There are various rumours floating about concerning leave. Mainly to the effect that I may get leave after 4 or 5 months. So cheerio. I am looking forward to it like anything. By the way I would very much like a knitted woollen helmet[159]—never mind I will see what I can get from Ordnance. It is by far the cheapest way of doing things. Dinner is just served so I must shut up. Very much love to you all.

Gilbert to Owen, 2 October 1918

My dearest Boy, I have just had Mother's wire of Sept. 23rd 'Owen France'. It has come at last—it never seemed to me in my heart that you would have to go. May God preserve you in all the dangers to which you may be exposed, and may you never fail to so behave that afterwards you can look back on your memories without regret. Tomorrow I hope to write more, just now I have no heart to write about trivial incidents.

On 3–4 October both Germany and Austria-Hungary sent notes to the Allied governments requesting an armistice on the basis of the 'Fourteen Points'. This was in part a result of German losses in the Allies' Meuse-Argonne offensive which had begun on 16 September and of Austrian losses in the Battle of Piave in June. Negotiations now began with London, Paris, and Washington.

Gilbert to Owen, 4 October 1918

I wonder when & where this will reach you, & what you will have gone through before getting it. I have just had your letter of Aug. 20 ... Yesterday

I had Mother's wire of Sept. 23rd—which I suppose, was the day you started—I don't suppose they give you much notice when they order you abroad. You are just in for the biggest fighting of all but also, as the news has come to us so far, the victorious fighting. Victory will have to be paid for dearly enough, no doubt, but till July 19th we were paying the price, but only getting defeat. It is a shame that India should have done so little to help.[160] It is the fault of the Government [in Whitehall] much more than of the Indian people, and least of all, of the British in India.

It has been pleasant to get away for a little from the steamy heat of Madras, into the slightly cooler and drier air or the Mysore tableland...We are...in the midst of the mining area. All the gold mines of India are just round, they extract about £2,000,000 per annum since the outbreak of the war [but] all the gold has been kept in the country. I shall go down a mine in a few days time. It is, I believe, the reverse of a pleasant experience, but not a thing to be missed.

I spent 3 days in Bangalore at the British Residency. It is quite a palace...I had the best guest quarters...But there came in suddenly & unexpectedly the Cossack general (with two members of his suite) who made that dash southwards through Persia to join the British forces when advancing on Bagdad after the surrender of Kut.[161] So I was moved to make way for him...I lectured 3 times in Bangalore on 'The Economic Problems after the War'...Now I fear I must shut up, to catch the post. I am hoping that it will leave India for home quite shortly. May it find you well and unharmed. I am not without hope that we may meet next April! Good luck, good luck, my dearest boy.

⸺⸙⸺

Gilbert to Violet, 4 October 1918* from the Kolar Gold Fields

You seem to have been very lucky in your travelling to Leyburn—everybody here reports getting letters that travelling at home is perfectly awful...Did Eliot do any farm work? I think he ought to & hope that if he has not yet he will get at it next summer holidays...I gave my lecture on 'The Economic Problem after the War' three times over, as arranged, and improved it each time. I think the last time it was good. But it was a great strain the last time, as I had just had the wire 'Owen France' ...

Gilbert to Violet, 5 October 1918*

Try to find out about Furniss standing for Parliament.[162] I don't think Furniss is at heart a bad sort, but very weak, and Mrs is, I think, a thoroughly vulgar woman, with considerable driving power, and I am sure she holds the reins very firmly. But if Furniss stands for Parliament, I presume he means, if elected, to drop Ruskin. That should be a comfort to Mrs Grafflin.

That, by the way, is a very interesting letter of hers which you enclosed. And I think she is absolutely right about all organised religion. You want to know how I feel about your joining the Quakers. Well I much prefer it should be the Quakers rather [damaged paper]

In the following letter the influenza pandemic of 1918 was mentioned for the first time. Estimates of those who died varied widely at the time and since, but it is fairly certain that at least 20,000,000 people perished worldwide, far more than were killed in the war. The illness, which particularly affected those between the ages of 20 and 40, was most severe in the combatants' armies and navies because men were gathered together in larger groups than ever before in history.

Owen to Patrick, 6 October 1918

I am so sorry to hear that you have got flu. I do hope you have been taking care of yourself & are nearly all right now. I suppose you have been reading a good deal. When you get time, & can do so please write to me as I am always wanting to have letters & it is miserable to have to do without. I have been having exciting times during the last two or three days marching an awful lot & working in mud & pouring rain. I wouldn't mind a bit if only one could get a hot bath & a good change & bed afterwards, but when you keep your clothes on for two days you never get them properly dry. Buck up & get well & don't please [forget to] work hard when you get well.

Owen to his mother, 6 October 1918*

I had to attend a military funeral today. So many things in the army seem barbarous rites—such as drinking the King's health in port whine—'Gentlemen The King' 'The King' which has to be gone through every guest night. At the funeral it is most barbaric. As propitiation to [the] god of Battles bayonets are fixed & then volleys fired…I…have heard from [Bella] Barnes & Uncle [Joseph].

On 7 October Owen was ordered to report to his company in France.

Owen to his mother, 8 October 1918*

I got my orders late last night. I go up to join my company sometime today. It will probably take me a couple days to get up. It is pouring as hard as it possibly can…I find that a man who was with me at Kelham is going to the same Division as I am which will be rather nice travelling together…I find I am starting this evening.

Did I tell you that I met a boy here who was at Oxford with me. We did chemistry at the same time. It was rather interesting meeting him though I don't like him particularly...I'm afraid that since I have my orders my capacity for giving news has dwindled away. We have just had a new lot of officers who arrived here today—nearly all of them are old acquaintances who were at Kelham with me. This is typical absolutely. One [damaged paper]

Owen to his father, 8 October 1918

You talk...about smoking. So far I have never had any inclination to smoke and what I have seen of others had rather disgusted me. It seems so hopeless to spend every available minute of the day smoking as a great many do here whenever there is a gathering of any number of men the atmosphere gets horrid in a very short time. Altogether I have not been struck in the slightest by any of the officers I have met so far. Everybody seems to take advantage of every opportunity to indulge in drinking and smoking and dissipation of every variety. One hears youngsters like myself saying 'Hooray tomorrow guest night and I can get tight!' And they carry out their intentions.

On a guest night at Chatham one might imagine one was attending some ancient barbaric ceremony, a feast to such and such a god. To start with there are three long tables...and they are entirely bare except that down each side runs a narrow table cloth on which are wine glasses and the various implements of eating. Down the middle...are placed various pots and silver ornaments most sumptuous and grand...When we come in and take our places the various waiters and waitresses all line up behind the top table and directly the President has said grace they turn to their right and file away to their different duties. About half a dozen WAACs[163] stand solemnly round the hall with their backs against various pillars—absolutely motionless during the whole of the meal—only moving their eyes. Dinner progresses in the usual way course after course and always on guest night there are ices to finish with...If you order a drink they bring you a separate glass suitable for the drink. When the eating is over these glasses are collected and the whole table cleared. Then at a given signal all the cloths are whipped off the table by a man standing at the end. Port wine glasses and finger bowls are solemnly placed on the bare board and mysterious drinkings of the King's health are gone through…Hereupon the band plays God Save the King and then everyone says 'The King!' and drinks. Then the smokers light up and this is where the WAAC statues come in. Each arms herself with a long silver snake with a methylated spirit flaming tongue and lights everyone's cigarettes or cigars. Finally after the Port has been round twice and one has sat smoking, drinking and talking for about half an hour the President rises and there is a general rush for the door.

However that is all about Chatham. I would like to tell you a little about my life although there is not much to tell. After I crossed the channel I spent a couple of days in a rest camp and then came on here where I have been waiting ever since to be posted to a company. For the first week [we] were under instruction in fieldworks & had practical examples & schemes to work out. We used to get off about 4 pm & then have about three hours writing to do before the volume was completed. The whole thing of course was absolute eye wash, because before each scheme we were told exactly the kind of thing that was wanted. After our field works course was over we were put onto riding & physical jerks. We went out on horseback every morning & in the afternoon had an hour's jerks. All this of course was most jolly & we managed to see quite a lot of the country round—all hilly & pine forests with glorious views whenever you came out of the forest on top of a hill particularly when you could see the river twining its way underneath you almost. By getting off at three o'clock it left us plenty of time to go down to the town. I have been down several times. The cathedral is glorious & there are several old churches & the law courts all wonderful pieces of architecture.

I had my posting orders two or three days ago & last night I had my actual moving orders. I have to go up to my company starting this evening & it will probably take me a couple of days to get there. I don't know where they are or what they are doing. I am rather funking things as I am more or less unprepared. All through my training I have had absolutely no experience in handling men. The whole thing, though is a great adventure & in a great many ways one learns a great deal, but I am afraid that when it is over it will be horribly hard ever to settle down to book work— even writing letters is an effort particularly if other things are happening at the same time.

There is a Y.M.C.A. hut here as you can see from the paper I am using, it is awfully nice as there is a room for officers with writing tables, chess & draughts, a billiard table & a piano. Just lately I have had a shot at billiards. It is very fascinating & apt to take up any amount of time.

I wish there had been a chance of my coming out to India but absolutely nothing doing. I should have loved to have come out & to have seen you in your native element & possibly to have come home with you when the war is over though I expect I shall get my discharge more quickly from France. I find my French wants polishing horribly badly. I'm not much good at it & unfortunately there are not many opportunities of practising... I am looking forward to leave like anything, though I hope peace will come before I am due to get any. On an average you are lucky you can get a fortnight in five months.

<hr />

Joyce Cockram to Owen, 9 October 1918 from Wallingford

I have made two futile efforts to write to you—which I'm not enclosing— I couldn't continue in that sheet of paper—because it gives the appearance of having been written by a raving lunatic... I was hugely bucked to get a letter from you this morning—& delighted that you are still in Rouen. That and Dad's remark—that he thought Peace wasn't far off— went far to raise my drooping spirits—due to a cold in my head—which is keeping me chained to the spot—so to speak.

I knew you'd got a lively imagination & that you were a bit of a poet, but have always got laughed at for saying so. Life seems to me to be so ghastly inconsistent. I'm perfectly awful myself I know. For instance, you talk about lying in the heather & having a sort of forest of little people. Well, lots of times if one's lucky enough to be alone at night in the country— you can hear the poet's 'Thousand Voices of the Night'[64] & feel the grandeur of a clear starry sky—but when you read in a book any description of such things you say to yourself—'What sentimental rot—I can't read that' & you chuck the book away—at least, I do.

And then I hate things in other people that I do myself...I hope it's only the inexperience of youth which leads me to making mistakes which I loathe myself for doing. Something always happens to spoil things like thinking, as you say. I suppose one can't go on ad lib apostrophising the stars, but I do think one might be let down without the usual bang. It's most annoying. Don't you find the 'bang' particularly obnoxious when you're getting confidential? I've just had an interruption—in the form of Mrs Read—& my pen refuseth to flow calmly any longer.

It may interest you to know that I'm a business woman now! This morning I have opened an account. After long deliberation I decided to put a deposit of at least some of my thousands in Lloyds—in other words I opened a Current Account with £20. I possess a cheque book & a pass book—like you...It is really rather a joke because I've got to pay everything myself—clothes, college fees, board & lodging etc.

It is all very well for you to laugh about me being a Spartan. It really will be an effort to dissect a spider. You needn't be so horribly cutting.

You may get your degree now before I am qualified: how long ought it to take you now? You've done some of the work, haven't you?

I'm going into Oxford on Friday and my goodness, I am pleased. I'm simply aching to get started...We went round to the Damans last night and had a gay time...we played a trio written with a piano accompaniment arranged as a duet...and I smoked a cigarette, so that life was particularly agreeable. As a matter of fact I like smoking *when I'm alone*. I've followed your excellent advice this morning & am thoroughly enjoying myself with a cigarette at the present moment...I must stop & do something to account for this morning. Mother wants the flowers done, I believe. It's sure to be some Early Victorian Upper Middle Class job like that...Mr Read has been hit in the right arm. Mrs Read was very anxious that I should tell you this, so I suppose I'd better. She always asks for you when she gets a letter from France; I don't think she can quite make out why he doesn't meet you!

During the late summer and autumn of 1918, public demands for a general election increased. Parliament, elected in 1910, had been sitting since 31 January 1911. The life of the 'Long Parliament' had been extended through a succession of five short Acts, each of which suspended the operation of the 1911 Parliament Act (forbidding any Parliament to sit for more than five years). Each of these Acts had suspended the Act for a set period although the government had wanted a suspension 'while the war continued'. The fifth extension, in July 1918, extended Parliament's life until January 1919. Plans for an election in late November or early December, without reference to the conduct of the war, were well under way by September. This altered state of affairs was reflected in Violet's increased work for the Labour Party.

Violet to Gilbert, 9 October 1918

I have just come in from giving a lecture on Land Reform...& am waiting for the kettle to boil for my footwarmer. I am thinking of the many times we did that together & how little we thought of the future being a sad and a terrible one. And now again I wonder whether we are to have any future together with our little family. This week has been very momentous with Germany's accepting President Wilson's 14 points as a basis for Peace.[165] Of course we have the same sort of fear & caution & such placards as the 'Allies say no'. It makes one full of hope & fear. I wonder if President Wilson can hold his War Hounds that have scarcely tasted blood & demand a spring offensive [to produce] a [crushing?] victory & a dictated Peace...It is ghastly when one thinks of what it means...I got on very well tonight & there were about 20 soldiers present as well as others. They were quite interested in getting at the land & one was not averse to the Russian Method—there was a good deal of discussion so that was all right. I felt myself to be a very incompetent person before I began but I had written most of what I wanted to say…I have enjoyed looking it up…How splendid it would be if he [Owen] could do all constructive work after Peace is declared…Isn't it lovely drinking the Kings health in 'whine'. Dear old Owen isn't much better than I am [at spelling]…I actually have engaged a maid…she comes tomorrow…I do hope Germany will give in though it really seems asking unconditional surrender [is] to ask them to clear out of everywhere before we even begin to talk. All this brilliant work means great loss of life & ghastly casualties. I must stop to catch the post.

Owen to his mother, 10 October 1918*

I was horribly sore & stiff this morning after my riding yesterday…We were let off very lightly…as the riding master himself was stiff…In the afternoon we had an hours physical training. We played a game called medical ball. It is an adaption of tennis. The net is made of wire & pretty strong about 5'6" high & the ball is pretty heavy—the size of a football made of old sandbags & in the middle some sand…You play four or three a side and throw the ball from side to side…It is quite energetic & rather exciting but it makes one's arms horribly tired…Beyond our riding & P.T. we have done nothing. I am going to a concert at the Y.M.C.A. which will probably be very good. I went to one two or three days ago at a Convalescent Hospital…There are not high class turns but there was one excellent [text ends]

Owen to his mother, 12 October 1918

I have not done any serious work yet; last night there was a stunt on but I was ordered [to] remain behind. All one does really, is to eat, drink, & sleep as the opportunity offers, not knowing from hour to hour what is going to happen & of course one is deluged with rumours the whole time, of every type & description...I have been reading *Peveril of the Peak*.[166] It took me a long time to get into it but really it is an excellent book...I have not got hold of my valise yet which is rather hard & beastly. For the last two nights I have managed to borrow a blanket; last night I managed quite well, had a rug to sleep on, took off my tunic & wore a leather jerkin & wrapped myself over with the borrowed blanket & my trench coat & lining & slept jolly well...You have read I suppose in your paper how the line has been advanced rapidly. We have moved from back areas where everything has been smashed to bits up to villages where everything is intact & civilians still hanging on. They rejoice mightily whenever a party of prisoners is marched away. The officers of the company now are all sitting round a table in a intact house in a certain French village all writing letters...When I get hold of some suitable paper & the opportunity I will try to do a hasty sketch of each of the different officers here...I do trust & pray that the war may be over by Christmas this year but as days go on we seem to be getting no nearer peace. If the allies held honourably to the war aims etc that they have published from time to time we ought to have peace by now but the more successful we are, the harder probably will be our terms.

The men in our company are a very decent lot particularly my section which is supposed to be the best of the lot. It is extraordinary how sappers make themselves comfortable. Two will go shares, rig up a tent under a hedge with a couple of ground sheets & a bed of straw. All that I have seen of the war so far is a sort of picnic & really a sapper is a fairly happy individual. Granted he lives very much like a rather intelligent beast he has no or very little responsibility, does what he is told when he is told & everything is arranged for him. One hears occasional gun fire & shells bursting & although the noise is unpleasant one gets more or less used to it very quickly—that of course is one of the greatest [word indecipherable] of the war—it blunts or destroys in most cases the higher parts of the intellect making one inclined to become very indifferent. Very much love to you all—in spirit at any rate I am at home, may I be there in the flesh very shortly.

Edna Brown to Owen, 12 October 1918

My dear Mr Slater, We were so awfully pleased to hear from you, we did begin to think that you were a 'Perfect Washout'. Here have we for nearly a month, twice a day rushed when the postman came in sight, & each time after she had passed, one would hear 'Oh, isn't he a froad,'[167] 'oh what a naughty boy [he] is'! We had given up ever hearing from you again… This last Sunday when we came home from Chapel we were very much surprised to find one of our very first boys here. By name of Sweetman. I believe you have heard us talk of 'The Mayor & Corporation of Bath' well he is one of the Corporation…You remember a Cpl Williams that was billited on us, who went to Mesopotamia, he is now in hospital in Cheshire. Last Monday Ida took her writing pad down to the school intending to write to Cpl. She no sooner got it out than a boy came up to her & said 'Doing yer 'omework', he being most inquisitive she was obliged to put it away…I do hope you will not be bored by this time.

    The boy stood on the burning deck[168]

    His --- --- --- --- --- shall I tell you the rest

I have ever so much to tell you but must save it up. With lots of love from all.

Gilbert to Violet, 12 October 1918 from Kolar Gold Fields

I have had a copy of 'Some South Indian Villages' sent up here, and have presented it to the Georges [his hosts]. When I get back to Madras I will see to the sending of copies home, both on my own account to you & my mother & others, and by the O.U. [Oxford University] Press for sale & review...News has been most hopeful lately—I wonder what will happen while this is on its way to you. Tell Owen I long to hear from him.

[P.S.] You will of course wire if there is anything. Otherwise I shall take no news as good news.

Joyce Cockram to Owen, 12 October 1918 from Oxford

Many thanks for letting me know your 'change of address' as one saith in the common tongue...I came in yesterday and am jolly thankful to be on the point of starting work again, having fooled round doing nothing for nearly 4 mths!...I'm absolutely terrified at the present moment because at 5 p.m. I go to see Miss Kirkaldy, the Science Tutor & then I'm going on to see Mrs Johnson, the Principal. I don't know in the least what I'm supposed to do...Then I am going on to see your Mother, unless it's too late.

Later. It's all over and everything at present seems most satisfactory. I duly arrived at...a minute and a half after five of the clock. Then I had to wait ages until she could see me...When I went into her room she struck me as being enormous & I felt a mere kid, but she grew shorter after a time and the atmosphere grew proportionately less strained...I really rather like her & hope she won't deteriorate. Then I trotted on to Mrs Johnson; she's old and white haired & a little deaf but quite nice too. She evidently considers Science & Medecine much below her notice and I expect to find her of little use to me practically; of course she keeps up the social side of the job more. And she obviously considers herself above modern side [science?] & reverts constantly to the Classics & the good old days.

All that probably doesn't interest you, so I'll stop. I was able to go on & see your Mother. I arrived and yelled 'Mrs Slater' all over the place. Suddenly a strange voice from the kitchen said 'Is that you, Miss Mollie?' I nearly had a fit, because it had been too dark outside to read the number & I suddenly thought I'd arrived at the wrong place. However there was nothing for it but to pretend I thought everything correct, so I went to the top of the kitchen stairs & said 'No, it's –it—it's Joyce Cockram.' Then to my delight Patrick appeared & made some cutting remark. I *was* glad to see him. The old girl who answered me is your Mother's maid. She seems awfully nice & homely—though rather ancient...then your Mother appeared...We had a long 'chat' and I got the...film I'll take to Druce on Monday. Patrick and I raised our voices in song and the beautiful notes of old folksongs from the boy's & girl's sweet voices rang in the clear frosty air—which isn't right because the sentence isn't balanced & we had a fire. However you gather that we gave a performance of 'The Jolly Waggoner', 'The wraggle taggle gipsies' etc. Your Mother showed me a letter from you which she had this morning, at least she read me extracts...I thought Mrs Slater looked tired but well and she seemed more cheerful than I'd expected as today has been rather depressing as regards weather etc. Patrick of course requires no squashing. I mean he requires a lot—but I think he's more obedient than he was. (You don't mind my saying so, do you? It's too late to cross it out.)

I saw Hugh yesterday...He & Joan [Anderson] both saw 'Dear Brutus' & didn't tell me it was here. I am so disappointed, as I wanted to see it awfully, especially when you'd said it was good...I'm frightfully fed up, because the nasty man who was staying here in the spring...is in Somerville[169] with a wound in his arm which will keep him there some time. Luckily he isn't up yet. When he is, he'll probably be down here every day & I loathe him. It's such an effort to be decently polite with some people to whom one has no aversion, but to a man like him—it's the limit...The Andersons send the usual messages. Joan is taking up music seriously.

Edna Brown to Owen, 16 October 1918

My dear Mr Slater, I have nothing of any importance to do this afternoon so I thought I would write to you, that is if you have no objection.

I have written this out once & Ida came in & said 'You had better be careful of your writting, don't forget Owen's a character reader,' so I am writing it again.

Last Monday all the family went down to hear Sapper Balderstone recite—it took place in the Chapel, he was ever so nice, I believe it was the night you came up to 29 & found us out that we went to hear him at the schoolroom.

Neither Ida or I told you that Aunty has been staying with us for a fortnight. Aunty foretold in my tea cup that a tall dark boy is going to fall in love with me but it is not going to be genuine... Our cousin Reg (Lieut. Hawes) is getting better. Things must be brighting up now, since I bought 2 lbs of cheese this morning. Everybody seems very hopeful about the war at present.

A man who calls daily with shrimps round Stuart Rd, one day he came calling the usual cry 'Fine *Large* Shrimps', Dorothy was sent out to buy some, & he remarked 'Tell yer Mother they're rather *Small* today.'... Every evening the schoolroom has to be closed promply by nine, owing to the shortage of coal & gas.

Lieut. Jeffrys had his arm in a sling on Sunday... he looked very unwell. He has one of his sons here, by name Norman, he is the one who was discharged from the navy, he is now in seconds [?] & expects to be called up any time. I like him ever so much, but it is not the one that is to fall in love with me, because he is fair. Did you notice any particuly dark person while you were here? I am most anxious to know him.

Ida Brown to Owen, 16 October 1918

As Edna is writing to you I thought I would just put a note in. By the way I hope you don't think you have to answer all these letters if so you will be feeling very bored. I believe you promised to write a letter once a week and a Field P.C. three times a day directly after meals. However we must not expect too much from you. I don't suppose you will often feel like writing.

Aunty has been staying here, but she developed influenza, spent several days in bed then went back to Portsmouth...She left Mother in bed with the same complaint.

Marjorie and I are off to Portsmouth next week...The 'flu' epidemic is very bad down there & they are having many deaths so its not a very cheerful outlook for us...Mother and I dreamt of you last night but Mother has forgotten hers. I dreamt you had come back. You were sitting in the easy chair & we were all so pleased to see you. You said that they had sent all the young officers back to England for Home Service and were only going to keep the old officers in France. Outside waited your motor car which was a lovely four seater. You had arranged to take us for a ride. When I said it was rather risky, you might be fined for wasting petrol you said: 'I don't care about wasting petrol. I'm going to take you all for a ride.' We were just putting our hats and coats on when I awoke. I should think that this portends you are coming home soon.

Can't think of any more this time. You know the saying 'A good beginning makes a bad ending'. I think it will be so in this case. This will be the fourth letter from 29 this week. We all send heaps of love.

P.S. We see by the morning paper that the Kaiser has to move. I wonder if he has found another house.[170]

―――∞∞∞―――

Joan George to Owen, 17 October 1918

I haven't written to you for some time so I am going to make a violent attempt to clear my concience now.

Mother & Miss de Brisay are gone to an Anthropological Society meeting this evening... & I am left with many instructions about kettles, gas, & making cocoa for their return—as usual I am wondering how many I will remember & quake in my shoes for their poor insides over the cocoa!!! I have done nothing but write letters all afternoon... I am tired & my head aches a bit, I am *sick* of writing letters but I just had to write to you tonight—it is such a glorious night. Do you remember what a glorious moon light—starlight night it was this time [in] 1916 when I went off to Darby [Derby?] the next day & I went to listen to you playing & then you came home (a very roundabout way) with me? *Do* you remember Owen? I often think of that night—you were such a dear to me Tufty.

Dear I must stop. I can hardly see what I am doing & I must go & make that wretched cocoa. I am sure to do something silly with it. I feel so wuzzy & tired! Such a sleepy girl it is!

Good night dear. God bless you & keep you safe. Your loving, Joan

Owen to his mother, 18 October 1918

A month ago I left England, to me it seems absolutely ages. I do hope the war will be over soon but everybody seems to be turning out rotters in the way they break all their original war aims etc & after the first touch of victory become perfectly reconciled to the use of unlimited force. As regards news there is precious little to tell you—the mail from Blighty has got hung up somewhere... Today for the first time I had a job to do—clearing out a drain—not a particularly elevating job I can tell you but not too bad... Life out here is in its way rather fun. I can now quite realise what Bilson said about being a father to your men. This evening I had the job of issuing rum. You wander round to the billets with the sergeant major when he dishes out a pannikin full to each man while you stand by to see fair play & make remarks. It is quite interesting. This afternoon I wandered up to an aerodrome quite close to us here to have a look round & also incidentally to see if I could get a joy ride but they were all too busy. I have just had a postcard from the Browns asking me for correspondence so I must make an attempt to write soon.

P.S. We are still out on rest.

Violet to Gilbert, 18 October 1918*

How I wish you were here to help in the fight there must be to gain a really democratic peace... I hope the very miserable moral quality of our men in power will awaken the best [word indecipherable] of those who have a spiritual vision to work & pray for a Peace Conference that shall be so wise in the decisions, so internationally just that we may get rid of the ghastly menace of possible war... We must not forget our own past that has helped towards the world catastrophe... We must not forget that we tried to starve Germany & Austria & apparently succeeded in doing so, their aged—women, children who have died... Well dear heart I believe you stand for International democracy. Each country has its War Party.

Owen to his mother, 19 October 1918

We are still out on rest thank goodness... Daily I am getting to know my section better though I don't know them all by names yet. The more I see of them the nicer lot of fellows they seem. This afternoon we had a shooting competition between teams of 8 chosen from each section & my 8 won... The prize is 50 francs between the 8.

Today I had a ripping surprise: I got a horse. Before I hadn't had a horse of my own but any old thing from the section & I had only ridden once. It is a ripping little black mare, quite young, about six years old & 14 hands high, a hand is four inches. I don't know what to call her, do suggest a name. The only thing I have thought of so far is Joan as she is rather like her [Joan George] in one or two ways; not particularly tall, well built & inclined to podginess, nevertheless in jolly good condition & quite strong. I had a little ride this afternoon before the shooting & enjoyed it like anything but I didn't get a chance of trying any jumps unfortunately. This morning I went to a Field Cashier to get a field cheque book & found that I can draw money to the extent of 125 francs [£5] a time three times a month, so under no circumstances can I spend very much.

Gilbert to Owen, 19 October 1918 from Bangalore

I am hoping that your job is that of restoring roads and bridges in the country over which the Allied armies have passed in their victorious march, so that you are able to help in the work of saving humanity & civilisation from Prussianism, without being in great danger yourself. It must be a wonderful experience, & I hope you are using all the French you know to the utmost. We have just had a premature report that the Kaiser has abdicated, and peace assured; which of course excited us as it must have the people at home, improbable as it was. Nevertheless the surrender of Lille [on 17 October] without destruction, of which we heard last night, shows that Germany knows she is beaten, and that additional crimes will bring additional punishment.[171] So there is good reason to hope for peace by Christmas, and I think it is now more probable than not that I shall be able to use my return ticket next March. I wonder how long it will be that you will be retained in the army. I presume the R.E. will be kept at work after the Infantry & Artillery are sent

home, but only a fraction of them, I suppose, will be needed, so that dis-
charges will be taking place gradually. Possibly they may give you the
choice of being discharged in France, and of receiving your return fare
and making your own way home—if so you might seize the opportunity of doing a little travel. It would be very jolly if this came off just as
I pass through France.

Mrs D. Brown to Violet, [20 October 1918]

Thank you for letter and photographs received this morning, it was so
very kind of you to let us read Owen's. We gather from that that the dear
boy knows that [what] it is to be close to the firing line, also that his
brother officers are not very companionable men for him which is a
great pity. Poor Owen used to get very homesick even here. We sometimes called him the 'homesick babe'—it was a name he gave himself.
We do indeed hope with you that our brave defenders will soon be
home again, events seem to be moving very quickly towards that end—
The wounded men and those coming into the town on leave are delighted with all that is happening and really seem more hopeful of an
early peace than the people who merely read the papers. We received a
letter from Owen on the 12th, the girls have written him and are
watching the posts in hoping to get another soon ... We receive a lot of
letters from the Front but must hand Owen the 'Palm' for his interesting
descriptions, his account of the voyage across was so realistic that as
someone remarked 'one could feel the ship rock'. More about the
photos, we think some of them are really good and should like to get
some enlargements. May we ask you for the films ... It is a wet and
dreary day. Three Scotchmen have just come in to enjoy our fire-side in
preference to their wet tents. They seem so loathe to put the men into
billets but if red tape says they must keep in tents until Nov: 1st well: it
must be right; and these brave fellows keep smiling, they are a lesson to

all of us who still enjoy our home comforts and an unbroken family circle. I don't know what the controller would say if he looked into our breakfast room & saw a large fire with 3 khaki coats round it trying to get themselves dry. I only hope we shall not have our gas supply cut off bye & bye as we have no cooking stove other than gas. However we must not look foreward to such a calamity especially as we may be eating turkeys etc by Christmas.

Mr Brown and the girls join in very kind regards to you. I am yours very sincerely D. Brown.

Gilbert to Violet, 21 October 1918* from Madras

I got back here yesterday morning & this morning [found your] letters…the last enclosing Owen's [orders for] his final leave and orders for the Front. I *am* glad to see that [he] is at first for more training…so try hard, dearest one, to be only a little anxious about him.

You ask me to tell you more clearly what I think [about] the war. I expect I have in previous letters, but one is always slightly modifying one's position. I am now much more hopeful that peace when it comes will be permanent. I believe in President Wilson, & don't at all think he has been rushed or carried [along]. I consider that he is practically in control of the Allied [Powers and that] no other ally can afford to quarrel with him, & I believe [he] has America as a whole firmly at his back. And I believe [that] his only aim is permanent peace. He will dictate terms while, of course, results may not come up to hopes, the fact [that] the terms will not be the ordinary compromise between [conflicting] ambitions, but worked out *in order to ensure* peace means a good start…I think that this experience of war will give [an impetus] to all efforts to perfect the Peace…There was hope that if Germany had given up submarinism, diplomatic pressure might avail…But as soon as it was absolutely [clear] that nothing would stop the war except force, he [had] to work to use force effectively to stop it. The only criticism one can make against America is that if America had [set] to work to arm at the very beginning of war, the mere [ability] to land 2,000,000 American soldiers in France, [with] another 3,000,000 to follow, without the actual [ending] of the threat, might have sufficed. A similar criticism can be applied to ourselves. If we had been prepared for war, the announcement that we would go to any length rather than allow France to be crushed would probably have prevented the war.

I agree that if there had been no corruption in British [word indecipherable] and no greed in British commerce that the war [would have] been over before this; though I am not sure exactly [words indecipherable] this. I mean that we should have had greater strength & so should have beaten Germany.[172]

Owen to his mother, 21 October 1918*

I sent you off a field card last night because I was too tired to do anything else…I was called soon after five in the morning & had to go out with another officer to do some reconnaissance. We had breakfast & got off at about 6.30 on horse back. It was really rather jolly riding. We went out towards the front line, left our horses behind the crest of a hill & then went forwards on foot to look at the different roads & bridges. I had my first experience of shell fire & I admit it fairly unnerved me. The nearest one was about a 100 yards away but the whole thing was an unpleasant experience. We got back to the company about 2 o'clock & found they had moved to a neighbouring village. I found my billet and went to bed and slept till about 7.30 and woke with a beastly headache & feeling of sickness, came up to the mess & sent off a field card to you & then went back to bed & slept in fits & starts till the morning. Now thank goodness I am feeling much better after a wash, a shave & breakfast. I am billeted at a house…& really am as comfortable as one could hope to be. Oudney who was out reconoitering with me is sharing the bed. [Violet Slater: It is to be hoped a room!] The woman who owns the house is awfully nice & dried our coats...& gave us coffee both in the evening & the morning. Yesterday I saw her roasting it & it was most excellent coffee—black & she offered us a bowl of sugar to help ourselves from. I have never enjoyed black coffee so much before. Even after my night's rest I am still as tired as anything & can hardly think. One cannot realize in the slightest what war is like until you have seen a little of it. I am sure I have seen quite enough & what little it was has made me feel quite different. I am afraid I can't explain in the slightest what I mean. Probably I shall have recovered completely in a couple of days.

I am awfully pleased with my little horse. I only wish I could keep it for good. It went rippingly yesterday though it got pretty well soaked...Still no mail has come in, the latest rumour is that it will arrive later this morning...The only way to avoid disappointment is never to expect a letter before it comes...I hope & pray that the war will be over this year. It is such a ghastly waste of everything & I am perfectly sure that if all the militarists in England experienced just a little bit of it they would seize any reasonable opportunity for making peace.

Owen to his mother, 22 and 23 October 1918

Just a line to give you my love. At the present moment we are out in the open more or less. We have got the cellar of a house that has disappeared & consider ourselves very lucky to have a table & two chairs in it. The sappers have dug themselves little holes in the bank of a road.

23.10.18. I haven't had time to continue before now so I will go on where I left off. Our cellar unfortunately was just at a cross roads which in this part of the country is generally rendered unhealthy by shells. However nothing landed nearer than 200 yards & only about three in the neighbourhood. The reason I couldn't go on with my writing last night was first that lots of senior officers kept looking in & monopolising attention, table, chairs, & light & afterwards I had to go out on a reconnaissance. It was quite fun being busy though I spent most of the night cycling about the country over cobbled roads & started off with my section soon after 7 o'clock. Now we are settled down for the night in a house & field the Germans were in [in] the morning. In consequence of all my exertions I am now pretty tired but not so until just now as I have been very busy nearly every minute. There is nothing exciting to tell you so I will send this off while I get the chance. By the bye with the ten letters I received a book from the Browns 'The Monastery'[173] & also the parcel containing the sketch book & helmet. I will thank Mrs Grafflin for it as soon as I get the chance & now I will hie me to my bed & sleep as long as I can. [This is the 'helmet' Owen requested on 1 October.] Sorry this isn't any longer.

⸺⸙⸺

Hugh Cockram to Owen, 23 October 1918

There is a rumour that D'oyly Carte's are coming next term, which is splendid. There is hardly anything worth going to this term except the Carl Rosa's,[174] which are rather expensive, I think! I have now formally joined the Oxford Bucks Light Inf. 1st Vol. Batl…By joining the thing I have been & let myself in for a lot. On Friday for instance, there is a 'full marching order & pack' inspection…Preparing for this we had to go to a parade last Friday at 2 & last Monday at 7.30 in the County Hall. That not being enough, tomorrow at 1.15 we have to join a procession canvassing for War Bonds in which will be a gun, R.A.F., Cadets & O.B.L.I.V.R. [Oxfordshire & Buckinghamshire Light Infantry Volunteer Regiment] & Boy Scouts etc. We have to walk round the town for 2 hours…We had a novel experience last night. In the words of my official report [as Senior Prefect]:- 'C. W. Bushell (i.e. tertius) was found to be the originator of numerous drawings on library property, an offence

197

which was increased by the fact that he had taken a map from the current issue of the Times without making any attempt to obtain leave first. As warnings against each of these delinquencies had been frequently made, a strong action was deemed necessary, & after being reminded of his right of appeal, he received 4 strokes of the cane from J. E. Bushell (maj) who discovered the offender.' What do you think of that eh? It was jolly funny seeing one bro. jaw another!…Brigger is now a Captain in the O.B. [Oxfordshire and Buckinghamshire]…Joyce is taken by Walden twice a week I believe, but he is all right with girls I believe!

Edna Brown to Owen, 23 October 1918*

Your letter to Ida arrived this morning. She as you know is in Portsmouth so we have sent it on to her…It is awfully lonely without the girls you cannot imagine what a miss they are. Mother has gone to a meeting this afternoon…so I am Mother for a short while. Poor old boy is home with a cold we do hope he is not going to have the flue—it is something dreadful in this country, but it is not so bad here as it is in other places. Norman hardly knows what to do with himself at present he is amusing himself by making a Calander for 1919.

We are looking forward to your coming home. When one thinks about it, it is really not very long before your leave…I do hope the War will be over before my sixteenth birthday so that we can have you here…This coming Sunday we are having Sapper Sweetman & his wife & Sapper Lilycrape to tea. I wish we were having you instead.

Last Monday evening Mother, Kervin, & I went to the Literary [Society]. It was question night, one of the questions which were asked was 'When is the war going to end'. Mother stood up & recited this little poem, I don't know whether you know it or not. 'Actual Evidence have I none, but my wife's washerwoman's sister's son, heard a policeman on his beat, say to a [housemaid in Downing Street, That he had a brother, who had a friend, Who knew when the war was going to end.]"[175]

———❦———

Violet to Owen, 24 October 1918

I am glad you have a little black horse. I hope she has a sweet temper and that you will love her and she you, it's very nice to have something to love. You will have to make her acquaintance carefully so that she understands. I suggest 'Black Beauty' for her name or 'Beauty', but 'Joan' isn't bad and is nice and short...I wanted to go to the Fellowship of Remembrance [Reconciliation] meeting. Oliver Sturt[176] is home and came in to ask me to go to the theatre with them...but I didn't feel inclined...my mind is the whole time occupied with the war and what one can do to bring about a better spirit because Peace will only be the beginning of our opportunity. I really think we must have a daily Labour paper.[177] And I think we must—those of us who care—try to get the truth told. At present the public are fed on just what is allowed mentally as well as physically. Are my letters to you censored? I wonder? Not that I would put anything unpatriotic in them. I consider that those of us who want to save the world from needless slaughter and misery are the true patriots. I cannot believe it is wise to stifle opinion...Oliver looks very fine in his naval uniform. He is home for 3 weeks because there was so much influenza at the Crystal Palace where he is training that 20 died of it so there was a panic and the others were all sent home and the whole place is being disinfected. It is quite a plague...We are taking quinine which I hope is a preventative[178]...I am so glad that you like your men and think them 'nice fellows'. I hope you will get to know them...Have you ever met a teetotaller or non-smoker?

———❦———

Ida Brown to Owen, 25 October 1918 from 'Somewhere in England', written on notepaper headed Royal Corps of Naval Constructors

Parsnips have gone up. 'Orace will miss Marjorie. Robin and Crusoe are singing a duet in the old yew tree. Turnips have gone down. 'Subtle very'. Mixed biscuits are 1/8 a lb. Oranges are very scarce. Unsweetened milk is still very scarce. Twinkle twinkle little star. Heads I close Tails I don't, it has come down heads so Goodbye. I.B.

P.S. I have imagined in the foregoing letter that we want to give you the name of the town where we are staying but it has to pass the censor. He would be very sharp if he saw through it. We are having quite a good time and the weather so far has been lovely. The first day … we went to Ryde … There are great doings here in connection with the War Loans. Every one is rushing to 'Feed the Guns'. At the Town Hall there is a great display of guns which have been brought back from France. Model dugouts and all kinds of various war trophies. At night they play search lights on to the Town Hall. It looks lovely, outlined against the dark sky.

Your letter has just come. I did not think you would get that post card because we had no address … The day after I posted it we had a letter from you saying you were just off up the line. You were feeling very blue and asked us to write. Well, I wrote a long letter that night and so did Edna. About three days after we both wrote again but evidently you have not received them … We have only received three of yours … We have written five times so there must be something wrong somewhere.

We are glad you have a nice lot of men. I hope they will take kindly to their new father. What about the officers, have you found a nice chum amongst them? It must have been a thrilling sight to see you clear that drain. What a lot of things one learns to do in the Army.

The 'flu' epidemic is very bad here. All the schools are closed and this week they are closing all places of amusement. It nearly always proves fatal, and hundreds are dying. We are taking every precaution. Marjorie had a letter from a friend at Chatham—she says whole families are dying. The schools are all closed…It seems to be all over the country.

One evening we went to the Promenade concert in the Town Hall. There were only two artists, the rest of the programme was filled in by the Orchestra which was grand. They played several pieces from Grieg, Beethoven, Tschaikowsky and Verdi. Mendelssohn's Bees Wedding [*Songs Without Words*, Book 6, No. 4, 'Das Spinnerlied'] was lovely and so was Handel's Largo. This letter is being written in installments. I started it two days ago but there is really no time for writing we are gadding about such a lot…really one soon tires of this sort of life…I am longing to get back to the [Sunday] school to serve lonely home sick Tommies with cups of tea…We have not found any one to take your place yet and I don't think we shall.

This morning we went over the Royal Yacht [*Victoria and Albert III*]. It is anchored right up the other end of the harbour so we went over in a steam launch. Uncle came with us but he had no sooner got on board when the Admiral sent for him so he had to go back. Of course everything is packed away. The carpets are all up and the furniture covered over, but it was well worth going to see. All the paint is white and instead of wall paper the walls are covered with chintz. In the Queen's bedroom are some lovely water colour paintings and several photos of different members of the family. We went into the room where the china is kept. There is a lovely tea service, each cup costs 27/-. The drawing room is not very large, but beautifully furnished. There is a lovely grand piano which we both played. There is a table which [Queen] Alexandra calls her kitchen table. This she uses when pasting snap shots in her album. We spent nearly two hours on board. We got down the companion ladder safely. Going up was bad enough. But coming down was far worse. There were 30 stairs nearly perpendicular. It was an awful sensation to stand at the top and look down…I'm afraid I feel awfully wicked enjoying myself like this in war time. I have just finished reading [E. F.] Benson's new book 'Up & Down'. It's rather good. I expect you would like it because there is no love story in it.

Sunday afternoon. We went to the dockyard Church this morning… After Church Uncle took us round the yard. It is very interesting to see the different types of ships in dock. There is a large American boat with the front part of the ship completely blown away, and several of our largest battleships in for repairs. There were two ships just off to France being loaded with R.A.F. motor lorries and ambulances, aeroplanes and coal trucks.

Owen to his mother, 26 October 1918

I'm so sorry I couldn't write to you during the last two or three days, but we have been having very exciting times & very busy. During the last two days I have been out with my section & another section away from the rest of the company. We have been working near the front line & luckily have only had one casualty. I have had a certain time for writing but unfortunately couldn't get hold of any writing paper. I did one or two sketches in my new book…We are going out tomorrow & I have to go out early to get billets. I shall hope to get a good letter to you tomorrow as on the whole I have a lot of interesting things to tell you. I have not got much time now. I have just marched six miles & had dinner & I want to go to bed…Please tell me whenever my letters are opened by the censor & if they are whether anything is cut out…I'm sorry but I must get off to bed.

On 27 October, Erich Ludendorf, who had been, with Hindenburg, the driving force behind the German war machine, resigned. The following day the crew aboard SMS Markgraf mutinied when ordered to get ready for another attack on British ships and the mutiny spread throughout the German fleet. Two days later Turkey, a major German ally, signed an armistice.

Gilbert to Owen, 27 October 1918

You must now have been in France for about 5 weeks. I suppose you are still receiving instruction, but perhaps they utilise even men under instruction in the work of repairing roads & bridges in the country from which the Germans have been driven. I hope you are able to contribute something to the needs of poor France; and that no mischance comes to you in the doing of it. The news of the surrender of Bulgaria came just at the same time as the wire; and now things are looking continually more hopeful in the direction of Austria. It is wonderful; how quickly the position has changed. Up to July 19 the Germans were, with minor set backs, continually victorious, & we seemed further off the end than ever—then, in one day, the tide turned, and already, in the space of little over 3 months, by far the greater part of occupied France has been liberated, & the coast of Belgium, & about half Serbia; &, for ought I know, peace may come before this letter reaches you...I hope you had a good time your last week of leave, and that just as you were lucky in finding friends everywhere in England, it may be the same in France. And I hope you will go as far as military etiquette will let you—and stretch it as far as possible—to get into friendly relations with any men you may have to command. Don't be shy with them, any more than you can help. Bear yourself as though you were quite sure of yourself, & don't be afraid of a joke.

My book 'Some South India Villages' got bound and delivered while I was away, which was rather a nuisance...The influenza has been as bad as a visitation of plague—between 3,700 & 3,800 deaths in Madras in a fortnight. Nobody knows what is the mortality in the villages. The people have poor constitutions, (owing to vegetarianism, dirty habits which infect them with worms, too early marriages of girls & sexual excess of boys & men, and malaria), & they knock under & have little notion of taking care of themselves. So it is no wonder they die, but the rate is enormous—last week's deaths, if continued at the same rate, would wipe out the whole population of the City of Madras in 5 years. If the monsoon come in earnest, it would probably do a lot of good. It might wash down the town, & diminish the disease germs, and it would give the people the idea that the gods—or goddesses—were becoming benevolent again, & they would pluck up courage.

I do wonder how you are getting on, & whether your French is good enough to be of any use to you—also in what part you are. Tell all you can, when you get opportunities of writing. God be with you, my dear boy, Your loving Father, Gilbert Slater

Owen to his mother, 28 October 1918*

As I told you we are out on rest & in consequence I have had any amount of letters from my section to censor. Today I have had a job erecting a stage for a Divisional Concert Party going by the name of the 'Shrapnels'…Next door to the house where my section is billeted, there is an old woman not at all old really with her husband & daughter, farmers but not doing anything now except in the garden. They are awfully nice & I go in & chat for an hour or so every day. There is a son who is in the French army & they have had no news of him for four years but now have had word [that he has got leave and can] visit them. They had hidden some grain for these years not being able to take it out for fear of having it confiscated & this evening *la fermiere* [ground some] in a coffee mill.

Violet to Owen, 30 October 1918

Auntie Agnes is here…Pat is much better today & I trust has not taken cold. I let him get up & while I was upstairs he went out on to the verandah & got sticks & I came down to find both door & window open. The danger of the 'flu' is when convalescent, an enormous number of people have died of pneumonia. It upset me very much for I have been taking such care of him & petting him, giving him all sorts of things & he is really old enough to know he was doing wrong [but] of course he did. Well never mind.

I do hope that the Paris conversations are going on well & that the armistice will come before long & the shells cease dropping & the guns firing & the boys come home. Agnes talks of sending a Christmas parcel! In my heart I am thinking that perhaps you will be home. I imagine it. One may as well. I find out how much I imagine it when other people talk as if the war were a permanence...Eliot is better. I had a card from him this morning—he said there were only 10 boys well in Grove House & no maids so the 10 boys had to be skivvies!...He doesn't mention any serious case—so I hope that they have none...Goodnight my darling. I remember that there was a Temperance song called 'Where is my boy tonight' that we used to sing at Band of Hope meetings...Anyway that is what I always feel. I long so much for the whole thing to stop & for the world to have a chance of becoming sane again.

Owen to his mother, 1 November 1918

The second little sketchbook also arrived & in that you asked me various questions which I shall endeavour to answer. To start with I have a section of nominally 36 men, 6 of them are N.C.O.s but there are usually about 6 men doing something special so that they hardly count as belonging to the section, as company postman or orderly officers, servant, officers, cook etc. My N.C.O.s consist of one sergeant, one full corporal, two second corporals & two lance corporals. They are all pretty efficient particularly my sergeant who is an old regular soldier who has been out all through the war. The majority of my men are about thirty...They are all very good fellows not a single one I would class as a rotter, though one or two are not quite up to the standard of the others.

Yesterday was a fairly busy day in so much as we did practically nothing. In the morning for an hour & a half I sharpened shovels or rather a couple of my men did. In the afternoon we had an inspection by some old general or other. We had to get to the parade ground abominably early, had an hour to wait & it poured with a steady drizzle that ate into the marrow of your bones…In the evening I patronised some officers' baths that have been rigged up here & had a sumptuous hot bath. This morning I had rather a nice job. I had to scrounge for shovels & picks: I sent out half a dozen men to wander over the country & search while I went on my dear little Joan. I had a ripping morning riding though I was rather rattled as two men disappeared. I found them all right when I got back to the billets. In the afternoon we had a memorial service for our poor old major in a barn with half the roof off.

I ought to have told you to start with that we are still out at rest but expecting to go in again any day. This evening I am going to a concert in the hall where I was rigging up the stage etc. I think I told you that I had made friends with an old French couple…I went in there the other morning & brought them a present of several boxes of matches whereat they were mightily bucked & gave me coffee & some strange salad…It is extraordinary how tired one gets. I generally go to bed at 9.30 & get up at 7.30 when I am lucky though occasionally I have to get up at 6.

Please…take care of yourselves against influenza. There is very little in the company only 1%.

Owen to his mother, 2 November 1918

We are still out on rest & rumours of peace keep flying around & by the men's conversation & letters they all seem to think that the war will be over this year. How unutterably glorious that would be. I had quite a jolly job today which involved my using my horse the only thing was that it rained most of the time…Our mess has hardly a single pane of glass whole & today the gaps have been made up with sheets of oiled cotton & now the room is very much darker but warmer thank goodness. Just outside runs the main street of pavé cobble stones & lorries & guns passing make a deafening noise so that you can hardly hear yourself speak.

Owing presumably to going occasionally for five or six days without a shave I can now scrape along without looking too disreputable with a shave every other day which is of course a saving of time & means that I can stay so much longer in bed. I sleep very well, but whenever I turn over or wriggle my bed makes the most horrible screeches.

Last night I went to a concert given by the Shrapnels, very good in its way & some of the turns were really excellent. One juggler was very clever but the best by far was a violinist who played most beautifully. The last half of the programme was entirely cinematograph which was not particularly high class.

On 3 November the Austro-Hungarian Monarchy signed an armistice agreement with the Allies in Padua.

Owen to his mother, 3 November 1918*

We are still out on rest...I am very sorry to hear that both Pat & Eliot have got flue. I do hope you won't get it...Wasn't it beastly for Uncle Harold having the whole family down with it & having to nurse them all. There is very little of it in the company & the few cases there have been are all going on well. We are all well fed & clothed & there are fires in nearly all the section billets so everybody is comfortable.

The end of the war seems very close now, most people here put it at about a fortnight to a month. I hope they are right. Though I am certain that we are absolutely defeating our ends in asking for unconditional surrender. That will just about firmly establish militarism in all the fighting countries. International socialism is the obvious remedy but everyone I have met out here so far is so unutterably pig headed. Speaking with the men you get on all right up to a certain point. Then they will suddenly make a remark that dashes one to the ground as far as internationalism applied to war is concerned.

One gets very little chance of sketching. I tried to get a glorious [word indecipherable] French peasant but before I could even get the outline sketched in she went off.

Owen to Mrs Grafflin, 3 November 1918*

This is just a very short note to thank you for the knitted helmet that Mother sent me from you some time ago. It is very comfortable & most useful as I wear it under my tin hat, a shrapnel helmet which is very large for me & it makes it a beautiful fit.

We are now out at rest & have been out of the line for several days & have been having quite a good time though we have not had any football matches & the whole company is feeling rather cut up because our O.C. [Officer Commanding] has died of wounds. He was an excellent [word indecipherable] father to his men & officers.

Agnes Peacock to Gilbert, 4 November 1918

I write in hope that you will get this in time for Christmas…It will indeed be a good Christmas if peace is assured by then; and surely everything points to that possibility. I am sending you a letter of Owens…I think he writes very nice letters & it is good that he is in better spirits, poor dear boy, than when he first went. It seems extra hard that all the boys in France & Flanders have to go on whilst there is cessation on the other Front. Of course I suppose our troops from Austria & Mesopotamia will come to France and so the Germans are up against a much bigger thing. It seems impossible that they can go on. However, long before this reaches you we shall know Germany's fate. I am not blood thirsty but I wish to goodness the Kaiser would fall into his own peoples hands. It is suggested he may take refuge in England & then I suppose we could place a Royal Palace at his disposal!

Violet will have told you I have just been three days with her in Oxford, the visit nearly did not come off because of Pat's influenza, but he was about well and I trust now that Violet is going to escape...Violet had several letters from Owen whilst I was there & two from you, one in which you spoke of the possibility of your tour with her to Japan, California etc. How deliriously thrilling it sounds. I began to consider whether it was worth while to be without one's husband more or less for five years to finish up so gloriously...I spent one day with Aunt Annie & had hoped to see Eliot, but unfortunately he was laid up just at the time. Influenza has been & is very bad here, Jim is going all the time. It is mostly children who are ill & of course they close the schools too late. There have been several very sad deaths...I am sending Owen's letter for Mary to see.

Gilbert to Owen, 5 November 1918

The mail leaves today, and it may well be the last before Christmas— though perhaps submarining will stop now[179]...I have had several of your letters to Mother from France, & your last from Chatham to me & the snap shots of the Browns. They are very jolly & one of Edna, apparently sitting on a see saw is particularly jolly. I do hope you get your Christmas leave; & that, what looks so very likely will come off—peace before Christmas...The Syndicate determined yesterday evening to ask Government to provide Rs 50,000 a year to establish a permanent Chair of Economics. It won't affect me, but it is a feather in my cap. It means that I have convinced *the University* that it is worth while to have a University department of Economics, & to spend three times (nearly) as much on it as hitherto...You are an awfully good boy to write so often. Try not to be homesick!

[P.S.] Here's to a Merry Christmas in Oxford for you, and a happy new year.

—◆◆◆—

Joyce Cockram to Owen, 6 November 1918 from Oxford

I was extremely bucked to get a field card from you yesterday. I hadn't heard for nearly a month! Mrs. Slater said I ought to write and say 'Don't trouble to write to me'; I know you're awfully busy and I can get all your news from your Mother.' Not I! I hope the letter, following at the earliest opportunity, will turn up soon.

I saw your Mother on Saturday. Miss (Bother, I can't remember her name. Patrick calls her 'Auntie' and your Mother 'Susie' I think.) was spending the week end with her, so she was exceedingly cheerful. Patrick has quite recovered—in fact he upset the kettle (the wretched boy fell over it) just before tea and we had a fine old time mopping up our only boiling water (you probably don't see the connection. I mean to imply that he is quite as wicked now as ever.) Mrs Smith amused me so much. I rushed downstairs for a bucket and floor cloth and tried to explain to her what had happened and all she could say was 'Lor Miss there now! You don't say so.' Meanwhile the whole of the dining room was being flooded out.

I am frightfully busy this term. Did I tell you that I am trying Chemistry, Botany and Zoology Prelims: this term? I am not particularly upset about the Chemistry and Botany…but I am afraid the Zoo is rather hopeless. We began with the frog. Mine rejoiced in the name of Amelia. (She is no more.)

—◆◆◆—

Violet to Owen, 6 November 1918

The papers are horribly disappointing, apparently the Allies are going to push the thumb screw on & make it as difficult as they possibly can for the

Germans to leave off fighting As Patrick says 'It's like kicking a boy after you've licked him.' The worst of it is that they get other people to do the kicking & to pay the penalty. Last week—November 1st—the D.N. [*Daily News*] says Our Lobby Correspondent predicts that Germany is nearing the end & that hostilities will end next week. But apparently the Versailles Council has decreed otherwise. I think that the epidemic of 'flu' is decreasing. Poor Dr Gillett looks awfully tired. He was at the F.o.R. meeting tonight.

We have had a beautiful autumn day. Patrick went back to school. There are only 36 & several masters are away so they have quite different lessons.

I have written a letter to the *Pioneer*…suggesting that all who care for Cooperation & Democracy should refuse to buy Northcliffe papers & only read them at the librarys & to buy the others (by the by I only know the D.N.[180] I believe the [*Daily*] *Chronicle* has been bought up) but out of 17,000,000 one ought to be able to make some reduction.[181] But really one sees what an enormous power the capitalist press wield. Also to support Labour Papers & to go for a daily Labour Paper. Well it is late & I must stop & fill my footwarmer & to go up to your little peaceful room where I am longing for you to be. Learn all you can from your men. I must try to remember that mouth organ.

Violet to Gilbert, 6 & 7 November 1918*

~~Last week the D.N. Lobby correspondent predicted that hostilities would cease in about a week's time. Apparently the wretched Versailles council are not going to stop the fighting yet in spite of the ghastly cost of going on.~~ I wrote this last night. Today we hear that the Germans have sent Military & Naval delegates to receive from Marshal Foch[182] the terms of an Armistice & that the Allies are at last going to be willing to discuss terms on Wilson's 14 points. Thank God for President Wilson!

H. G. Wells has a splendid article on the Great Powers Idea [of] a League of Nations & the Foreign Office.[183] I must send it to you though I want to keep it to send it to Owen…it's an article I should like you to read because it represents so largely my views & whenever I've tried to argue on them people misunderstand & think I am desirous of finding fault with my own nation which is not the point [missing text] our sin is common [and] the whole method & spirit has to be changing & we must right it.

I have just been down to collect our ration of coal—they allow us 5 more tons so I am sure we shall have enough & they say I may [make] special application when you come home… so don't stop away for fear of cold. My darling of course I want you home at the end of five years—I shouldn't mind you stopping until March, and it would be glorious if we could go to Japan & America… You need not make definite plans so soon. Dear heart will such happiness come? And if only our boy can come back whole and safe. God grant it and yet my heart breaks that so many must mourn their loss. And if we had to be counting the number we should all the more set ourselves to make a better world. I long to help on a big scale, not all these necessary but tiny patching up. God bless you dear heart.

On 7 November German authorities opened negotiations with the Allies for an armistice while revolution broke out in various parts of Germany. Two days later Kaiser Wilhelm II fled to the Netherlands.

Owen to his mother, 7 November 1918

We have moved up towards the line but are still about the same distance away from it owing to an advance on the part of the infantry. We had an abominably long tramp mostly cross country owing to traffic on the main road. We have not done any work yet but will probably start to-morrow on uninteresting jobs of clearing roads… after arriving in our billet this evening a mail came up & I had your letter of the 29th which told me mainly about influenza. I do hope Eliot & Pat will have completely recovered by the time this arrives… I will try to get you a description of a shell some time when I am not so tired or so busy.

Violet to Owen, 7 November [1918]

At last there really is going to be an end. It must mean if Germany has sent Military and Naval Delegates to receive from Marshal Foch the Allies terms of armistice but best of all the Council of Versailles have agreed to President Wilson's bases. I thank God for President Wilson. I of course feel as if it is Peace already. But surely it does mean a cessation of fighting & that is what is wanted by all humane people…I have yours of 2 Nov. I hope you are still safe my darling. But today I am happy. The end is coming Thank God. 'Bow we our heads and humbly pray, That, if this terror may pass away, We may not preen our horrid pride, That fortune fought upon our side; Rather, God grant we may begin, To expiate our common sin, And guide our souls, which still the flesh, Must captive hold in quivering mesh, To bow to His eternal plan, And better love our brother-man.'[184] This ought to be written in verse but never mind. This is the spirit we want—we must recognise that individually we have good & evil in us & so nationally. It is common sin…God bless you dearest boy, your loving Mother

Violet to Owen, 7 and 8 November 1918 [10.30 p.m.]

My darling boy, the Toynbees have just been in to tell me that it is all over: that the German army has been cut in two and that it is 'unconditional surrender'. It is a ghastly finish, and will have cost many many lives and I suppose this is what we have been fighting for. My feelings are such a mixture. I am elated beyond words that all this shocking murder—for be sure it is nothing better—is ended that please God you are saved from a fate that has met so many. I am filled with fear that we may want a revengeful peace that will be no peace but a slumbering hate. God grant us something better! They said 'now you will sleep tonight' but I don't think I shall. I shall pray that we may be humbled as a nation and choose a better way…My boy we must all learn to consecrate our lives to the service of Christ in man…'In as much as ye do this unto the least of my brothers ye have also done it unto me' like the simple story of Tolstoy's old cobbler just every day to see Christ in our fellows…I pray that this terrible experience that you have gone through will have given you a vision of what is worth while and what is of no value.[185]

8 November 1918: This morning no papers arrived and I ran round to Mrs Grafflin's only to find that the report last night was not correct so the fighting must go on though the end must be very near. Still when I think of what it means it seems so unbearably cruel to go on after we have broken the Germans…I went round to give Joan and Mrs George your photographs…Mrs George was typing. I had a little talk with her but it isn't much good; she is a nice kind old thing but she is very imperialistic.

Violet to Gilbert, 7, 11, and 12 November 1918*

The Toynbees have just been in to tell me that the Great War (as Patrick calls it) is over, that the German Army has been cut in two by the Americans & it is 'unconditional surrender'! It is ghastly—an awful finish. I suppose we shall all rejoice but it is like the tearing down of a beaten animal by other animals for we might have saved many thousands of lives if we had stopped when we had beaten them. I suppose we have might…I feel ashamed. And yet I rejoice beyond all words that it is all over…Mrs Toynbee said now you will sleep…I can't possibly go to bed. My fire is nearly out &…I am cold. I have just made myself some bread & milk & I wish with all my heart I could sleep in your arms tonight & that I could just get you & Owen here. I wonder if you have heard…It may seem remarkable to you but I cannot help thinking of those defeated nations, how appalling it all seems. We must somehow refuse to build up another idol to crash to the ground. It is staggering to think of the heaped up dead, all the result of definite action not the result of any one nation alone. Our common sin.

11 November. Now the real thing has come that first report wasn't true the next morning we had it contradicted. Since then we have been on the rack not knowing what was coming…the war has ended. But what happenings! What is the future going to be? It does indeed seem as if it were all the birth pangs of democracy. There are possibilities of a magnificent future if only we get the right spirit to bring it in. One doesn't feel that our statesmen are suitable. The only suitable person is President Wilson. One wants someone better than poor old Balfour & the old diplomatists.[186] It looks as if the secret treaties will have to go. Our thoughts tumble upon each other; things have moved so quickly after the long dreary reign of evil…Oh how unspeakably relieved I shall be to hear that Owen is safe.

12 November. But you and I will never know in any way the horror of war. Of course the papers are full of the jubilation of the crowds & Bella Barnes wrote that London went mad. I heard some girls & I suppose men coming along they were singing 'Ho! Ho! Ho! He! He! He! Good old whisky's done for me.' 'I came rolling home' or some such worse than rubbish with no tune…All the flags are waving (of course we have some too!) & the city looks very gay with them. It was full of people standing about or walking or cycling up & down, undergraduates in taxis waving flags & shouting on top as well as inside, and best of all cadets marching along…now happier. The present attitude of Labour & the growing discontent in the Army makes one wonder what changes will come…Such idiotic things are said & the policy of thinking we can starve everyone [by the blockade] without having to pay for it is quite mad. As we have sown so shall we reap. In my opinion the bombardment was as bad as the sinking by U boats [text indecipherable]

The following letter refers to an emergency which Owen had to surmount when he was driving a 'tool cart' drawn by four horses. He was on a bridge which crossed a water-filled shell crater when a beam broke and two of the horses fell into the crater. He thought he would have to shoot them but in the event he managed to free them from their traces, replace the beam, and carry on.

Joan George to Owen, 14 November 1918

Thank you most awfully for your two letters…It is ripping of you to write to me so often and I do so love having them as you know. Poor horses dear—that fell into that crater because the beams gave way. I did feel so sorry for them!!! Don't you feel inclined to shout and dance—even though it is three days after the Armistice has been signed I feel so pleased and yet so very very sad

Last Saturday I cycled to Oxford [from Watlington] after work. I did wish so on the way too that you were there to keep me company for it is 14 miles and was very very dark and I had trouble with my lamps the whole time!! (Good Lorrd!!! Here's Crackers. Help and he is trying to telephone. Oh my I'll tell you about him in a minute!!) Finally I stopped at Stadhampton, found the 'Smith at his house and asked him to help me…We cycled into Thame last night Miss Coleman and I and I was just a-stopping to light my lamp again when 'someone' on a bicycle coming very quickly down the road jammed on brakes and said 'Hellow Hellow Hellow is that Miss Coleman?' and she said yes—I said 'Horrors!!' and it was Crackers—the last person we wanted to meet…Oh he's a jewel he is!! When he tries to phone he nearly kills me with laughter because he keep saying 'Hello are you there, are you there?' every few seconds. He starts like that every time he speaks into the receiver and he gets frightfully excited over anything…This is a frightfully unsatisfactory letter I am afraid.

L. R. Sofield to Owen, 14 November 1918
on mourning stationery

Dear Sir,
I thank you very much indeed for your most kind letter I received this evening. As you say I have heard of my dear brothers death[187] and I need

not tell you what a terrible shock it as [has] been for me, for I did think after all this time, and so near the end, that God would spare him to me. After losing our dear mother, he seem[ed] the only one that I had to look to and now I have lost him.

I think it is too hard to bear but I am so glad he is buried and perhaps some day God be willing I shall at least have a look at his resting place.

I hope you wont think me too hard if I ask you to let me know, if he was able to speak or tell you anything at all or was he unconscious to all his pain.

And I might add, if you could let me know at all if he had anything on him that we might keep in remembrance of him. I hope you will give my thanks to all his comrades for their sympathy & I must ask you to accept the same. I will now conclude in Sorrow. Yours Sincerely, L. R. Sofield.

⟨⟩

Violet to Owen, 15[?] November 1918

I am so rejoiced to have your letter of the 11th and 12th and to learn that you were safe. I only hope that the attack of flu' is over and that you are feeling quite A1 again. I dare say that you will have plenty to do. I wonder if you are going forward again perhaps into Germany. I do hope that the poor things are getting fed and settled down wisely. I wish that we could hear more of what is going on...I dug the end of my potatoes out of our allotment. Mrs Sturt is a great potato eater, she says she would starve without a potato so it is a good thing that we have some...I saw Mrs George. Joan is at Watlington...I went to see Mrs O'Sullivan today. She was affectionate in her enquiries. I showed her 2 of your letters which she was pleased to read. Today came letters from Father which I en-close. You see that they are written just after he had the cable. Now I shall cable 'Owen safe'...Do not run unnecessary risks with equipment or explosives...Do you want any more books?...We are in a very vigorous time—a General Election. I don't think they are going to take the soldiers' vote. Labour is coming out of the Government I am glad to say.[188]

Owen to his mother, 18 November 1918*
from 20th General Hospital

I am so sorry I haven't been able to write to you during the last two or three days but I have been on the move & as a result of my wanderings I have come down here. How long I shall stay I don't know in the slightest. There is just a chance of getting back to England which seems almost too good to be possible.

I am rather afraid that I may have lost my company and may be kicked off to join [text indecipherable]…as regards myself I am fairly all right now; my temperature appears to have gone & I have a fairly good appetite. I do hope you have escaped this abominable influenza. I am longing to get letters & to know how you have been getting on. The last I heard was a letter written on the 8th. I am in a ward of thirty beds & very comfortable. The only thing is that at present it is horribly cold.

Letter writing I find is jolly tiring so I will stop [text indecipherable]

Joyce Cockram to Owen, 19 November 1918
from the Slaters' home

Hurrah three cheers Congratulations on winning the war for us, any other old exclamation which will make a row!…I'm incapable tonight—I simply can't write a connected letter for some reason. Next time I write would you like a letter full of woe and troubles…On Saturday I went to my first Opera—Tales of Hoffman. It was a gorgeous show & I enjoyed it hugely.

Have you seen it?…I was at home when the news came through. In fact I was in the Garden saying goodbye to Mother just before biking back to Oxford. Consequently I was able to embrace every one there and every one here.

⸙

Violet to Gilbert, 20 November 1918

We have just had your letters Sep. 22, 24th, Oct. 2nd all together. Nearly 2 months ago. The last was when you had just heard of Owen going to France…Much as you fancy you have realized the horror of war you know that it is infinitely more vivid when your own boy is in it. I felt as if I could not see or talk or write to anyone and almost that I hated all the good people who still believe that war [was] inevitable but that it was and is the only way…I think the problem has to be settled and that we must have unconditional disarmament if we want to get rid of war really… Owen is in hospital with 'flu'. I had not heard from him since just after the Armistice was signed & he told me that he was sick & had diarhioa that was on the 12th. But he did not get into hospital until the 17th & so had 5 days hanging round…I wish he had got in sooner…I have just come in from [a] J.D.R. meeting…we had a very interesting & lively meeting. Alderman Carter and a Rev'd was holding forth on the Church & the Labour Movement. We had a very keen discussion & there was another clergyman who spoke & several N.C.C.[189] men as well as others…Of course on these occasions it is the discussion more than the address that is important…No letter from the War Office or Owen. I shall write again if I have any.

⸙

Violet to Owen, 20 November 1918

I had a notice from the War Office via Field P.C. [post card] & letter from you this morning, a letter written on a leaf of the little sketch book. I am

219

very glad since you had 'flu' that you are in hospital. I sincerely hope that you will only have a slight attack & no complications. It is a nuisance that it takes so long to hear. I must however be thankful that it doesn't take as long as to hear from dear Father... I know that you will write to me every day if you can. I am sitting in the drawing room to listen to Patrick while he plays Beethoven's Rondo which you learnt once... I have received your College dues from the Non. Col. [Non-Collegiate] people. I shall try to see Dr Pope when I pay & see if I can get any information about undergraduates with temporary commissions...I am going down to the F.o.R. meeting—it is to be a rather interesting subject tonight. I [shall] tell you about it tomorrow. This afternoon I was sewing shirts for C.O's I don't know when they will let them out of prison but I suppose they will when Peace is declared.

Edna Brown to Owen, 22 November 1918

So sorry to hear you have flu & hope that you will be well again when you receive this. The flue has been very bad in Gillingham. We are very fortunate to have escaped it, so far... We have very few soldiers at the Schoolroom now; it is hardly worth while going down. Last Monday Ida did not go, & I went to the Literary. We had fine fun on Victory Day. It is awfully nice to think that you will not be needed to fight. They are still sending the men to France from here. Two young men who are billeted in Rock Avenue are expected to go to India... Yours Very Sincireley, Edna

---

On 25 November 1918 George V dissolved Parliament and campaigning for the long awaited general election began. The government announced a special 'motor spirit licence'. Rationing of petrol was lifted for bona fide candidates and their agents and each was allowed from eight to ten gallons of petrol, depending on the size of their constituencies.

Violet to Gilbert, 26 and 28 November 1918

I have been busy sewing shirts for Conscientious Objectors this last 2 Wednesday afternoons at Mrs Howse...Her son was a Johns man a blue who stroked the Oxford crew & rowed for the Varsity at Henley & they have pictures & oars etc & also some interesting relics of his prison experience. He is now doing work under the Home Office. The Conscientious Objectors are not allowed liberty yet & will probably not be allowed until after the elections. I have been trying to see what...the Liberal candidate is like...& went last night with Mrs O'Sullivan to hear him speak at St Paul's school in Jericho. It was a small meeting & held in semi darkness. He isn't bad but not exciting. I don't like his view about the importance of trying the Kaiser & everyone before a tribunal of the nations. Though what is to become of the Kaiser & the Crown Prince I don't know. But it seems to me useless to try to spend our time trying to punish individuals. We shall certainly let most of the worst villains go and are sure that they are all on one side...I hope the coalition will not get as big a majority as they expect they are doing so much to poison people's minds about the real issue. I wonder what you feel and think of D.L.G. [David Lloyd George]

Owen to his mother, 27 November 1918

I have arrived at what is called No 3 Medical Board Depot & I go before a medical board probably on Saturday. As far as I can make out between now & then I have practically nothing to do beyond a parade at 9.30. I am just outside Etaples & had a ripping ride here in an ambulance, my kit following me some time or other...I am awfully annoyed I bought that beastly camp bath [and] wash stand bucket, as I never have used any of them. Thank goodness I never bought a bed. There are washing bowls in the mess & one can always get hold of a bath or a bed...You can't imagine the waste of everything that has been going on...Yesterday at tea in

Hospital I met Love. Love is a very quiet Scot, rather tall & solemn. He was a Cadet with me at Newark & was in the same room, we came out to France together… & here we meet again. I am expecting him to follow me down here in a couple of days time. I have still a chance of going to Mentone, I do hope I do in some ways but to start with at any rate it is rather expensive. After all one must expect to pay for some of the good things in the world. I wrote to Eliot a day or so ago. You might just tip him the wink to write to answer me some time soon. Just think of the expense you might have gone to in postage & stamps for letters to me. 7*d* a week. What extravagance one would consider it if it was spent on a 7*d* novel a week. I shall be interested to hear what Dr. Pope said when you saw him. I think I ought to pay my college dues myself. I have forgotten how much they are. I do wish I could have joined some college, a mere prejudice of course, but I always dislike it when people say 'Were you ever up at Oxford?' 'Yes' 'At what college?'… How is Pat getting on at school. Did you keep that wonderful letter he wrote & got birched for?

Annie Hersch to Violet, 30 November 1918*

I hope Owen is quite recovered from the influenza, it can be so serious. Laurie wrote that he has had it, after he was better; he did not go into hospital…We have quite interesting letters from him since the censor restrictions have been relaxed…Isn't it a wonderful relief that fighting has ceased? Let us hope for ever & ever if we get the right Government…And haven't you really one Labour candidate? We actually have three! I wish I had time to work all day to get Rhondda Williams [in], he is opposing Eric Geddes[190] for the Borough…The other two are Stubbs, a real working man, who is standing against Montague for the county, & a man named [J. C.] Squire for the University.

Owen to his mother, 4 December 1918

I have had a most useful job to do today I don't think. With 13 other offi-cers I conducted a party of about two or three hundred men from the parade ground to their work a distance of about half a mile. I left them & got back just in time to see the RE's disappearing for their morning ride. I must try to get back in time tomorrow to go out with them.

One interesting thing about my morning's work among the men I found one of the men of my section who had come down sick. I had quite a nice little chat with him & he is a very decent fellow...I do want to get some riding some time soon, also to get back to my company, I expect I shall just about get there nicely for Christmas.

Violet to Gilbert, 4 December 1918*

The fates are against my having a quiet time for writing to you...I went to pay Owen's university [fees and] I saw Dr Pope and asked him about the possibility [of Owen's coming] back to take up his studies. He...[said he could] come back if he desires to do so [after] a year in the army. I believe he will gain exemptions. However about that I will write to Dr Pope again...I shall definitely ask Owen if he would like to come back as soon as possible or leave it until later as Dr Pope says...I hope to enclose various cuttings from the D.N. [*Daily News*] You see Furniss is standing for the university [of Oxford]. I heard that Gilbert Murray was standing. I should suppose that they are opponents—Furniss Labour and Gilbert Murray, Liberal certainly not Labour. He, I should think, is of course the better man though I don't think Furniss would be bad.

Good night dear husband. Let us try to understand each other if we cannot think alike. Love from your loving wife, Violet Slater

Ida Brown to Owen, 5 December 1918*

Hurrah! Another letter from you this morning! That is five this week and I have only written to you twice. I feel an awful slacker. But as a matter of fact there is nothing to write about. Gillingham is such a sleepy old town…We are sorry to hear you are feeling so blue, but who wouldn't after such a miserable journey. When the effects have worn off your spirits will rise no doubt.

We have not done very much cycling lately as the roads are getting so muddy. 'Joyriding' started last Sunday within a radius of 30 miles. Dad risked it and took Mother and me…Norman is home from school today, and well we know it [end of text]

Owen to his mother, 6 December 1918

I am picket commander today, turn of duty 24 hours which means that if any fire breaks out I am in command of the fire picket & have to be in on the scene at once. In consequence I am not allowed to leave the camp. I don't mind much but it is unpleasant to know that if you do want to go out you can't. I hope there will be no fire, still there are very little chances of one.

I am wearing my new waistcoat & it is just glorious. I am afraid it will be a Christmas present to myself. Oh dear, oh dear the more I think about presents the more I am bewildered…I really think the best thing for me to do will be to write letters to everyone, send cards & give presents when I come on leave. Of course I shall keep my eyes open for anything nice I can find but all the shops try to be as English as possible & as expensive. One can't help being expensive once in a way but to repeat the offence is dangerous.

I am parading my fire picket in about half an hour, after that I shall have tea & then I hope to be able to get to work solidly & polish off a nice little lot of letters.

My pass book ought to arrive in a day or two. I am excited to see what my credit is. I feel that when I do come back to England for good & go on with my work as an undergraduate I must manage to make an income some how—if it is only by means of a hobby of some sort. I shall never be able to consider myself as a child with precious little thought of caring for itself. However!

I do wish billiards was not so fascinating a game to watch—it makes letter writing fifty times more difficult, especially when there is a piano going at the same time. I believe I shall be leaving the depot for a couple of days tomorrow, on duty taking a party of men somewhere or other so it ought to be rather fun.

I saw a girl in the tram yesterday & she was carrying four pots of the most glorious chrysanthemums, I did envy the person they were going to. There is an officer who came into the board depot two or three days ago who has very curious tastes & has decorated his hut with coloured material for wall paper & vases of imitation flowers. Some knut for the front line, if he ever gets there.

Violet to Gilbert, 7 December 1918

I expect that they are working very hard in Woolwich for the 2 Labour men, Crooks & Alec Cameron.[191] I don't feel very enthusiastic about Crooks…I hope the Coalition will not get as big a majority as they expect; they are doing so much to poison peoples minds about the real issues. I wonder what you feel & think of D.L.G. [David Lloyd George] nowadays. I told you that Joseph [Violet's brother] has joined Labour & of course Sidney Webb & Bernard Shaw.[192] J. A. Hobson[193] is standing for the University. I daresay you would have been asked to stand had you been in England. How would you have liked it?…I hope Owen has written to you direct. I shall try to enclose some of his letters. He's been in hospital 10 days now. I hope he will not lose his company & little Joan the black mare.

—◦◦◦—

Owen to his mother, 10 December 1918

For a wonder to-day I have had nothing to do so far but this evening I have to go on escort duty. I wonder if you remember I was on escort duty once or twice at Chatham. All I had to do then was to go out for a walk with the officer in question once in the morning & again if he wanted in the afternoon. Here it is a much more important duty. There are three of us to form the escort of one for a prisoner. We have to be with him every hour of the day & night. We take it in turns. He has a hut to himself & one of us has to sleep with him every night. My turn starts this evening.

I am now on duty as escort. The hut is quite comfortable & the bed all right & an oil stove going strong—actually not making smoke & smell. This evening I went to a concert at the Y.M.C.A. hut. It was awfully good but unfortunately did not begin till 7 o'clock & mess is at 7.30. I enjoyed it so much that when it came to 7.26 I determined to stay on & go without dinner & I am very glad I did so…It was just glorious to hear good music well played & to see the pianist's fingers frisking & twinkling over the notes made one horribly envious. I really must put in a lot of practice when I get home…I wrote for my pass book some time ago & as soon as it comes I will send you a cheque. My pen has gone dry & also I must off to bed.

—◦◦◦—

Philip Oakeshott to Violet, 10 December 1918*
from Oakland, California, USA

This is to wish you all the happiest of Christmasses. I [have] no doubt it will be a happy one for you, the happiest you have had for four years at least. I suppose Owen will be [home]…When do you expect Gilbert back?

It looks as though the Allies may have to occupy Berlin before things are settled in Germany. They seem to be in a terrible turmoil at present by all reports. But one cannot tell how much truth there is in them and how much propaganda. They are doing a great deal of squealing about the harshness of the Armistice terms but I hope that they will believe us to mean [?] every particular, and that the peace terms may be severe enough to completely destroy all military ambition. President Wilson has so far proved himself a really big man, don't you think so? He should be in Paris in a few days now. Agnes told me of Pat's prayer 'that the war may end sooner than we expect'. It certainly was answered wasn't it?

We all join in love and best wishes for Christmas & New Year to all of you and hope you may all be united soon. Your loving brother, Philip S. Oakeshott

---

Maurice Adams to Violet, 10 December 1918

We were pleased to get your letter with the enclosed from Gilbert, & the little calendars…What is going to happen? You ask. When I read this to Ada she said 'wait & see'. That's what we shall have to do, but things look very unsettled & this attempt of [Lloyd] George & of the Tory Party to jockey the country is not likely to make for peace, or for any good to the people.[194] Perhaps, however, the attempt will fail & a strong labour contingent be returned to Parliament. It looks as if Wilson were the only Statesman who realised the seriousness of the crisis & who will really work for a permanent peace & for the salvation of civilization, & *he* is opposed in his own country by blatant wind-bags like Roosevelt & by the Capitalist & military interests.[195] 'Ah, it's a mad world'!

Owen to his mother, 12 December 1918

For the first time I managed to get a ride. It was just glorious & I enjoyed myself immensely. We went miles through the forest & then came out over fields down to the river & then back again by a different way…I had an appointment with the dentist…& was not more than a few minutes late…The dentist was very decent & after a few days I shall have all my teeth in tip top condition & the beauty of it is that I pay not a farthing. There was precious little to do in the afternoon but directly after tea I went down to Rouen with my friend Love. Everything went well, we caught a motor lorry which took us down…& we then proceeded to wander round the town. It always looks very pretty in the lamp light, particularly the cathedral with its towers & spire gradually fading into the mist & night …The soldiers vote is causing a good deal of beastliness, everyone is fed up about it. Myself, I have had no notice of anything about the election except what you have told me in your letters.[196] As soon as I get back to the Co'y I shall make every endeavour to leave it for good.

[P.S.] Please send me all particulars about the smash my bike has had.

Eliot to Owen, [12 December 1918?]

Thanks awfully for the five franc note. I am going to get one of those Swedish knives with it. The Morrisons invited me to a dance on Saturday to be held in St Mildreds Hall in the Turl.[197] It was fine fun. The room was a ripping one and the boards were beautifully slippery…I have just received an invitation to go to the Lynams dance. Hum said he wanted any 'young fellah' he could get. I hope you will like the plum-pudding, toffee etc. Your loving BRAT, Eliot Slater.

Owen to his mother, 13 December 1918

Today we had quite a lively change from the usual run of things. For the usually strictly masculine Mess...was enlivened by a touch of femininity. Lina Ashwell's concert party gave a concert this evening which most of the officers...attended.[198] It was very good...The hall was packed, men were crowding round the open windows & every performance was encored...After the concert L.A.'s performers, 6 ladies of various ages, came to dinner at our mess. Altogether you can imagine it was a pukha (proper) dinner, umpteen courses & of course champagne & cigarettes...It was a great change to hear the chatter of feminine voices. Everyone was hilarious & after dinner by way of a finale we adjourned to the ante room & proceeded to have an impromptu dance. Most unfortunately for me I had to depart & go & guard the prisoner. Here I am in a close uncomfortable hut in my pyjamas with a very smoky smelly oil stove going at full pressure. To add to my annoyance my fountain pen is not behaving as it ought to. I told you about seeing the dentist yesterday. My tooth has just started to play tricks. I'm so cheerio as they say.

On 14 December the general election took place. With the passing of the 1918 Representation of the People Act (8 Geo. V c. 64) for the first time women over 30 who met certain qualifications and all men over 21 were entitled to vote. A special provision in the Act specified that for this election only men over 19 serving in HM forces could vote. Likewise for the first time polling in a general election occurred on the same day in every constituency. However, the count would not begin until 28 December.

Owen to his mother, 14 December 1918

I was on escort duty last night from after dinner until after breakfast this morning. I was tired & breakfast did not come in to the hut till after 9. At two minutes to 10 I remembered I had an appointment with the dentist so I fairly rushed, a wash & hasty dress & then a quick walk down the road to the D's. On the way down an A.S.C.[199] lorry passed me & I doubled &

hopped in beside the driver. The poor man was horribly bored & annoyed but couldn't actually kick me out as I was an officer. Finally I got down to the dentists…when I got there he said he didn't want me till Monday & would let me have a week end in peace.

In the afternoon I was again on duty. I took my prisoner for a walk. He very much wanted to have a ride so we went down to the Remount Depot & asked the C.O. [Commanding Officer] but were told very curtly that it was quite impossible. So we wandered off through the forest for a little way & then came back & watched a football match. The match itself was not interesting a bit but there was one player who was horribly amusing.

FIGURE 13 'My Prisoner': the Bavarian officer whom Owen guarded (taken by Owen on his VPK).

He was about 6 ft. & very fat—couldn't run for toffee, he got knocked over several times & looked absurdly funny & once he got his chance of getting a kick in, he kicked mightily hard but unfortunately the ball went straight into the face of a man on his side a few yards in front, knocked him flat & bounced back into the hands of the enemies.

My tour of duty ends tonight directly after dinner & tomorrow I have a free day & hope to go down to Rouen...I had Sinclair Uptons [Upton Sinclair's] little paper, it is rather brilliant in its way isn't?[200] Please don't forget to tell me about the smash up my bike appears to have had. I am feeling rather anxious about it, as I'm not quite sure of Eliot's knowledge of the temperament & behaviour of bikes.

Technically speaking my leave is due on February 20th about, I may possibly get it before. I don't believe there is any chance of getting back to my Co'y before Christmas now, the dentist will probably want me for a good ten days more.

Violet to Owen, 14 December 1918

No letter from you today...It seems as if I have been writing for weeks & always hearing that you have had no letters...We shall look forward to February & if the weather is fine you will have to cycle over to Wallingford & to Eliot at Leighton Park...I do hope my letters will turn up. I asked you to let me know at once if you want to get back to University work as soon as you can. I saw Captain Fife & Dr Pope—the former said that you must fill in forms at once because it will take probably months. I asked you to write to the Rev Dr Pope & ask him to put the matter in hand as soon as possible. He thought it was just possible you could get out & begin in Jan!!! Hamilton Fife thought Easter or October. I feel sure you will wish to get out of the army as soon as you can...(By the bye you said the other day that you still felt week. I suppose you know it shd. be weak. Its a pity you all take after me in spelling.)...I...got up early so that I might be first at the poll. I had to vote in Leckford R^d Schools, but though I got there first at 8, almost before there were 6, 3 of us being women. Not bad was it? I tried to get in a few voters this afternoon but I was not very successful. I went to Union S^t.[201] Such miserable houses I saw & some of the people dirty with that sort of dirt that means never a bath or thorough wash. Isn't it a disgrace that in the seat of learning—the hub of the Universe as Oxford people think, they won't allow children to play in The [University] Parks & give them no public baths or wash houses & such miserable badly built, ill equipped houses. Many have one w.c. between several houses—& then houses often belong to the Colleges. I was talking to a man today & he said the poor law [word indecipherable] was disgraceful, some only get 3/ or 4/- allowed by the Guardians.[202] I have always thought that the Poor Rates here were very low. One does feel that we want to make a clean sweep & get new people & fresh institutions, if possible something small & direct, not…like the officialism of the army. Do you hear serious talk on any subject?

[P.S.] I feel inclined to put on my envelope: For goodness sake find the boy & let him have this letter.

⸛

Gilbert to Owen, 15 December 1918 from Rangoon

I am sending this [letter] home, because it seems an even chance whether it will get to you quicker that way than if addressed to B.E.F [British Expeditionary Force]…I suppose you are probably somewhere on the Continent, but whether in France, Belgium or Germany, one cannot guess. I only hope you are getting some useful and interesting work to do, & also turning your French into a means of communication with the people & making something of it…I am impatient to hear all that happened to you between getting to the Front and the signing of the Armistice…I wonder how you feel about taking up engineering as a profession. I think it might suit you excellently, only the best openings for young men seem to be away from England. I should not recommend the P.W.D. [Public Works Department], which is the Indian engineering dept. I suppose there is little doubt that the Indian is going to be top dog in India, and things are not likely to be comfortable any more for Europeans. Ceylon or Burma might be all right, if Burma is made a Crown Colony, which would suit everybody far better than remaining part of India under a new regime. A very Happy New Year, my dear boy!

Owen to his mother, 15 December 1918

I have been seriously considering the question of my demobilisation & from all points of view I think I had better try at once to wangle it. It is bound to take some long time to go through so in no way will it interfere with my ordinary leave which will come off in February…I am writing to Dr Pope today to get all particulars. According to the little leaflet which he enclosed under C[over] I can get a degree without doing any further exams but all I shall probably use my service for is to get off Divers which seems rather a pity in a way. At any rate under all circumstances the sooner I get back to work the better as at present though I may be learning a certain amount, my time is nearly all wasted…I have just had *Bleak House* from Aunty Mollie. I am still on escort duty. The court martial comes off on Tuesday so I won't be in this job much longer. Have had a letter from Eliot dated Nov 5 & hope to answer it tomorrow. My word I have hosts of letters to write.

Joyce Cockram to Owen, 16 and 17 December 1918 from Wallingford

I am sending you this awful scrawl—to show that I really made an effort to write before, but apparently I really did go to sleep—I should think it highly probable. You will possibly have heard from Hugh, that I ploughed in zoology. I feel annoyed but not sick with myself (awfully good of me I know). I hadn't much hope anyhow, and I did such a rotten practical paper that it would have been a distinct stain on the University's reputation, had they passed me.

[17 December] This is utterly hopeless—if I get interrupted again— I shall just stop in the middle of a sentence. Hugh is in bed with flu—or rather he was in bed when I got home on Saturday. He is quite recovered now...Eliot turned up earlier than I expected...He has grown horribly and I begin to realise what I may expect when you come home. I gave him Oxo and toast, cake and jam and then biscuits and then biked part of the way with him...I can't see myself having time to write again before Christmas somehow. Mrs Read is going away probably and there is tons to be done in the house. I'm rather a knut at making it look nice nowadays! The cooking still beats me. I must therefore wish you as good a Christmas as you can expect under the circumstances and as speedy a return to Oxford next year as possible...Hugh has just arrived downstairs so this is the end of my peaceful time.

Violette Bossy to Violet, 16 December 1918, Serrières près Neuchâtel, Switzerland

The joy for your letter and the photograph of the family gave me, you can hardly realise. I felt I had no right to an answer and scarcely expected it, and now it is written as if I left England not six years, but six months ago. And the kindness of your words concerning everybody in this sad world, and the way you consider the future have been really like fresh air to me. I am so sick of breathing nothing but hate, revenge, and this horrid feeling which is said to be the exclusive property of the German—schadenfreude [gloating over others' misfortunes]—so sick of being considered the victim of some incomprehensible folly...What a joy to see Owen come

safe home after this awful trial. I certainly shall write today to him…
I must tell you how happy we have been of the Armistice. The flags of the
Allies floated high on the house tops…People were beaming in spite of
this shameful and happily unsuccessful attack of bolchevisme, in spite
of the awful number of dead caused by the plague [influenza]. Now all the
prisoners interned here are gone. We miss the gay uniforms and the idea
they incarnated, though I believe it to be a relief for many fathers and hus-
bands. You know how horn buttons are always jealous of metal buttons.
We see everyday long trains of French, English and Americans going
behind our house with loud clamours of joy…For myself these days were
darkened by the death of two very dear friends, both Allies, very shortly
before the Armistice and other such things…Now I must stop such a
long letter, or you will be bored. The censorship has accustomed us so
well to short messages!

⁂

Violette Bossy to Owen, 16 December 1918*, Serrières près Neuchâtel, Switzerland

What am I going to tell you first, now that the communication has been
cut such a long time? Congratulations on the Armistice—congratulations on your coming safe out of this 'confounded job'. (Would you not
say so?) or on being grown such a big fellow, as the photo your mother
sent me shows you, or on having the same good face which I have known
in Oxford?…You may believe that I have often been anxious about you,
counting on my fingers how many years old you must be, and what
chance you had to escape the War…do you remember you once wrote
Latin to me which was rather bad and impertinent to a not blue stock-
inged girl, that you will perhaps correspond in French. Do you still want
to come to Switzerland or are you tired of the Continent…We are now
content to see the War ended. The Armistice has been one of our happiest
days. Everywhere manifestations, in some towns, delirium. Departure of

French, English etc etc interned prisoners, for the joy of the ones and the sorrow of the others. There have been broken hearts enough to pave the roads of all Switzerland. A try of our international social anarchists to upset everything here on the very day of the Armistice. Lack of taste. The Army tired of being sentinel would fain have made an end of the disturbers.[203] This too is rather an antique English isn't it?...I wish you a merry Christmas, at home if it is possible, or at least in the now peaceful camps.

Owen to Eliot, 16 and 18 December 1918

My dear brat-as-you-call it Eliot,

Your letter of the 5/12/18 arrived this morning—many thanks for it. From the data you gave me it seems that you went home yesterday—presumably biking. A few days ago I had a letter from you to Mother in which you say something about a boy having to pay umpteen shillings on repairs to my bike. I am very anxious to know exactly what happened, what damage was done & how it was repaired. Don't forget that its still my bike & I shall want it a lot when I come home.

18.12.18

I have no particular news to tell you—Mother gets all I can manage. I am enclosing the fallacy [trick question] you asked me for also another one I saw for the first time the other day. I am just off to take some troops from here to Boulogne—look it up on the map. The journey takes about 14 hours & you travel at night. I start this evening, get to B. tomorrow & come back either straight away or spend the day in B. & return the following day. For all my trouble I am paid 12 francs travelling allowances.

I am enclosing a five franc note as a Christmas present for you & Pat. Mother will be able to get it changed for you. You ought to get something like 3/10^d for it now.

You can guess I'm in a hurry so good bye & a Merry Christmas & a happy & prosperous new year. Your loving brother*, Owen

*NOT BRAT

Owen to his mother, 17 December 1918

Today was rather interesting as I attended my first Court Martial. It happened to be my turn of duty as escort when the affair came off so I had to conduct the prisoner to the court & stand at his side during the whole of the proceedings. There were about a dozen witnesses but as he pleaded guilty none of them were called in to their disappointment. It was rather interesting [to] look on though of course I had to stand strictly to attention the whole time. Everything went with a swing so utterly different from the petty fogging procedure in a civil court. The case didn't take longer than twenty minutes & then we went back & carried on the old routine…I had the afternoon off so I went down to Rouen, got some money which I hope will last me some time & wandered around the town…Tomorrow I have the interesting job of conducting a party of men from here to Boulogne.

[Violet's marginal comment about the court martial:] An officer who had gone off to Paris for a week. Seems he had once been wounded in the head & was some times 'a creature of impulse'—this was said for him by the soldiers. He was let off & told 'not to do it again'.

Violet to Gilbert, [18 December 1918]

We are now a complete little family—all there are of us in England. Eliot arrived yesterday at 2.30. It is very nice to have him but there is no getting anything done, so to speak…I think this morning we have been down to get presents but we haven't got many. Owen sent some money so I gave them each some of it to help because it is a real pleasure to be able to spend and almost impossible to save out of their small allowances. Tomorrow…we hope to make some cakes and puddings, much better than none which was our share last Christmas…I have done nothing about game of any sort for Christmas. I've never bought a turkey or anything of the sort. I wish someone would invite us out for the meal…One cannot altogether count this a peace Christmas while war is going on in poor Russia and war conditions obtain…I shall try …to have a little Christmas tree and to have a nice cosy time. I must find a really nice ghost story to tell I think…Your books and the very beautiful silk arrived…the white silk is very pretty but it is almost too thin for a blouse. I must think of something to use it for (the boys' talk makes it difficult to write).

I don't believe I sent you any of Owen's letters last week. I had such a lot to send I will try to make up a nice bundle this time. Since last I wrote we have had the election. I told you that Mary Pask, a nice intelligent and interesting Quaker girl, gave leaflets out at the meetings. We went to 2 or 3 in all and heard the candidates. They were not good…Of course Marriott was the best Quaker.[204] But the whole thing was taken up in demanding revenge on the Germans and lauding Lloyd George. We got quite sick. I could not stand more than 1½ hours of it and then came out. It will be most interesting to see what happens but I expect it will be [a] short lived government. I sincerely hope that President Wilson will have a real influence on the Peace and also that the demand for a Labour [word indecipherable] be set out at the same time will be granted. The Peace discussions are now put off while the ministers rest on the shores of the blue Mediterranean. I expect that they have had a very fierce time. But I wonder who pays. The poor workers get no pay for their holidays.[205] Well goodbye dearest. A happy New Year to you and may we all meet.

Mrs Brown to Gilbert, 19 December 1918

This awful war seems to have made almost the whole world kin, and it has found for us so many friends that otherwise we never should have known. Owen for instance: we thought that when he went to France, in all probability he would forget his friends at Gillingham, but instead of doing so he seems to have created an interest in us among his people which I am sure we do not deserve, but we fully appreciate it and indeed hope that some day we may have the pleasure of meeting you all.

We thank you very much for your kind thoughts and good wishes.

Please accept the enclosed group [photograph]—it is Owens work. Mr Brown & the family join in wishing you a Very Happy New Year.

Owen to his mother, 19 December 1918

I am now for the moment at Boulogne. I reported for duty yesterday at 3 pm & the train did not start from Rouen before 8 oclock... We travelled all night & I'm afraid I hardly managed to sleep at all... We arrived here at about 10 oclock & I had to march my men whom I then saw for the first time, to a rest camp. There were about 700 of them, by far the largest party I have ever had to deal with but as they were going on leave they all behaved excellently (most unusual nowadays). As my train starts back between 4 & 5 I have plenty of time to wander round the town. I have already seen a fair amount of it. The docks are just typical, one mass of masts & rigging of the fishing smacks & here & there a larger boat glorying in its black & white camouflage... Now for a few business questions. How much do you pay for vests & pants (good woollen ones). I am enclosing a snippet of velvet. Will you give me by return some idea of its quality & suitability for riding bags. It is a ripping colour but I am afraid it is not quite close enough. It is 20 francs a metre... & a little under 16/- a yard... I found this at a little French shop in the back streets of Boulogne—just the place where they make workmens bags & one so often sees the most disreputable looking men in glorious velvet trousers. According to these prices I could get a pair of riding bags for about £2.10 instead of … £4.4.0.

Ida Brown to Owen, 19 December 1918

Just a hurried note to say that your adopted family will think of you on Christmas Day and hope that you will have as good a time as possible away from your own people. We are not sending cards this year but we wanted to send you some little remembrance … we eventually decided on a book which we sent some days ago … Edna and Dorothy are both down with the 'flu'. They both collapsed on Monday. Dorothy is a little better today but Edna is still very ill. So all our Christmas plans are upset. We are hoping they will be able to come downstairs for the jollifications and not spend Christmas Day in the bedroom … With best wishes from all, your affectionate sister, Ida

P.S. We have had Xmas greetings from your father.

Owen to his mother, Eliot, and Patrick, 20 December 1918

I wish you all a very Merry Christmas & a happy & prosperous New Year when it arrives. I only wish that I could be at home with you & Father too, so that we could eat our Christmas dinner as a complete family.

I remember I spent my last Christmas day in bed so I hope you will all be perfectly well & fit & have a jolly time. I wish I could send you holly & mistletoe for decorations. There is not much holly [here] but all the or-chards & big trees are full of mistletoe. I am afraid this letter will come too late to help you provide Christmas decorations but if you want to put any up for the New Year the best place I know of to get holly at all close is on the top of Shotover Hill past the Jacks' house & right on top, also there is some on Horspath Common which is down on the right when you get on top.

I have just come back from Boulogne & I had a most miserable journey. The train was supposed to leave at 4 oclock in the afternoon but actually did not leave before 8 at night. It simply crawled & got in here a few minutes before 4 this afternoon. I have had nothing to eat between tea yesterday & the tea I have just finished here in the officers club Rouen...I am hoping to see a Lena Ashwells concert this evening.

Very much love to you all & a jolly Christmas from your loving son & brother, Owen

---

Owen to his mother, 21 December 1918

I have had a day of rest, nothing to do for a wonder but to make up for it tomorrow I am orderly officer which means employment during most of the day...I have heard from the Browns a few days ago & talking about my leave; they seem to have almost forgotten that I have a home in Oxford to go to...I have written to Dr Pope & I wonder when I shall get an answer. I should like to get my release just at the beginning of the summer holiday...then I could have a good holiday, do a certain amount of work during the latter end of it & then start right away in the autumn term. I don't believe I told you about the job Love got. Some few days ago he had to take a draft of men to England. He embarked here at Rouen & has not yet returned. It must be very jolly—a long trip down the river & then crossing probably to Southampton. I expect he will manage to get a couple of days in London. Wouldn't it be jolly if I managed to get the same job & pay you a surprise visit.

Owen to his mother, 23 December 1918

By some unaccountable turn of fate or fortune I am orderly officer again today which means getting to bed again after 11 pm.

I visited the dentist again today & he has actually finished with me. I suppose now that in a day or two I shall transfer next door to the REs. I shall be glad in a good many ways but I don't want to move before Christmas day...& besides Love has turned up from England...One thing when I do get next door I shall get plenty of riding though probably not so comfortable a hut to live in. I am rather afraid that the present lot of officers there are not particularly congenial company.

A moment ago I told you that Love had returned. He appears to have had a ripping time in England, getting four days in London. It would be just ripping to get four days at home now & then my proper leave shortly afterwards.

As I am orderly officer I have been able to do nothing all day. Most of my time has been spent in sitting in the mess & reading *Bleak House* that Aunty Mollie sent me. It is a most interesting book & a change from the one I was reading immediately before. On my way back from Boulogne I bought Thackeray's Book of Snobs & Barry Lyndon.

A man has just been ragging me about my letter writing, saying that he has often seen me start a letter in the morning & do any number of other things in between & finish last thing at night. It is not quite true but most of my letters do take me ages...I haven't been down to Rouen for several days now & when last I went I bought about half a dozen cards & seemed to spend no end of money.

I wrote to Grinles [C. H. Grinling] a few days ago...I enclosed £3 for the *Pioneer* which I suppose I shall never see again.

There is a concert on tonight at a neighbouring hospital & everyone in the mess has gone to it except about four of us...These performances are not generally first class but never the less very enjoyable.

Owen to his mother, 24 December 1918, Medical Board Base Depot

Christmas Eve! An awful day, blustering wind & rain now but early this morning heavy white frost & all the puddles frozen over. I took a party of men up to the Bull Ring—a broad open expanse of flat sand—where they played football & PT games for an hour. Just when their time was up it clouded over like anything, so I fell them in at once & doubled most of the way back. By the time we got to camp it was coming down in bucketfuls so we just managed nicely. This was my job for the day & it has been impossible to do anything outside. I have been reading *Bleak House* in the mess most of the time.

Next door the RE's have been putting up a new & larger mess & have been working at it all day & night to get it finished in time for Christmas. It has sounded so weird to hear hammers going on all through the night, like the ghost of some buried monk trying to hew his way from his living tomb. Why is it that ghosts & Christmas are inseparable? Have you ever read that book of Jerome's on ghosts?[206] I read it during the first few days of my time at the C.C.S. [Casualty Clearing Station] It was very witty in his usual way.

Your toffee arrived yesterday & was too scrumptious for words. I am afraid that Love & I finished it before midnight & we both enjoyed it immensely. Its one fault was its excellence & hence its short life.

I don't know why my tunics should feel more uncomfortable now than at any other time but they both are intolerably tight round under the arm...I had a small split in the seam of one & this afternoon while wrestling & having a rag with Love the seam burst halfway down to the elbow & a quarter way round the arm so I just had to set to work to sew it up again.

The M.O. [Medical Officer] here is a funny old curmudgeon who wears a beard & nothing looks more out of place than a beard in khaki: he's rather fat & quite interesting. I am expecting to leave the medical board base depot where you know I am at present to go to the R.E.B.D. [Royal Engineers Base

Depot] in about 3 days, staying there for something like a week & then of course join my Co'y. I only wish it were leave, but that won't be long now.

<hr/>

Violet to Owen, 25 December 1918

My dearest Owen boy, We have been sitting by the fire made of a big Yule log of the Chestnut tree. We first of all had tea by the light of the little Christmas tree lit up with candles then we told stories by the fire light; then we thought of yr. Father in silence & lit up & wrote to him. Again we had fire light & thought of you & now we are writing. Pat began his day at 4.15 a.m. At least that was when I heard him going to his stocking...outside the nursery door. Of course I sent him back to bed but he had got hold of various things...It was a glorious morning & yesterday too was beautiful. Magdalen tower looked so beautiful both days...yesterday in the warm light of a reflected sunset it looked perfect—the houses just sank into insignificance in a misty blue shadow & made a lovely contrast. I felt as if it were a sin to go home...I hope I wasn't too generous with your money for our boys. I think that they told you what their presents were...Goodbye dearest boy. I shall hope to hear shortly from you what you did on Christmas day. Do not promise to go to the Browns [during his forthcoming leave]. I do not know how long you will have but I think if you are not likely to return for good quite soon you ought to go & see dear old Grannie & of course the Leyburn people want to see you & the Browns have seen you much more recently.

<hr/>

Violet to Gilbert, Christmas Day and Boxing Day 1918*

We have been sitting by the fire in the drawing room, a fire made from the fine big log off the chestnut tree, the wood that Owen cut down. We have been telling stories, they had to be sort of ghost stories…We have had our pretty little tree alight for tea. And yesterday while I took some Christmas presents the boys cycled up to Shotover and picked holly… Mrs Grafflin gave me some lovely white chrysanthemums…[and] a 1lb box of delicious dessert chocolates…Perhaps I told you that old Mrs Franklin, the choir woman we know in Portland Rd (with whom I have kept in touch by way of little gifts of apples, she was living with her married daughter, a young woman (husband killed in the war) there are 4 children) [died]. The funeral cost £8 insured so that paid most of the expenses. So I gave Mrs Green [the daughter] 10/- and the children some little things…Well when I got home I got the little tree ready a bit so that the boys saw it from the garden as they came in. They were delighted. I dressed in my pretty blue coatee…decorated with the gorgeous Indian gold necklace that Lord Pentland sent Patrick. After tea we visited Mrs Grafflin…We took her some holly & a Yule log & Margaret a little present & we sat by her fire.

Pat went out to look for his stocking at 4.15 am. Of course it was more or less moonlight in his room so he thought it was day light…the stocking was on the banister…I made him go back to bed but…I think he had raided the stocking and got a book and lit a candle but Eliot made him put it out…We had pork sausages and plum pudding and custard. Though not a grand dinner [it was] a very nice one the boys thought. Turkeys are 2/8d a lb. I really can't buy them.[207]

Owen to his mother, 26 December 1918

Christmas day is over & it has been quite a jolly one. In the morning Church Parade with not a particularly brilliant sermon. In the afternoon I went down to Rouen with Love & for the first time I went inside the Church of St Ouen—it is simply glorious…There was a service going on. It was really rather ripping—a perfectly glorious organ. The only word that I could understand was Amen. We went round, meandering through little back streets & ever & anon coming out into an unexpected little square with perhaps a statue or a fountain in the middle. We went to the Club for tea & got back to camp just at 7 o'clock. My thoughts flew homeward though I was busy changing. I suppose you were all sitting round the fire, probably in the drawing room. I wished I were at home instead of going to a concert though the concert was very good, one of Lina Ashwell's concert parties. They all came into [a] dinner dance, it was a great pity we did not have more & as it was we did not leave off till about half past twelve. It is horrid dancing in boots especially if they have rubber soles. However it was all great fun. We finished up with all joining hands & singing Auld Lang Syne. Today I am picket officer so I am not allowed to leave camp. There is precious little doing…I am bound to stay over the New Year now but soon after I expect I shall go back to the Co'y.

———— ⊗⊗ ————

On 30 December the results of the general election that had taken place on 14 December were declared. Candidates in parties loyal to the Coalition had had official letters (nicknamed 'coupons') from their party leaders. The coalition government were returned with a massive majority of 526 seats out of a total of 707. The Opposition was led by Labour, which not only had more MPs than the anti-Coalition Liberals under Asquith but a much larger popular vote. The 73 Sinn Fein MPs refused to attend.

Joseph Oakeshot to Gilbert, [*c.*31 December 1918]*

The General Election was sprung upon the Country in the most unscrupulous way and the wildest promises were made by L.G. which did the trick of getting votes. Locally we hurriedly formed a Labour Party, frightened a prospective Liberal away, got a candidate, my old friend Jesse Hawkes of Maidstone, who got nearly 3000 votes at the first trial. The Tories are in power under the camouflage of a coalition and we are in for troublous times: the Army seethes with discontent; we have had the spectacle of semi-mutinous deputations of soldiers obtaining concessions from the Generals who when the war broke out were boasting that industrial disputes would get a short shrift after the war…Labour [working people] has the whip hand, is quite aware of the fact and will use its power, perhaps not too wisely. By the way I had a visit from my cousin James Field, the head of the Indian Aerological Laboratory, who is doing some 'super-confidential' work for the Admiralty. He is a high Tory and said that in ten years time a Labour Government will be in power.[208] He thinks England is played out for the middle classes, in which opinion I am inclined to agree. He recommended emigration to any colony where it is possible to grow apples, & thought that I was not too old to do it.

Violet gave us the volume of Indian Essays which are of great interest You must be making quite a name for yourself in Indian affairs on the economic side…I have written to Owen once or twice and have heard from him…As a matter of literal fact the War is not over whatever it may suit L.G. to say.

⋘⋙

Marjorie Brown to Owen, 3 January 1919

A happy New Year to you and may you soon be home to enjoy this year of Peace after all the months of fighting.

I hope your Christmas Day was as gay and cheerful under the circumstances as you expected. The Browns spent a very quiet holiday owing to Edna and Dorothy being unable to leave their bedroom, and everybody else rather 'blue'…Dad has been home since Monday with a slight attack of 'flu' but is better now.

I suppose you are counting the weeks now, instead of the months for the time when you get your leave. We are learning the songs in the Scottish Students Book[209] so that we shall be able to sing them all when you visit No. 29.

The weather here is dry but very cold, just right for a long walk but objectionable to one who has to sit in an office all day with a small electric radiator which is supposed to heat the place, but it does nothing of the sort as it only reminds and makes one long for the fire which one knows is burning brightly and keeping every one warm in the office behind this one.

Horace goes to Sandhurst on the 17th of this month so there will be no more half-past nine stunts for me or going to the post at the corner and finding a new way home. I shall grow awfully good...I suppose Ida told you that the rest room is closed so you see we shall all grow good together and stay at home every evening...With love from us all including Horace, Your loving sister, Marjorie

---

Gilbert to Owen, 3 January 1919

I am here in Bombay for the 'Annual conference of the Indian Economic Association' [for] which I have done as much as anyone else, I suspect, to bring into such a sort of existence that it is likely to be permanent[210]... I suppose you will not be specially interested in our Congress proceedings. We had, mostly, good papers and good discussions. I drafted the constitution and got it adopted, & we raked in over Rs 200 in subscriptions...I am sending this home, but I hope to send another line or two direct, as I do not know which is the best way of reaching you.

Owen to his mother, 3 January 1919

I have put in my papers for demobilisation this morning so if all goes well I may be home soon. It is rather exciting but from all I can hear there is going to be a certain amount of trouble about demobilisation etc. The

C.O. [Commanding Officer] didn't seem to fall in love with the idea anyway. It is extraordinary the difference in the discipline here & the discipline at Rouen which was hopeless. Here when you speak to a man he springs to attention & answers you decently instead of mumbling & grumbling some remark with his hands in his pockets…The Company is employed in a pretty extensive job—a delousing station supposed to be able to deal with 3,000 men a day. I went down this morning and had a look round & tomorrow take my turn of being in charge. We keep pretty early hours here—reveille 6.30, parade for work at 7.30. We have to march down a mile or so to the work, knock off work at 3.30 & come home to dinner.

Violet to Owen, 6 January 1919

I am afraid I am rather stupid tonight. I can't get Eliot off to bed & it takes all my attention off. I've had more letters from Gilbert today, such nice ones only he fears that he will not get a passage home…I hope if you get leave you will not lose your Co'y. The shorter the time you have to be in France the nicer it will be to be with people you know rather than with new ones. But I expect the men are rather fed up with being kept abroad still. I do hope that they will set you to real work; there must be lots of interesting things to be done. I wonder how Peace conversations are going on & what will happen. I do wish we could feed Europe.[211] I am afraid I am in a hurry for reforms of all sorts. The whole machine of life has become too complicated so that the little things take a long time like the motor lorry & ½ dozen men sent to get 1 lb. of paint that Harry Joseph told us of.

Eliot began to paint your cycle today. I noticed he was getting his hands in a great mess & I find that the only brush he could find was unsuitable so he was dipping a piece of rag in & painting with his fingers.

Owen finally got leave and returned to England on 6 January 1919.

Owen to his father, 8 January 1919

At last my leave has come through & I am at home for 18 days total leave. I say at last but that gives you an entirely wrong impression. In normal war time circumstances or if I was with my Company I would have to stay in France for five months before getting leave. But an order came out some time ago—leave to be every three months so being at the Base I put in for leave and got it…I had a pretty unpleasant journey…I was not sick myself luckily but lots of the troops were…I arrived at Dover and did not take the leave express to Victoria but a pretty fast train to Chatham where I…went up to the Browns. They were very glad to see me and welcomed me with open arms & it was very jolly altogether. We all sat up to after midnight & then went to bed…Everyone at home is very well. I saw Eliot cycling down the Banbury Road so I commandeered the bike and cycled home. I was pretty fagged walking up from the station with a pack on my back & a heavy haversack over my shoulder.

I met a certain Joan Anderson in the town this morning & she says she is cycling over to Wallingford to see the Cockrams tomorrow & I shall bike over with her…I don't believe you know the Cockrams at all except from photos I have sent you. The girl Joyce is very jolly & interesting, while the boy who is a great chum of mine is more or less quiet and reserved. At present he is working for a schol. in Maths. I hope to see Dr Pope in a day or two & will write at once…I am afraid I am more or less satisfied with my position in the army. Besides 11/- a day is not to be sneezed at. All the same as soon as I get back I shall get out as quickly as I can & Hurray for civilian life & impecuniosity!

———∞———

Violet to Gilbert, 9 January 1918 [1919]*

I have had 'lots' of letters from you & I cannot answer them as I should like because Owen has come home unexpectedly…& there does not seem a minute…I am glad that I did not go [to Wallingford]. It is best to leave the young people to themselves tho the Cockrams are very nice—they always go together, Mother, Father, Joyce & Hugh. Mrs. Cockram is something like me—younger but they all go on excursions & Joyce is so sorry if they can't. Owen is going with Joan Anderson who is going today & will return tonight I suppose…The unrest in the army seems to be coming to a head.[212] I am very thankful they are making a protest…I daresay you have your own opinion about our Russian interference[213]…I am crying out over the ocean to find a common ground & you always want to put me right. I am persuaded that we do agree essentially when you have changed your opinions. Have you read 1914 in some verse[214]—that epitomises largely what I mean by Germany not being the only one to make war. Bernard Shaw said we have all been making war for 23 years. We can't go on in the same way & not get war again—that is what you have always said.

Gilbert to Eliot, 9 January 1919

We now have regular mails leaving for England once a week from Bombay on Saturdays, so we have to get off our letters by the Bombay mail leaving Madras on Thursdays. Then the mail is supposed to take about 23 days… as now they are to be carried by rail across France.

I have just had a nice little lot of letters from you, telling all about the flu & being an orderly & the boy who was so dangerously ill. I hope he got through it in the end. I think your school was rather lucky in getting through the epidemic as well as it did; it was a devastating plague

---

Violet to Gilbert, 15 January 1919

This morning Owen & I went into Bell & Co.[215] to ask about passage to India. There is a lady clerk there who is very anxious to do all she can to [help] everyone but she said that it is quite impossible to do anything now but that she understands that more ships will be put to the purpose of carrying passengers later on so that if you get back she thinks that there will be no difficulties but she advised me to make arrangements immediately I hear if you are able to come that you will cable. There are two months before you could start so that is not bad... Letters are coming through much quicker. We received the picture of you [?]... which you sent on the 8th Dec. last, last Saturday—it only took a little over a month. That's a comfort... I hope that your Burma trip was altogether a success... Owen's leave is slipping away quickly... He put in a little time digging in the allotment one morning & went over to Wallingford for the day & stayed the night, returning today to dinner. Then the Cockrams came here and went to the theatre—they stayed the night. Mrs Briggs [the boys' piano teacher] came as usual & Owen has had a little music... It's just dinner time & the boys have come in so I must stop. The Museum this afternoon. I shan't go.[216]

⟨⟩

Ida Brown to Owen, 16 January 1919

Ten thousand thanks for the book. It was very good of you to think of us and we are all delighted with it, *only* you should not have bought it.

I have consulted my Mater and Pater as you requested and the result is—they thank you very much for remembering them but really there is nothing they want so please don't buy anything.

We are glad you are having such a good time. We thought about you last night at the dance.

Horace has actually spent two evenings under the roof of his beloved and is coming tonight to bid the family farewell.

Remember us all to your Mother and brothers. With heaps of love from all, your affectionate sister, Ida

P.S. Suppose there is no hope of us seeing you on the way back?

—∞—

Peace negotiations began at Versailles on 18 January in the midst of continuing violence in Germany, Russia, Hungary, the former Ottoman Empire, and Scotland as well as in the new republics of Latvia, Czechoslovakia, Estonia, Lithuania, and Yugoslavia. The defeated powers were not allowed to send delegates.

Violet to Owen, 18 January 1919

I am sending a tiny letter to greet you [on your return to France]. Perhaps it will cross with you … I hope you will do your best to get your discharge & get back to work. Don't bother about money. It is no doubt useful but is better to come back to the work you have made up your mind to do… I shall be really glad to have you back to help to train young Patrick. I do feel that the boys are losing a great deal by not having their Father with them. Of course I feel very differently about your going this time & I know you do, still it is all so indefinite & unsettled abroad that I do not feel that you are going to have exactly an easy time. I hope that you will be attached to your old company & that you will be able to get into sympathetic relations with your men & 'work hard & be kind & honourable to your men' which is what little Pat usually prays for you. It will be infinitely nicer for you to be in a civil relationship with men than military. I hope you will get through your course of 'Rural Economy' & become an agricultural adviser. You will have the chance of an agricultural scholarship & go abroad which will be interesting.

—∞—

Gilbert to Owen, 19 January 1919

I expect I can still address this to B.E.F. The last I have seen in the papers which throws some light on your probable whereabouts is that those who have had least of the fighting will be kept longest. I hope they aren't keeping you idle, as there must be plenty of engineering work to do, if it is only filling in shell holes in roads & repairing bridges. Also that you have 'Joan' still & your new section, though I suppose men will be picked out of that for discharge…It is pretty clear I shall not be able to come home this year. I must make the best of a bad job, & hope both to save money & get some permanent work done. What I am at (apart from my classes, which take up a good deal of energy) is trying to get the future of Economics in the University put on a definite basis. But I hope to do some writing in the summer holidays…I am off tennis just now through tennis elbow…This does not prevent other exercise & I had 3 golf matches last week & won them all.

I was interested in your padre telling you about plant pathology being a big new field of work. We are getting the influence of the movement here, though mostly in the restricted form of study of funguses and other definite plant blights. I think the development of a similar movement in England is bound to come; & if you are attracted to that sort of work probably to get back to Oxford, complete your Science degree, and then peg away with Somerville[217] would put you in touch with such developments. You don't want to begin specialising too early, but gradually to narrow your field of study as you discover which possible opening gives you the work you can go at year after year without getting sick of it.

No mail this week…but it is rather disappointing after we had got used to the idea of regular weekly mails both ways.

[P.S.] It has just occurred to me that I don't know what the postage is! I put on 2½^d to make sure.

―――

Hugh Cockram to Owen, 21 January 1919

If you find yourself feeling very generous and your funds permit it, could you send us the suggested cash as soon as possible? You suggested

20 francs; suppose you send a *little* more, and then we would make up the difference and we could then take Tidswell with us. He was with us you see when we arranged, & it will seem funny that we didn't ask him. And he *has* improved; and he is gym captain so perhaps he would do something in your permanent cup idea. Nevertheless, now don't think I am presuming upon your generosity, 'cos I am not! But an offer's an offer you know, & I am sure you would call me a damned fool if I did not seize my opportunities.

I am writing to ask you to send cash now because [G. L.] Deuchar [the chaplain at Magdalen College School] is awfully keen on the idea, & is getting tickets for everyone at any theatre that week…He is going to four nights & is taking various members of a suggested glee club. Tidswell, Bushell ii etc. By the way Tidswell's a prefect.

The field will be flooded tomorrow so napoo [no chance of] to hockey for sometime to come.

Violet to Gilbert, 21 January 1919

I particularly want you back to discuss Owen's plans. He would have liked to discuss his future with you which I hope he has written about with Dr Pope and Dr Sommerville…When we were going to the theatre with the Cockrams Owen and I were arranging how to sit. Of course Owen had taken Joyce on his right…at least I thought so. Owen was going after Eliot. I said 'of course both the young would rather sit by you' and Owen came and put his arm round me and said 'you are so delightful that I am sure anyone would be glad to sit by you.' He said it so quickly and sincerely it did make me happy.

But he is very keen to stay on in the Army for a little while for the…pay and the easy laziness of the life which I fear is demoralising. He says (I have read in his letter) that he seldom does it, only has to see that it is done. Here is your hot water Sir, shaving things, clothes and all! He is overfed with butter and cream and dinners and if he liked he could drink (he doesn't) he told me that he has nothing stronger than your 'soda water' you spoke about in the Army. He says he can't talk to his men. Except when they were together up at the Front under fire when sometimes they slept together and messed together. I feel that it is very important that he shall begin his real training for his work...He is a dear charming boy. I am proud of him. I do feel proud that he hasn't taken to smoking and drinking.

Gilbert to Patrick, 23 January 1919

How are you getting through the winter? Have you had much skating? Are you going ahead like one o'clock in school work...We have now finished our cold weather...Already it is so hot that my shirt sticks to my back nearly all the time. I have now only 8 weeks before the summer holidays, & if there were ships enough I should then be off for home, but as it is it will most likely be a case of going up to the hill instead.

On Monday there was to have been a great reception at Government House & everybody was going in all their best. I had made all my arrangements, & had got into a starched shirt & white tie & swallow tails all very swanky & proper, and had made arrangements with a man who has a fine big motor car & chauffeur to drive me to Gov't House, when I met a man in the corridor who told me it was all off because little Prince John had died.[218] Now we are all supposed to go into mourning. Mourning in India does not mean that you put on black clothes generally, but just a black neck tie, & you must wear black boots or shoes & not brown ones. People in uniform put a black band round one arm.

Owen returned to France on 23 January 1919.

Owen to his mother, 25 January 1919

I have heard today that I am going to proceed to join my company either today or tomorrow, in fact as soon as there is a train to take me. I shall be awfully glad when I actually do get there.

I have had a horrible misfortune—my valise & all it contains, which is everything barring what I bought on leave, through some ill chance & the carelessness of a batman got placed with the kits of officers being demobilised & has gone off with their kits to Le Havre. I have telegraphed after it & I hope of course to get it all right when I get there but it may have gone on to England or goodness knows where…I have done nothing all day except rushing round after my kit & sending telegrams & this evening I have to go on picket duty.

Owen to his mother, 26 January 1919

Yesterday I was on picquet [picket], which was not at all too bad. I had to guard a hospital. I placed my men out & then spent the rest of the time in the officers mess where they gave me dinner. One of the hospital patients—a prisoner, escaped & I went all over the hospital & grounds with the orderly officer but I failed to discover any trace of the man. I got to bed at just on midnight…As regards the tickets for Pat & yourself for the G[ilbert] & S[ullivan] Opera you had better get them & take the cash for them from the next cheque I send you—whenever that may be.

I heard rather an amusing story. A sergeant wanted a party of men for fatigue duties & they all refused to come [to] work so he had a brainy notion. He ordered all miners to parade & of course hosts turned up expecting early demobilisation. 'Are you all miners? All right then—coal fatigue.' An officer was taking a parade & ten men were absent. The sergeant said they were not warned for duty at the right time. 'No' said the officer 'I suppose they all had prior engagements.'

⁂

Violet to Owen, [late January 1919?]

Your letter from Boulogne came today. It contains a pattern of corduroy velveteen. It is a jolly colour but I have my doubts about it being suitable for riding bags. I'll try to take it in to Woodwards and ask the tailor there. I'll send back the pattern. Do you want some vests and pants? I might get some at Jaegar's sale…I should say about 7/6 per pair, but that was pre war. I daresay they would charge you 3 or 4 times that. Things are dearer than ever I believe.[219]

I have been sending off all sorts of things to various people today and still have about 10 letters I ought to write. As soon as you can get back to your Co'y. I'll send you the fountain pen that Uncle Harold sent to you. It's a Waterman…I enclose letters from Father—they ought to have come to you a week ago…I had a letter from Joyce today. Hugh had a relapse—a nuisance.

[P.S.] Send back the letters from Father for me to take care of.

⁂

Hugh Cockram to Owen, 29 January 1919

Thanks awfully for the cash; it was very good of your to send even that amount, & truth, we did not expect any at all. Thanks awfully & think of us during the week of the 10ᵗʰ–15ᵗʰ, won't you dear. I have been playing hockey for Ch.Ch. [Christ Church College, Oxford] the last 2 halves! On Saturday 7 of us helped Christ Church to lose about 20 to 1 to a military team from Cambridge…Jax has decided to write to you, so don't get a fit! But you see we are so damnably bucked at the idea of Doil Ecart[220] that God help us if we survive.

Owen to his mother, 29 January 1919

I am still at Rouen though I hope to get off now in a day or two's time & join my company. I had to go through gas this morning—a most absurd proceeding & I was presented with a bran new gas mask which cost the Government 17/6. However! The interesting thing about it was that I found inside it a note from some munition girl in Nottinghamshire to the tommy who should get the mask wishing him good luck & a safe return which was really rather amusing.

I am most anxious to hurry back to my company as then I shall be able to get letters & also to get my 'Demoralisation' papers through. I don't think it ought to take long. I also am most anxious to get my little mare again.

I got your parcel yesterday & at the present moment I am using the fountain pen which is excellent. Thanks awfully for the cakes, pudding etc. I am going to have a cold feast tonight & wish you luck.

Owen to his father, [29 January 1919]

Here I am back again in France after my short leave. I enjoyed myself immensely though…14 days had gone almost before I realised they were half past.

By far the most important thing about my leave was my interview with Dr Pope. He told me that I could now obtain a degree in Agriculture—a new arrangement about a week old. So I went round & saw Somerville of the School of Rural Economy & he said that my two prelims [preliminary examinations], Physics & Chemistry (really prelims for a degree in Natural Science) would exempt me from the prelim. in Agriculture & that I could set to work at once for the final exam which would come off in July 1920, when I could take it if I had done enough work. I think that sounds a very good plan indeed, especially as I believe that if I take Divinity & French [as an] extra subject I can get a degree in Natural Science without further exam. I am not absolutely certain on this last point but that is what I understand from a paper Dr Pope sent me.²²¹ On strength of all this I am putting in an application for demobilisation in the near future so that I can hope to get out of the army in time to begin work next term or in October.

I am still learning such things as management of men & technical & practical engineering & also getting a fairly good screw of which I ought to save £5 to £10 a month but don't always succeed. At present I have £40 invested in the Co-op under Mother's name.

———

Owen to his mother, 29 January 1918 [1919]

I am still waiting to get away from Rouen but there appear to be various difficulties. However I have still hopes of going tomorrow. I have seen every one I possibly can see about going & all I can do now is to wait.

I told you I think that I was on escort duty, taking care of a couple of officers under arrest. Well, it is not much fun, I spend most of my time in the mess yesterday. I read *Quinney* by Horace Vachel.²²² Also I have been reading botany but some cad has bagged my writing pad containing my notes so I must start again…I actually had egg & bacon for breakfast, in fact the food is quite good what there is of it. At present I am being as economical as anything. I only hope it lasts.

———

Edna Brown to Owen, 29 January 1919

All the family are well with the exception of Aunty Kate...Your poor old friend Mr Green has left the Chapel & is working for the Council, he got fed up with the rest room. Last Sunday when we went into the school room from Chapel, there were only 6 soldiers their. We expect that it will be closed altogether now for it is not worth while keeping it on.

One evening before the Armistic was signed Horace & Marjorie went down the High St. Marjorie had to go to Vinalls [grocery]. It was a very dark night being no lamps lit. While Horace waited outside for her, a woman came up & took his arm—they both walked a few steps when the woman said to Horace 'Liz is that you.' One can imagine how Horace felt. Of course he told her he was not 'Liz'.

We had a ripping time at the social last Wednesday....Kervin sang twice, 'The Valley of Laughter' & 'Beyond the Dawn'. We hope you have found your kit, we wish that it had been you demobolised instead of that. We all send our love & hope to see you soon.

P.S. The Boy stood on the burning deck

His ----- ----- ----- ----- -----

As you said in one of your letters that he was a Lucky Fellow but I am afraid he was just the opposite. E.A.B.

Ida Brown to Owen, 29 January 1919

I have been meaning to write a long letter but have not found time; now Edna is writing...I am just writing this short note to tell you I have freely forgiven you for all your cruel remarks. I am only waiting for an opportunity to pay you out. Thanks ever so much for your letters. I should think they would demobilise you as they have demobilised your kit. Shall us hope so? Yes! Lets. No more now as I am in an awful hurry. Love from all, Your Affectionate Sister, Ida

———

Gilbert to Owen, 30 January 1919

The other day a letter came through from you without any from England…but the contents were only a letter from Eliot & one from Pat forwarded. Thanks for sending them on, but I wish you had just, however much in a hurry, just scribbled a few words to say how you are in health & spirits & whether much occupied. I cling to the hope that you have been getting some useful & instructive work to do. The chance of your being released soon seems rather to recede & time goes on, like my chance of getting home…What a lot of experiences you have gone through since I last arrived home in April 1917!

   I am…making arrangements for a series of articles in a local paper 'The Hindu'[223] on Indian Poverty, which I hope I may afterwards be able to publish as a book. I am getting a little golf & have spent Sunday evenings on the River Adyar. That is still open to the sea, so that the tide comes in & out & it is full of fish which sometimes jump right into your boat. We had two in last Sunday, when I rowed Collins down to the bar & sailed back with the sea breeze…I have had no mail from England for over a fortnight, but one is expected on Sunday or Monday, just three weeks after the last. As you are so fond about writing home, I expect to get quite a budget of your letters, which will be very jolly.

———

Hugh Cockram to Owen, 2 February 1919

I have just received your second letter, dated 30.1.19…and hasten to thank you most awfully…It is terribly decent of you, and in view of your present

262

position financially we both feel little short of cash. Nevertheless thanks awfully, I will think of you at the time *sine dubio* [without doubt].

As you mention the moneys of yours in my possession, and as you seem to be suffering a financial crisis, would you like me to send on to you some or all of the cash? None of the War Savings Certificates have yet increased in value, but I might see my way to granting a small interest if you are in need of ready money.[224] Be sure to let me know.

Everyone here is ill…on Friday…Brigger returned with a temperature over 4 degrees above normal, and is still in bed. Meanwhile I was in bed Friday and Saturday, but have got up today feeling rotten and Jacks is about to take my place in bed directly a bed is made up for him…But I am tres bucked by your letter, and with many, many, many thanks, yours v. affectionately, Hugh.

Violet to Owen, 4 February 1919

If you can get a *fairly cheap* pair of gloves for him [Patrick] you might do so say about 5/-. It's no good getting rotten ones & no good getting them at 7/6 unless you shell out! Well old man I'm glad that you have at last joined your Co'y. What a pity you do not know German so that you could speak to the prisoners. It's certainly interesting. Did you meet old friends—are your men friendly? I am glad you are doing work & learning to build huts. Don't you ache to do some of the work yourself & not only watch…You will need a good deal of pluck & determination to set to work in earnest. Bilson said…a number of men from the army in the Forrestry are getting schols. He isn't because he still gets army pay. So do see if you can do any-thing of the sort in Rural economy or Agriculture or whatever they call it. Do a little hard reading daily. Tomorrow if I can I will send you a book on the League of Nations…& some tales of Tolstoy which you haven't read, they are interesting & vivid though rather terrible still he is such an artist in sketches of human beings…I met Joyce…she looked rather sweet, she sometimes has such a pure look, I think it's the fineness of her skin & perhaps the cheap rimless glasses. She's a nice girl. She has such kindly impulses. Well I must stop. Goodbye dear son of mine. Much love from your loving Mother, Violet Slater. It's freezing again I think.

———

Owen to his mother, 6 February 1919

The weather is horribly cold and rather miserable alternately snow, thaw, rain, freeze. You seem to be having skating which must be very jolly—here there is no ice at all fit, only frozen marches etc. Besides the work is always going on very energetically. It is most interesting especially now it is nearly finished, every day makes so much difference. I do hope Pat has managed to get to the Gilbert and Sullivan opera all right…I'm sorry this letter isn't longer but I'm horribly tired—I think it must be the cold.

———

Joyce Cockram to Owen, 9 February 1918 [1919] from Oxford

Many thanks for your letter of 30.1.19. Since then I believe you have gone to Harfleur—at least I think your Mother said so—& have sent in your demobilisation papers. I suppose you may get home at practically any moment now. Just think of yourself up here [Oxford] properly and settled next term!

I should have written before; unfortunately I have been busy and incidentally so fed up that I daren't write to anybody. Joan [Anderson] is going away, probably some time this week for four or six months. She is going to do Y.M.C.A. work down at Hindhead in Surrey. She is not on duty till 3.30 pm & only has to play accompaniments etc. then. For this she gets £1 a week, room & meals provided—except breakfast. I ask you! & I have to go on doing rotten jobs like Physics and interesting but

264

obviously obnoxious jobs like Anatomy for nothing for five years, with no prospect at the end except of an exceedingly busy life! Sometimes I can't help wondering whether the game is worth the candle (but of course I *know* it must be. I am only feeling properly sick with life.)

You probably know that Hugh & Jacks have been ill with bronchial ---itis. They are together in a pink sick room with some of the plaster knocked off—showing white spots! I went down with oranges yesterday and saw Matron, as I wanted to know what was really up. She told me to go up and see them. I nearly had a fit and thought Hugh would swear, but he seemed quite bucked and asked me to go again today. I went up when I got back from home and found them up and better...they were munching cake cut with a rusty pocket knife: they offered me some in a tentative fashion so I knew I was on dangerous ground & refrained from having any. (The relief on their faces was well worth the sacrifice—for I was mighty hungry.)...They are going to various D'Oyly Carte things. I am going on Tuesday to the Gondoliers...but I expect that's all. I am sorry you are missing them, & that your Mother can't get seats too. The 1st man in the queue bought 176 tickets, so it was pretty hopeless!...by the way, many thanks for the Scout button thing [Turk's Head knot]. I hope to make some in the near future. I went to see *David Garrick* again last night— for the third time. It's a gorgeous play and Martin Harvey is perfectly topping.

Violet to Owen, 9 February 1919

Earlier P[atrick] and I went to a Serbian service at the Cathedral. A translation was given of the service. That old man who prayed for the warriors' graves gave the sermon which was in English. The musical part of the service was unaccompanied & was rather weird but very nice. We enjoyed it. Father —— gave a sermon on brotherly love quite a nice simple sermon. We had quite a noisy meeting at the Friends. I should like to tell you about it.

[P.S.] I hope your valise has turned up long ago & that you manage to keep warm, & are kind & honorable to your men! As Pat prays you should be & 'work very hard'.

Patrick to Owen, 9 February 1919

We went skating in Long Meadow and as I had sore legs I put on some bandages, so every body cept [kept] on asking what was the matter. One boy (Angus MacDougal) found a strap and went towing every body about, some people, when they cought hold first called out 'Carriage full no more room!' With Lots of Love From Pat

---

Owen to his mother, 11 February 1919

I am having a pretty busy day today. To start with up early & parade for works at 7.30—a horrible effort on these cold mornings. Down at the works I was kept pretty busy though nobody came round as I was half expecting. Generally I have a sapper to look after the fire in the office but today I had a Bosche [prisoner of war, a Bavarian officer]. He was rather a nice old fellow with a ripping complexion & beard, looking very much like a typical grandfather. He showed me a photo of his wife & two kids. Finally I took his photo, hope it comes out well…after tea I had to read out pages of stuff inciting men to volunteer to join the armies of occupation.[225] Now in the evening I am going with the Major to a couple of dances. The first will only last an hour or so as it is a practise in one of the YMCA huts in the valley. The one afterwards is quite a small affair but a pukha dance given by & for Waac officers.

The whole question of demobilisation here in the Co'y seems to be in a hopeless muddle & the same everywhere else, nobody knows exactly what is happening or understands the arrangements. Daily the O.C. [Officer Commanding] sends off messages & inquiries, so far without result. Meantime we just carry on. Comparatively few of the men have been demobilised as yet & the best men seem to be the first to go.

Violet to Owen, 11 February 1919

I had your letter this morning wherein you tell me that your valise has not turned up...I hope sincerely all those nice things are not lost to you... I ran down to the town & went to Woodward's. They say they have not been able to make the bags because the pattern comes from a wholesale firm who want them to buy a whole 'piece'. Of course they do not want to do that now; he said that probably they would be able to arrange & then they would only be 2 or 3 days...We, the Friends, are going to try to do something in connection with the 'Fight the Famine' committee. We shall first have a meeting at which various people will be asked to speak who have been in Russia. I will tell you about it later when we have got the speeches etc.[226] On Sunday a certain Langdon Davis[227] a young man you may easily know by sight. He has a rather fair curly hair, low forehead, keen grey eyes & bright complexion. He has rather a straight-direct look. I've seen him about a lot. He had been in Glasgow during the strikes & not only told how the leader was knocked down by the police with batons while trying to keep order but he also described the truly appalling slums of Glasgow.[228] You ought to visit them. It was rather graphic to hear these things from a eye-witness.

If you are writing any time send things that seem interesting to Father. He said in his last that he would like sometimes to see cuttings that I think good...Have you the least idea when you may get sent home? I'm glad that you are busy & that it's interesting work. That's good.

Owen to his mother, 12 February 1919

I had a fine time yesterday at the dances. The first was by far the most enjoyable. We arrived at the YMCA & after waiting there were about 50 of us. Three YMCA ladies undertook the job of teaching us & we started with some Morris dances. I don't remember ever having seen any before much less taken part in them. It was awfully jolly, excellent exercise & the enjoyment most infectious. They seem to go on the principle that if you dance about & hop & skip & run you must feel happy & you do. I am most certainly going to the next practice which will probably come in a few days time. After the Morris dancing we had a certain amount of instruction in modern dancing—waltz & one step, which was quite helpful. All this only lasted a little over an hour & then we went along to a Waac camp. There were very few there & the hall we had was abominably cold but the floor was simply ripping. We went on there till 12.30 & then had to walk home. It was, as always, a tremendous tug coming up the hill. As a result this morning I didn't want to get up at all, so had breakfast in bed & arose at about 10.20 or 11.0. We have been having jolly good food lately, quite a large amount of eggs.

Owen to his mother, 13 February 1919

Another hard day on the works...I shall be glad when the job is done as one is apt to get rather fed up with it...There is a little Irishman in the company who is employed at present in making me my valise, by name Delaney. He is an awfully amusing little fellow, he has a high squeaky voice & is an excellent scrounger, which I am afraid is almost synonymous with 'thief'. But in the army it is not exactly the same thing. For instance at the works there is a large pile of timber that is of no use for building purposes so we sent down a wagon to-day & removed a full wagon load for fire wood for the company. That comes under the heading of scrounging, which really is stealing government property for the use of troops & also may be expressed by the word salving or salvage.[229]

This evening I got that pamphlet in agriculture & have filled in the application for £175 scholarship. No harm in applying but it is extremely doubtful whether I shall be able to get it.

Gilbert to Owen, 13[?] February 1919

I think I had better send this to Oxford as the safest way of getting it to you. I am so glad you got that leave in Jan...About the Cockram family, I have met Hugh, he came to tea one day when I was at home & I remember him fairly well. I thought he was a very good sort. As for Joyce, although I have not seen her, what with photos & scraps about her in letters, I feel I know her quite well, but I am hoping some day—not this year, alas—to have opportunities of making her much better acquaintance. If you are writing to her you can tell her so, & you can tell her that I think you are lucky to have such nice friends as the Cockram family.

Your Aunt Gertrude in a letter I got on Saturday says she was very glad to hear that you intend to stick to Engineering. Do you? I think it might be wise, but I have heard nothing from you to that effect. It seems to me that you have as your three most obvious lines, (1) sticking to engineering, (2) chemical research (3) the original agricultural plan. Of these engineering is the biggest field, then chemistry, then agriculture. With regard to the attractiveness of the life, I should put agriculture first, engineering second, & chemistry third. On the whole I think chemistry comes after engineering. You have made a beginning in each, but I think your R.E. course would count more than what you have done in chemistry. We have, however, also got to consider to what extent these three professions are likely to be overcrowded, & I think engineering very likely *may*. There are so many coming out of the R.E. like you, & many with a good deal more experience. On the whole agriculture is the most risky, but also it may turn out very well. I think you must try to settle it according to your tastes, the one you like best you will be able to work at hardest & that will probably yield the greatest success. I have sent some advice to Mother as to what you should do if in the end you hit upon Engineering. Don't pass by any good opening that comes along without due consideration, but try not to let any hesitations prevent you from working your best. Nothing you learn will come amiss.

I have put down a motion for the March meeting of the Senate for a degree in Economics. I hope to carry it by the Indian vote. It will be very unwelcome to a good many of our official conservatives. But the debate should be interesting. I generally find myself hitting right & left, at officialism on one side & the anti-official party on the other; but in that motion I hope to have all the antis with me.

I do wonder where you are now & what you are doing. I hope it is not bitterly cold, or wet & gloomy. It is hard to realise in our successive days of autumnal sunshine.

Violet to Owen, 14 February [1919]*

I am so disappointed to get such a shabby few letters from you now-a-days. We are interested in everything. Sometime I should like to know how your day is usually spent. It is just these commonplace things which are interesting. Also one would be interested to have an idea what the men & officers are like. Have you any time for any work—book work? Are there any facilities for learning anything, either for men & [or] officers? If you stay on a while *do* try to do some steady grinding work. It would be worthwhile I think to try to get saturated with French—to read some good French books, & if you could, get conversational French. It will be such an opportunity that you may not have again...This afternoon Mary Pask[230] & I went to the prison to see a poor Conscientious Objector who has already been imprisoned 3 years & has just been given

1 year more. He is allowed one letter a fortnight & 3 visitors once in 3 weeks all at once. He is not allowed to read the newspapers so he was tremendously keen to hear all about things. The curious part he seems to know quite a lot. Our interview [missing pages]

I enclose several letters you may feel interested to read if you are not much occupied. *Destroy them*. I don't want them back. The Censor very much opened your last letter [and] scarcely shut it again.

Owen to his mother, 16 February 1919

Sunday & a fine day. My day off again so stayed in bed respectably late but got up for breakfast & went to a Communion Service after Church Parade…After tea I went for a short walk with the Major but it turned dark very quickly & miles away you could see heavy rain over the sea so we turned back. The country just round here is not pretty; the hill we are on is a plateau…& the stray houses…are hideously ugly… like one of those paper covered bricks kids play with. Very close to us there is a huge camp of German prisoners…tents enclosed by high barbed wire entanglements & then a path round which armed sentries march, & then a ring of very high electric lights. At night time they really look very pretty, hundreds of these bright lights in the open country—one might almost imagine it was a fairy ball which in day time nothing more hideous could be thought of.

Violet to Owen, 17 February 1919

You will be surprised to have a letter from Joyce in mine. She will probably have told you that she came in after tea & stayed to supper, that Hugh is better & went to the theatre 3 or 4 times, that Mrs. C. was ill with toothache

& had her tooth out, that Pa Cockram has had all his out & now for a new set. She brought up Vaughan Williams' *Sea Symphony*. It is very nice & the words of Walt Whitman are beautiful.[231] I wonder if you know them. They are so descriptive. I should think his words would inspire music. I did not write yesterday & I have not heard since Sunday morning. Never mind. I hope I'll hear tomorrow...I went to tea to Mrs Grafflin yesterday. It was a miserable wet day. We talked single tax.[232] Did I tell you that on Saturday there was a conference at Barnet House[233] on the Housing Q[uestion]. I asked the lecturer who never mentioned the land and how it was to be acquired...She did not think that the question of Land Values was at the root of the matter. She was Eleanor Rathbone a C[ity] C[ouncillor] for Liverpool.[234] She said well 'Land Nationalization' will take a long time. I rose again & said *'Why not take the land?'* It is extraordinary how sacred the landlords' rights have become. Few seem to think about the matter at all.

I wonder if you will be moved on from Harfleur? Do you expect to be? And mind you tell me what you hear about demobilization. Have you heard from Love? You should write to him & send on the Glasgow cutting. I suppose your valise will turn up?

Joyce Cockram to Owen, 18 February 1919
from the Slaters' home

Your Mother suggested that I should write to you and even produced paper, a block to write on—*and* her fountain pen; so I ask you! What is a poor weak minded maiden to do? You mustn't expect a coherent letter from me as Patrick insists upon doing all his work aloud and has just reached the mighty conclusion that as $-44y = 88$, $y = -2$. Between us we have discovered that if a man is 3 times as old as 12 years hence as he was 12 years ago—his present age is 24!

Joan [Anderson] went away last Tuesday. She has quite settled down and enjoys the life tremendously; she has a thoroughly slack time, gets up at 9.30 & begins work at 3.30, & earns £1 a week with everything found; whereas I get up at 8—nominally—& work all day & have to pay for it into the bargain!

Hugh has quite recovered. I think the 4 theatres in 3 days last week did him pots of good; he enjoyed them thoroughly. I saw the *Gondoliers* with the Dixeys[235] & should have 'stood' for the Pirates, only I retired to bed with a cold: incidentally with Joan away I haven't the necessary chaperone at hand. The Gondoliers was topping.

I am awfully busy with Physics & am at present worried with Electricity—the exam is in 3 wks time & yesterday I did Latent Heat of Steam and got an error of 7% in my 2nd experiment which was a bit worse than my 1st—& I went away nearly in tears! It is a ghastly thing to do accurately.

Have you ever seen polarised light? I saw it the other day through crystals of tartaric acid—a double oxalate of Potassium & Chromium—Epsom Salts—a whelk's tongue etc: Dr Dixey's polariscope belonged to W. S. Gilbert. It is one of the most wonderful & beautiful shows I've seen. If you ever get a chance you should see it if you haven't done so. I was surprised to find how beautiful it is.

Pat & I are just going down to supper—so I'll stop.

Edna Brown to Owen, 18 February 1919

Thank you ever so much for your letter of the 2nd & the 7th. I was awfully pleased to have it…We are all looking forward to your coming home & do hope you will come to see us…Norman wishes me to give you a piece of poetry which he has composed, it goes to the tune of 'O Happy Band of Pilgrims'

> O how lovely to be in Heaven
> My Mother says it's nice
> She knows all about it
> She's been there once or twice.

Sapper Fisher took us by surprise the other evening; he has just come from a hospital in Wales. The second evening he came, Ida, Norman & I were in the dining room with him & Norman started reciting 'your favourite poem' 'The boy stood on the burning deck' we tried to stop him but he would not, & he said it all through. We girls did feel horrid. I fortunately was reading so I kept my face hidden. I could not see how Ida took it. I cannot write anymore as it is supper time. ~~Perh~~ Probably you will be glad it is supper time. Heaps of love from all. Your Sincere Friend, Edna

---

Gilbert to Owen, 19 February 1919*

I have now heard that I cannot get a passage before June, which rules it out for this year, as I have to be back by the middle of July. I shall manage things so as to clear off in 1920 by the middle of March to get home, I hope, at the beginning of April. Mother is most anxious for me to get home to help decide on your future plans & I wish I could. My advice to you is, unless you hear of some good & attractive opening, to get back to Oxford for the October term, and work hard for the Agri. Sci. degree. If you are demobilised sometime before, you might perhaps get a temporary job at engineering. If not, at least you might do some agricultural work; it is all good & educational. Meanwhile I am wondering whether you are beginning to entertain in your mind any matrimonial project. The names of various girls, all evidently very nice girls, have come into your letters, but the only one that suggests something serious is Joyce Cockram. Of course there is no hurry for you to be thinking about marrying, & no chance of any very early marriage; all the same a good wife is a very precious possession and the wise young man, when he finds the right girl, makes up his mind with great determination to win her if possible. And the best way to succeed is to let that determination be quite clearly understood.

274

Also it is very foolish to put off marriage until you can start married life with swank & servants etc. A little roughing it, with good health and a determination on both sides to make the best of life & of one another makes a good foundation for happiness. My father told me so when I was your age, and I know it by experience. So when you do want to marry, if it is Joyce or some other nice girl, I shall do my level best to help you to the fullest extent I can.

Owen to his mother, 21 February 1919

A pretty miserable day & my turn on the works…The delouse was finished on Saturday.

Peter Russell, a full Lieut., is expected back from leave any day now & Jenkins is requesting to go & is terribly worried about his souvenirs as to how he is going to manage to get them home because there is an order of long standing that if anyone is caught taking home rifles, shell cases, nose caps,[236] bombs etc his leave is cancelled & he returns to his unit at once.

I don't know whether I have ever told you about our officers. First there is the Major as he is called. Major J. O'Sullivan & Irish of course, tall, fair haired & blue eyed. Then Johnny who has now left us. Captain H. G. Johnson, tall dark broad redfaced & extraordinarily energetic, a bit of a bird or a knut.[237] Then Peter, who is away on leave, about my height, fair & rather ugly & a Scotchman, Lt Peter Russell. Then Tick as he is called, Desborough, Lt. short & ugly & fair. Then Jinks or Jenkins short, dark, a Welshman, rather older looking with a bald patch, quiet, voted Labour but doesn't agree with strikes & is called a Bolchevist.

Today I saw Delaney who is making me a valise & really he has made an excellent job of it.

Hugh Cockram to Owen, 22 February 1919

Many thanks for your letters. I have in my pocket 4. I can say that I have answered one only for certain…so will content myself with your last letter solely.

As regards Jacks' & my sickness, I believe we missed bronchitis by the skin of our teeth, that's all. We were away for a week, & I returned on the Thursday of Gilbert & Sullivan week! I had intended to go to *Iolanthe* (Monday night), *Mikado* (Wednesday aft.), *Trial by Jury* & *Pirates of Penzance* (Friday night) & *Gondoliers*, Sat. Mat. Of course the first two were washed out. However I did jolly well. I came out of the sick room Thursday morning…that evening Deuchar and I went to Gondoliers; afterwards Jacks, Tidswell and I went to [the] Cadena to tea;[238] we then rushed back to theatre, & joined Filsell, & we all four stood for 'the Gods' in the *Yeomen*. So I did 4 theatres in 3 days, not so bad. They were all topping. One A1 whimp[239] Catherine Ferguson who took Phoebe Meryll in the *Yeomen*, & Pitti Sing in the *Mikado*. I was absolutely gone on her.

By jove, thanks awfully for the cash. We enjoyed it tremendously; I cannot tell you individual things on paper, but when we next meet, I'll give you nothing save D'Oly Carte.

I hope to see your Mater in the course of a very few days, & find out about the bike.

By George I am longing to see you. I'm so sorry to hear that in all probability the Summer vac. stunt will be 'washed out', yet I hope we shall have another chance next year. With love, in haste, yours as ever, Hugh

---

Violet to Owen, 22 February 1919

I had 2 letters from you this morning one telling about Morris dancing & the other about your ride on Lucy. I'm jolly glad you did not get hurt. It seems a bit risky. I hope the Major won't think you such a bad rider that he won't invite you to ride again. I suppose you can't go off on your own. Naughty little creature. You will have to keep a sharp look out if you ride her again…Now for a few questions which please answer:

1st. Have you heard anything about your demobilization papers. What happens?

2nd. How about your valise? Have you heard where the others were going when yours was taken? Can't you claim any compensation if it doesn't turn up? Ask the Major!

3a What is the Major like? How old. Do you like him? What do you talk about when you go for a walk.

3b What work have you all been doing? Huts?

4th. Aren't you doing any French of any sort?

5th. Have you heard from Love or written to him

I had a rather full day on Saturday. In the afternoon I went to the Sheldonian Theatre to hear --- Fisher[240] Minister of Education hold forth on the Place of the University in the Education of the future. All the old fogies were there of the University…& undergraduates & common town people like myself were in the gallery which was only scantily & partially full. He is a man of about 50 with a very superior Oxford manner, rather good looking & clean shaven, pale. Of course he put Oxford in the forefront of the Universities & spoke of the liberal education that Classics give in contrast to the materialistic science though he thought that necessary. He wanted to see the teachers of all grades able to have a University course. It was all very academic & as he spoke of '30 years hence' as if the same old traditions just a little modified & broadened were going to persist. I could not help thinking so [how] ignorant he was of the great revolutionary movement that is sweeping along & how remote of [from] actuality he was. How ignorant the 'liberal education' of Oxford leaves most of the men who go through it…These people not only know little or nothing of big working class movements, or of industrial conditions, or of economics moreover don't want to & so the young undergrads go on in the same way.

In the evening I went to hear Sylvia Pankhurst[241] in the...Town Hall. She was lecturing on Russia. It was a contrast. It was most exciting. I wish that you had been there. There were a great many undergrads & soldiers & a few women. Of course there was a certain amount of game [barracking] going on, a little bell that was tinkled & the lights going up & down but they were much too interested to really interrupt. She was out & out revolutionary, she is a very clear, vivid speaker, very simple & direct & very good at debate. In the questions after the lecture she came off well. She gave an account of the Soviet government & of their rules & regulations for the official documents that they have issued. She gave an account of the Revolution & disposed of a good many lying statements that have been made about Russia more particularly about the Soviet government when disorder has occured is just where the Soviet has not had control—from all reliable sources it is apparent that the Soviet is not only the popular form of government but the only stable one. Under it, miners & others who do the rough & hard work are paid more than those who do the lighter & more pleasant. She was very fascinating though not exactly pretty. It was a treat after the Sheldonian & Fisher—one feels that these people are only half alive. Goodbye dear boy & good night.

<hr />

Owen to his mother, 22 February 1919

A perfectly beastly morning when I woke up...I went for a walk with Desborough down to the valley & wandered about for miles going from one place to another making arrangements for clean underclothes, games, baths & dancing for the men. The only way we can get underclothes for the men is to send them through a delouse & bathe and have their khaki disinfected & new underclothes dished out to them.

Just a few words about our Mess & sleeping quarters. The Mess is a hut about 20 feet long by about 18 feet wide...it is covered with felt & built of wood. It consists of three rooms...A is the mess. B is an unused sleeping room. C is a cubicle now used as a coal & wood shed to supply the stove…The sleeping hut is exactly the same…but is divided into four cubicles with one window to each…My cubicle is by far the best as I have lined the walls with green canvas & the roof as well & it looks rather ripping. All I want to complete it is a few bright coloured prints preferably with reds & oranges in them.

Peter Russell came back off leave today. He is a lively bird, a Scotchman & fond of the whisky & generally dances in the mess every night in a state of semi-intoxication. Quite a good lad in his way.

Owen to his father, 23 February 1919

I have just had a letter direct from you. I don't know how it comes, whether through England or not but it arrived on a day when I had no other letters. I am a very lucky individual as very rarely a day passes without a letter for me.

You must have heard from my letters to Mother what I am doing at present & where the company is. The delouse we were building is now finished & in full swing. Tomorrow all the men of the company are being put through it as for one thing they will get a bath & for another this is the simplest & quickest way to get clean new underclothes.

We are now employed on jobs quite close to our camp which is much pleasanter though the work is not nearly so interesting.

A few days ago I went out for a ride with the Major, both our horses had not had exercise for some time & mine was particularly frisky. I am sorry to say that through an unexpected buck I was thrown, however I managed to land on my feet & to retain my hold of the reins so I was all right, but later on, on the same ride we were having a fine gallop down a path through a wood when my mare swerved at a cross path & I fell headlong. The horse scampered off. The major, lucky man, had a glorious gallop to catch her again & I had a 3 mile walk before I met him again. I am taking the next available opportunity of going out on that horse & not being thrown.

Have you heard of a Miss Scott, a famous militant suffragette? She is now an administrator to a Waac camp very close to us & is a little quiet meek looking woman & awfully nice.[242] I am sending on various letters from home & cuttings Mother has from time to time sent me.

⁂

Violet to Owen, 25 February 1919

I had 2 nice letters from you today. It is *so* nice to have letters. These told me about the officers & the mess & cubicle etc. I…got those Danish pictures…& I send you the best in case you like to put some up in the mess or in the 'cubicle'…Everyone is getting 'flu' again it is a nuisance, some cases are very bad apparently Pat says 100 boys are ill at school…I think he must have made a mistake. He says he counted on his fingers who were away—quite a good memory test if he can remember 100 names. We are going to have Land Value people down, Scotchmen from the Highland League for the Taxation of Land Values[243] so I have been trying to get & see people to ask them to turn up…Tomorrow I'll try to remember to send Sylvia Pankhurst's paper—it's lively. Send Jenkins some of the papers if you can. I hope you get the 'Herald'. Why does he disapprove of strikes? What other way have the workers got? Surely if men are not slaves they have a right to cease working. And people are so blind they do not choose to believe that the housing conditions are as bad as they are, or indeed anything that it is unpleasant to believe.

⁂

Edna Brown to Owen, 25 February 1919

We are wondering how you are getting on—it is quite a long time since we heard from you. Every member of the family are all round the fireside talking to Sapper Fisher. Dorothy is quite well now, & Ida is not very well tonight but hope she is not going to have flue. Last Sunday night the Rest Room was closed for good. We girls went down & Dadda. It was not very nice. Mr Sander's gave a description of all that had happened during the four years.

Our cousin Reg is still very ill & is not expected to leave the hospital for another year. They have had to put him on his face again because he faints when he is on his back. Regie's little baby is a darling—he is just turned a year old...Dadda brought your camera home today & we are sending it to Oxford.

Gilbert to Owen, 27 February 1919

I have been thinking a good deal & talking a little about careers. People generally seem to think that engineering will be rather overcrowded with people placed like you are, & that our original plan is very good—an expanding and important field of work, & not too many workers. Anyway I don't think you can do better than go ahead. I have asked Mother to get Dr Somerville's advice about books & give you a present of them from me & send you as many as you can do with, in the hope that you may get some time for reading. And I think it is pretty clear that you had better, when released, go back to Oxford, and go for your degree in Agriculture as hard and quickly as you can.

I have been asked to put in a week at Bangalore for the Y.M.C.A. & am inclined to do all I can for them in gratitude for what they have done for Tommy Atkins and all Second Lieutenants.

Violet to Owen, [late February 1919]

I have just sent off a parcel containing various things you asked for...I've been putting a footwarmer in your bed thinking that you might come in any time. I hope that you are wrong about the position but you will see.

Donne & that other boy came up to ask for your address. Donne has been in Brussels & enjoyed himself mightily of course. They are both working at New [College, Oxford]. Donne is in digs. I've had a full day today as there has been the Friends Quarterly meeting...& then...a 'League of Nations' meeting. Gilbert Murray is speaking.

Owen to his mother, 1 March 1919

By the way I don't believe I ever acknowledged the receipt of the pyjamas socks shirts etc. Thanks very much. Also I was very glad to get the pictures you have sent; they are not exactly the type of picture that is popular in messes but they have jolly bright colours.

I have had a fairly busy day. Work all the morning...In the afternoon I went for a ride with the Major & had a perfectly ripping time going through some silver birch & oak woods. Tonight I am going to a dance with the Major at Miss Scotts which is only about 5 mins. away. I am told it is informal so it won't matter wearing my canvas shoes.

Don't forget to ask Dr Gillett about the lime juice as everybody swears it is bad for one & that whisky is better; I must pop off now & get changed for the dance so good bye.

Owen to his mother, 2 March 1919

I can't write much of a letter today as I am feeling abominably seedy. I have a cold coming on & so am going to bed very shortly.

The dance last night was great fun though of course I did not enjoy it so much as I would have done if I had been fit. We got there soon after 10 pm

& went on til about 1.30 by ordinary time but by 2.30 by the new time. We all changed our watches to summer time at eleven o'clock.[244] There were very few at the dance, as a whole bunch of Waac officers failed to turn up so in the end there were 3 ladies & 5 gentlemen. However we managed all right. As a matter of fact I found I danced much better with a masculine partner than with a feminine one though all the ladies...danced very well.

Violet to Owen, 4 March 1919

I am glad you are training & having Morris dancing. I hope you have an adequate amount of under-clothing & can get a good wash down: *don't* wear dirty underclothing. I daresay I can send you a vest [?] & pants if you want any, only try to think of all you want at once because it is rather extravagant to send so often & takes a lot of time...Goodnight dear boy. I am glad that you have had a little riding. I haven't heard about your bags. I'll call in again tomorrow if possible.

Ida Brown to Owen, 4 March 1919*

Didn't you know I have a propensity for falling in love with nearly everyone? I am afraid I could not count the times I have been in love but I have always managed to get out alright...You seem to have had some thrilling adventures on horse back. What about poor little Joan; have you discarded her? We three girls went over to the 'Math'[245] last week to see a play—written and staged by the boys. The proceeds went towards a memorial to the memory of old boys who have fallen in the war...I think it is going to be produced again on a more elaborate scale....The weather is as you say 'depressing'. It has done nothing but rain all day. I hope it will be fine tomorrow because I am going to Town for the day. 'Flu' has began its deadly work again. It seems to be more fatal than ever here. In London it is very bad and I am really rather nervy about going especially to a theatre but Dad and Mother think it alright. I certainly don't want to die yet; life is too sweet.

Cant write any more because it is tea time. We hope you are keeping well. Don't get the 'flu' again!

―――∞∞∞―――

Violet to Owen, 5 March 1919

I asked Dr Gillett this evening about drinking lime juice & he said it was excellent & would do you no harm, fruit juice was very good for the body, & that you were not likely to take sufficient to be anything but good for the system. So that's all right. On the other hand he said that whisky & spirits of any sort enlarge the arteries & bring the blood to the surface, they also quicken & dilate the heart, & so weaken it... he has come to the conclusion that spirits should be used very cautiously... I sent off your shoes & hope that they will arrive as soon as this. I was very sorry that you were not feeling well. I hope that you have not got 'flu' & that you are all right again. Don't forget to be particular about your underclothes. If you dance & get hot & sweaty you are liable to take cold unless your skin is cleansed & your clothes dried or clean. Of course woollen clothes are not so bad as cotton.

I hope I acknowledged your cheque for £5–0–0. I wish you would give it to the Fight the Famine fund. What do you say?

―――∞∞∞―――

Violet to Gilbert, 6 March 1919*

Each time a letter comes I seize it & hope that you may say 'Coming home'. But alas each gives less hope. Still I hope that a cable may come...I do want you so much…I can't help feeling that it is right for you to come back to the boys…Pat is in so many ways such a splendid little chap & yet something is wrong either with the education or with home life—he is very difficult.

The whole tragedy of Europe starving, of revolution & pestilence is so unspeakably ghastly when those who have the power are just fighting over the spoils. We shall be thankful to get Wilson back[246] but whether he will be able to do something to bring sanity into the turmoil remains to be seen…Pat is such a darling I love his bright boisterous ways & I *hate* & detest to be such a severe disciplinarian & a policeman as I have.

Gilbert to Owen, 6 March 1919

I am sending this home because there is a possibility of you being demobilised, according to your last letter. It has been very comforting to see by the trend of the news that chances of any fresh outbreak of war appear to diminish, & it would really look as though what remains to be done will be mainly done by freshly enlisted troops. The sooner you can get back and tackle your studies the better. I hope you will find you *can* mug in at books & lectures all right…I suppose there would be no chance of your getting a schol. but it would be nice for you to be able to get into a college for at least one year. If it can't be done perhaps you will be able to stir up the Non. Coll's to put a boat on the river…When you get demobilised, I want you to take a hand in getting all arrangements put straight for Mother's coming out to India. There are your own lodging arrangements to make—Pat to be boarded somewhere—Christmas arrangements for all three of you. Then I should very much like you to escort Mother through France and see her off at Marseilles. If you could manage it I should like you to take the Ostend, Bruges, Ghent, Brussels route, & then Paris, Lyons, Marseilles—or instead visit Le Cateau, or whatever other place it was where you saw action. But the other would be most interesting to you.

When I see you again I suppose the strong officer surface they have put on you will be quite rubbed off, so that I shall never know what you were like in that stage, & there will be instead the up-to-date Oxford under-grad of the post-war type. Changes are so quick in young men nowadays that one requires to be on the spot all the time to know one's own son. Well, I am very glad that in little over a year I shall be with you, & then our next parting will be but a reasonably short one.

Edna Brown to Owen, 10 March 1919

Ida received your letter this morning. We are very glad that you are well & hope you will not be so unfortunate as to have flue again…tonight some of us are going to see Mary Pickford.[247] I suppose you know she has had flue awfully badly but suppose she is well again. We heard that she had died but that was not true…On the 29th of this month the time is going to be altered, we are starting the summer time. It does not seem much like summer coming. We are having rather cold weather lately…There is an awful shortage of coal in England. Dadda ordered ours last summer & we have not got them yet…If they don't come soon we shall have no fire. We have enough now to last us about a week.

I must get the tea now so goodbye. Heaps of love from all.

Violet to Owen, 11 March 1919

I have just had your letter all about the grand dance. I am glad that you en-joyed it & got fairly suitable shoes. I only hope you did not wear them out. They sound very thin!…I am sending a letter of Eliots which I intended to send sooner. Will you send it on to Father. It is sad that he has had to give up the idea of coming. He now fills his letters with my coming out to him...It will be a great adventure & very delightful in many ways but I shall not like having to leave you all. I do wonder how long it will be before you get out of the army. I hope not long. I am sure you will find it difficult to sit down & work hard at books. I only hope you try to discipline yourself to do some now though I'm sure it must be most difficult. Apparently some people do. Aren't there any lectures or classes going. Do try to find out.

The Friends are getting up a meeting to be held next Monday in aid of the Friends Emergency work.[248] I have been making some calls to ask people to come also to deliver letters, rather leaflets, with the invitation. Miss Pask & I are doing it. Do not forget to tell me if you will make a contribution & how much. Also answer my other questions dear boy. I've made some toffee & will try to remember to send some to you.

Tomorrow we are to have 2 speakers down from the Highland Land League to speak at the F.o.R. meeting. Mrs Grafflin has asked them & me to supper first & Dr Gillett is going to take us down to the meeting...Mrs Grafflin is greatly excited about it. Mrs Morrison came today...I suppose you know that they are leaving Oxford for America in April. Mrs Grafflin goes in May.

Gilbert to Owen, 13 March 1919

I was sorry to learn about your disappointment with regard to demobilising, but I never supposed, myself, that there was much chance, & I hope at any rate you are getting interesting work & are not like the infantry, who are said to have nothing to do except kill time.

You are approaching your 20th birthday, and I wonder whether you would like me, for your birthday present, to pay for the Pitman[249] course for you. According to the information that reaches me it is quite good, and does enable those who go through it to learn things more quickly and easily than they would otherwise be able to do.

I am going to give a fortnight of my precious holiday to the Y.M.C.A. as a thank offering for what it has done for you & for some millions of other young men.

Violet to Gilbert, [March 1919]*

It is dreadful to have the fate of millions of men women and children [and] the whole well being of countries in the hands of a few statesmen. They are supposed to represent the people but they never do. I wonder if we shall live to see some great and good changes. One has always a faith that we shall…God bless you & keep you my beloved one. V.O.S.

Violet to Owen, 18 March 1919

I got your letter written with a made up pen. Bertha brought it up to me & said 'that be some funny writing'. There was not much news to comment upon. If I send sheets it seems no good sending only 2 for you would have to have a change. I'll look out what I have—these things are so expensive to buy nowadays, but I dare say you are longing to have something better than an army blanket. You seem quite a pal of the Major's. Do you like him? I am glad to have some snaps of your fellow officers. We had a very good meeting on the land question yesterday. I went to Mrs Grafflins to dinner & met the two speakers & Dr Gillett called with his car & drove us down, also drove them to the station & took Mrs Grafflin & me home, so we did the thing comfortably. They were both good speakers & we had an excellent discussion afterwards. There were from 30 to 60 people there, a good many N.C.C. [Non Combatant Corps] men I think. I undertook to send an account of the meeting to the *Oxford Chronicle*[250] so Mrs Graffin & I did it this afternoon. I wrote & she typed & I took it down to the office. If it

288

comes out I'll send it along. I am now enclosing a bit from Upton Sinclair's paper—its the best statement of the Russian business that I've seen. You might send it on to Father when you write[251]... I am going to Headington to see Mrs Margoliouth[252] who has got home from India. I want to hear how she got home & all about [it]. As Father wants me to go this autumn I must find out about all I can.

Aunt Annie to Owen, 19 March 1919

I am afraid I have been owing you a letter for long...I've not been forgetting you, though, and am glad you have had a time at Rouen; it is one of the only 3 French towns I have ever stayed at...only 2½ days, but I was *very* interested in it...I expect you walked down the Rue de la Grosse Horloge [la rue du Gros Horloge] many many times, & admired the carvings on the roof of the arch under the clock. What a grand old street...Oh dear! I do like to remember the *few* things I have seen.

But I am glad you are wanting to be back at Oxford, & I *do* hope you will get the £175 grant for land work that you have applied for. Also it was good for you that you were interested in that big hut you were helping to build for the doctors' work & the disinfecting etc. work for the poor soldiers who were so badly needing such ministrations. It must have been so good for you to feel you were not merely 'marking time' while you waited for Peace & demobilization, but were helping in such eminently useful work. I wonder whether you are long enough with the same set of men, to get to *know* them & like them & feel you & they are friends? I hope so. I think you must have some weary, empty times over there, sometimes— but I'm glad you have the enjoyment of horse riding—for to tell you the truth, I *don't like* all the things in a young officer's life & I think the Y. O. himself cannot like them either. I *imagine* there is too much *purposeless* time in it. Am I wrong, I wonder?—or are you saying to yourself 'Poor old Aunt Annie! How little she knows!'

I wish you would come across some of your relatives over there: for instance, Theodore Meas...he is I believe called a 'Commander' & is teaching about 300 engineering...Cyril Berlinshaw Smith is still over there, but *not* in the Army of Occupation, as he hoped to be...He has gained the Military Cross...for 'Gallantry in Action', a few days before Nov. 11—Eustace Dodd is expecting to be sent over to the Rhine, in the Army of Occ: before long...Now I must close—with love from me in wh. Miss Cooper joins, I am, dear Owen, Your very affectionate Aunt Annie.

Gilbert to Owen, 20 March 1919

I wonder how things go with you. Before this reaches you spring should have come in full blast, and the peace settlement may be well on, and a lot more demobilising done. Each month that passes seems to show more clearly that the army in the field can be cut down without danger. The war has shown that if any great power has conscription all must, and it has been good news to read that the Paris conference has practically decided that none shall.[253]

The more I think about it the more I am disposed to conclude that the agricultural line is likely to be in the end a very satisfactory one, though there may have to be a good deal of patience. Certainly there are very big openings in India for agricultural progress—improvement of wheat, cotton, jute, rice and sugar have all been taken up by various governments, and with very remarkable results. When India tackles problems of this sort, England cannot long continue its attitude of sloth and apathy. Of course ordinary farming in England is far better than in India, so the field for improvement is not so big. Still it is a very big one.

On Thursday I attended a meeting...to discuss the food problem...So far as I can make out there is probably, with old reserves, enough grain in the country for everybody, and so measures for coping with profiteering are what are mostly needed. But if we have another bad monsoon this year, things will be very different. There will be an absolute deficiency of food in India, i.e. no matter how well the food is controlled and distributed, *millions* of people will probably die of famine, unless they can be fed on imported food. And with the miserably low level of wages it is tremendously difficult for the people to pay for imported food. With practically no taxation the Government is almost powerless for want of funds. What India wants is a just distribution of the land tax…If the landholders had to pay more they would produce more.[254]

Gilbert to Owen, 23 March 1919

I have unexpectedly heard of a chance of getting home. The 'Ormonde' assigned to clear off women & children has accommodation for a number of 3rd Class passengers which the people who have priority are turning up their noses at—but it should be good enough for a man. If I get the passage I have wired for, you will have had the information earlier by wire. If you have not had that, you may infer that I could not get it. But if I do get my passage I sail on April 8th. In that case I shall enquire in Paris for your whereabouts and the possibility of meeting.

Hugh Cockram to Owen, 28 March 1919

I really must apologise for not writing before. I know we have not exchanged views for over a month…I made a great effort about a fortnight ago & visited your mater & found her flourishing; & Joyce & I went out there to tea last Thursday week. She asked me to inquire about your bike which I promptly did next day; of course the blighter has not touched the thing yet, but I told him you were returning in a fortnight & *must* have it!

I shall have to do the Dickens of a lot of work next term. My pater came over to see George Wood yesterday re. my chances of a schol., & I am to stay on till Doomsday provided that my prospects at the end of next term are fairly bright. Otherwise God help us! I am going to work jolly hard, I can assure you.

Am longing to hear from you, & will write again early in the vac.

—⊶—

Violet to Owen, [late March 1919]

I am sending a letter to you from Father. He mentions the 'Ormonde'… Today's '[Daily] Herald' speaks of men being called up for Russia. What horrible madness it is & what fools the men are not to all turn Conscientious Objectors It is disgusting to be a piece of machinery that can be used just as those fire eaters like. I wish the men would be like the things in that old song of the pig & the stile, that the men would refuse to go [to] the railway and to move the munitions & the sailors to take them. It is just a attempt to get rid of a Socialist government. I hope indeed that it will fail… Your 2nd parcel came today; it contained a new trench coat. What is the meaning of it? Well I am very tired so I will stop.

—⊶—

Violet to Owen, 13 April 1919

I hope you will get the letter that I sent though I did not put Tournai or Belgium. I thought you might receive it in France. I did not realize that you would have such a long journey to take. I hope you will have fairly comfortable quarters & a nice Y.M.C.A. hut or something of the sort. You really had a very pleasant time at Harfleur & will miss your jolly rides & teas & dances etc. But I hope you will find something else. I have of course been thinking of you very much also of dear Father sailing on the ocean. It is lovely to think that he is coming towards us every day.

As soon as you tell me that I can safely send I will send the breeches & sheets so mind you tell me when you write dear boy.

Edna Brown to Owen, 13 April 1919

Marjorie received your letter three days ago, we were awfully glad to have it, as we begun to think something must have happened...I am no longer at home now you will probably be surprised to know that I am in the Medway Insurance Office, Chatham. I have been their a month now but I think I would rather be at home.

Mrs Collins had a little baby son last Monday but it only lived eight hours. It is a great disappointment to both of them, she had made all its little clothes. He was to be called Rodney but it had on the coffin Harry Collins age eight hours. They sent a telegram to the Major to say it was born & then Tuesday another was sent to say it had died & Major did not receive it, & on Thursday he came home expecting to see his baby & when he was told it had passed away he broke down. He is home for good now.

Horace is home he looks ever so nice in his uniform...Cant you get your leave this month, I thought you had leave every 3 months...Sapper Fisher went away to Horsham for a short time, & is now here waiting to go to Russia. Our cousin Reg is progressing fine, the other day he was put on his spinal chair & then went down to dinner. Please write soon & how is Joan & Lucy?

Violet to Owen, 18 April 1919

I am writing to you with your new address & I hope that my letter will reach you. Your 2nd letter said that your orders were cancelled so I expect you may still be in Harfleur but I dare not address you 11ᵗʰ Field Co'y any more...As soon as I hear that you are really settled I will send those new breeches...& some sheets etc. I do wish you were coming home, it's perfectly sickening to go on hanging about. I do hope that you will be doing some interesting work. You must tell me what you think of all Father's plans for you...I expect the lack of privacy makes any sort of study quite difficult...I am glad that you had that beautiful walk to the sea. Didn't you want to swim across?

I was at a most interesting lecture on Russia at the FoR meeting. The lecturer was a Tolstoyian & had been in Russia,. The room was full & was electric with interest. The audience bombarded the lecturer with questions. I do hope Labour will make a very definite stand against going to war against the Russian soviet Government.[255] It is too terrible to keep up the blockade.[256] Really the Devil seems loose.

In late April Gilbert arrived in Oxford on leave, which meant he was not in India when the Amritsar Massacre took place on 13 April.

Violet and Gilbert to Owen, 1 May 1919 from Gilbert's mother's house in Plymouth

We have had such a delightful day & have many times wished that you & Patrick were with us...We are anxious to know when you will be coming home. Tomorrow I shall write & ask Mr Evans if Eliot may stay until Wednesday in Oxford. I do wish that you could come home before. It would be jolly if you turned up on Saturday. Perhaps tomorrow will bring me a letter...After tea today we all worked in the...garden & yesterday afternoon we worked in an allotment that Auntie Maud has here. It is really very satisfactory work. We dug...& I planted 2 rows of potatoes & one big row of peas. Well when you think of what that represents it is a pity that they don't make officers and men work on the land. Father dug a good bit & he & Eliot sharpened pea sticks & put them in another row that had been planted...We hope each day to hear of your coming to England...I have a good many letters to write so will leave Father to fill in this sheet...Your loving Mother, Violet Slater

Do try to use your time to good advantage, and if you can get no useful classes, at least read some science, & seize opportunities of improving your French. You will regret all your life not having done this to better effect than you have hitherto. Try hard for demobilisation, & failing that, leave. Your loving Father, Gilbert Slater

---

Gilbert to Owen, 16 May 1919 from Oxford

We are awfully disappointed that your prospects of early leave are so poor. I intended, as soon as you got leave, to concoct with you a letter asking for demobilisation on compassionate grounds. I have seen Hamilton Fyfe[257] and his next of command, and they both think it is worthwhile to make the effort. I enclose a draft, which you can send in by your commanding officer—unless he tells you to send it direct. Mind the cap. Y & S in 'Your most obedient Servant'. Fyfe, whom I have seen this afternoon, suggests enclosing a note from Dr Pope, so I shall see him to-morrow, and try to get it, & then forward it.

In spite of difficulties try to the utmost to make some good use of your time. If there are lectures or classes available take them—or get to some public library if any one is accessible.

[P.S.] Don't worry about the bike. We found the old hub and I have taken it to [word indecipherable], where Moore the younger is, to be replaced, & shall doubtless have the bike available in a day or two.

Violet to Owen, 16 May 1919

Perhaps this will reach you on your birthday & perhaps the enclosed note will be a really valuable birthday present. I hope so. I feel quite sick about your still being in the army & not doing anything. If you were working hard on reconstruction work it would not matter as much. Can't your superior officers get at the work? There must be no end that wants doing…We had two letters from you this morning. The situation of your camp sounds delightful but don't you feel it is hateful to be doing nothing. Can't you make me a nice little hot water can out of one of those horrid shell cases just a straight up one like the sort of vases you sent only it must have some sort of a handle. I must try to design some.

I shall send you a tiny greeting tomorrow & I hope it will reach you on the 20th. It seems that we must wait patiently until we hear or perhaps see you. It is particularly awkward because Father wants to be doing ever so many things in & about London & elsewhere.

Father & I worked in the allotment for a short time this morning. It wants no end of work & it is wonderful how soothing work with the earth is. It always does me good. I went up properly sick with your prospects & more with the cruel indifference of governments to the suffering of starving peoples. I found myself comforted—there is something so sane about agricultural work. God bless you dear boy. I hope you will have a useful happy life.

The Revd R. W. M. Pope, DD, to Owen, 17 May 1919 with letter enclosed

Dear Mr Slater,

Your father asks me to send you a letter supporting your request for de-mobilisation. So far as this term is concerned, you would not gain much advantage (if any) as nearly half of it has gone. With sincerest [?] regards, Yours very truly, R. W. M. Pope

Sir,
I beg leave to support Sec. Lt. O. R. Slater's application to be demobilised, and confirm his statement as to having passed his Preliminary Examinations. Yours faithfully, R. W. M. Pope, D.D., Censor

⁂

Israel Hersch to Violet, [17 May 1919] [forwarded to Owen]

What can be done. Z.15 must be filled up & while Owen is still in the army but other forms when he is admitted as a student at one of the colleges or as a Non-Coll. I [It] should make no difference at all.

⁂

Joyce Cockram to Owen, [18? May 1919] from Oxford

Very many happy returns of your birthday! I had a pathetic post card from your Mother saying that you were not coming home just yet, yesterday, so I bethought me of your birthday and have taken up my pen to write a letter.

Why on earth do you get shoved round into new companies like this? It must be absolutely sickening for you. I suppose you get moved on when your leave is just arriving into a company where you won't get leave for ages. I wondered whether you had been ordered to go to the Army of Occupation. People seem to be expecting some great excitement about the signing of the Peace Treaty.

I have just come in from the University Service at St Mary's.[258] I have not heard such a magnificent sermon for ages. It is not common to get an absolutely frank man in the pulpit, who slays the clergy for their intellectual insincerity. The Vice-Chancellor was awfully sick… Eights[259] begin on Monday May 26th and are to last only 4 days this year. However there are to be 4 races instead of 3 every day, 2 with fixed seats and two with sliding seats. I wish you could get home for that.

Did you know that Joan [Anderson] was teaching music at Lynams [the Dragon School]? She enjoys the work on the whole, but finds her mornings trying when boy after boy plays the same discords in the same places...I have a horrible amount of work to do: I have two exams at the end of term, zoology again and organic for the first M.B. [Bachelor of Medicine] I loathe organic chemistry frankly and wholeheartedly: one lives in the atmosphere of such smells as ethyl benzoate, etc, SO_2 [sulphur dioxide], H_2S [hydrogen sulphide], acetic acid and chloroform all mixed up. I am also dissecting a lower limb; females are not allowed to smoke in Oxford—it is the only medical school with such a rule, I believe.

Yesterday I went to see 'Daddy Long Legs'[260] with the Anderson party. I had seen it before so perhaps that accounts for the fact that I didn't enjoy it frightfully...This week I am taking most of these people to see 'Quality Street' (J. M. Barrie). I had hoped you would be able to come. I went to one done by Somerville, 'The Jilt' by Arnold Bennett and 'She Stoops to Conquer' at St Hugh's. I believe Lady Margaret Hall are doing *Clementina* by A. E. W. Mason.[261]

As a matter of fact I haven't told you that I went on the river last Sunday with your Mother and Father and Pat. Your father ridiculously resembles Pat. We had a gay time only Pat kept on giving me awful shocks by trying to stand on his head in the punt. And when he and I were paddling he was about the limit, he back handed until the boat was about to charge the nearest tree and then left me to put her straight! My attention had to be riveted on the punt all the time; and we kept on charging innocent canoes. I was frightfully bucked with myself for keeping my temper.

Violet to Owen, 19 May 1919

I am writing early as I woke at 4.30 and could not get to sleep so at 5 I got up. Father and I are going to London on Wednesday until Saturday & there are so many things to see to...You will be pleased to hear that we found your hub & Father had the bicycle which was a great comfort. Up to the present he has had to walk everywhere when he could not have my cycle. We have been doing what we could with the allotment but at present it has very little in it.

P.S. I am glad you had such luck in meeting the Colonel.

———∞∞———

Gilbert to Owen, 19 May 1919

I see Mother has told you everything except what is most important. As soon as we heard from you that your leave is not likely to come immediately, we arranged for the necessary visit to town [London]. We shall go up first on Wednesday 21st, stop at Woolwich that night, at Harpenden on Thursday night, and at Streatham on Friday, & pick up Eliot, as he has Saturday evening & Sunday as an 'Exeat', though he has to be back on Monday night.

Mother is too pessimistic about the allotment. It is going to be beautifully dug all over, and therefore should also get reasonably well planted. Yours with love, Gilbert Slater

———∞∞———

Ida Brown to Owen, 25 May 1919

I have had three letters from you and I have not answered one yet. I resolved to write to you but something came along and prevented. For one thing we were passing through that critical time known as spring cleaning...As I told you before all Mother & Father wanted was to see you safely home again. It's awfully good of you to want to buy them something but I'm sure they would be very cross if you did; and as for giving you the dates of birthdays really Owen I can't let out family secrets.

How they do keep putting off your leave. What disappointments one has in life, but I suppose you will get it one day. We are very much looking forward to seeing you and your Father, we do hope you will find time to come.

I think we will all spend our holiday at Trouville, if you are still there…We are staying here [Wigmore] for the week end, the first time since the war. The other hut is finished and we have had them both painted…Several friends came out yesterday …After all our friends had gone we had our supper in the twilight. We were sitting there quietly listening to the birds. The cuckoo could be heard very distinctly. Norman broke the silence by saying 'Blow that blooming cuckoo. He woke me up at quarter past four this morning and he has been at it ever since'…Much love from all, your affectionate sister Ida.

Violet to Owen. 19 June 1919

I was very interested to see the letters that your Batman had written to you, it showed you as well as him, showed that you had been sympathetic & interested in his affairs. I remember as a little chap you used to be tremendously friendly & sympathetic with everyone who came to work in the houses & it was so nice. Your father is always so ready to give himself…& is so extraordinarily free from any self indulgence of any sort. I feel that you have been brought up to be very careful. We had a very small income when you were small—being careful is apt to make one mean. I am always trying to be on my guard against it. Formation of character is the only investment that pays. It seems to me that the life of an Officer in the Army in Peace is not calculated to develop helpfulness & service. Do try to seize opportunities to help other people…I shall be very much with you in thought & shall hope to see you back before long! I do want to cable 'Demobilized!' to Father.

Violet to Owen. [June 1919]

I wonder why you write so seldom now a days. Do try to send a letter more often even if it is only a short one. I want to know what is going on in the army and am always glad of personal news…I wish we could settle your future. I do hope you are at least desiring to get out as soon as you can. Can't you do anything through the C.O [Commanding Officer]? What sort of a person is he? It is so ruinous to be slacking all this time but I hope you are doing your best to accustom yourself to doing some work. Are you doing any practical work? Have you any other books. Don't forget to tell me how you like *Walden*[262] or if you found it so little to your taste that you haven't read it at all…Goodbye dear boy this isn't much of a letter. Ever so much love from yr loving Mother Violet Slater

A clue to the irregularity of Owen's letters may rest in three snapshots which were found among Owen's papers. They show an attractive young girl in a summer frock and in one photograph she is in a garden, smiling and looking directly at the photographer while she attempts to spray him with a garden hose. On the back of one photograph someone, presumably the girl herself, has written 'À ma petite carotte—souvenir de notre séjour'. She is referring to his reddish-gold hair.

Eliot Slater to his parents, 22 [June 1919]

I nearly yelled for joy when I got your letter, as it was I made inarticulate gurgling sounds, and people asked me whether I was mad, when I got your letter. How glorious, how ripping of you. Still there will…[be] a touch of sadness, when Father goes…Nowadays I never read trash but only books out of the central library such as:-

Mohammed	[D. S.] Margoliouth
History of the French Revolution	Carlyle
Germ Life	[H. W.] Conn
Scientific Romances	[C. H.] Hinton

Rhyme? & Reason?	[Lewis] Carroll
Tales & Phantasies	[R. L.] Stevenson
Midnight House & Other Tales	[W. F.] Harvey

et cetera, et cetera.

For Peace celebrations, Two Days, the seventeenth & 18th of July, will be free from work. On the first, there will be rag sports & in the evening several scenes, in one of which I am taking part, and everybody must get into Fancy Dress. The Second Day there will be a river excursion. What shall I wear for the Fancy Dress? I would very much like to be a Devil, you know the rig up, and it strikes me as rather simple. However, all these things we can discuss when we meet. Oh, won't that be a treat!…Your loving son, Eliot

———

On 23 June the German delegation to the Peace Conference accepted that they could not have forty-eight hours to consider their options and agreed that they would sign the Treaty of Versailles. Rumours then exaggerated their willingness to sign into the actual signing.

Owen to his father, 24 June 1919

Peace was signed yesterday but we heard nothing official till after midnight. In the way of celebrations & holidays we have the day off to-day & I have just returned from a dance at a neighbouring hospital which I enjoyed immensely…I do hope you have it fine for your crossing & that this will reach you before you leave home…I have done a certain amount of work but it is most difficult. I just pray for demobilisation & hope to be able to work better at home. I am afraid it will be impossible for me to meet you at Havre…My best wishes for your voyage & time in India. I am looking forward to taking Mother to Marseilles, I only wish I could come with her all the way.

———

Owen to his mother, 24 June 1919

I am sorry I have not written to you more regularly lately, especially at a time you want letters most but... I haven't had so much work for ages. The captain thinks he is being demobbed soon & that I may have to take over from him & in consequence tries to make me go into all details & he is particularly fond of details. For example he spoke to me half seriously & half in jest about wearing slacks before 7 pm. & also about wearing a Sam Brown without a shoulder strap.[263] At last the motor bike has arrived & will come in very useful both for work & recreation... At present an awful lot of time is wasted by going to & fro between different jobs; when you have to walk 3 to 4 miles between whiles it is tiring.

Gilbert to Owen, 24 June 1919 from Oxford

In two days I am off, & most things are done, bar packing. We had strawberries and cream today, as a farewell treat for Pat. We have arranged for Eliot to come up to town & are going to take him to 'Abraham Lincoln'[264] at Hammersmith theatre. As it is suburban, we hope to get seats easily... You know what time I pass through Havre (I don't) but I fear I shall have no chance of seeing you en route. Well it won't be so long as last time before we meet again... I have sent off the last scrap I am going to with regard to the 2nd Ed^{n}. of my book.

We were very glad to get your letter this morning. You were quite right to get at the reading immediately. I hope you will be able to stick at it all right. The more thoroughly you work at it—drawing all the illustrations, & getting more from nature & all that sort of thing—the more interesting you will find it.

Joyce Cockram to Owen, 25 June 1919* from Oxford

The Organic paper wasn't bad, but the practical was appalling…However I got through alright. The Zoology paper was pretty bad & yesterday the Practical was the limit—in the first place it was too long. I had spent a whole morning revising the dog's skull and they gave us a frog's skull instead and I hadn't looked at one since the 2nd week in October 1918!

Don't have too great a shock! I am going to a dance tonight—a Commem Week dance at Trinity College, from 9–4; or something equally unearthly; (& I've got a viva tomorrow!) We dine at the Randolph [Hotel] first. I wish to heaven I hadn't said I'd go, now! The thing was that I hoped Mrs Johnson would decide for me by refusing permission…to my surprise she said…'Oh yes! That will be quite alright. I do hope you will enjoy it, dear child! But will you have a chaperone? And will someone see you home?' She was really excited when I said that it was my first dance. Joan [Anderson] has a rotten time trying to teach me to dance properly!!

I must stop because I want to mug up the Zoo paper. Joffre, Haig, Beatty and crowds of other statesmen, soldiers and sailors are here today for honorary degrees—huge excitement of course.[265]

On 26 June Gilbert left Oxford to return to Madras and Violet began to make plans to join him there in September. Two days later, on 28 June, the fifth anniversary of the murder of Archduke Franz Ferdinand and his wife, the Treaty of Versailles, between the Allies and Germany, was finally signed.

Violet to Owen, [29 June 1919]

Already 2 nights & one day have passed since Father left & I suppose he is, or will soon be on the 'Monora' & sailing away. I wonder if you saw him. I hope you may have. As you travelled by the same boat you will know the time he reached Havre. But perhaps it wd. be impossible …The papers have had all sorts of rumours of the [German] Crown Prince escaping & fighting in Berlin & Hamburg etc. But I hope Peace will be signed & that things will become more settled. But there is to be a big fight between Employers & Labour & the East[266] is still all war so we shall not really have Peace.

Patrick to his father, [3? July 1919] from Putney Hospital

I am, as you can see, in Putney Hospital. It is quite nice in here but we do not get Butter attal. The person next door is called Croxford and he is jolly nice he has given me 3 apples at different times and several other things, in return for which I have lent him my 'Puck' and *Childrens Newspaper*[267] & some grapes.

I suppose you know that we bussed from 58 Holland Park [where Violet's brother lived]. Well, I do not remember anything from then until the next morning! There are lots of flies in here and I have killed 14 today, 2 yesterday, 0, day before.

I am rather sorry I had that accident because of my Diary, but it's quite decent here and the grub that mother brings is jolly good. Excuse writing. With lots of Love from Pat

[P.S. from Violet:] You see he is getting on famously & the original wickedness is returning. He looks much better.

Gilbert to Owen, 8 July 1919

We have just got to the neutral centre of the Red Sea, which has a habit of having a wind blowing in at each end. Just now it is sweltering. I had the following judicious lunch today: (1) a little soup. 2) an ice. 3) a slice of water melon. 4) an iced lemonade. Between meals I take cold baths. We have had a little improvement in some respects in our arrangements recently. We meal in two batches, each pretty crowded and the original arrangement was for a bell to be rung for the first batch, and then the second lot, in which I am, had to look out about half an hour later to see the first batch come up on deck, and sit in their places until we got served. Now we have a bell of our own, and a little tidying up is done before we come down. Also the worst bounder of the lot has been mercifully removed. Some first class passengers got out at Port Said and he got the vacant berth. But last night, as old Tait says, we got a lesson not to grumble. Some humourist in the electrical department was determined to show us, as Tait says, that however bad things were we had to be thankful they were not worse, for suddenly in the midst of dinner out went the lights, and the fans also struck work. I was one of the lucky ones. I had just secured a helping of tough fowl, and potatoes and cabbage and bread and salt and water—everything that had to be scrimmaged for, and it was not too dark for me to see my plate. So I ate away while the steamy heat increased, till I had cleared my plate, and then decamped while I could still breathe.

And I tell you this by way of encouragement; because I fancy the difficulties of doing any work must be as great, or pretty nearly as great, on board the S.S. *Manora* as under your conditions.

So it may be a fair match between us, my longer experience matched against your young manhood, as at tennis, to see which of us can do the most work. I have had nine days at sea, and have written some nine or ten thousand words, or about the equivalent of four or five newspaper articles taking a column of the *Daily News* or [*Daily*] *Chronicle*, for which I used to get three guineas each…So you play up and whenever you see a tennis racket remember that you are going to lick me at this game as well as at tennis.

On 19 July the United Kingdom and the Empire celebrated Peace Day. In London the Victory Parade marched past and saluted a wood and plaster model 'cenotaph' (or empty tomb) set up to honour the dead. It was designed by Edwin Lutyens and was one of several temporary monuments specially erected for the occasion. Its design was so effective and popular that it was used for the permanent national memorial to those who had died in the war. This was unveiled by King George V on 11 November 1920.

Israel Hersch to Violet, 19 July 1919

This is just a brief note on Owen's account. I cannot understand his difficulty in getting release from the army. Immediately the armistice was declared Caius college claimed Laurie as a student and he was released at the
end of January. There are simply hundreds of these here who obtained
release in the same way. Has Owen's college claimed him? If it has not,
bother the people there until they do. If he were coming to Cambridge I
am sure I could do much to help him. But I do not know anyone at
Oxford.

P.S. *Take very real care, in any event, that Owen & Owen's college claim for him a
grant from the government for his university training.*

———◦◦◦◦———

Owen to his mother, 20 July 1919

I wonder how Peace celebrations went off in England—more particularly
at Oxford. Here, they were almost entirely a wash out. To start with it was
a general holiday which meant that nobody knew what to do in the
slightest & secondly it was cold & rained nearly the whole day long…In
Trouville as in England we were going to celebrate Peace by bonfires &
during the whole morning there were lorries collecting scrap timber etc
and men building a huge bonfire on the Bluff which is a high hill over-
looking the sea with Blenville [Blonville?] underneath, Villers to the left &
Trouville & Deauville to the right. At about 5 o'clock messages were flying
about all over the place cancelling everything. I forgot to mention that 8
tons of German flares had been distributed along the shore…to be lit just
after the fire. Well a miserable lot of French people found the flares &
started lighting them & as it was fine then (about 9.30) it was decided to
have the fire after all…I was wandering along towards the Bluff at 9.30
when I met a car from Honfleur containing a Miss Barker—an adminis-

trator I had met at Havre. They were looking for the fire...so I got in & went off miles down the beach...then came back to the hospital to see if any one was about...We then met an H.L.I. [Highland Light Infantry] officer who told us of the cancellation & the wash out of the cancellation. We then all went off down into Deauville to the Casino...& we all went into a small café for refreshments & finally back to the Bluff where we found they had just started the fire...after the bonfire—at about 12.30 we all, i.e. sisters & nurses & officers went down to the sisters Mess of 72 General Hospital & had refreshments of sandwiches, cakes & tea. I left there at 1.30 am & got back to my bunk about 2 o'clock this morning. Needless to say I had breakfast in bed this morning & got up at about 11. So that was how we celebrated Peace in Trouville. A thousand & odd pounds worth of fireworks were wasted by the French. The more I see of them, the more despicable they seem—they really are a nation of cads. However! Much love to you all.

[Note by Violet written before she sent the letter on to Gilbert:] I'm sorry he thinks so badly of the French. He sees all one sort & does not realize that they are terribly poor & so careful & thrifty that they have the vice of their qualities.

Violet to Owen, [20] July [1919]

We had a letter from you this morning telling of your trial trip on the motor bike. It must have been quite an excitement. I wonder what you do all day in the hospital? You don't tell me half what I want to know. Did you take your books? Do tell me how you are getting on with your reading. Of course in hospital you can't make any practical experiments but I should like to know what you are thinking about. You see dear boy you have got to live in the world & you must do your bit to the formation of the future good or bad. You are going on towards 21 and you ought to be attempting

FIGURE 14 Owen on leave outside 4 Park Crescent. He is wearing the gauntlet gloves suggested for him by his mother: 'I hope you have plenty of warm things. *How about gloves*. I saw a rather jolly pair of gauntlet fur lined riding gloves…if you will keep them I will get a pair & send for a Christmas present from Father & me.' (Violet to Owen, 28 [29] September 1918, p. 169 in this volume).

to understand what sort of a world you want to help to make. You must throw your weight somewhere—the one great snare to avoid is to drift. I am going to send you a page of the 'Herald' it is full of meat. You can give it to anyone to read. Don't destroy it if you can't pass it on to anyone you know; just send it to Father. I know he would like to see Robert Minors[268] little article about Russia…What newspapers do you get a chance of seeing? Do you ever see 'The Nation'?

We had simply a soaking wet Peace day…I took Pat down to see the decorations, which were very poor on the whole, & then Mrs O.S[ullivan]. called us in & we watched the procession of troops from her window. It was long in coming & was quite ineffective, but I hoped might make people realize that the once idealized Tommy was now the average working man (there was very little Khaki most of the men were in mufti) so now their sympathy should have some concrete result in understanding the position of the 'wicked miners' etc.[269] We had intended to spend the afternoon on the river but of course could not. Bertha went down to see the illuminations in the evening, but came home with tales of drunkenness more than anything else. Pat & I stayed at home.

I fear I have told you this before so it's rather [a] waste of time [?] This morning I had a letter from Ira Hersch which I shall enclose. *You must send it on to Father.* Auntie Agnes also tells me that Colonel Parry has got his boy out to try for a scholarship at Cambridge. I am sick to the bottom of my soul that you don't get out. I wish you were only getting 1/- a day. I hate you to be getting money for such work. Leave no stone unturned dearest boy & make yourself work. The demoralizing influence of being too well fed, too well paid, is I believe worse than the reverse.

The roof leaks & 2 ragged trousered workmen[270] have come to mend it. One has scarcely any teeth. His clothes are appalling. I think I shall give him one of your coats! I don't suppose he gets money enough to even buy himself teeth. Isn't it abominable. Give some of your money away. Much love from your loving Mother, Violet Slater.

<hr />

Violet to Gilbert, 24 July 1919

The boys are on the river...& I am having a quiet morning ignoring housework as much as possible...I wonder where you are in politics now & what the people you know think. Have they come to the conclusion that it is time we tried argument as well as force? I am certain that the powers that ran the war are more afraid of an international labour conference & the result of mutual understanding of the workers of the world than of anything else. We are having strikes. The truth is that there is a desire to conscript labour & create a servile state. Are we to go on with the war with only Americans are left to fight? It is raining hard—what a nuisance.

Violet to Owen, 30 July 1919

I cannot imagine why you write so seldom, not even *once* a week & not in reply to my letters. It gives one a horrid feeling. Don't my letters reach you? Or do any of yours go astray?...The last letter we received from you was telling of the Peace celebration so you can calculate how long that is. Please write more regularly & tell us something about yourself. You never told us you were out of hospital & well, but I suppose you are.

Do you know that since Peace was signed a new order has come out which allows all who want to get out of the army to come out 3 months after. That would mean about the end of September. I hope to go up to London & to the War Office & get at the Demobilisation R.E. Dep^{nt} & see if I can't get you out at once. I wish I could get you out in time to come with us to Painswick on the Cotswold Hills for one holiday & then you would be able to help get things ready before I go to India.

Would you like to get *into* [a] College? If so which? I went and interviewed Major Bishop [?]...and he tells me (1st that my idea of going to the W.O. was quite good), 2nd that if you are to get a grant for your University course it must be made on Form Z15 [and] *must* be made through your C.O. [Commanding Officer] & the College or Non-Collegiate must be stated. I could get the head of some College to accept you. Would you rather go to Cambridge & I will get Ira Hersch to get you into a College. *Answer this by return.* You have never acknowledged the letter I sent on to you from Ira Hersch. It makes me feel as if you are quite asleep to the great importance of your future. You must be up & doing & not drift.

We hope to go to Painswick on the 13th or 16th.

[P.S.] I think if you try Oxford College either [St] John's or New.

Israel Hersch to Violet, 3 August 1919

As far as I know Owen ought certainly to fill up Z.15 as soon as possible. Laurie filled up this form as soon as it was issued. At the same time I got a certificate from Caius College claiming him as a student on their books and this I took to the Appointment Board here. As soon as he was 're-leased' or shortly afterwards the college sent him a 'D.O.' form which he had to fill up claiming a grant. This was returned to the college and pre-sented by them to the Committee appointed by the University to consider these applications on behalf of the Board of Education. About a month ago we were informed that the application had been granted. I understand that all applications (apart from Z.15) have now to go through *The College* authorities. All the colleges in Cambridge are full to overflowing at pre-sent. It might be possible to get Owen into St Catharine's or Downing pro-viding *he can find his own rooms*: rooms are the almost insuperable difficulty. Both these Colleges are cheap, I may say. If you will let me know as soon as possible I will see [what I can do].

Annie Hersch to Violet, [3 August 1919 included in Israel Hersch's letter]

I hope you will be successful in your interviews with the War Office. I am so sorry for you; it's a wretched business. Can't you get a man friend who lives in London to do it for you? I wish you could. What about your brother Joseph. He has a son about Owen's age hasn't he?

Hugh Cockram to Owen, 3 August 1919

Joyce has just torn up her letter which she has been writing to you for the past forty minutes, & has just started afresh. I hope I shall not do likewise.

I know you are calling me all sorts of names under the Sun for not having written to you, & I own I have been terribly negligent...I even expect I should not have written today, but for Joyce's urging me, as she herself is writing or trying to write.

The Certificate papers were moderate, distinction ones distinctly (excuse the pun) hard, & na poo for me in that quarter. The other ones easy on the whole.

At any rate I am carrying on next term, with renewed vigour and strength, & am trying for a Schol. in December for which I am doing some work this vac; & next term I shall have to slave. I hope to be going to Scotland at the end of this month...but it is not settled yet. I am looking forward to it most awfully. Other delightful members of the School will be there I hope...To pay for part of my expenses I intend to go on the land for three weeks or so...I only wish you were going to be here too; for I shall get very bored alone I am sure. After all that, I shall have to do three months solid very hard work, which I mean to do very conscientiously for Dad's sake as well as my own and the School's. I am afraid you will see in the *Lily* that your name was left out in the list of Old Boys who had been in Oxford last term. The Editor apologises. Otherwise I think it was a very good *Lily*, don't you? Please congratulate me.

'Tis rumoured that D'Oyly Cartes are coming to Oxford the 1st week of term. I hope you'll be back by then. Now that you have a letter from me, you have no excuse, so buck up & write; I am longing to hear your news. Love, yrs very affectionately, Hugh

---

Joyce Cockram to Owen, 3 August 1919 from Wallingford

Many thanks for your last letter. I was glad to have it, because I hadn't heard for such ages...I am sorry you have been in hospital. Bad luck! Do you still have to walk about with an interesting limp...I've lost your letter, but I rather think you asked about our domestic troubles. They are very happily settled for the moment. We have a smiling new maid, who is quite pretty and very tidy…I do all the housekeeping now; the actual job isn't so bad but accounts are the limit.

Hugh is trying to be funny and has just fought me. I unfortunately have got rather knocked about! …

I went up to see your people on Monday evening and incidentally to fetch my photographs. Did you mean me to have those films? Your Mother assures me that you did. Thank you most awfully for them and for the loan of the Camera…I was also presented with one of the smaller brass shell cases which Mrs Slater said was destined for me. Again thank you awfully. I am going to clean it, to use for flowers at home. I think it will be very handsome!

Owen to his mother, 4 August 1919

I can't understand why you have not received any letters from me for such a long time. I certainly have not written every day but since I left hospital I have written approximately at least twice a week.

Today your letter arrived containing all the information about demobilisation etc. The Army Order you mention has not yet reached us but the G.R.O. [General Routine Order] containing all the corresponding information arrived around the same time as your letter and in fact I read it first being business. I enclose the order and as you see I applied this morning for release under this order so I may yet get away soon. However please notice under 7195 para. 2 it definitely states that the date of release is entirely individual and may be now or in two or three years time, the date being entirely regulated by the number of volunteers. As regards the application for training at an University I have already applied in February but got turned down. However I have met an Officer at Headquarters who has all this subject at his finger ends and I am seeing him tomorrow. Now as regards a college I would very much like to go into college and would prefer New to any other. I don't know much about it but I believe Hertford is jolly good too but I certainly back my money on New.

I do hope I shall get demobilised before you have to go to India. Of course I should have loved to come with you to the Cotswolds [Painswick] but that is almost an impossibility. Work has got more and more as the days go on—we have had a considerable number of reinforcements and have work going on at a place about 10 miles away which has to be visited pretty often as there is no officer to stay out there with the detachment. This of course entails the use of a motor bike which is rather enjoyable.

You don't seem to have had my letter which I wrote directly I came out of hospital. I was in for just a week and was then discharged for light duty for 5 days but really took up my normal work at once...I have found two rather nice play boxes [Magdalen College School slang for tuck boxes] which I am packing and sending home, partly because they will be useful but also because I have such a lot of stuff that when I am demobbed I will have an awful job getting it hence.

Violet to Owen, 7 August 1919

Now about your demob business. I went to the Demob. Centre for R.E. and asked for the top official and so to a certain Colonel Street. He was most kind and sympathetic and told me to write out a letter...I took it again today and boldly asked to see him (I feel a bit like Queen Esther).[271] He was however quite friendly and pleasant. He says that is all we can do and hopes it may be effective...Now old man I want you to tell me what you feel about it all: they could not trace your letter asking for compassionate release. Can you remember what date it was that you wrote and sent it. I mean the one Father concocted.

Violet to Owen. 13 August 1919 from London

I have got Patrick out of hospital this afternoon. He was rather exhausted & he can't walk very well. I had a taxi & it cost 7/- so altogether the whole affair of coming up to London to get you out of the army has cost a good deal. Of course I gave a subscription to the hospital & I must taxi to Paddington & from Oxford [station] home & then again both ends for Painswick. However it seems little when one thinks that it might so easily have been so terribly worse. A few inches more & the motor would have run over him. I hope to get him to Oxford tomorrow & to Painswick on Saturday morning.

Dear one it will be lovely if we are ever all together again. Don't forget that it is Eliot's birthday on the 27th Aug. I want a shell case cut to the height of the trunk in the dining room—it would be most useful. By the bye I got the £25 cheque. Do send some money to give away sometimes. Wouldn't you like to give something more to the Emergency Com'tee? Are you doing any work in reading. You say you are too busy to bathe that seems an awful pity. What are you doing to be so 'busy'.

✆

While on holiday in Gloucestershire in August Violet learned that Owen had finally been demobilized and telegraphed to Gilbert.

Gilbert to Violet, 3 September 1919

When I got to my office from Coonoor on Monday morning I got your letter of Aug. 7…Your letter was also full of disappointment about the prospect of passage. But when I got to my office I got the longed for telegram 'Demobilised' & saw it came from Painswick. So I do hope that you were able to finish up your holiday with a blessed relief in your mind, enabling you and the boys to get some real good out of it.

I expect, in view of what you write, that this will reach you in Oxford. I recommend you to go round *with Owen* and see people about his getting into a College and getting Gov^t. money to help him with his education. Your going and seeing people in London was evidently what was wanted about demobilisation…Dons etc. are all human; and Owen is a nice looking, well set up lad, and his rowing is a possible asset to a College. A little delay in your setting out [for India] will be cheap if you can get him really satisfactorily arranged for. But I am not so pessimistic even about that. As I pointed out last week, if I make the arrangement to stay on till March 1921 as I think in fairness to the University I should, and then make up my mind to get to America by the end of April…I can use my return ticket by P. & O. in 1921…I have made definite arrangements to be able to house you as soon as you come…It will be a great thing for us to have a little stock of Indian memories in common…I calculate that your wire left Painswick about Aug. 25, but I could find no date in it. I hope Owen was able to get there before you left, & help to enhance the quality of your holiday.

Gilbert to Owen, 7 October 1919

My last letters were those of 10th September just as you and Hugh Cockram returned from your trip in the New forest. I suppose I must wait for several more mails before getting your important news about settling in in Oxford, and only hope that when the news does come it will be good…I have written to a Madras publisher, offering to let him have some of my recent lectures and newspaper articles to make a little book. If he takes it, I expect it will sell well. Soon after I return to Madras the October meeting of the Senate takes place, and on the agenda will be, I presume, the proposal of the syndicate for my extra 6 months. As soon as that is settled I shall make arrangements for 1921.

L. to Violet, 22 October [1919] from Hasserode, Wernigerode, Saxony, Germany

My dear old VO, I am getting a very bad correspondent. Here is your dear letter from August still unanswered…As you see from the above address I am now happily settled at home with Sister Emma…she is so frail & delicate & wants me badly…At present I am the housemaid & the cook. In the afternoon I go out & get fir cones…& E. is glad when I bring home the treasures of winter fuel…Next week I shall begin looking for some lessons or rather pupils. Things are getting dearer every day & our valuta[272] is almost at 0. I sometimes wonder if our enemies will ever be satisfied with sucking our life blood & draining our resources. And they call this—Peace—It is worse than war. But I will not talk about politics. I know your kind heart suffers pangs of agony. The Quakers have been our best friends & still go on doing their truly Christian work among the children & the poor…I have been reading a delightful book to E. on Oxford by a German scholar written before the war. I had my pretty book of Oxford views beside me & revelled in all the dear familiar sights…Dear V.O., how I should like to see you all again. I send this letter through Ada Adams…From Sister Hanne we get many letters, parcels & dollars: she is helping us splendidly. Give my love to the boys & thank Eliot for his nice letter. With fondest love, ever yours, L.

AFTERWORD

Margaret Bonfiglioli

The letter from Violet's German friend reminds us of her desire to renew and restore old friendships rent asunder by a war she had so hated. The letter also gives us an insight into the hardships faced by Germans after 1918, hardships that helped to prepare the ground for that country's tragic future.

Demobbed in August 1919, Owen was in time for the beginning of term and undergraduate life in Oxford—a university renewing itself. His decisions were his own. His father's dream of reading agriculture faded with the memory of hard labour, strengthening biceps, and pleasure in handling livestock on Mr Tweddell's Yorkshire farm. He resumed his membership of the Non-Collegiate Society, already on its way to becoming St Catherine's College, and started a shortened degree course in Physics, something which would not cause him too much trouble.

The university needed time to recover from the huge changes war had brought to its established ways and from the army's requisitioning of academic buildings for medical and military use. Familiar sounds and sights began to return with the former soldiers: bells could ring out again joyously while gowns now competed with military uniforms. War-wounded men marked with arm bands walked the streets and Ruskin College arranged a summer school especially for them. Owen's beloved rivers, the Cherwell and the Isis, called him. In preparation for this in 1918 he had bought a beautiful carvel-built canoe, imported from Canada. This later became the very canoe in which we children, once we could swim, learnt so much river craft. It was, he told us, the first substantial thing he had

319

FIGURE 15 A photograph taken toward the end of the war showing, from left to right, Owen, Patrick, Violet, and Eliot Slater. On seeing them again in 1919 Gilbert remarked on Eliot's growth since he last saw him, reaching 5ft 11 inches at the age of 16 and now the tallest of the family. Owen's adult height was 5ft 8 inches.

bought with his own money. He was soon energetically involved in the university's rowing scene and in the St Catherine's Boat Club with the revival of Torpids in the spring of 1920 and Eights in the summer, races which had been in abeyance since 1914. By Hilary Term 1920 he was coaching a new team for Torpids, cycling along the tow path shouting exhortations and encouragement through a megaphone, a familiar noise of an Oxford summer in peacetime. He invited the Browns to Torpids and this was, almost, their last appearance in our story. As Vice-Captain it was hard work to be a father to the new St Catherine's eight. Six of the crew were ex-soldiers who had served variously in France, Belgium, and Egypt. One had been an ambulance driver. The former 2nd lieutenant had to discover a new authority, one not based on military discipline. Subscriptions had to be collected and crews rounded up for training regardless of the rain. The Boat Club minutes ring with anti-authoritarian voices: 'impropaganda' is quashed, meetings 'disintegrate' in time for the

FIGURE 16 Owen (second from left) with oarsmen and boatmen of the St Catherine's Boat Club.

FIGURE 17 The St Catherine's Boat Club Eight starting the race.

'bachannalian orgy'; 'their names are writ in pewter [beer mugs]'. Sometimes Omen, Caption of Boats, has to be put on his feet again to be heard.

Owen's first summer vacation was not devoted solely to the 'steady reading' Gilbert advised. There was time for a camping trip on the Thames to the first post-war Henley Regatta. Snapshots show the party's tent and two punts, one equipped for camping. Frank Howse, an Oxford Blue who had done time in a stone quarry as a conscientious objector, and his sister Marie, a singer who never married, can be identified. With them are a handsome mystery man and a smiling girl under a large sun hat holding a tin of corned beef. Could she be Joyce with her love of hats?

Violet's frustratingly delayed passage to India finally began in September 1920. This was only arranged, Gilbert recorded, after she had insisted on a private interview with the head of P&O. Back home, Owen continued his mother's enthusiasm for the Fellowship of Reconciliation although in February 1921 he told his parents that Miss Pask and he had 'decided we ought to wind up our active work'. The following year, as

FIGURE 18 Punt camping to Henley for the first regatta after the war.

Captain of Boats, Owen was proud to secure a new coach for the Eights crew, an older military veteran, the Revd H. C. Wace, the eccentric Chaplain and Bursar of Brasenose College. Not just a rowing man, Owen had also been making good use of St Catherine's Clubs, joined the St Catherine's Music Society, and took part in the International Society whose aim was 'promoting international friendship in the Non-Collegiate body'. Here he could expound the 'internationalism' which the men at the Front, those whom he had found so 'pig headed', didn't want to hear. He also joined the Debating Society, which asked if, in a time of rising taxes and wide-scale unemployment, 'A friend in need is a friend *not* in need.' They tackled independence for Egypt and the 'Irish Question', when members asked a loquacious Irishman if he was suffering from 'Ulsteration from swallowing Orange pips'. Society Minutes tell us about one debate on 20 May 1922 (his twenty-third birthday) that 'Mr O. R. Slater believes in loving our enemies and cursing all hecklers, which he does with vigour.'

New freedoms came to him as his mother set off to join Gilbert in India. The Park Town house was let while Eliot returned to Leighton Park and Pat became a boarder at the Dragon School. Apart from reporting on the well-being of the cat and dealing with some household bills, Owen's domestic responsibilities were light. As a Non-Collegiate student he lived 'out' and shared digs with 'Tugger', as yet unidentified. Notes to parents mention décor and the arrival from Park Town of his bureau and the piano, the upright on which he and Pat had learnt to play so exuberantly. He invited friends for teas and occasionally for breakfast which his land-lady provided at 6*d.* a head.

The delightful cache of letters from Owen's young friends—Joan, Basil, Hugh, Joyce, Marjorie, Ida, and Edna—had kept him connected to the warmth, humour, jokes, theatre, singing, and punting of civilian life in Oxford and Gillingham. These treasures from the trunk helped make the man he became. Sadly we now say goodbye to the people whose words have made themselves so alive to us. No more of them is to be found in the family papers, so far, although we are working on other ways of tracing their histories. The exceptions to this are Hugh, his school friend and exact contemporary, and Hugh's sister Joyce, whom Gilbert had rather startlingly suggested Owen could marry.

While Hugh went on to become, like his father, a bank manager, Joyce was pursuing her studies to become a 'lady doctor'. Like other women in the Society of Home Students (later St Anne's College) she had to live either at home or in approved households with some chaperonage. Joyce was a pioneer in reading for a science degree and she finally finished her med-ical studies at King's College Hospital in 1925. Ironically the undergraduate who hated spiders and had trouble with frogs' skulls was for many years resident pathologist at the West Suffolk General Hospital. She became a JP, a school governor, the President of the Medical Women's Federation, and a lay canon of St Edmundsbury Cathedral. She organized blood banks and when occasion arose volunteered her chauffeur as a donor. She retained her 'twinkling sense of humour' and strong religious faith. When she was an undergraduate she could not be married and later marriage might have been incompatible with her career. Among Cockram family photographs (shown me by Joyce's nephew and Hugh's son, David) is one showing

Owen balancing on the end of a punt, arms folded and smiling compla-
cently. David Cockram believes he was 'the one'. Whether he was or not,
we have no letters after 3 August 1919 and she never married: another
'might-have-been'. Joyce died in 1975 and is commemorated as a 'much
loved physician and friend' by a plaque in the Cathedral she served so well.

In India, when the time came for Gilbert to leave the university in 1921,
Lord Willingdon, the Governor of Madras, invited him, as a man with 'a
shrewd mind behind observant eyes', to take on a new role as Publicity Officer for the Madras Government. This was a job he took up with zest. It
involved widespread and efficient diffusion of government information
and advice on matters sanitary and agricultural and also the explanation
of government policy. (He had already served on the Madras Board of
Agriculture.) In addition, he was co-opted as a member of the Provincial
Legislature. His new work meant he had to defer his return home. When
he did return he immediately began lecturing on Indian subjects at LSE
and continued his life as an independent scholar. He brought out books
on the politics, culture, and economics of India along with studies of
armaments, poverty, currency, and Shakespeare. He acted as a tutor and
lecturer and he supervised new editions of earlier histories. In 1936 he
brought out *Southern India: Its Political and Economic Problems*. The book
has engagingly autobiographical passages, including Violet's visit in
1920, all described with a self-deprecating humour alongside detailed
analyses and new perspectives on Indian affairs. He concluded by saying
that he was 'loathe to leave beautiful Madras, but eager to be at home
again'. In 2010, his description of a just settlement to the fighting, *Peace and
War in Europe*, which originally came out in 1915, was republished: it was for
this short book that he was later praised by *The Times* as 'the spokesman of
a large and then growing body of democratic opinion'. In 2012, *The Making
of Modern England* was also republished. Since his leaving India there has
been a succession of studies of village life, all drawing on his original idea.

Violet continued her active passion for making a better and more humane post-war world through the Society of Friends. She served on many
committees, was one of two representatives on the International Council,

FIGURE 19 Dr and Mrs Slater home at last in Park Town Garden.

worked to arrange Saturday and Sunday evening meetings in the Oxford area on disarmament and on the Russian famine. In one 1921 meeting, 'crowded but orderly', £33 10s. od. was collected for Russian relief. In 1922 she became responsible for arranging village meetings, involving her in numerous bus journeys. In June 1923 Mary Pask and she were chosen as representatives on the Interdenominational Committee for Social Reform for the next twelve months.

FIGURE 20 The heavy bridging of the Royal Engineers for crossing war front craters gives way to light bridging for lads crossing rivers. Owen as Scout Master (to the left of the photograph, looking on) taught the right knots for the purpose.

Owen left university with a third in Physics and Natural Sciences while Eliot followed Gilbert to St John's College, Cambridge. He qualified as an MD and went on to have a distinguished career as a psychiatrist. Patrick followed Eliot to Leighton Park School and then went on to Oriel College, Oxford. After that he got his doctorate and became a psychologist who specialized in the new field of psychometrics. Owen began a lifelong career teaching maths in boys' schools and in adult education classes. He made good use of his training with the Royal Engineers when he trained as a Scout master. To supplement his income he gave private coaching and marked exam papers. He got his first teaching post in 1921 at King William's College in Castletown on the Isle of Man. There he met Nando MacLauchlan, his future wife and our mother. Their relationship prospered when he abandoned a walking tour in Ireland and stayed on in Cork where he met her parents and became friends with her four younger sisters. One day in 1980, I called round to see my father and found him much distracted. He was feeling 'strange' and said, 'I am in the 1920's.' He then showed me a small cardboard box which he had just retrieved from the garden shed, a no longer visible building collapsing under a weight of Russian vine, but fortunately still weather proof. On what impulse he had found his way inside it he did not say. The box contained letters our mother and he had exchanged during their courting days. He allowed me to read them and I was amused by our mother's shaky spelling—I had so often relied on her for spelling help. There are touching details of purchases for setting up house together: a pair of brass candlesticks, bookshelves, and so forth. Here was the beginning of my mother's fascination with auction sales and antiques. Since that day I have not seen those letters again and my father said nothing of any other family papers.

By the 1930s Owen was teaching at Oxford's Southfield Boys' Grammar School and he and Nando took on the end of a 99-year lease at 12 Bradmore Road, Oxford, where their three children—Martin (1933), Margaret (1935), and Eithne (1940)—were born. The house was a short walk from Gilbert and Violet in Park Town. Here our parents consumed detective stories by the fire on winter Sunday afternoons. The only First World War book which resonated with our father's experience was Robert Graves's *Good-Bye to All That*, which came out in 1929. Despite Violet's hopes, both our parents did enjoy a drink and both smoked. The drinking was convivial and moderate; the smoking was heavy. Our drawing room, only once redecorated in thirty-five years with beautiful silvery white wallpaper, gradually turned a dark amber colour. From time to time Owen would stop smoking to prove that he was not a slave to the habit. Nando became so addicted that one would see her fumbling to start on a new cigarette when she already had one in her mouth.

For me, childhood, old age, gossip, memory, and facts connect in exploring the mystery of my father's character and in what we inherited from him. Gossip from my brother tells how at MCS Owen took his bike to the top of Founders Tower and rode down the spiral staircase, emerging seated and still spinning. An insignificant piece of folded paper, an after-find, opened to add a further glimpse into the unwritten mystery of Owen's life. In this pencilled and undated scribble from Basil we can only wonder what the two friends were up to in early December 1919:

Good my Slater,

This is in case I don't see you before 7.0 p.m. There is a bit of a breeze on about last night. I evidently woke the skivvy (in that lower bedroom & she saw the torch light as I went out) then rushed to Ma Cooper's room saying 'Oh God, the house is full of men!'

Our greatest piece of luck is that Pa Cooper wasn't in the house (sleeping at Keble) so Audrey alone searched & found the note, which is the sole trace.

Ladder was found next morning & police phoned for. Now if they put two & two together they'll connect us with the two people who were seen waltzing about with a ladder in Bardwell Road. But I don't think they can get any further than that—but it would perhaps be as well if we weren't seen about together.

About tonight: Audrey was awfully angry & I was very sorry I had done it—it wasn't fair on her—but the cloud will clear I hope. Her Mater had a slight heart attack over it & so they are not having anyone for dinner this evening unless *perhaps* me. I am sorry. It would have been good. When I have got full partics. I will tell you all about it. Yours, Basil

Gymnastics was Owen's first favourite subject at school, from which his confidence grew, and so from him we children learnt that balance and coordination have values beyond their physical basis. He taught us how to stand on our heads with ease and we taught this to other children—the secret lies in the unmentioned role of the hands. By example and a bit of showing off he taught us all manner of bike tricks—riding backwards seated on the handlebars. We felt fit to join the circus. He also taught us to swim, to use, maintain, and value tools, to mend punctures, to wire electric plugs and change fuses, to recognize and name plants and wild flowers because many were edible but some were poisonous. He never fostered fear of danger but rather a rational understanding of how to deal with it. He explained geometric solids, map reading, and the uses of knots like the 'Scout button thing' that had fascinated Joyce. He never suggested that there were things girls could not do just as well as boys and he had a much respected gift for coaching girls for O Level maths. I once asked him how he did it. He said he would find out the point at which a pupil had had confidence in the subject and lead them forward from that point. He also conveyed the idea that maths was enjoyable and intriguing. I hadn't heard that girls were no good at maths. In a family expectation is sometimes more powerful than injunction and his personal influence and example are active in the lives of his children and grandchildren to this day. 'Owen was magic,' as his brother Eliot said, yet occasionally he would balk at something he didn't want to do. He would then end all discussion with a curt, 'I'm sorry. It is quite impossible.'

After Eliot qualified as a physician he went to Berlin in 1934–5 to study psychiatry. While there he met and married Lydia, a biochemist, daughter of the painter Leonid Pasternak and sister of the novelist Boris. As Russian Jews Lydia's sister and her family, along with their parents, soon had to leave Germany and came to live with Gilbert and Violet in Park Town. Other families fleeing Nazi rule started to arrive and some were allocated to live with us. Our own house got so full that we sat down fifteen to meals at two tables in the big kitchen. The so-called Breakfast Room had lost its function and became a bedroom for ever afterwards. During the Spanish Civil War my parents again opened their home, this time to refugees from Franco's Spain. There was a constant to and fro between the two houses. My childhood recollection of Gilbert is of a frail old man, seated at a small table covered with papers, with a shawl round his shoulders. His health had never recovered from his time in India and Owen regularly walked round to Park Town at night to carry his father up to his bedroom as the stairs had become impossible. Gilbert died on 8 March 1938 four days before Germany's seizure of Austria. In time Eliot, based in London, bought his parents' house on the understanding that Violet would continue to live there and that he would use it as his Oxford home. Gilbert's sons had all married foreigners: Owen married an Irishwoman; Eliot married a Russian; and Patrick married an American. Internationalism on a family level.

During the Second World War Owen served as air raid warden and fire watcher. His delight in dancing, discovered at the WAAC dances, combined with the injunctions to 'keep the home fires burning' and not to spread alarm and despondency, were inspiration enough to set up monthly roll-up-the-carpet, dress-up-and-dance evenings. A group of young couples took it in turn to host dances. When our parents' turn came round we children were allowed to sit on the stairs in our pyjamas and watch the grown-ups looking thrillingly beautiful in evening dress. The garden was dug up for vegetables and given over to increasingly free-range hens. I can still remember our mother in a very pretty dressing gown standing by the gas cooker boiling up a large bucket of disgusting scraps to feed them. We thought the hens mildly interesting, but their eggs were an essential part of our diet. Our mother studied food values and catered for an increasingly complicated household with variable help. American friends left Oxford while fear of invasion sent children we knew to America and Canada, and the children of our parents' friends came to stay with us and became our friends. Cast iron railings were carted off to make submarines, or so it was said, and at school we suddenly had new arrivals from Malta. Whenever there was an unexpected bang from a desk lid they dived to the floor. Something had happened to them which had not happened to us.

Violet continued to play a big part in our lives as most days she visited our mother for morning coffee and to share with her the *Daily Worker*, its significant passages already underlined in red. For us children she chose little books with good illustrations, so we came to know the works of Arthur Rackham, Edmund Dulac, Randolph Caldecott, and Heath Robinson. She invited us to hold them in our hands and study the pictures accompanying stories from the Bible and Beatrix Potter. Later she read Tolstoy's stories to us: perhaps these were the same stories she had advised our father to read in 1919. She often walked us round to Park Town and back, hidden underneath her charcoal grey cloak, naturally bought at Jaeger's, with its arm slits at the height of our heads. Progress was slow but we enjoyed looking out from peepholes which to outsiders appeared to be pockets. These walks always included one beautifully silver-wrapped tablet each of Callard & Bowser's butterscotch. When Martin and I were in our cots suffering from an unexplained fever she brought us each a small bunch of grapes to tie just in reach above our heads, conjuring up a warm vineyard to surround us. Once a week Granny had a day of rest: we were allowed a short visit and could open her treasure box to take out the seahorse and unfold papers with the silky baby curls of our father and Uncles Pat and Eliot. Uncle Pat's were the nearest to red gold. Violet died in 1950.

After the war Owen carried on at Southfield School and tried to retire three times, each time being called back. It was toward the end of this period, in 1962, that a new English teacher was employed with responsibility for Religious Education, a subject not much liked by some of the staff. Although by now Owen had little time for religion, he nevertheless came forward with his support for the young man, who was intrigued to notice that when his senior colleague returned from his lunch break he always had a damp upper lip. There was a simple explanation. The school had been built with a headmaster's bathroom which was no longer required. Always fond of a bath from his youth up, Owen even now did not miss an opportunity for a hot bath which also helped to reduce the strain on No. 12's antiquated boiler.

In 1963 my father finally retired from teaching but carried on tutoring and examining. In 1978 Nando died, a victim of emphysema and a stroke. Once, after her death, when my father was approaching 80, I was passing No. 12, a four-storey house. Glancing up a long extended ladder to roof level I was aghast to see my father at the very top inspecting guttering repairs. I dared not call up to him. Instead I went round the block, coming back to find him sitting calmly in his chair. This incident was 'character isolated by a deed', an insight into a trace of private rebellion, doing something quite against all normal advice, a reminder of his method of dealing with parental pressures when young and with children's pressures when old. Not long after this incident Owen died quietly in his bed. He had never talked about his time in the Royal Engineers. Had he forgotten those years altogether? Not completely. Soon after his death we had a phone call from Edna Brown's housekeeper to say that the young girl who had so enjoyed

Owen's parody of 'The boy stood on the burning deck' had just died. There would be no reply to my father's recent letter to her.

When Owen was on his deathbed my sister and I were reading silently in the room, aware of his gentle breathing and the ticking clock. The clock struck ten and when the chimes ceased there was absolute silence. Earlier in the day he had sat up beside me on his bed to drink some water while I had my arm round his shoulder. He waved his right hand vaguely in the air and said 'It is so hard to signify.' Those were his last words.

NOTES TO PREFACE AND INTRODUCTION

1. Gilbert Slater to Owen Slater, 14 Nov. 1917, and Violet Slater to Gilbert Slater, 9 Oct. 1918, Slater MSS. *Echoes of the Great War: The Diary of the Reverend Andrew Clark 1914–1919* was edited by James Munson and published by Oxford University Press in 1985.
2. For the wide range of opposition to the war see Martin Ceadel, *Pacifism in Britain, 1914–1945: Defining of a Faith* (Oxford, 1980), and Adam Hochschild, *To End All Wars: A Story of Loyalty and Rebellion, 1914–1918* (2011). For the Nonconformists' difficulties see Adrian Gregory, *The Last Great War: British Society and the First World War* (Cambridge, 2008), 173–7, and James Munson, *The Nonconformists: In Search of a Lost Culture* (1991), 291–4.
3. The difficulties involved in generalized comments about people's reactions and feelings in 1914 are best analysed in Gregory, *The Last Great War*, 9–39.
4. For the importance of letters see Alexander Watson, *Enduring the Great War: Combat, Morale and Collapse in the German and British Armies, 1914–1918* (Cambridge, 2008).
5. *The Daily Telegraph*, 12 Jan. 2013.
6. The most recent discussion of the war's many-faceted origins is found in Christopher Clark, *The Sleepwalkers: How Europe Went to War in 1914* (2012). A thorough analysis of the atrocities committed by German soldiers is in Alan Kramer's *Dynamic of Destruction: Culture and Mass Killing in the First World War* (2007). For attacks on hospital ships by the German navy see Richard Crewdson (ed.), *Dorothea's War: The Diary of a First World War Nurse* (2013).
7. Joyce Cockram to Owen Slater, 25 Feb. [1918], Slater MSS.
8. Basil Donne-Smith to Owen Slater, 25 Feb. 1918.
9. Anon., 'Cheveley Hall School, Mannamead, Plymouth' (n.d.). This two-page prospectus was probably written in the 1880s.
10. The Fabian Society had only been established on 4 Jan. 1884.
11. School Boards (to which women could be elected) were allowed by the 1870 Education Act. They could be set up in areas where it was felt existing provision of elementary schools, almost always provided by the Church of England, were

insufficient. Essentially Boards provided schools for working-class children paid for by middle-class ratepayers. The elections, fought every three years, were highly controversial and electors (which included female householders) had as many votes as there were members of their area or of the whole Board in rural areas with only one or a few schools. Board schools were allowed to provide non-denominational religious instruction if they wished. For an insight into the religious debate see J. E. B. Munson, 'The London School Board Election of 1894: A Study in Victorian Religious Controversy', *British Journal of Educational Studies*, 23 (1975), and 'The Unionist Coalition and Education, 1895–1902', *Historical Journal*, 20 (1977).

12. Undated obituary notice from the *Sunderland Echo*.

13. Gertrude Slater, Chronology, n.p., Slater MSS. For the Labour Party in Woolwich at this time see Anon., 'The Woolwich Labour Party, 1903–1951', in David Clark (gen. ed.), *Origins and Developments of the Labour Party in Britain at Local Level* (1982), 9.

14. O. R. McGregor, 'The Social Sciences', in F. M. L. Thompson (ed.), *The University of London and the World of Learning: 1836–1986* (1990), 211–12. See also John Burrows, *Adult Education in London: A Century of Achievement* (1976), 1–44, and J. H. Burrows, 'The Teaching of Economics in the Early Days of the University Extension Movement in London, 1876–1902', *History of Economic Thought Newsletter* (Spring 1978), xx, *passim*.

15. *The Times*, 3 Nov. 1903 and 10 Nov. 1905. The University of London introduced the D.Sc. in 1860. At first it was equivalent to a master's degree, gained by examination after two years graduate study. The independent research component became ever more important and from the 1880s the degree was generally awarded on the basis of a thesis alone. In 1919, the university introduced a Ph.D. This replaced the D.Sc., which became a 'higher' doctorate awarded in recognition of significant published work. In recent years the D.Sc. has been awarded by London University only as an honorary degree.

16. Violet Slater, *Sketchbook* (n.p., n.d.), Slater MSS.

17. Gilbert Slater to Violet Slater, n.d. [?Feb. 1916] and Ellen Slater to Lilian Slater, 19 June 1913, Slater MSS.

18. Robert Owen (1771–1858) was a utopian socialist and social reformer famous for his concern for children and for his work at the New Lanark Mills near Glasgow. There he established decent housing, education, and working environments for his employees. He later moved to the USA to set up the 'New Harmony' commune in Indiana which failed miserably.

19. Ellen Slater to Lilian Slater, 28 Aug. 1914, Slater MSS.

20. *The Times*, 22 and 18 Sept. 1914.

21. Perhaps the best discussions of this question are in Roger Chickering and Stig Förster (eds.), *Great War, Total War: Combat and Mobilization on the Western Front*,

1914–1918 (Cambridge, 2000), and Roger Chickering, 'Total War: The Use and Abuse of a Concept', in Mannfred F. Boemeke, Roger Chickering, and Stig Föster (eds.), *Anticipating Total War* (Cambridge, 1999). See also Stig Föster and Jörg Nagler (eds.), *On the Road to Total War* (Cambridge, 1997), and Roger Chickering and Stig Föster, 'Introduction', in Roger Chickering and Stig Föster (eds.), *In the Shadows of Total War* (Cambridge, 2003).

22. J. M. Winter, 'Oxford and the First World War', in Brian Harrison (ed.), *The History of the University of Oxford*, iii: *The Twentieth Century* (Oxford, 1994), 6–7. Estimates for the number of refugees vary from 160,000 in Ian F. W. Beckett, *The Great War 1914–1918* (Harlow, 2nd edn., 2007), 397, to 265,000 in David Bilton, *The Home Front in the Great War* (Barnsley, 2004), 217. The total of 200,000 is the total Winter uses and seems a reasonable estimate. Ellen Slater to Lilian Slater, 14 Nov. 1914. Slater MSS.

23. The *Ruskin Collegian* was a bi-monthly magazine established in Jan. 1911 for students and supporters of Ruskin College.

24. Ellen Slater to Lilian Slater, 28 Aug. 1914, Slater MSS.

25. Henry Sanderson Furniss (1868–1939) was Vice-Principal. He came from a comfortable upper-middle-class background and became Principal without pay in 1916. In 1918 he stood as the first Labour candidate for the University of Oxford seat. In 1925 he resigned as Principal and in 1930 was created a Labour peer, Baron Sanderson of Hunmanby, Yorkshire, by George V.

26. Gilbert Slater to Ellen Slater, 20 Apr. 1915, Slater MSS.

27. *The Times*, 10 Mar. 1938.

28. Dr S. Narayanan, Research Fellow, Institute of Advanced Study and Research, University of Madras, to James Munson, 10 Mar. 2012.

29. Owen Slater to his father, [Nov. 1915], Slater MSS.

30. Owen Slater to his mother, 18[?] Sept. 1918, and Gilbert Slater to his father, 4 Nov. 1916 and 5 Dec. 1917. Slater MSS.

31. Owen Slater to his mother, 23 Apr. 1918. Slater MSS.

32. Gilbert Slater to Owen Slater, 25 July 1918. Slater MSS.

33. Owen Slater to his father, 8 July 1918. Slater MSS.

34. Owen Slater to his mother, 21 Oct. 1918, 22 Oct. 1918, and 3 Nov. 1918. Slater MSS.

NOTES TO LETTERS

Unless noted otherwise, the place of publication is London.

1. Isabella Barnes was born in London where she trained as an artist and became a friend of Violet Slater. She was known for her pastels, watercolour portraits, and landscapes. She had exhibited at the Royal Academy and the Suffolk Street Gallery in 1890.

2. The Presidency College in Madras was established in 1840 as The Madras Preparatory School. In 1841 it opened a High School division and eventually offered university-level courses and granted degrees. When the University of Madras was founded in 1857 the college became affiliated to it. Presidencies had been units of government under the East India Company.

3. John Sinclair (1860–1925) was a Liberal MP 1892–5 and 1897–1909. He was Secretary of State for Scotland 1905–12 when he was appointed Governor of Madras, an office he held until 1919. In 1909 he was created the first Baron Pentland of Lyth. In Madras he appointed a town planning adviser (who also worked to improve sanitation) and encouraged industrialization.

4. RMS *Persia* was a passenger ship en route from Marseilles to India when it was torpedoed by a German U-boat on 30 Dec. 1915. Of 501 passengers and crew, 335 were drowned. (*The Times*, 3 and 7 Jan. 1916.) The commander of the U-boat, Max Valentiner, was put on the Allies' list of war criminals for not firing a warning shot before sinking an unarmed ship. He escaped justice and went on to serve the Nazis in the Second World War.

5. Ernest Thompson Seton (1860–1946) was a keen naturalist, born in South Shields, whose family emigrated to Canada when he was 6. He was later sent to live in the USA where he became a founding father of the Boy Scouts of America as well as a highly popular author of adventure and naturalist books. *The Trail of the Sandhill Stag* was his sixth book, first published in 1899.

6. Rudyard Kipling's *Jungle Book* was first published in book form in 1894 and *The Second Jungle Book* appeared the next year. Rikki-Tikki-Tavi was the pet mongoose of an English family in Bihar which fought off cobras who wished to kill the family and repossess the garden from which they had been expelled.

7. 'Brigger' and 'Old Brigger' were nicknames for C. E. Brownrigg (1865–1942), Headmaster of Magdalen College School from 1900 to 1930.

8. The University of London initiated examinations for school pupils in 1838 when the London Matriculation Examination was introduced. Its aim was to examine candidates who were seeking admission to university. But as the 'London Matric.' was open to anyone over the age of 16 it quickly became used for purposes other than university entrance and became a qualification in its own right.

9. Hobble skirts were close fitting-skirts popular between 1910 and 1914. They had a wide band below the knees and above the ankles which severely restricted a woman's ability to walk normally.

10. 'The Kitchener' was a name for the type of cooking-range with closed tops and fitted with various appliances such as ovens, plate-warmers, and water-heaters. It was patented by the Exeter ironmonger George Bodley in 1802 as the Bodley Range. The term does not refer to the field marshal but to the medieval term kitchener, which survived into the 1880s. This was someone who was in charge of a kitchen, especially in a monastery.

11. Grand Admiral Alfred von Tirpitz (1849–1930) wanted restrictions on German U-boat attacks on British shipping to be lifted and when this was not agreed he was forced to resign on 15 Mar. 1916.

12. The Dead Sea Apple (*Poma Sodomitica* or 'Apple of Sodom') was beautiful to the eye but would dissolve into ashes when touched.

13. The Fourth War Loan consisted of 4.5% State Treasury Bonds and 5% State Loans. The issue raised £535,600,000. This bond was deemed a success because the number of subscribers (5,279,645) was far greater than for earlier loans. *The Times*, 2 Mar. and 8 Apr. 1916; The German University League, New York City, Bulletin No. 6 (Sept. 1916.)

14. Annie Besant (1847–1933) was a left-wing activist who dropped agitation for Theosophy and from the 1890s took up Indian Home Rule. She spent much of each year in India and was interned in May 1917. She was released in August when Parliament voted for 'progressive' self-rule in India.

15. Gilbert was here probably referring to the Revd A. J. Carlyle (1861–1943), Chaplain of University College, Rector of St Martin's and All Saints, then the City Church of Oxford (1895–1919), and a lecturer in economics and politics. He had been an active supporter of Ruskin College from its inception and was a consultative member of the Executive Committee although he did not have a doctorate until 1934. Harold Pollins, *The History of Ruskin College* (1984), 10, 21.

16. In the Church of England one cannot be confirmed unless one has already been baptized. Although Gilbert's background was Congregational he does not appear to have been an active chapel-goer for many years and had forgotten that Congregationalists also practised infant baptism. Magdalen College School was

of course a Church of England institution and at this time it was customary for boys to be put forward for confirmation unless they or their parents objected.

17. The SS *Sussex* was a ship sailing between Folkestone and Dieppe. On 24 Mar. 1916 she was torpedoed and badly damaged but stayed afloat and was towed into Boulogne harbour. At least 50 people were killed and some estimated as many as 100. As letters to India were sent through France to Marseilles the post would have been affected.

18. The School Certificate and the Higher School Certificate were created by the Consultative Committee of 1911 in its Acland Report. Its aim was to simplify and co-ordinate the various examinations begun in 1858 by Oxford and Cambridge to improve teaching in schools. The School Certificate was for 16-year-olds who were leaving school; the Higher School Certificate was for those staying on.

19. The Friends' Ambulance Unit was established in 1914 by individual Quakers as the Anglo-Belgian Ambulance Unit. It eventually had some 1,000 men involved, most of whom were men registered as conscientious objectors.

20. Howard Slater was Gilbert's younger brother and a physician who had joined the Royal Army Medical Corps in July 1915. This had been formed in 1898 when the Army Medical Service was reorganized. In the event the corps lost 743 officers and 6,130 men during the First World War so it was not as safe a bet as Gilbert thought.

21. 'The Skipper' was a nickname for C. C. Lynam, Headmaster of the Dragon School where Eliot and Patrick Slater were still pupils. He was an accomplished yachtsman, hence the name.

22. *The Draconian* is the magazine of the Dragon School. It began in Apr. 1889 with two issues a term. By 1916 it was being published once a term. *The Lily* was the magazine of Magdalen College School and began life in 1870 as the *Magdalen College School Journal*. Its new title became permanent in 1888 (R. S. Stanier, *Magdalen School: A History of Magdalen College School Oxford* (Oxford, 1940), 183, 183n.).

23. Gilbert Slater was referring here to the Brusilov Offensive. This carried on until late Sept. 1916. It was one of the most deadly series of battles in the war and Russian casualties are said to have reached 1,500,000. It broke the back of the Austro-Hungarian army and forced Germany to shift troops from Verdun to the east.

24. Henry Tregelles Gillett (1872–1955) was an Oxford GP and the Slaters' doctor. He was active in the Religious Society of Friends.

25. The Volunteer Training Corps began independent of government supervision as a type of 'Home Guard' in 1914 to defend the country against invasion. National organization followed and in July 1915 local battalions became Volunteer Regiments. In Aug. 1916 they were fully integrated into their local county infantry regiment. In Owen's case this would be the Oxfordshire and Buckinghamshire Light Infantry, the 'Ox and Bucks'.

26. The National Council for Combating Venereal Disease dates from 1914 and had its first AGM in 1916. See *The Lancet* (31 Oct. 1914), CLXXXIV.4757.

27. The Madras Club was established in 1832 and was the social centre for the resident British community.

28. Coimbatore Agricultural School was started in 1868 at Saidapet in Madras and in 1905 was moved to specially built premises in Lawley Road. In 1920 it was transferred to the University of Madras and in 1971 it became Tamil Nadu Agricultural University.

29. Gilbert was right in saying that after the Battle of Jutland the threat from submarine warfare would increase.

30. Gilbert is referring to the Women's International League for Peace and Freedom, which began life at a conference in Washington, DC, in Jan. 1915 as the Women's Peace Party. It advocated the establishment of a committee of neutral nations to negotiate a peace and had as its ultimate goal an investigation into the causes of war and the establishment of a 'permanent peace'. It also advocated women's suffrage. In time it became the International Women's Congress for Peace and Freedom. In 1919 it became the Women's International League for Peace and Freedom and continues to this date.

31. The Kellett Institute is a Christian boys' school in a poor part of Madras. It began life as the Aryan High School but in 1899 was renamed the Wesleyan High School. It took its present name in honour of one of its most dedicated teachers, F. W. Kellett.

32. *The Madras Times*, an English-language paper with liberal views, was founded as a weekly in 1859, became a daily in 1860, and carried on until 1921 after which it was merged with *The Mail*. *New India* was a home-rule periodical started by Annie Besant. It was sympathetic to the Brahmins, the highest of the four castes which traditionally constituted Indian society and which got the majority of posts open to Indians under the Raj at this time.

33. The island of Heligoland, some 29 miles off the German coast, was ceded to the UK by Denmark in 1814. In 1890 Britain transferred the islands to Germany and in 1914 the first naval battle was fought just off the island. It then became an important naval base for Germany.

34. This refers to a 1916 'memorandum' organized by the Revd Joseph Estlin Carpenter (1844–1927), who was a Unitarian minister, scholar, and Principal Emeritus of Manchester College (now Harris Manchester College) in Oxford. It argued for a negotiated settlement and a post-war reconstruction of international relations. Supporters were defined as 'democrats, writers and Quakers, female as well as male'. Israel Zangwill, 'The Principle of Nationalities': The Conway Memorial Lecture, 8 Mar. 1917 (1917), 13–14. They included Thomas Burt, MP, Edward Carpenter, J. A. Hobson, and George Lansbury. In Gilbert's case there may have been

a personal element because Violet regularly worshipped in Manchester College Chapel. See *The Socialist Review* (14) and *The Spectator* (17 Mar. 1917). The third year of the war had given rise to much talk of peace settlements. In May the US President Woodrow Wilson would address the first annual conference of the League to Enforce Peace although he did not then advocate the use of force to maintain peace.

35. Gilbert is referring to the War Office's decision in Aug. 1916 to convert the Volunteer Training Corps into 'Volunteer' regiments of their local county regiments. See n. 25.

36. When it came to 'difficulties & dangers' Gilbert was wrong to think that Owen would be safer as an officer. Because of his training in the OTC and Cadet Battalion scheme Owen would enter the army as a second lieutenant. If he were in the infantry he would be, as a junior officer, in the group which suffered the highest rate of casualties. See John Lewis-Stempel, *Six Weeks: The Short and Gallant Life of the British Officer in the First World War* (2011).

37. In 1916 German and Austro-Hungarian submarines sank 415 ships in the Mediterranean. These formed half of all Allied ships sunk in all theatres that year.

38. Bahman Pestonji Wadia (1881–1958) took over his father's Bombay textile firm when only 19 and became independently wealthy. He took up Theosophy and in 1907 started working with Annie Besant. He followed her lead in turning from Theosophy to Home Rule and made Madras his centre. In 1918 he helped to establish the first trade union (for textile workers) in India and in the 1920s became a leading figure in Indian public life.

39. On 7 Dec. 1915 the garrison at Kut (manned by the British and Indian armies), on the left bank of the Tigris River, 100 miles south of Baghdad, had been surrounded by Ottoman forces. After a siege of just over twenty weeks and despite major efforts to relieve the garrison, Major-General Townshend surrendered his forces to the Turks on 29 Apr. 1916. It was the British army's greatest defeat to date. Kut was retaken by British forces on 23 Feb. 1917. Gilbert's optimism about the defeat of German submarines was premature: shipping lost to the U-boats in the waters round the UK would rise between Jan. and Apr. to its highest peak and the convoy system, which would do so much to undermine the German strategy, was not introduced until May 1917. The Battle of the Ancre from 13 to 18 Nov. 1916 was the last stage of the Somme Offensive. British successes raised spirits in the Empire, reaffirmed Britain's commitment to the war, and weakened German forces in this part of the line.

40. These two lines occur in Shelley's sonnet 'England in 1819' but in the second line 'helpless' should read 'fainting'.

41. Lionel George Curtis (1872–1955) was a Fellow of All Souls College, Oxford, and a well-known advocate of greater unity within the British Empire. In 1909 he

helped to establish the Round Table movement in the UK and throughout the Empire to promote that unity. Curtis felt that federalism, self-government, and social reform were inseparable. He came to India in Nov. 1916 to promote his recently published books and the Round Table movement and while there he advocated a degree of self-government, a policy that would be adopted in the 1919 Government of India Act.

42. Gilbert's letter was published in *The Times* on 6 Feb. 1917. Other than 'a small quantity of patent infant foods' there was no need for exports to India: limiting them would reduce losses in ships and keep food where it was most needed.

43. The phrase 'wait and see' had become famous in 1910 when used by the Prime Minister, Asquith, to fend off questions from Unionists regarding the government's policy over flooding the Lords with new creations to force the budget through the upper chamber.

44. Sir John Wallis (1861–1946) was the Advocate General in Madras 1900–7, Vice-Chancellor of Madras University 1908–16, and Chief Justice 1914–21.

45. Dravidian is the term usually applied to the languages and culture of southern India and northern Ceylon. In 1924 Gilbert would publish *The Dravidian Element in Indian Culture*, a major study of Dravidian civilization.

46. India, which then included modern Burma, Pakistan, and Bangladesh, contributed some 1,000,000 men to the Allied war effort. In 1914 the Indian army had only 150,000 men. Indian troops fought on the Western Front, in the Middle East, and in Africa. The number of men who died in all theatres came to 74,187. Lutyens's famous India Gate in New Delhi commemorates those who lost their lives.

47. Gilbert had presumably not heard that in Jan. Germany, reluctantly followed by Austria-Hungary, declared unrestricted submarine warfare. By Apr. the Central Powers would have some 28 submarines in the Mediterranean and Allied losses there would reach a peak of 94 within a single month. The Allies were helped by the presence of Japanese and Italian warships.

48. In 1916 India introduced a graduated income tax on incomes over Rs. 2,000 and there would be further changes in 1917 and 1918. As Gilbert's annual salary was £1,000 he would obviously have been subjected to the higher rate of 25%. Had he been taxed in the UK he would have paid only 15% or 3s. in the £ although by 1918 this would have risen to 30% or 6s. in the £.

49. *The Times*, 2 July 1917.

50. Leighton Park School, in Reading, is a Friends' boarding school, originally for boys, founded in 1890.

51. The Officer Training Corps dates from the Haldane reforms of 1908 and was a response to the shortage of officers during the Boer War. The corps were divided into a senior division (for certain universities) and a junior (for certain public schools).

52. Rabindranath Tagore (1861–1941) was born into a Pirali Brahmin family in Calcutta. He became famous as a poet, writer, and essayist and his work was much loved by the Slaters. In 1913 he was the first non-European to be awarded the Nobel Prize in Literature and in 1915 he was knighted by King George V. In the West he was regarded as something of a seer and he remains one of the most important literary figures in recent Indian history.

53. After 1864 Simla was the summer capital of India. During these months it was also the headquarters of the Commander-in-Chief of the Indian army. Its position in the Himalayas with an altitude of some 7,900 feet made it a healthy escape from the summer heat of Calcutta, capital until the inauguration of New Delhi in 1931.

54. Boars Hill was historically a hamlet on high ground some 3 miles south-west of Oxford. It was well known to local people as a picnic spot and was famous for its view of the Oxford skyline, a view which also inspired Matthew Arnold's *The Scholar Gypsy* and *Thyrsis*.

55. In 1917 H. G. Wells approached *The Times* regarding an article on a peace settlement but the paper turned him down. He then had a letter published in the *Daily Chronicle* on 4 June 1917 with the heading 'Wanted: A Statement of Imperial Plans'. This was later published as a pamphlet which had a print run of 100,000. In the following year he expanded his ideas into a book, *In the Fourth Year: Anticipations of a World Peace*.

56. The Boer, or South African, War began in Oct. 1899 when the Orange Free State and the Transvaal Republic declared war on Britain. Its root causes included Boer fears of expanding numbers of British residents in their 'republics' and the growing strength of British colonies in southern Africa. The war dragged on until 1902 and it had been strongly opposed by left-wing people in Britain and by many in Europe. This meant that in 1914 three factors applied: people's memories of war were of one that had lasted for two years and seven months; (2) opposition to a British war by British people in 1914 was not something new; and (3) the basis for opposition to war—peace movements, religious bodies, newspapers etc.—was in place in Aug. 1914 and many leaders and organizers had had experience in 1899–1902.

57. The reference to 1864 is to the complicated Schleswig–Holstein dispute between Denmark and the German Confederation as to the suzerainty of the two duchies. The second war between Denmark and Prussia was fought between Feb. and Oct. 1864 when Denmark was defeated by a coalition of Prussia (under the Chancellor, Bismarck) and Austria and lost the two duchies. In 1870 Napoleon III, Emperor of the second French Empire, was defeated at the Battle of Sedan in Sept. 1870, again by the forces of several German states led by Prussia under Bismarck. Napoleon was captured at sedan but the newly proclaimed Third Republic

carried on fighting until 27 Jan. 1871 when Paris surrendered. After this the German Empire with the Prussian King as its Emperor was proclaimed. To Gilbert, German militarism could have been halted if Britain had stood up to Prussia in 1864 and in 1870–1.

58. The University of Oxford entrance examination paper in 'divinity'.

59. 'The Man Who Stayed at Home' by Lechmere Worrall and J. E. Harold Terry was premiered at the Royalty Theatre in London in 1914 and ran for 584 performances. It was later made into a film.

60. The series of five articles appeared under the title 'An Allied Peace' in the *New Statesman* between 9 Sept. and 14 Oct. (VII.179–81, 183, 184). An inspiration for these discussions had been Woodrow Wilson's speech of 27 May 1916.

61. Yarnton is a village some 4 miles north-west of Oxford.

62. Here Gilbert was seriously mistaken. The Royal Flying Corps and the Royal Naval Air Service, which were united on 1 Apr. 1918 to form the Royal Air Force, suffered horrendous casualties during the war: in 1917, the year he was writing, 1,094 men were listed as killed or missing. Between 1914 and 1918, 9,378 men from the RFC, the RNAS, and their successor, the RAF, were listed as killed or missing, with 7,245 wounded. The average life span of a pilot was eleven days. See Ian Mackersey, *No Empty Chairs: The Short and Heroic Lives of the Young Aviators Who Fought and Died in the First World War* (2012).

63. The Revd Dr R. W. M. Pope (1849–1923) was Censor [Head] of Non-Collegiate Students, 1887–1919. The Delegacy of Non-Collegiate Students was established by the university in 1868 as a way in which men unable to afford college fees could get a university education. They sat the same exams but were not matriculated through a college and had to find their own accommodation. In the event students formed a club and met in St Catherine's Hall in Catte Street. By Owen's time this had many of the characteristics of a college and in 1962 the Delegacy became St Catherine's College and the 'censor' became the 'master'.

64. Wytham Park adjoins Wytham Woods, a forested area some 3 miles north-west of the centre of Oxford beside the village of Wytham. The woods are a favourite picnic spot for Oxford people.

65. The Rt Revd Ulric Vernon Herford (1866–1938) was one of the irregularly consecrated Episcopi Vagantes and sailed under the splendid title of Mar Jacobus, Bishop of Mercia and Middlesex, Administrator of the Metropolitan See of India, Ceylon, Milapur, etc., of the Syro-Chaldean Church and of the Patriarchate of Babylon and the East, and founder of the Evangelical Catholic Communion. None of this was recognized by either the Church of England or the Roman Catholic Church. Herford came from a Mancunian Unitarian background, was trained for the Unitarian ministry, ordained a Presbyterian minister, attended St Stephen's House, the High Church Oxford theological college, for a year, and

was pastor of the 'Church of the Divine Love' in Percy Street, Oxford, before his consecration. He was also kind to animals.

66. Kelham Hall, in the village of Kelham, is some 3 miles outside Newark. In 1914 the hall, home of the Church of England's Society of the Sacred Mission, was taken over as a military training centre.

67. St Ebbe's parish, now home to the Westgate Shopping Centre, then contained some of Oxford's worst slums and cheapest digs. It also featured Cape's, a general store famous for its millinery and copper pneumatic tubes which took customers' cash to the office.

68. The George was a fashionable restaurant and tea room at the corner of George and Cornmarket Streets in Oxford famous for its trifles and vol-au-vents.

69. Knuttily is the adverb of knut, a slang term for a fashionable, showy, or socially adept young man. The term appears to have been first used in 1911.

70. The Jaeger chain of outfitters was established in 1884. The name honours the German zoologist Dr Gustav Jaeger, who advocated the use of clothing made from animal fibres, e.g. wool, rather than plant fibres, e.g. cotton. Its clothing was looser fitting and 'advanced' in style, e.g. women's dresses did not require corsets to be worn. It appealed to the intelligentsia and those like Violet who enjoyed beautiful clothes yet eschewed 'fashion'.

71. After Aug. 1914 the Friends' War Victims' Relief Committee, first set up in 1870, was restarted by the Quakers. Its agents provided not only food but medical treatment to refugees and victims. After 1917 it was aided by the American Friends' Service Council.

72. The reference is to the opening lines of Horace's *Odes* (I.5). The translation Joan would probably have used was that by the Revd E. C. Wickham which she could have found in a variety of editions published before 1918. The relevant lines read:

> What delicate stripling is it, Pyrrha,
> That now, steeped in liquid perfumes,
> Is wooing thee on the heaped rose-leaves in some distant grot?
> For whose eyes doest thou braid those flaxen locks, so trim, so simple?

73. Thomas Allinson (1858–1918) was a Scottish physician who urged healthy eating, brown bread, exercise, vegetarianism, and birth-control and opposed smoking (as a cause of cancer), vaccination, spirits, tea, and coffee. He milled his own flour and set up a bakery, both of which became more popular during the war because of the restriction on imports and the recognition that brown flour was healthier.

74. Botley Road is the main road out of Oxford to the west. The houses which were built on both sides were described by C. S. Lewis as a 'mean and sprawling suburb'. *Surprised by Joy* (1955), 184.

75. Shotover is a forested area with a hilltop common which was a favourite spot for picnics. It was historically part of Wychwood Royal Forest, and is to the east of Oxford, beyond Headington.

76. Cowley Road is one of the three roads that fan out from 'The Plain' (now a round-about) on the eastern side of Magdalen Bridge which crosses the Cherwell River at the end of Oxford's High Street. The other two are the Iffley and Headington (or London) roads. The Cowley Road heads south-east. Like Botley Road at this time it ran through a mainly working-class district. In all these cases the roads originally led to villages that were at one time outside Oxford.

77. The Oxford Picture Palace was a cinema on the corner of Cowley Road and Jeune Street. It opened in 1911 and closed in 1917.

78. Easton's Syrup (or tablets) was often taken for anaemia. It contained strychnine (a stimulant), iron phosphate (a 'brain food'), and quinine (an appetite and general stimulant).

79. Percy Alfred Scholes (1877–1958) published *Everyman and his Music: Simple Papers on Varied Subjects* in 1917. Scholes was a musician, music historian, and critic. He remains best known for writing *The Oxford Companion to Music*, published in 1938.

80. T. W. Robertson's comedy *David Garrick* was first staged in 1864. It enjoyed many revivals of which this was one. John Martin Harvey (1863–1944) got his start in Sir Henry Irving's Lyceum Theatre Company and toured with his own company after Irving's death in 1905.

81. G. C. Druce (1850–1932), MA (Oxon.), FRS, set up his chemist's shop, Druce & Co, at 118 High Street in 1879. His shop had one of the earliest telephones in Oxford (number Oxford 12) and like many chemists he developed film. He was also mentioned in Max Beerbohm's novel of Oxford life, *Zuleika Dobson*.

82. The Revd G. L. Prestige (1889–1955) was a Fellow of New College from 1913 to 1920, editor of *The Church Times* 1941–7, and Canon of St Paul's Cathedral 1950–5.

83. 'House' or 'The House' is Oxford slang for Christ Church College while 'Togger' was the slang term for Torpids, the boat races held in Hilary Term.

84. Winnie or Winifred Slater was Eric Slater's daughter and from time to time stayed with Violet. Rationing was finally introduced early in 1918 in response to the German U-boat attacks on Allied shipping. Sugar was the first item rationed and by the end of April meat, butter, cheese, and margarine were added to the list. Ration cards were issued and everyone had to register with a butcher and grocer. Sugar and butter would be rationed until 1920.

85. Robert Louis Stevenson's *Familiar Studies of Men and Books* was published in 1882. His *Travels with a Donkey in the Cévennes* was published in 1879 and was based on his time in the Cévennes mountains in France in 1878. Stevenson's novella *The Strange Case of Dr Jekyll and Mr Hyde* was published in 1886.

86. St Giles is the principal street leading north out of Oxford. Within a short distance it divides into roads to Banbury (to the right) and Woodstock (to the left). For The Plain see n. 76.

87. The Labour Party was divided over the war and the leader, Ramsay MacDonald, who opposed it, resigned in 1914. The new leader, Arthur Henderson and after him George Barnes, supported the war and served in the Asquith and Lloyd George coalition governments. The much smaller Independent Labour Party consistently opposed the war.

88. 'Schemes' were training assignments such as building bridges, drainage, etc.

89. As is usual with slang terms 'tchacooning' had a variety of meanings: (1) taking a long time over any mental task; (2) 'mugging up' a subject; (3) being at a loose end; (4) pretending to a knowledge or skill one hasn't got; or (5) having no established order—a free-for-all. This was the use in Magdalen College School where the term was held to be derived from *chacun à son goût*. In this letter Owen seems to be using it in the first sense.

90. St Edward's School, in the Woodstock Road, Oxford, was founded in 1863 by the Revd Thomas Chamberlain, a student of Christ Church and Vicar of St Thomas the Martyr, a slum church in Oxford. Chamberlain was a leader in the High Church revival and St Edward's had a High Church ambience. It is claimed that during the war the school sent *pro rata* more men into HM forces than any other independent school.

91. The Religious Society of Friends, commonly called Quakers, is a Christian sect established in the 1640s by George Fox. Quakers believe in the priesthood of all believers and assert that there is something of God in everyone. It is traditionally pacifist. It has no ministers, sacraments, or ordered worship but 'meetings' in which those present speak if inspired. The Quaker meeting house in Oxford is in St Giles. Quakers have for many years been associated with progressive causes and for much of their history could only marry fellow-members, thereby helping to create wealthy dynasties such as the Cadburys, Trittons, Barclays, Gurneys, Rowntrees, et al. The denomination's affairs are carried on through monthly, quarterly, and yearly 'meetings'.

92. Gilbert Murray (1866–1957) was the Regius Professor of Greek in 1918 and a keen supporter of the Liberal Party and in time of the League of Nations. As his wife was a daughter of the 9th Earl of Carlisle she should have been referred to as Lady Mary Murray.

93. Chatham became a Royal Engineers Establishment in 1812 and was renamed the School of Military Engineering in 1868. In 1962 it was granted the prefix 'Royal' by the Queen. The Headquarters of the Royal Engineers moved to Chatham from Woolwich in 1857.

94. 'Hum' was the nickname for A. E. Lynam, the son of C. C. Lynam, Headmaster of the Dragon School. He would succeed his father as headmaster in 1920.

95. The lyrics to which Violet objected first appeared in *The Gentleman's Magazine* of 15 Oct, 1745 with no attribution. The verse which Violet found offensive would have read: O Lord, our God, arise | Scatter his enemies | And make them fall | Confound their politics | Frustrate their knavish tricks | On thee our hopes we fix | God save us all.

96. 'Aunt Sally' is a traditional game often played in pubs and fair-grounds. Contestants throw sticks at a ball or 'dolly' which balances on top of a post. Originally sticks were thrown at a clay pipe which was affixed to a woman's head which rested on top of the stick.

97. Emmeline Pankhurst (1858–1928) is generally regarded as the founder of the suffragette movement. In 1914 that movement split on whether to continue or suspend agitation. Mrs Pankhurst and her daughter Christabel opted for suspension and became warm advocates of the war while her other daughter Sylvia, who had already been expelled, opposed the war as a pacifist and socialist.

98. In Dec. 1917 Gilbert was invited to a garden party in Madras for E. S. Montagu, Secretary of State for India, and Lord Chelmsford, the Viceroy. Montagu had been sent to India to work on proposals for the 'increasing association of Indians in every branch of the administration and the gradual development of self-governing institutions with a view to the progressive realization of responsible government in India as an integral part of the British Empire'. The two men were instructed to draw up a report on reforms and issued the Montagu–Chelmsford Report in 1918. This became the basis for the Government of India Act 1919, which extended the franchise and gave increased authority to the elected legislative councils. This meant that in the provinces ministers of education, public works, agriculture, etc. were made accountable to the assemblies. Ministers concerned with finance, home affairs, etc. were still appointed by the Viceroy, who was himself still accountable only to Whitehall. These ministers tended to be British.

99. J. M. Barrie's play *Dear Brutus* opened in London in Oct. 1917. Variously described as a fantasy or comedy, its setting was a country house party in which the guests were transported into a magical wood in which they were offered a chance to relive their lives.

100. Strictly speaking the only boys involved were those studying engineering and they only made *parts* for ammunition. Ironically the headmaster who ordered this, F. W. Sanderson (1857–1922), was famous as an educational reformer who had among other things introduced engineering to the curriculum. He was praised by H. G. Wells, who sent his sons to the school and who based the headmaster in his 1918 novel *Joan and Peter* on Sanderson. By 1918 Sanderson had lost one son in the war.

101. In fact the former Prime Minister was exceedingly fond of his drink and had a long-standing relationship with the much younger Venetia Stanley and then with her elder sister Sylvia. The 2nd Earl Selborne's judgement of politicians was often unsound: the former First Lord and High Commissioner for South Africa wrote in his MS memoirs that Lloyd George was a great family man, apparently unaware that he had two families. See Selborne MSS 191–2 in the Bodleian Library, Oxford.

102. The Fellowship of Reconciliation was a pacifist movement which had been established by a conference which met in Cambridge in 1915. The F.o.R. resolved as one of its founding tenets that 'as Christians, we are forbidden to wage war'. While the movement was non-denominational its leading lights were Quakers. The Revd Walter Lock was Warden of Keble College, Oxford, from 1897 to 1919. W. B. Selbie (1862–1944) was a Congregational minister and scholar who was Principal of Mansfield College in 1918. He would become the first Nonconformist to receive a DD from the University of Oxford.

103. By 1918 there were two aerodromes near Croydon: Beddington, set up in 1915 to attack Zeppelins, and Waddon, set up in 1918 for test flights. After the war Beddington and Penshurst would be combined to form Croydon Aerodrome.

104. The Hon & Rt Revd Charles Gore (1853–1932) was Bishop of Oxford 1911–19 but in Sept. 1918 he would leave for a ten-week visit to the United States where he was to deliver lectures on a 'league of nations' based on his pamphlet arguing for the same.

105. The threat from Zeppelins had been neutralized by 1917 but in that same year the Germans began a new bombing campaign with aeroplanes that took off from occupied Belgium. In May 1917 bombers, en route to London, were forced by bad weather to drop their bombs round Folkestone resulting in 113 deaths. There would be more raids over London in June and July. By Feb. 1918 the Germans had stopped the raids because of heavy losses although there was one final raid on London on 19 May 1918.

106. Since the 16th century it has been the custom at Magdalen College, Oxford, for the chapel choir to greet the sunrise at 6 a.m. atop Magdalen Tower. The choir sings a Eucharistic hymn and crowds gather below. The Slater family would traditionally go by boat along the Cherwell to be there by 6 a.m.

107. This was presumably a reference to *Erewhon*, Samuel Butler's 1872 utopian novel.

108. Carfax, at the opposite end of High Street from Magdalen College, is regarded as the centre of Oxford. There are differing views about the word's French origins: *carrefour* (cross-roads), *quatre-face* (four face) or *quarter vois* (four views). Another school argues that it is derived from the Latin *quadri furcus* (four forked). Whatever the origin, Carfax is where four streets—Cornmarket Street from the north, St Aldate's from the south, High Street from the east, and Queen Street from the west—converge.

109. Northmoor is a village some 6 miles west of Oxford.

110. Charterhouse School was established in 1611 on the site of the former Carthusian monastery in Charterhouse Square in the City of London where it became a public school. In the 19th century it moved to Godalming in Surrey.

111. Dante Gabriel Rossetti (1828–82) was a poet as well as a painter but it is for his painting, and his establishment of the Pre-Raphaelite Brotherhood, that he is mainly remembered. His paintings featured women, some of whom were voluptuous and others, ethereal. Edgar Allan Poe (1809–49) was one of the most famous American Romantic writers. While he is now remembered for his short stories using 'Gothic' themes, he began his career as a poet and continued to write verse. He often wrote of lost love and highly romanticized women.

112. Arnold J. Toynbee is now remembered because of his twelve-volume *A Study of History*. In 1918, however, the former Balliol Fellow was working in the Foreign Intelligence Department of the Foreign Office and writing on the war and international relations. In 1918 Arnold and Rosalind Toynbee and their two sons lived at 14 Park Crescent, Park Town, Oxford.

113. William Butterfield (1814–1900) is one of the architects most closely associated with the 19th-century Gothic revival. While he is much maligned, his aim was to restore a sense of life and colour into churches left bare after the Puritan horrors of the 16th and 17th centuries. His buildings were famous for their use of red brick into which were set patterns and lines made of polychrome bricks. Keble College was constructed in the 1860s and 1870s and was very controversial when built.

114. The correct wording, 'The trivial round, the common task,' occurs in John Keble's poem 'Morning' in his collection *The Christian Year…* (1827). Joyce could have known it as poetry or as lines in the hymn 'New Every Morning is the Love', No. 4 in *Hymns Ancient and Modern* (1861) and No. 260 in *The English Hymnal* (1906).

115. *The Town Labourer 1760–1832: The New Civilisation* was by J. L. Hammond (1872–1949) and his wife Barbara (1873–1961) and was published in 1917. It followed their earlier study *The Village Labourer 1760–1832: A Study of the Government of England before the Reform Bill*, published in 1911. Both volumes were highly influential studies in the developing field of social and working-class history.

116. Wigmore is a village near the Medway and 4 miles from Gillingham. In a field near the village which bordered on a river the Browns had built huts for family holidays and picnics.

117. The Army & Navy Stores were a chain whose main store was in Victoria Street, London. It had been founded in 1871 as The Army & Navy Co-operative Society by officers and was originally confined to them. It was patterned on the Civil Service Supply Association. [See n. 149.] In 2005 it was renamed House of Fraser after the group that had bought it in 1976. The store to which Owen referred

must have been the one in Maidstone. Two reasons for the scarcity of matches were the transformation of the giant Bryant & May factory in London to munitions and the phenomenal growth in cigarette smoking among all ranks in the armed services.

118. Shepherd & Woodward was, and remains, a clothing outfitters at 109–13 High Street, Oxford. It traces its origins to 1845.

119. Responsions, nicknamed 'Little Go' in the 19th century, were the first examination for the BA degree which undergraduates sat shortly before or soon after matriculation. It examined Latin, Greek, and mathematics and was abolished in 1960. By 'certificate' Hugh meant the Higher School Certificate. See n. 18.

120. Violet is here quoting lines 10 and 11 from the fifth stanza of William Wordsworth's *Intimations of Immortality*: 'Shades of the prison-house begin to close | Upon the growing Boy'.

121. The conference had begun in Nottingham on 23 Jan. and after two days had adjourned to meet again in London on 26 Feb. Its third session took place between 26 and 28 June.

122. Alexander Kerensky had been de facto Prime Minister of Russia after the republic was established in 1917. He was ousted by the Bolsheviks and eventually escaped to Finland from which, in June 1918, he went to London for medical treatment. He addressed the Labour Party Conference on 27 June 1918.

123. The Women's Co-operative Guild was established in 1883 by Mary Lawrenson and Alice (later Lady) Acland. By 1910 it had some 32,000 members and agitated for minimum wages and maternity benefits. In Apr. 1914 they sent delegates to an International Women's Congress at The Hague which passed a resolution condemning war and advocating a 'partnership of nations, with peace as its object'. In the 1960s the WCG became the Co-operative Women's Guild.

124. Lambert's was a boot- and shoe-making shop at 70 and 73 St Giles, Oxford.

125. 'Etons' was the slang term for an Eton suit which consisted of an Eton jacket (short, black, open at front, and with wide lapels) similar to the army's 'bum freezer', which was worn with long trousers.

126. 'Smalls' was the Oxford term for Responsions. See n. 119.

127. Aldershot's history as the home of the British army dates from 1854 when the first permanent training camp was established. During the First World War it was the Mounted Depot for the Royal Engineers. A photograph of 'The Officers' Ride', which showed all the officers being trained with Owen, on their mounts, has survived in the Slater MSS.

128. By 'valise' Owen does not mean the more modern overnight bag but, as the *On Line OED* describes it, 'A cylindrical cloth or leather case adapted for carrying the kit or outfit of a soldier, esp. of a cavalryman or artilleryman'. They were large enough to act as a form of sleeping-bag.

129. Dutton Speedwords was a form of shorthand in which ordinary Roman letters, as opposed to symbols, are used to stand for the semantic qualities of words, as opposed to the phonetic as in the Pitman system. This meant that the system, unlike Pitman's, was designed as an 'international language'. In it the same letters could stand for the same words but in different languages: the sentence 'That was good' is rendered 'k y gu.' This would in theory be as intelligible to a German speaker (meaning 'Das war gut.') as it would be to an English speaker. As someone who ran a shorthand and typing school (Slater & Baker of Plymouth) Aunt Maud would naturally have been interested in the new approach.

130. Local Women Citizens' Associations date from 1913 and followed the initiatives begun by Eleanor Rathbone in Liverpool and Manchester [see n. 234]. In June 1917 the National Union of Women Workers set about creating a national organization of local WCAs. Their aim was to encourage women to take an interest in social and political issues pending the introduction of their right to vote, which would occur on 6 Feb. 1918. After that they also worked to encourage women to register and vote.

131. C. C. Lynam was Headmaster of the Oxford Preparatory School from 1886 to 1920. It had been founded in 1877 as a private prep. school and was frequently called Lynam's. C. C. Lynam was succeeded by his son A. E. Lynam, who served from 1920 to 1942 when he was succeeded by his son J. H. R. Lynam, who served from 1942 to 1965. In time it became known as the Dragon School and is located in north Oxford beside the Cherwell River and near the Slaters' home.

132. Stephen Leacock (1869–1944) was born in England but was taken to Canada as a small child. He eventually taught political science at McGill University and was one of the best-known humorists in the English-speaking world. Basil is probably referring to Leacock's *Frenzied Fiction*, which was published in 1918.

133. New College Lane opens into Catte Street under this name but actually begins in High Street as Queen's Lane. It winds its way between New College and St Edmund Hall when it is Queen's Lane and between New College and the backs of All Souls and Hertford Colleges on the other when it is New College Lane.

134. *Songs of the Blue Dragon* was compiled by C. C. Lynam and was published in 1917. The text was taken from his earlier work, *The Log of the Blue Dragon*. This had been published in three volumes in 1907. The *Blue Dragon* was the name of his yacht. [See nn. 21 and 131.] Frederick Marryat's *Masterman Ready, or the Wreck of the Pacific* was first published in 1841 but remained popular throughout the century and beyond. William Morris's poem *The Life and Death of Jason* was first published in 1867. Patrick was probably given a copy of the 1914 Oxford University Press edition prepared by E. Maxwell.

135. *The Loom of Youth* was the first novel by Alec Waugh (1898–1991), elder brother of Evelyn. Published in 1917, the book was set in a public school and drew on the

author's time at Sherborne. Waugh openly discussed sexual relations between boys. The school's old boy association expelled him while he was in the army in France, and the book was roundly denounced. Waugh, as is said, laughed all the way to the bank.

136. The College of Preceptors was established in 1846 as 'The Society of Teachers' in Bloomsbury and in 1849 changed 'teachers' to 'preceptors'. In 1998 it reverted to 'teachers'. Its aims were 'to promote sound learning, especially among the middle classes, by the instruction of teachers, and by the examination of pupils at stated times'. Benjamin Vincent, *Haydn's Dictionary of Dates and Universal Information* (1892), 778.

137. Violet was probably referring to the *Daily Herald* (1912–62), a Labour daily which became a weekly during the war under George Lansbury's editorship. It opposed the war and conscription while supporting conscientious objectors and the Russian Revolution. In 1962 it became *The Sun*. She would also have approved of *The Herald of Peace and International Arbitration*, a monthly newspaper published by the Peace Society between 1819 and the Society's collapse in the 1930s.

138. On 20 July there was a strike call from the Amalgamated Society of Engineers for skilled workers to come out in Birmingham (and later Coventry) in response to one company's misinterpretation of a Ministry of Munitions embargo circular on the further employment of skilled labour in certain areas. This was seen by the union as a general threat to all skilled workers and also brought underlying resentment into the open. By 29 July men were returning to work after the Minister of Munitions, Winston Churchill, said the government would use its powers to dismiss the strikers and replace them with workers already called up, thereby leaving the strikers liable to be called up. This was the only time during the war that this threat was made. A government committee was set up to investigate working conditions and pay. Earlier in the month there had been a strike of 10,000 wood-workers in London aircraft factories over the dismissal of a shop-steward. In 1918 about 6,000,000 working days were lost to strikes.

139. The Battle of Soissons took place between 18 and 22 July 1918 when the French-led forces fought to cut off the German salient aimed at Paris. Despite heavy casualties in dead and wounded (125,000 Allied and 168,000 German) the Allies regained most of the territory lost to the Germans in the previous May.

140. *The Nation* was a Labour and Liberal weekly newspaper and was published between 1907 and 1921. One of its supporters was J. A. Hobson. In 1931 it was merged with the *New Statesman*.

141. The 'someone or other' was Joseph Wells (1855–1929), Warden of Wadham College, Oxford, from 1913 to 1927. His *Oxford and its Colleges* was published in 1903. Edmund New (1871–1931) was famous as an artist and illustrator for his pen and ink drawings. He had adopted the black and white style of the Arts and Crafts movement.

142. After 1882 'Inter' meant the Intermediate Examination which was the first of two examinations required for the University of London's BA or B.Sc. degrees. Owen's interest in the 'Inter' might have been because he wanted to collect another qualification or because he was considering applying for the University of London. The surviving letters do not make his thinking clear.

143. Owen is referring to *Profit and Loss*, a collection of verse published in 1906 by the poet John Oxenham.

144. In 1918 the Oxford B.Sc. was in fact a graduate degree. It is now the M.Sc.

145. Mongewell Park was a country house located 1 mile south of Wallingford in Berkshire (Oxfordshire after 1974). It became a military hospital after the owner, Alexander Frazer, died in 1916. The hospital was closed in 1918. Between 1948 and 1997 it was the home of Carmel College.

146. The words are a paraphrase of Isaiah 7: 15, which reads, 'to refuse the evil, and choose the good'.

147. Walt Whitman's 'Song of Prudence' first appeared in the 1856 edition of *Leaves of Grass*. The relevant lines read:

> knows that the young man who composedly peril'd his life and lost it
> has done exceedingly well for himself without doubt,
> That he who never peril'd his life, but retains it to old age in
> riches and ease, has probably achiev'd nothing for himself worth mentioning.

148. The Royal Military College was founded in 1802 as a training school for officers and moved to Sandhurst in Berkshire in 1813.

149. The Civil Service Supply Association was established in the 1860s as a cooperative venture by civil servants in London in imitation of existing stores in Lancashire and elsewhere. It was a cooperative retail chain open to civil servants for an annual subscription of 2s. 6d. A limited number of members' friends could be admitted for a fee of 5s. a year. It was also known as the Civil Service Stores.

150. Newspapers in the Allied countries generally ridiculed the overtures from Kaiser Karl for a peace settlement. He had written to Woodrow Wilson on 15 Sept. asking for a peace conference but five days later Wilson rejected his offer. The Emperor had earlier valiantly tried to pull Austria-Hungary out of the war but his secret attempts were made public by the French in Apr. 1918. In addition Germany had offered to withdraw from Belgium but without reparations and only if Belgium remained neutral, thereby making an Allied invasion of Germany that much more difficult. Germany also proposed that Belgium negotiate a peace settlement.

151. Field Service Post Cards were given to soldiers by the army to allow them to keep loved ones informed. One was only allowed to write the date, sign one's name and mark through statements that were not appropriate. For example under the

statement 'I have received no letter from you' the soldier could strike through 'lately' or 'for a long time'. The first statement was 'I am quite well' and underneath were statements about his health if he were ill or injured.

152. Cox & Co. began in the 18th century as 'agents' or provisioners serving regiments in the British army. By 1914 the established role as paymasters meant the company was now functioning as a bank for 250,000 members of HM forces.

153. Edwin C. Armstead was a cycle manufacturer at 9 Broad Street, Oxford.

154. A 'Home Student' was a member of the Society of Oxford Home-Students, established for women in 1879. This was four years after the university passed a statute which allowed the creation of examinations for women which were equivalent to those set for men. It would not be until 1920 that women could become full members of the university and take degrees. The SOH-S allowed young women to study at Oxford without becoming a member of one of the women's colleges. In 1952 the society became St Anne's College.

155. *Woodstock; or The Cavalier: A Tale of the Year Sixteen Hundred and Fifty-One* by Sir Walter Scott was published anonymously in 1826.

156. The importance of letters and an indication of the number written is seen in statistics published in July 1915: troops received 7,500,000 letters and 700,000 parcels each week and they sent 5,000,000 letters home each week. These figures do not include the 40,821 letters and parcels to POWs and internees in the UK and the letters and parcels sent to the 30,710 British POWs as of July 1915. *The War Illustrated* (22 July 1915).

157. The railway strikes, led by engineers and firemen, began in South Wales on 24 Sept. 1918 as a protest against the settlement reached between the government and the men's unions regarding the additional 'war wage'. It quickly spread throughout the country but ended two days later on 26 Sept.

158. The *Continental Daily Mail* began publication as a daily paper in 1905 and quickly became the most important English-language newspaper in Europe. *The Bystander* was a weekly magazine published between 1903 and 1940 when it was merged with *The Tatler*. During the war it was famous for Bruce Bairnsfather's 'Old Bill' cartoons. *The Sketch* was an illustrated weekly which ran from 1893 to 1959; it was noted for its reports of the aristocracy and of Society's doings and was somewhat 'arty'. *Punch; or, The London Charivari* was a humorous and satirical weekly which ran from 1841 to 1992 and was well known for its cartoons based on contemporary events and behaviour. It was revived in 1996 but closed in 2002.

159. By 'helmet' Owen meant a knitted woollen device made to be placed as a lining under a soldier's 'tin hat' (actually made of steel). These linings not only provided warmth but made the 'hats', many of which did not fit well, fit better.

160. Gilbert is being rather unfair here. See n. 46.

161. At the time British forces surrendered Kut to Ottoman forces, General Nikolai Nikolaevich Baratov was leading a Russian relief force made up mainly of Cossacks, but he turned back.

162. In the event Henry Furniss did stand as the Labour candidate for one of the University of Oxford's two seats in the 1918 general election. The Universities of Oxford and Cambridge each had two MPs from 1603 to 1950. All MAs were electors. Other universities in the UK were also represented and in 1918 7% of the population had more than one vote. Voting would take place on 14 Dec. and the two successful candidates, Lord Hugh Cecil and R. E. Prothero, were both Conservatives. The Liberal candidate Professor Gilbert Murray got 812 votes on the re-count while Furniss came bottom of the poll with 352.

163. The Women's Army Auxiliary Corps was created in 1917 and in 1918 was renamed Queen Mary's Army Auxiliary Corps. Over 57,000 women joined between Jan. 1917 and the end of fighting. The first women to go to France arrived in Mar. 1917 to serve as cooks and waitresses. The QMAAC was disbanded in Sept. 1921.

164. This is presumably a reference to Henry Wadsworth Longfellow's Prelude to his first collection of poems, *Voices of the Night*, published in 1839.

165. Woodrow Wilson (1856–1924) was US President from 1913 to 1921. In the UK and France he initially received unlimited adulation as a messianic statesman who was going to change international relations through his famous 'Fourteen Points'. The statement that God had been satisfied with ten points while Wilson needed fourteen has been attributed, among others, to Oliver Wendell Holmes and to Georges Clemenceau.

166. *Peveril of the Peak*, the ninth and longest novel in Sir Walter Scott's Waverley series, is set in the time of the Popish Plot of 1678.

167. A froad is defined as an amphibian indistinguishable between a frog and a toad. The word may be derived from the medieval *froud*, another term for frog. The last recorded use is given in the *On-line OED* as 1496. Assuming a correct reading, this is an interesting survival.

168. 'The boy stood on the burning deck' is the first line of Felicia Dorothea Hemans's poem, properly entitled *Casabianca*, which was first published in 1826. It is based on an event in the Battle of the Nile in 1798: the son of Louis de Casabianca, the commander of the French ship *Orient*, remained on the stricken ship's deck. Having promised never to abandon ship until ordered by his father, who lay dead below, the boy perished. The poem became famous and remained so well into the 1950s. It was endlessly recited and parodied, and the quote here obviously refers to a parody, possibly ribald, recited by Owen.

169. Somerville College, named after the mathematician Mary Somerville, is in the Woodstock Road, Oxford. It was established as the second women's college in

1879 and during the war it became a hospital. Patients whom Joyce might have preferred seeing included Siegfried Sassoon and Robert Graves.

170. This may refer to reports in papers that some captured German soldiers were saying that 'the Kaiser must go, and with him the Crown Prince, whom all seem willing to allow to drop into oblivion' [The Times, 16 Oct. 1918]. The Crown Prince, Wilhelm (1882–1951), was a much hated figure in Britain. From Aug. 1914 to Nov. 1916 he was in command of the 5th Army. Ironically he was quoted in an English interview early in the war that 'this was the most stupid, senseless and unnecessary war of modern times'.

171. While Lille was not levelled by the Germans as they retreated, over 2,000 buildings had already been destroyed by German artillery earlier in the war. After the Germans captured the city they had destroyed an entire section in retaliation for the French having tricked them into thinking the city had more than one piece of artillery.

172. By 'corruption' Gilbert was probably referring to the 'shell crisis' that broke in May 1915 over the lack of shells. This forced Asquith to restructure the government as a coalition and to create a new Ministry of Munitions with Lloyd George as minister. All the warring nations faced severe problems with the supply of ammunition and in some cases this led to major political scandals.

173. The Monastery: A Romance was set in the 16th century by Sir Walter Scott and was published in 1820.

174. The Carl Rosa Opera Company had been founded by the German-born musician Karl Rose in 1873 as a touring company which also had a London season. It presented opera in English at reasonable prices and continued touring until 1960.

175. Because the rest of this letter is missing the editors have provided the missing text of this poem, on which there were many variations. It was written by Reginald Arkell (1882–1959), a British humorist and, later in his career, screen-writer who was in the army at the time. It first appeared in Arkell's collection of verse All the Rumors, published by Duckworth in 1916, with the title 'When the War Will End?' Mrs Brown used 'wife's washerwoman' for the original 'aunt's charwoman'.

176. Oliver Sturt, the son of a neighbour who lived at No. 5 Park Crescent, had been on HMS Nicator, a destroyer which had seen action at Jutland. He was demobilized in time to be matriculated into the University of Oxford on 14 Sept. 1918.

177. The Daily Herald was still being published weekly. It would resume daily publication with peace.

178. Quinine was one of the drugs doctors used to treat influenza. Later, in the 1940s, researchers testing mice argued that quinine did have a slight retardant effect on influenza but was not a preventive. See A. O. Seeler et al., 'Effect of Quinine on Influenza Virus Infections in Mice', Journal of Infectious Diseases (Sept.–Oct. 1946), lxxix.2: 156–8.

179. On 14 Oct. President Wilson demanded that Germany stop all submarine attacks against Allied shipping and on 20 Oct. this was agreed.

180. The *Daily News* began publication in 1896 and was founded by Alfred Harmsworth, Lord Northcliffe (1865–1922), the first British newspaper mogul. By 1918 his newspaper group owned not just the *Daily News*, but *The Times*, the *Sunday Times*, the *Evening News*, the *Weekly Dispatch*, the *Observer*, and the *Daily Mirror*, which he established in 1903. His papers supported the Boer War (1899–1902), attacked Germany before 1914, and were uncompromising in their support of the war between 1914 and 1918. Northcliffe was instrumental in toppling Asquith in 1916 and in putting Lloyd George into Downing Street. Afterwards he was put in charge of the British propaganda effort.

181. Here Violet is referring to Lloyd George's campaign to oust the editor of the *Daily Chronicle*, Robert Donald. The paper had been started in 1872 and by 1914 supported the more advanced wing of the Liberal Party including Lloyd George but this did not stop Donald from criticizing the government. A group inspired by Lloyd George bought the paper in Sept. 1918 for £1,800,000 in order to get rid of Donald. If one assumes the rather odd figure of 17,000,000 is meant to refer to the circulation of the Northcliffe papers it might have been reached by arguing that (1) the 1911 census showed that England, Wales, and Scotland had a population of 40,831,000 and (2) Northcliffe's papers made up some 40% of all papers sold there. This would produce a figure of 16,332,400 although admittedly this would have included all ages.

182. Maréchal Ferdinand Foch (1851–1929) was in the early years of the war a French hero because of his defence of Nancy and his victory on the Marne but he suffered an eclipse after the Somme and was removed from power. He was reinstated as Chief of the General Staff in 1917 and was eventually made Generalissimo of the Allied Armies.

183. Wells's article was one of a series published in the *Morning Post* on 6 Nov. 1918. In it he analysed the Foreign Office's attitude towards his vision of world government and attacked 'the Great Power idea in human affairs'.

184. Violet is here quoting the fifth and final verse of Frank Sidgwick's poem '1914' which was published in book form in *Some Verse* by 'F.S.' in 1915. Frank Sidgwick (1879–1939) was both a poet (known for lighter verse) and novelist as well as the founder of the publishing house Sidgwick & Jackson, which he started in 1907.

185. Christ's words are found in St Matthew 25: 40. 'Where Love is, God Is' is the 1885 short story by Leo Tolstoy in which the central character is the cobbler Martin Avdéitch.

186. Arthur James Balfour (1848–1930) had been the Tory Prime Minister 1902–5. He was First Lord of the Admiralty 1915–16 under Asquith, Foreign Secretary in Lloyd George's coalition government 1916–19, and Lord President of the Council from 1919 to the breakup of the Coalition in 1922, in which year he was created Earl of Balfour.

187. Mr Sofield's brother was presumably the one casualty to which Owen referred when writing to his mother on 26 Oct. 1918.

188. Violet's information was incorrect. There were six Labour ministers in the coalition government at the dissolution before the general election of 1918.

189. The NCC or Non-Combatant Corps was formed in Mar. 1916 for pacifists. Its members were part of the army and wore uniforms but did not carry weapons and did no fighting. Instead they worked in building, cleaning, and loading or unloading (except ammunition). An alternative was the Royal Army Medical Corps. Those men who refused either option were usually called 'Absolutists' and faced courts martial and, if convicted, possible imprisonment. The NCC was nicknamed the No Courage Corps.

190. Sir Eric Geddes (1875–1937) had been a high-ranking official of the North-Eastern Railway. He was put into the civil service in 1915 and was famous for his administrative skills. In 1917 he was brought in as MP for Cambridge Borough and appointed First Lord of the Admiralty. During the campaigning in 1918 he became famous for his statement regarding reparations from Germany: 'we will get everything out of her that you can squeeze out of a lemon and a bit more.' In later speeches this became 'squeezing Germany like a lemon until the pips squeak'. In the event these were not Geddes's original views: he had doubted the economic value of German reparations on the British economy and he had been accused of not demanding punishment of Wilhelm II.

191. Will Crooks (1852–1921) was the famous East End political activist who became the first Labour mayor (of Poplar) in what was then the London County Council. He was a Labour MP from 1903 to Jan. 1910, and from Dec. 1910 to 1921. Violet would have disliked him for his support of the war and his continuing links with the Liberals. Alec Cameron was the Assistant General Secretary of the Amalgamated Society of Carpenters and Joiners and stood in West Woolwich while Crooks stood in East Woolwich. Cameron only got 34.5% of the vote, losing to the Conservative candidate. Anon., 'The Woolwich Labour Party, 1903–1951', in David Clark (gen ed.), *Origins and Development of the Labour Party in Britain at the Local Level* (1982), 13.

192. Sidney Webb (1859–1947) and his wife Beatrice (1858–1943) were by 1918 the Labour Party's leading socialist intellectuals. Sidney was a founding member of the Fabians and worked to create the London School of Economics and Politics (LSE). He supported the war and the growth in state control which it produced. In the 1930s he and his wife became apologists for Soviet Communism. George Bernard Shaw (1856–1950), a Fabian socialist, was a friend of the Webbs. While he is now remembered as a playwright, he was equally well known by 1918 as a novelist and controversial journalist. He argued for a negotiated settlement as early as Nov. 1914.

193. John Atkinson Hobson (1858–1940) was a Liberal writer and economist, famous for his New Liberalism in the 1890s and later for his theory of under-consumption. He opposed 'imperialism' and the war and joined the Union of Democratic Control which Violet would have approved. The UDC had been set up by Charles P. Trevelyan, who had resigned from the Asquith government, Ramsay Macdonald, Norman Angell, and E. D. Morel. Its aims included a full and open discussion of war aims and opposition to conscription, censorship, and excessive state regulation. Like Gilbert, Hobson had been a university extension lecturer before the war. He was also a founding member of the Sociological Society at which Gilbert lectured and was on the Executive Committee of the New Reform Club with Gilbert.

194. The 1916 coalition government headed by Lloyd George was kept in office by the support of the Unionists (Conservatives) and some Liberal and Labour MPs. The 'jockeying' reference was to the decision to have a general election so soon after the signing of the Armistice in order to cash in on the 'war spirit'.

195. Theodore Roosevelt (1858–1919) had been the Republican President 1901–9 and during the war bitterly denounced Wilson's policy of neutrality and his 'Fourteen Points'. He favoured a more realistic post-war League of Nations. The 'military interests' refer to those in America who argued that whatever happened in 1918 the Allies should carry the war on into 1919 in order to invade Germany and bring the war home to the Germans.

196. It appears that Owen did not vote even though he was entitled to do so. The 1918 Representation of the People Act stipulated that any man serving in HM forces could vote if over the age of 19, not 21 as was the stipulation in the Act for men outside the forces. Many men thought like Owen: it is estimated that two-thirds of those in the military did not bother to vote. Martin Farr, 'Waging Democracy: The British General Election of 1918 Reconsidered', *Cercles*, 21 (2011), 86.

197. St Mildred's Hall was at 11 Turl Street. Whilst it provided some accommodation it was better known as a venue for meetings and events. It was also the site of Henry Thomas de Blois Leach's dancing school which perhaps explains the 'slippery' floor. The Hall was later pulled down by the site's owners, Lincoln College, for redevelopment.

198. Lena Ashwell (1872–1957) was an actress who became a theatre manager in London. In 1915 she became the first person to organize travelling companies to entertain troops in France. By 1918 she had twenty-five groups. She also organized all-male concert parties to perform near the Front.

199. The Army Service Corps as it operated at the beginning of the war was established in 1888. During the war it was responsible for getting food, horses, forage, petrol, office supplies, etc. from Britain to the various fronts. At its strongest it consisted of 10,547 officers and 315,334 men as well as local employees. In 1918 it became the Royal Army Service Corps and is now part of the Royal Logistics Corps.

200. This probably refers to Upton Sinclair's 1917 essay *The Profits of Religion: An Essay in Economic Interpretation* in which he surveyed the American religious scene in 1914.

201. Union Street is in Cowley, the working-class part of Oxford east of the centre. It was then filled with 'two up–two down' terraced houses. Its name reflects its nearness to Oxford's Workhouse.

202. Under the 1834 Poor Law Amendment Act parishes in England and Wales were grouped into Poor Law 'unions', each of which had an elected Board of Guardians. These had the power to set rates and to establish the 'workhouses' which were so hated by the poor. The Guardians could still give 'out relief' or grants to individual families and this is what Violet is referring to here.

203. The presence of Bolshevik activity led the Swiss Federal Government to break off relations with Russia on 8 Dec. 1918.

204. J. A. R. Marriott (1859–1945) was a history don at Worcester. From 1895 to 1920 he was also the Secretary to the Oxford Extension Delegacy and involved in the same sort of work that Gilbert Slater had undertaken. In 1918 he was the sitting candidate for Oxford City as a Coupon Conservative. Presumably by saying Marriott was the 'best Quaker' Violet meant the best from a Quaker point of view.

205. The Bank Holidays Act of 1871 recognized only four holidays in England and Wales: Easter Monday, Whit Monday, the first Monday in August, and Boxing Day. Christmas Day and Good Friday were already recognized as Common Law holidays. There were no annual paid holidays for workers until the 1938 Holiday With Pay Act.

206. Jerome K. Jerome's collection of ghost stories *Told after Supper* was first published in 1892.

207. If one uses the Retail Price Index as a guide with 1913 at 100, by 1919 this had risen to 211. In very rough terms retail prices had more than doubled. Stephen Broadberry and Peter Howlett, 'The United Kingdom during World War I: Business as Usual?', in S. Broadberry and M. Harrison (eds.), *The Economics of World War I* (2003), table 10, p. 39. <www2.warwick.ac.uk/fac/soc/economics/staff/.../wp/wwipap4.pdf>.

208. In the event Labour formed its first government on 22 Jan. 1924. The general election of 1923 had given the Tories the largest number of seats but not a majority. Labour, with more MPs than the Liberals, therefore formed a minority government which lasted until 4 Nov. 1924.

209. *The Scottish Students Song Book* had a sixth edition in 1897 and another, undated edition, followed.

210. The Indian Economic Association was started in 1917 and continues its work today. The IEA has some 3,500 members, holds annual conferences, special seminars, and lectures in different parts of India, and publishes the *Indian Economic Journal* quarterly.

211. The Allied blockade of German ports was lifted on 17 Jan. 1919. However, imports, including food, would only be allowed after the new German Republic accepted the Allies' restrictions which it did on 12 Mar. 1919. After that date food imports were allowed. All restrictions were lifted on 12 July 1919 after the signing of the Versailles Treaty. The suffering in Germany and Austria, especially in the cities, was appalling. Estimates of those who died from starvation and illness caused by the blockade between 1914 and 1918, just in Germany, vary from 424,000 to 763,000. It is estimated that a further 100,000 Germans died between Nov. 1918 and July 1919 and this estimate does not include Austria.

212. In late 1918 there had been general unrest and small-scale mutinies in Calais and Folkestone, along with a demonstration by some 3,000 soldiers in London, over plans for demobilization. Things improved when a new scheme for demobilization was announced in Jan. 1919.

213. By July some 30,000 men from Allied armies, half of whom came from the British Empire, were entering Russia to protect Allied materiel sent there and to put down the Bolshevik rebellion against the Kerensky government. They were later joined by ships of the Royal Navy.

214. Violet is referring here to Frank Sidgwick's poem '1914'. See n. 184.

215. Bell & Park were passenger and shipping agents at 137 High Street, Oxford.

216. It was a custom that after each Christmas the family would go to the Natural History Museum in Oxford for the lectures being given there.

217. Sir William Somerville (1860–1932) was the Sibthorpian Professor of Rural Economy at Oxford and a leading figure in improving British agriculture.

218. Prince John, George V's youngest child, died on 19 Jan. 1919. Because of his epilepsy the prince had led a private life on the Sandringham estate.

219. If prices had increased fourfold, 7s. 6d. would have become 30s. Using the Retail Price Index as a rough guide, 30s. would in 2010 have become £53.76. No wonder Violet was concerned.

220. The D'oyly Carte Opera Company was established in the 1870s to perform Gilbert and Sullivan's operas and continued until 1982. The company was revived in 1988 but sadly closed in 2003. By 1918 it was a touring company.

221. On 19 Nov. 1918 the University of Oxford brought in special 'Privileges Granted on Account of War Service' to those whose education has been interrupted or postponed by military service. The residency requirement could be reduced from the usual nine terms down to four, depending on how long a person had been in HM forces. In Owen's case he could be excused the first (of three) examinations if he went for the Pass degree and the first and second examinations if he went for an Honours degree. He could also take a shortened Honours course but would then not be placed in a class after his final examination.

222. *Quinneys* was a comedy by Horace Annesley Vachel (1861–1955) which opened in the West End in 1914. It would be made into films in 1919 and 1927. Vachel was a highly successful novelist as well as a playwright.

223. *The Hindu* is an English-language newspaper founded in 1878 as a weekly and published in Madras. In 1889 it became a daily and is today the third most popular English-language paper in India.

224. War Savings Certificates were introduced in 1916 to help finance the war. The certificates paid 3.5%, cost 15s. 6d., and could be bought at any money order Post Office or bank. They were advertised by the government as 'everybody's investment' and the investor was issued with a small War Savings Certificates Book. The scheme proved very popular and by Nov. 1918 £207,000,000 worth of certificates had been purchased. In 1920 they were renamed National Savings Certificates.

225. The Armistice agreement (Clause V) called for German evacuation of all territories on either side of the Rhine within thirty-one days and for an Allied military presence in the liberated countries, at crucial crossings, and along the Franco-German border. British occupying forces entered Germany on 3 Dec. 1918 and in Mar. 1919 the British Army of the Rhine was formed with its headquarters in Cologne. The other occupying armies came from Belgium, France, and the USA. The occupation lasted for twelve years.

226. The Fight the Famine Council was set up at the end of 1918 and held its first meeting on 1 Jan. 1919. The movement was led by Eglantyne Jebb and her sister Dorothy, wife of the Labour MP Charles Roden Buxton. Its aim was political, to urge HMG to lift the blockade, which was done on 17 Jan. 1919. In Apr. 1919 the Council went on to set up the Save the Children Fund as a relief agency aimed not at Russia but at Germany and Austria.

227. John Langdon-Davis (1897–1971) had been an Oxford undergraduate when called up. He became a conscientious objector who was imprisoned and then discharged on medical grounds. He went on to become a well-known anti-militarist lecturer and writer although he was awarded an MBE for his services to the Home Guard in the Second World War.

228. The strikes began on 27 Jan. in support of a forty-hour week. (A forty-seven-hour week had been introduced that same month.) The violence referred to here was the 'Battle of George Square' in which one union leader, David Kirkwood, was knocked down by the police and arrested. After the Scottish Secretary described the event as a 'Bolshevik' uprising the government sent in 10,000 troops to keep order. The strike was a failure.

229. While scrounge, meaning 'to seek to obtain by irregular means, as by stealth or begging; to hunt about or rummage (*for* something)', is associated with troops, its first citation in the *On Line OED* is from 1909.

230. Mary Pask was a very active member of the Society of Friends and became a family friend of the Slaters.

231. Ralph Vaughan Williams (1872–1958) composed *A Sea Symphony*, his choral symphony, between 1903 and 1909, and it was first performed in 1910. He took his text from Whitman's *Leaves of Grass*.

232. The 'single tax' proposal, also known as 'Georgism', was a politico-economic movement which advocated a single tax system based on the value of land which, it argued, belonged to everyone in a society and should not be privately 'owned'. Its most important proponent was the American economist Henry George (1839–1897) in his 1879 book *Progress and Poverty*.

233. Barnett House was established in Oxford in 1914 as a tribute to the Revd Samuel Barnett, founder of Toynbee Hall in London. It was a centre for the study of social and economic problems.

234. Eleanor Rathbone (1872–1946) came from a wealthy Liverpool Unitarian merchant family. She devoted herself to social causes including a system of family allowances and women's rights. She also worked to support the families of soldiers during the war and from 1928 to 1945 was an independent MP for the Combined English Universities, which included all English universities except Oxford, Cambridge, and London.

235. Frederick Augustus Dixey (1855–1935) first concentrated on optometry but changed to become a leading entomologist and a Fellow of Wadham College, Oxford. He was an expert on White butterflies.

236. A nose cap is a protective metal cap fitted to the 'nose' of the wooden stock of a gun.

237. 'Bird' was originally a US term equivalent to 'cove' or 'bloke'.

238. The Cadena Cafes were a chain of tea and coffee shops, famous for the quality of their coffee. The shops frequently had small string ensembles and appealed to a middle-class clientele. In Oxford it was located at 44–6 Cornmarket Street.

239. The *On-Line OED* defines the public school slang term 'wimp' or, as here, 'whimp' as an abbreviated corruption of woman or girl and cites its first usage as 1923.

240. H. A. L. Fisher (1865–1940) was an Oxford history tutor and a member of the Liberal intelligentsia. When Lloyd George formed his coalition government in 1916 he asked Fisher to become President of the Board of Education, in effect Secretary of State for Education. Fisher agreed and a constituency was found for him. Fisher's lecture was published later in 1919 by Oxford University Press with the title 'The Place of the University in National Life'. The Sheldonian Theatre in Broad Street was designed by Wren and built in the 1660s. It is named after Gilbert Sheldon, Archbishop of Canterbury and Chancellor of the University at the time, who also paid for it. Its main function was not to be a theatre in the usual sense but to house university ceremonies.

241. Sylvia Pankhurst (1882–1960) worked with her mother and sister in the Women's Social and Political Union, the leading suffragette movement. Unlike her mother and sister she was a socialist and supporter of the Labour Party and in time left the WSPU to establish her own suffragette organization in London's East End. This became the Workers' Socialist Federation in 1917. She opposed the war and did much to help the wives and widows of men who had been called up. She used her artistic talents to portray working women. She later supported the Bolsheviks and in 1920 her Federation would become the Communist Party (British Section of the Third International).

242. Arabella Scott (1886–1946) came from a Scottish Unitarian background and had an MA from Edinburgh University. A teacher in Leith, she became one of the earliest and most militant suffragettes. She acted as a 'bodyguard' to Mrs Emily Pankhurst, and was arrested and imprisoned seven times (once for attempted arson). When the movement split over the war she followed Emily Pankhurst's lead in supporting the war effort and became an officer in Queen Mary's Army Auxiliary Corps. In 1934 she married a man from Johannesburg and emigrated to South Africa. She later moved to Australia. *The Sydney Morning Herald* (14 July 1978).

243. Violet probably meant to write the Highland Land League, also called the Crofters' Party, which campaigned for lower rents and better terms for tenants in the wake of land clearances and famine in the Highlands. It began in the 1880s as a protest movement based on the Irish Land League. In addition to political work, including parliamentary campaigning, there were rent strikes and illegal occupation of land.

244. British Summer Time was introduced on 21 May 1916 and after that date clocks went forward by an hour on the last Sunday of every March. In France, however, the date in 1919 for putting watches forward was 11 p.m. on 1 Mar.

245. The Math is a nickname for Sir Joseph Williamson's Mathematical School, a boys' grammar school founded in the 17th century in Rochester.

246. Woodrow Wilson had left Paris in Feb. 1919 to return to the USA to cope with those in Congress who were opposed to the treaty and especially to the proposed League of Nations. He would return to France on 13 Mar. to face French demands for heavy reparations from Germany.

247. Mary Pickford (1892–1979), whose real name was Gladys Marie Smith, was born in Toronto and became, with Charlie Chaplin, the most famous Hollywood 'star' in early silent films.

248. Friends' relief work took place in Austria, Germany, Poland, and Serbia where volunteers worked alongside other relief organizations from the UK and USA.

249. Sir Isaac Pitman (1813–97) invented a course of shorthand in 1837 which eventually took his name. He also advocated spelling reform, vegetarianism, teetotalism, and the Swedenborgian religion.

250. The *Oxford Chronicle & Berks and Bucks Gazette* began in 1837 as *The Oxford City & County Chronicle* and was published until 1929 when it was amalgamated with the *Oxford Times*. In 1919 its offices were in St Aldate's.

251. Violet's cutting has disappeared but 'Sinclair's paper' was the *Appeal to Reason*, which was established in 1895 as a socialist weekly and carried on until 1922. It was the voice of the Socialist Party of America and by 1910 had a paid circulation of 500,000. It published many of Sinclair's essays and the one which Violet sent was probably 'The Case of Russia', which he wrote in 1919. It was included in his collection *The Brass Check*, which would be published in 1920.

252. Jessie Payne Margoliouth (1856–1933) was the wife of the Revd Professor David Samuel Margoliouth (1858–1940), the Laudian Professor of Arabic from 1889 to 1937, who was also a Church of England priest. She was a distinguished Syriac scholar in her own right and Professor Margoliouth and she were ordered by the War Office to lecture in India during the war. He returned in 1917 and she, in 1918.

253. In the event the Conference forbade conscription in Germany, which was allowed a standing army of no more than 100,000 men, but did not forbid conscription by the victorious powers.

254. In the event Gilbert's fears were unfounded. The next major famine to hit India was in 1943–4 in Bengal when between 1,500,000 and 4,000,000 died from starvation, malnutrition, and disease.

255. Violet need not have worried. The Labour Party already supported the 'Hands Off Russia' movement, which had started on 10 May 1918 when East End dockhands refused to load supplies onto the *Jolly George*, which was taking arms to anti-Bolshevik forces. The party campaigned to withdraw British troops already sent to Russia and joined with the TUC in threatening a general strike if more troops were sent.

256. While the blockade of Turkey was lifted on 21 Jan. 1919, the blockade of Germany was not ended until 12 July 1919.

257. Hamilton Fyfe (1869–1951) was a journalist and between 1903 and 1907 he transformed the ailing *Daily Mirror* into a highly successful paper. In 1907 he moved to the *Daily Mail* for which he acted as a war correspondent. Like the Slaters he was a supporter of the Labour Party and eventually stood as a Labour candidate for Parliament.

258. At this time the University Sermon was preached every Sunday in term in the University Church, St Mary the Virgin, in the presence of the Vice-Chancellor and Proctors or their representatives.

259. Eights races, named after the boats with eight oarsmen, take place toward the end of Trinity Term each year. The object is to 'bump' (touch or pass) the boat in front and if possible to go on to 'bump' the next boat (an 'over-bump').

260. *Daddy Long-Legs* was a silent film released in 1919 which starred Mary Pickford. It was based on the 1912 American novel of the same title written by Jean Webster.

261. J. M. Barrie's play *Quality Street* opened on Broadway in 1901 to a mixed reception and in the West End in 1902. There it was highly successful and ran for fifteen months. It was frequently revived and is now remembered because its title was used for a collection of sweets produced by Mackintosh. If Joyce got the title right, *The Jilt* was a five-act comedy written not by Arnold Bennett but by Dion Boucicault. It was first produced in 1885. If she got the playwright correct but the title wrong, plays by Arnold Bennett which she might have seen were *What the Public Wants* (1909), *Cupid and Commonsense* (1912), *Milestones* (1912), *The Great Adventure* (1913), or just possibly *Judith*, which opened in Eastbourne on 7 Apr. 1919. The play at LMH would have been based on *Clementina*, A. E. W. Mason's novel about Maria Clementina Sobieska, the consort of 'James III' (The Old Pretender), which had been published in 1901.

262. Henry David Thoreau's *Walden; or, Life in the Woods* was first published in Boston in 1854. It describes his two-year life in a cabin he built near Walden Pond in woods 2 miles from Concord, Massachusetts. His aim was 'to live deep and suck out all the marrow of life, to live so sturdily and Spartan-like as to put to rout all that was not life, to cut a broad swath and shave close, to drive life into a corner, and reduce it to its lowest terms', etc.

263. The eponymous 'Sam Brown Belt' was created in India in the 1850s. After being adopted for general use in the Indian army it was adopted by the British and Empire armies during the Boer War. A wide belt is accompanied by a strap worn from the left of the belt and over the right shoulder, diagonally across the chest.

264. *Abraham Lincoln* was the first really successful play by John Drinkwater. It opened in 1918 and was made into a sound film in 1924.

265. On 25 June 1919 the University of Oxford conferred Doctorates of Civil Law on the Prince of Wales, Generals Joffre, Monash, Wilson, and Pershing, Field Marshal Haig, Admiral Beatty, Herbert Hoover, and J. R. Clynes, the Labour MP and Minister of Food Control between 8 July 1918 and 10 Jan. 1919.

266. The reference was to the civil war in Russia and to the war between the new Republic of Poland on the one side and Soviet Republics of Russia and the Ukraine on the other. After the Polish victory in the Battle of Warsaw and a new offensive eastwards the Bolsheviks sued for peace. The Treaty of Riga would be signed on 18 Mar. 1921.

267. The 'Puck' to which Patrick is referring is probably Rudyard Kipling's historical fantasy *Puck of Pook's Hill*, first published in 1906. *The Children's Newspaper* was a newspaper aimed at children under 13. It began in 1919 and carried on until 1965.

268. Robert Minors (1884–1952) was a radical American cartoonist and journalist who had been a war correspondent. By July 1919 Minors was a communist who, while visiting Russia in 1918, had worked for Lenin.

269. By the third week of July, miners' strikes in the West Riding, Derbyshire, and Nottinghamshire had forced the government to bring in demobilized naval ratings to keep the mines open. Estimates of those on strike ranged from 25,000 to 45,000 although many did not strike. In addition that summer saw a cotton workers' strike in which 450,000 workers struck for eighteen days and a policemen's strike in Birkenhead which led to rioting and looting.

270. Violet is here recalling Robert Tressell's famous 1914 novel *The Ragged Trousered Philanthropist* in which the author lambasted capitalism and especially workers who 'gave' their labour for insufficient wages—the 'ragged trousered philanthropists'.

271. In the Old Testament *Book of Esther* the eponymous heroine stood up to King Ahasuerus to save her father from execution and her fellow Jews from massacre.

272. A currency's valuta is its value defined by its exchange rate with another currency.

INDEX